D1226314

BACH'S FEET

The organist seated at the King of Instruments with thousands of pipes rising all around, hands busy at the manuals and feet patrolling the pedalboard, is a symbol of self-sufficiency yielding musical possibilities beyond all other modes of solo performance. In this book, David Yearsley presents a new interpretation of the significance of the oldest and richest of European instruments by investigating the German origins of the uniquely independent use of the feet in organ-playing. Delving into a range of musical, literary, and visual sources, *Bach's Feet* pursues the wide-ranging cultural importance of this physically demanding art, from the blind German organists of the fifteenth century, through the central contribution of Bach's music and legacy, to the newly pedaling organists of the British Empire and the sinister visions of Nazi propagandists.

DAVID YEARSLEY is the author of *Bach and the Meanings of Counterpoint* (Cambridge University Press, 2002) as well as numerous essays on European musical culture in the seventeenth and eighteenth centuries. Active as a performer on organ and other keyboard instruments, his recordings are available on the Loft and Musica Omnia labels. Mr. Yearsley has been an Alexander von Humboldt Fellow at the Humboldt University in Berlin, a Wenner Gren Foundation Fellow at the University of Gothenburg, and an American Council of Learned Societies Fellow. He is Professor of Music at Cornell University.

MUSICAL PERFORMANCE AND RECEPTION

General editors John Butt and Laurence Dreyfus

This series continues the aim of Cambridge Musical Texts and Monographs to publish books centred on the history of musical instruments and the history of performance, but broadens the focus to include musical reception in relation to performance and as a reflection of period expectations and practices.

Published titles

BACH'S FEET

The Organ Pedals in European Culture

DAVID YEARSLEY

CAMBRIDGE
UNIVERSITY PRESS

CAMBRIDGE UNIVERSITY PRESS
Cambridge, New York, Melbourne, Madrid, Cape Town,
Singapore, São Paulo, Delhi, Tokyo, Mexico City

Cambridge University Press
The Edinburgh Building, Cambridge CB2 8RU, UK

Published in the United States of America by Cambridge University Press, New York

www.cambridge.org
Information on this title: www.cambridge.org/9780521199018

First published 2012
Printed in the United Kingdom at the University Press, Cambridge

A catalogue record for this publication is available from the British Library

Library of Congress Cataloguing in Publication data
Yearsley, David Gaynor.
Bach's feet : the organ pedals in European culture / David Yearsley.
p.   cm.
Includes bibliographical references (p.   ) and index.
ISBN 978-0-521-19901-8
1.   Organ music – Germany – History and criticism.   2. Organ music – Europe – History and
criticism.   3. Organ (Musical instrument) – Pedaling – History.   4. Organ (Musical instrument) –
Germany – History.   5. Organ (Musical instrument) – Europe – History.   6. Bach, Johann
Sebastian, 1685–1750. Organ music.   I. Title.
ML626.Y43   2011
786.5094–dc22
2011015549

ISBN 978-0-521-19901-8 Hardback

Contents

Figures

Acknowledgements

This is a book about making music at the organ with the hands and the feet, a unique form of musical performance that I learned from a series of inspiring teachers: Katherine Fowler, Edward Hansen, Christa Rakich, William Porter, Harald Vogel, Kimberly Marshall, and Robert Bates. Among the many scholars who helped me in numerous ways, I would like first to acknowledge Peter Williams, who shepherded a version of this book's Chapter 1 into his *Organ Yearbook*, for more than four decades the most important scholarly publication devoted to keyboard studies. As guest editor for a special Buxtehude anniversary issue of *Early Music*, Stephen Rose helped along an essay that formed the core of Chapter 3. Wm. A. Little, whose definitive study of Mendelssohn and the organ appeared just as this book was going to press, offered valuable advice and corrections, especially on my treatment of nineteenth-century developments. Master organ-builder Munetaka Yokota was generous with his unsurpassed knowledge of seventeenth- and eighteenth-century north-German instruments. Andrew McCrea was my main informant on matters British, masterfully guiding me through the significant holdings of the Royal College of Organists where he is librarian. The staff of the music division of the Staatsbibliothek zu Berlin were unfailingly helpful during my two years in Berlin under the auspices of the Alexander von Humboldt Foundation and my host Hermann Danuser. The Herzog August Bibliothek in Wolfenbüttel provided invaluable support during my fruitful stay at that most civilized library. During several extended periods working in the British Library, the Kennington Centre for Eighteenth-Century Studies in London bolstered me both intellectually and culinarily. I am indebted to John Butt and Laurence Dreyfus, and to Victoria Cooper of Cambridge University Press for supporting the project, and especially for defending its title. Various Cornell University grants generously aided research, writing, and publication. I must mention, too, the artistic contribution of Loretta Roome, whose evocative photo of my trusty organ shoes, recently retired from active service, can be admired on the cover. Thanks are due also to my Latinist, Erik Kenyon; to Andrew Dawes for copy-editing the manuscript; and to Zachary Wadsworth for setting the musical examples. Thanks also to novelist and musician Brian Hall for rescuing a rare trove of antique nineteenth-century pedal tutors from a Boston attic, and giving them to me.

I dedicate these pages to Annette Richards and to our daughters, Elizabeth and Cecilia. Annette gave generously of herself to this book about an instrument we are both fascinated by; indeed, one that brought us together more than twenty years ago.

Abbreviations

BD	*Bach-Dokumente*. 5 vols. Ed. Werner Neumann and Hans Joachim Schulze. Kassel, 1963–2007.
BWV	Bach Werke-Verzeichnis. Compiled and ed. Wolfgang Schmieder. *Thematisch-Systematisches Verzeichnis der musikalischen Werke von Johann Sebastian Bach*, rev. and expanded edn. Wiesbaden, 1990.
NBR	*The New Bach Reader*. Ed. Christoph Wolff *et al*. New York, 1998.

Introduction: the guardian of the organ loft

The feet are indispensable to so many human activities that their almost complete lack of direct involvement in music-making in the Western classical tradition is astonishing. Since humans first began moving their bodies to musical sound, the feet have been crucial to expressing the power of song through dance. Yet the feet, capable of so many skills, now lie largely unused but for a few musical acts. At the piano and the timpani, for example, they discharge an important, but still secondary function; on both instruments, pedals were introduced relatively recently, at the beginning and end of the nineteenth century respectively. The modern harp, too, requires the use of the feet, but not to play independent polyphonic lines or to break into solos during which the hands are idle. Vital to countless quotidian tasks, the feet of most classical musicians remain as immobilized as those of their audiences. It is only at the organ that the feet are given the chance to pursue their musical potential. The most energetic form of musical performance, playing the organ unites dance and music.

It might seem logical enough that organists use their feet in ways that other musicians do not. The organ is the largest instrument, its mechanism the most involving for the player. Stacked in front of the player are often multiple keyboards – two, three, four, or as many as an outlandish six at the John Wanamaker Store in Philadelphia, where the behemoth, said to be the largest organ in the world, inhabits the seven stories of the building's central Grand Court. Below an organ's manuals is a keyboard for the feet whose standard compass on modern instruments extends to two-and-a-half octaves. In the course of this book, we will meet many amazed witnesses lucky enough to have been invited up to the organ loft to take in the spectacle of four-limbed musical performance at close quarters. For these spectators the organist appears as much an acrobat as a musician. The ability to play with all the limbs together, but also to make music with the feet alone, impresses witnesses even more for its gymnastic virtuosity than its musical eloquence. Those organists who play without using the pedals at all, or who merely hold down an occasional note with the left foot, usually consider themselves – and are considered by others – not really to be organists at all. The modern organist must be able to use his or her feet independently from the hands;

the fully certified virtuoso can manage scales, leaps across large intervals, contrapuntal lines in each of the two feet simultaneously, even ornaments such as trills, and myriad combinations of these and other figures.

Nearly all organ competitions today, from Finland to Australia, place the music of J. S. Bach at the core of the repertoire; inevitably, works by Bach are to be played in the opening round. Take, for example, the required pieces for the first stage of the 2008 Musashino-Tokyo Organ Competition:

> Olivier Messiaen (1908–1992): *Le banquet céleste*
> Johann Sebastian Bach: Praeludium et Fuga in a, BWV 543
> Johann Sebastian Bach:
>   Choose one chorale from the following:
>   – Komm, Heiliger Geist, Herre Gott, BWV 652
>   – An Wasserflüssen Babylon, BWV 653
>   – Schmücke dich, O liebe Seele, BWV 654
>   – Nun komm, der Heiden Heiland, BWV 659
>   – Allein Gott in der Höh sei Ehr, BWV 662
>   – Allein Gott in der Höh sei Ehr, BWV 663

After the centenary of Olivier Messiaen's birth is marked by the intensely slow *Le banquet céleste* of 1928, the competitor must tackle Bach's Prelude and Fugue in A minor, BWV 543. The work opens with a display of manual figuration, much of it heard above a long note held by the left foot alone, before a short but arduous pedal solo charges the two feet with mimicking what the fingers have just tossed off (see Examples 1a and 1b). The Prelude enacts the words of Bach's Obituary, published in 1754, a document whose title describes the deceased expressly as "A World Famous Organist": "With his two feet, [Bach] could play things on the pedals that many not unskillful clavier players would find it bitter enough to have to play with five fingers."[1] In Bach's organ music the feet and hands oscillate between contest and cooperation. Once the hurdle of the Prelude's first pedal solo has either been cleared or has felled the aspirations of the competitor, the piece commences a concerto-like dialogue between hands and feet, with short solo bursts interjected by the feet. This multi-voiced texture demands exact coordination between hands and feet: what the pedal previously did alone when first announcing its solo skills it must now do with the manuals. After these diverse obstacles have been dealt with, a lengthy and spirited fugue rises up to test the player, whose feet must keep meticulous pace with the racing polyphony of the upper parts before a final pedal solo, the most perilous of the entire work, marks the finish line (see Example 1c). Bach's Prelude and Fugue in A minor is a musical decathlon unto itself, requiring speed, endurance, suppleness, poise, balance, coordination, marksmanship (where is that low pedal E in the last solo passage for the feet?), steadiness, strength, and, perhaps most important of all, confidence.

---

[1] *NBR*, 306.

Example 1a   J. S. Bach, Prelude in A minor, BWV 543/1, opening manual figuration, bars 1–3

Example 1b   J. S. Bach, Prelude in A minor, BWV 543/1, first pedal solo, bars 23–29

The Bach chorale preludes also on the Tokyo competition's required list are more introspective. But they also have obbligato pedal lines that demand perhaps even greater attention to the nuances of melodic contour and articulation. In this first round of an international competition, as in so many others, the feet must not only amaze with their dancing accuracy, but they are also charged with moving the listener with their subtle expressivity. In the Tokyo competition, as at almost every other event like it in international organ culture, the *pedaliter* music of J. S. Bach guards the entrance to the organists' fraternity,

Example 1c   J. S. Bach, Fugue in A minor, BWV 543/2, final pedal solo, bars 138–150

not only because of its overall musical qualities – chief among them contrapuntal craftsmanship – but also for the purely physical reason that it provides
the classic test for the independence of the feet. There are more difficult pieces
when judged in purely statistical terms: more notes, to be played faster, with
more accidentals. But in the exposed writing for the feet and the requirements

of aligning them deftly with a relentlessly exposed counterpoint, no prior or subsequent body of organ works has surpassed Bach's in gauging technical sufficiency with two hands and two feet. "Real" organists must show that their feet can do what Bach's could do.

ORIGINS AND ADAPTATION

The purported universality of Bach's music, and its ubiquitous presence in the international organ repertoire since the nineteenth century, tend to obscure the culturally specific origins of this often flamboyant, pedal-based approach to the instrument. Equipping organs with full pedalboards and a battery of independent pedal stops and playing on them with great musical force and finesse became the standard across western Europe only by the second half of the nineteenth century. While the association of the organ with monumental pedal pipes and the dazzling footwork of the organist has attained pervasive recognition in both high and popular culture, in literature, film, and music, this conception of the instrument and its player was a German one before it became global. At least three hundred years before the modern German nation was forged in the late nineteenth century, the people living in the cultural-linguistic area known as Germany believed that they had been responsible for the invention of the pedal in the fifteenth century; they boasted that this development had revolutionized the musical possibilities afforded by the organ.

No instrument has changed as much as the organ, not only over its long history of two millennia, but even over the last one hundred years. The modern Steinway has arguably more in common with the first Cristofori pianos from the early 1700s than the giant organ in the John Wanamaker store in Philadelphia does with the Silbermann organs known to Bach. Yet a well-trained organist should be able to perform a Bach fugue, that by-now timeless standard, on both instruments. None of these variables is more unsettling or requires greater adaptability on the part of the organist than playing pedalboards with their disparate compasses, layouts, octave widths, and key sizes. Those of Bach's time were flat and had wide keys, though their size was by no means standardized from country to country, or even region to region or builder to builder (see Figure 1). In the nineteenth century various innovations led to new forms: curved pedalboards brought the upper and lower notes of the pedal somewhat out from the console and up towards the bench, supposedly allowing for easier access, since organists' legs as they splay describe an arc. Extending this thinking into three dimensions – as the legs splay they not only rotate back but also upward – produced the most typical arrangement on modern organs, standardized by among others the American Guild of Organists: the radiating and concave pedalboard (see Figure 2). Imagine confronting a flat piano keyboard one day and a curved one the next. Sitting down at the organ and surveying the unfamiliar

Figure 1   Munetaka Yokota organ, 2011, Anabel Taylor Chapel, Cornell University,
based on Arp Schnitger, 1708

terrain – the spread and placement of the registers, the distance between manuals, and legions of other aspects of this new landscape – was and is a bracing, often unnerving experience, especially when a concert must be played within hours of this first encounter, or if a host organist, or other onlookers, experts and amateurs, are listening and watching. Trying out an organ for the first time is an adventure like none other in music. All musicians need to have their wits about them when playing a new instrument, but none so much as the organist, who must have a body trained in the art of

Figure 2   Aeolian-Skinner organ, 1940, Sage Chapel, Cornell University

adaptability and a temperament eager for the unknown. To be a traveling organ virtuoso – and we will meet many in this book – was, and is, to be a brave soul, willing to face diverse hazards.

The most fundamental differences in organs across national traditions were found in the pedal. Compared to the relative standardization of the twenty-first century – a partial uniformity that is breaking down somewhat with the revival of interest in historic repertories and organ building – the differences in pedals were enormous until the nineteenth century, during which the German-style pedalboard was adopted across Europe. I examine aspects of this transformation in Chapter 5. With very few exceptions, English organs were without pedals; English organists sat at their instrument as if it was a harpsichord, with their feet planted on the floor. Italian pedalboards were small both in the size of the keys and in the compass, typically of an octave; the keyboard for the feet was often canted upward (see Figure 3).

Figure 3   Italian organ, c. 1700, Memorial Art Gallery, Rochester, New York

Most often there were no independent stops, but rather "pull-downs" permanently coupling the pedal to the manual.

Spanish organs of the sixteenth and seventeenth centuries had minimal pedal, often of only a few pipes, or had no pedal whatsoever. The large instruments made by the Flemish builders Gillis and Hans Brebos were anomalies with respect to Iberian traditions; their instruments from the late sixteenth century in El Escorial had full northern pedalboards and plentiful allotment of independent stops.[2] One wonders what Spanish organists, from whom no *pedaliter* music survives, did with such an organ, though they must have used this unexampled pedal division, if only to reinforce cadences or powerfully deliver *cantus firmi*.[3] The two keyboards for the feet on the late eighteenth-century organ in Toledo cathedral were exceptional, but the small keys did not allow for rapid, virtuosic playing[4] (see Figure 4). The organs of Bohemia and Austria also had smaller pedal compasses than German instruments, and did not foster a tradition of vigorous independent pedaling.

French organs did have independent pedal divisions, though they were proportionally far smaller in terms of the number of stops allocated to the feet; the pedalboards had small, button-like keys, not conducive to the kind of elaborate playing common in north and central Germany (see Figure 5). There are a few examples of demanding pedalwork in the French classical tradition of the seventeenth and eighteenth centuries, but even a bravura display piece such as the *Grand prélude avec les pedalles de trompette meslées* from Jacques Boyvin's *Livre d'orgue* (Paris, 1689–90), did not measure up to the difficulty and panache of the German tradition (see Example 2). An important feature of this piece that distinguishes it from the music of Bach (who knew Boyvin's music and apparently admired his work, as well as that of other French organists)[5] is that the lowest manual voice, played largely with the little finger of the left hand, essentially doubles the pedal when the harmony changes. For the Germans, pedal-playing was not only a matter of what the feet could do, but that they could assert polyphonic independence from the hands even in quick-moving fugues. Louis Marchand, whom Bach met and supposedly vanquished in a playing contest in Dresden in 1717 (see Chapter 4), began his first suite for organ with a piece for double pedal. But the feet of the German tradition, both in staid contrapuntal works and in virtuosic showpieces, were far more ambitious; for Bach and for many of his

---

[2] Susan Tattershall and James Wyly, *The Brebos Organs of El Escorial* (Richmond, Virginia: OHS Press, 2006), pp. 212–213.

[3] Peter Williams, *The European Organ* (Bloomington, Indiana and London: Indiana University Press, 1966), pp. 240–243.

[4] *Ibid.*, p. 263.

[5] George Stauffer, "Boyvin, Grigny, D'Anglebert, and Bach's Assimilation of French Classical Organ Music," *Early Music*, 21 (1993), 83–96.

Figure 4   Toledo Cathedral, José Verdalonga (1796–1797)

German predecessors and successors, the pedal was not an ornament to be brought out on special occasions or only in particular genres, but was an aesthetic necessity, even if it too could be deployed for astonishing, rather than erudite, effect. The pedal-centric views of the organ that long

Figure 5   St. Jacques and St. Christophe, Houdan, Louis-Alexandre Clicquot, 1733

dominated the instrument's historiography continue to be revised as we learn from the revival of diverse repertories and performing and building traditions that pre-date the ascendancy of the German pedal ideal. But the hierarchy remains in place: to be a "real" organist requires mastery of the feet, even if one specializes in historic repertories played on instruments with small pedalboards, or none at all. Bach's music remains the standard of "complete" organ performance, his pedaling the ideal.

Example 2   Jacques Boyvin,*Grand prélude avec les pedalles de trompette meslées*, from *Premier livre d'orgue* (1689–90), bars 18–23

For only about the last century-and-a-half, then, has the concept of the "organ" necessarily meant an instrument with independent pedals to be exploited by obbligato playing with the feet. The universal adoption of north-German-style pedalboards had a decisive effect on the historiography of the organ. The author of the section on Italy in the lengthy article on the organ in the 1960 edition of the German-language music encyclopedia, *Die Musik in Geschichte und Gegenwart*, was Renato Lunelli whose work I draw on in this study; though Lunelli was the leading historian of Italy's organ past, he accepted the German teleological model: "it was only at the end of the 19th century that Italian organs began to be equipped with a *normal* pedal" (my emphasis) – that is, with a German-style pedal with separate stops and a compass of at least two octaves.[6] While the Early Music movement has broadened the sense of what constitutes a legitimate organ, Lunelli invoked a norm still operative today.

That the organ eventually allowed, indeed demanded, the feet's equal involvement in music-making on a keyboard designed for their use was in no way predestined. The instrument's origins were in classical antiquity, where it had been used as an all-purpose noise-maker in warfare, gladiatorial combat and training, and in ceremonial events such as processions and investitures.[7] After several centuries of silence, the organ was reintroduced

---

[6] Renato Lunelli, "Orgel: Italien" in *Die Musik in Geschichte und Gegenwart*, vol. x, cols. 281–284.

[7] Peter Williams and Barbara Owen, *The New Grove Organ* (London: Macmillan, 1988), pp. 42–58; and Peter Williams, *The Organ in Western Culture, 750–1250* (Cambridge University Press, 1993), pp. 1–16, 137–144.

into the West in the middle of the eighth century when Byzantine ambassadors dispatched from Constantinople by Emperor Constantine V brought an organ to the court of the Frankish king, Pippin.[8] This new musical technology quickly began to be cultivated within the European monastic tradition, and by the second millennium of the Common Era organs were visually and sonically adorning large churches. By the fourteenth century organs were being equipped with pedals, though the Germans claimed that it was in the late fifteenth century that they developed the more substantial keyboard for the feet that allowed for a complex, multi-limbed approach to making music, seemingly unprecedented and still unique in solo musical performance.[9] This book considers the entwined ideological and musical aspects of this unique form of music-making. My central claim is that the pedal served as the most potent symbol of the instrument's musical and cultural significance in Germany – and later beyond – for players, listeners, and spectators. More than that, Germans saw the pedal as their vital contribution to, and a reflection of their standing in, European musical life. Organ performance with hands and feet was long praised in Germany as one of its greatest contributions to music and culture more broadly: I want to take such claims seriously and suggest reasons why Germans were so proud of what they could do with their feet at the organ.

A CONGRESS OF FEET

One can get a sense of the central importance of the pedal in Germany from a singular event in the history of organ building and playing, which took place at the end of July 1596 in the castle church at Gröningen in central Germany.[10] It was here, in his favorite residence, that Duke Heinrich Julius of Braunschweig-Lüneburg, employer of the first organ historian Michael Praetorius, convened a gathering of leading organists from across Germany to dedicate the newly finished instrument by David Beck, a well-known builder resident in nearby Halberstadt. The participants called by the duke represented a vast geographical area extending the length and breadth of Germany: the musicians came from Augsburg, four hundred kilometers south of Gröningen, to Danzig, some six hundred kilometers to the northeast. Several of the players came from cities near the mouth of the Elbe (two

---

[8] For a skeptical view of the story of the organ's reintroduction in 757, see Peter Williams, *The Organ in Western Culture*, p. 58.

[9] The other instrument that requires the use of hands and feet is the drum kit, equipped with two pedals only from the 1920s. But only the organist uses all the limbs to produce melodies.

[10] See David Yearsley, "An Ideal Organ and Its Experts Across the Seventeenth Century" in Kerala Snyder (ed.), *The Organ as a Mirror of Its Time* (Oxford University Press, 2002), pp. 93–112. See also Wolf Hobohm, "Zur Geschichte der David-Beck-Orgel in Gröningen" in Eitelfriedrich Thom (ed.), *Bericht über das 5. Symposium zu Fragen des Orgelbaus im 17./18. Jahrhundert* (Michaelstein: [n.p.], 1985), pp. 50–70.

from the famous organ center of Hamburg), and others journeyed from their homes near the Baltic coast (Lübeck, Rostock, and Schwerin). Directly to the east, Brandenburg and Leipzig were represented, as were many central German towns – Wolffenbüttel, Braunschweig, Halberstadt, and Helmstedt, among a dozen others. From these far-flung locales the participants traveled to Gröningen to test a massive and daringly innovative instrument in an atmosphere of celebration, collegial exchange, and, one suspects, competition.

The lavishly appointed Gröningen organ, its stunning case richly decorated with carvings and gold leaf, was a striking adornment to an already resplendent church. The building had been renovated and expanded under Duke Heinrich Julius's auspices in a project he began almost immediately on his accession in 1589; work on the organ started three years later. For almost two centuries after its inauguration the Gröningen organ was recognized as a landmark; its extraordinary disposition was printed in several important treatises from the seventeenth and eighteenth centuries, including *De Organographia* (1619) by Michael Praetorius, himself a participant at the congress, and the *Musicalische Handleitung* (1721) by Friedrich Erhard Niedt, whose compendium of organ specifications was collected and collated by the book's editor, Johann Mattheson. On his way to Leipzig in 1706, the young Mattheson had made a point of visiting Gröningen to play the instrument; half a century later he would leave money in his will for the construction of one of the largest organs in Germany, in Hamburg's Michaeliskirche, which we will also visit on more than one occasion in these pages.[11] Mattheson included the Gröningen disposition among the "Sixty (mostly) Famous Organs" of his day.[12]

Of the twenty organ specifications collected by Praetorius in *De Organographia*, the Gröningen Castle church organ was the largest, exceeding the size of the monumental instruments in Hamburg's Jacobikirche and Danzig's Marienkirche by several stops. But the Gröningen organ's remarkable nature had as much to do with its scope as with the kaleidoscopic timbral potential immediately apparent from the unprecedented specification (see below).

The most striking aspect of this instrument was its behemoth pedal containing twenty-six stops, nearly half of the organ's total; these pedal ranks were divided between side towers, a chest inside the main part of the case, and compartments placed on either side of the keyboard. Here, too, colorful reed stops abounded: seven in total, offering three distinct options at 8′ pitch. But the extreme value accorded to variety of sound and the

---

[11] Johann Mattheson, *Grundlage einer Ehren-Pforte* (Hamburg: the author, 1740), first modern edn., ed. Max Schneider (Berlin: Leo Liepmannssohn, 1910), p. 195.

[12] Friedrich Erhard Niedt, *Musicalische Handleitung*, 2nd edn., ed. Johann Mattheson (Hamburg: Benjamin Schiller's widow, 1721), trans. into English Pamela L. Poulin and Irmgard C. Taylor as *The Musical Guide* (Oxford: Clarendon, 1989), pp. 106–107.

Specification of the organ in Gröningen Castle church, David Beck, 1592–1596 (Andreas Werckmeister, Organum Gruningense redivivum *(Quedlinburg and Aschersleben: Struntz, 1705), paragraph 11)*

Oberwerk	Rück-Positiv	Pedal
Quintathön 16′	Quintathön 8′	Quintathön 16′
Principal 8′	Principal 4′	Principal-Bass 16′
Rohrflöt oder Gedackt 8′	Gedackt	Sub-Bass 16′
Groß-Qüer-Flöt 8′	oder Rohrflöt 4′	Groß-Gemß-Horn 16′
Gems-Horn 8′	Gems Horn 4′	Octav-Bass 8′
Octava 4′	Octava 2′	Klein-Gemßhorn 8′
Kleine Querflöte 4′	Spitzflöt 2′	Super Octav 4′
Nacht-Horn 4′	Quinta 1–1/2′	Klein Quintathön 8′
Quinta 3′	Sifflöt 1′	Grosse Quer-flöt 8′
Hohlflöth 2′	Mixtur IV	Klein-Gemßhorn 8′
Mixtur VI–VIII	Zimbel III	Super Octav 4′
Cymbel II	Sordunen 16′	Gedackt 4′
	Trompet 8′	Hohlflöt-Baß 4′
Kleine Brust zum	Krum-Horn 8′	Nachthorn 4′
Ober-Manual-Clavier	Singend Regal 4′	Quint-Bass 3′
Klein Gedact 2′		Gedackt Quint 3′
Super Octav 1′		Hohl-Quint 3′
Zimbel II		Gedackt Quint 1–1/2′
Mixtur III Repetirend		Bauerflöt 1′
Zimbel-Regal 8′		Posaunen-Bass 16′
Groß Regal 8′		Sordun-Baß 16′
Rancket 8′		Trompeten Baß 8′
		Krumhorn 8′
		Rancket 8′
		Schallmeyen-Baß 4′
		Klein Regal-Baß 2′

technological capacity to achieve such refinements can perhaps best be seen in the seemingly esoteric inclusion of no fewer than three 3′ flue stops, playing a twelfth above 8′ pitch, in the pedal alone. One marvels, though perhaps not without a slight shake of the head, too, at the resources poured into the pedal even at this unusual pitch level. One is hard-pressed to conceive of the ways in which these stops might have been used. Still, the message is as clear from this unusual trio of registers as from the entire outsized pedal division: the feet were capable of great things, and should be given the chance to explore new territory.

The conception of the Gröningen instrument might be seen as an extreme manifestation of the pride German musical culture derived from what it saw as its unique contribution to organ design and playing. For Germans, the independent pedal was an essential feature in the most famous exemplars of their universal musical tool, and a more complete pedal than at Gröningen could hardly be imagined. With nearly half the entire stops of the instrument assigned to the pedal – and these were certainly the most expensive parts of the project, since the larger pipes required more metal and were most difficult to fabricate – this was a giant edifice largely dedicated to musical feet. It was not simply for geographic and linguistic reasons that all the participants called to Gröningen in 1596 came from German-speaking Europe. It was a matter of performance: only German organists would begin to know what to do with such outlandish pedal riches.

While vibrant organ traditions have flourished across Europe, it is only in Germany that a performance tradition based on the elaborate and demanding use of the feet has been cultivated for half a millennium. The mechanical advances that allowed for use of the feet were universally attributed to Germans and remarked on by European writers when Germans attempted, though without enduring results, to introduce these developments beyond their borders as early as around 1500 (see Chapter 1). While foreign visitors marveled, Germans were even more emphatic in their praise of their organists' footwork. In Nuremberg, an important center of organ-building, clock-making and other advanced technologies, the Meistersinger Hans Rosenplüt singled out the organ in the Lorenzkirche in his 1490 *Lobegedicht* (Poem of Praise) commissioned by the city fathers. With its "massed choirs of pipes," the Lorenz organ, one of the largest and most magnificent in Europe with a massive 32′ open Principal stop in the pedal, crowns Rosenplüt's list of the city's treasures, and it is the extraordinary mode of performance it inspires that fires Rosenplüt's imagination: "One touches it with hands and feet, praising God and His Mother."[13] Paeans would be sung in praise of J. S. Bach, but Germany's recognition of its organists' unique skill with four limbs had been inaugurated long before him. Technology and technique united to allow the German organist to pursue his unique mode of performance to the astonishment of his countrymen and foreigners, from Rosenplüt's time into our own. It was the pedal that allowed the Germans to make a claim to their privileged status at the organ. The importance of the pedal in creating a sense of German pride, not only at the organ but also in musical culture more generally, is the central theme of this book.

ITINERARY

While various uses of the feet at the organ pedalboard will be treated in these pages, this book is only tangentially concerned with issues of performance practice, among them perennial questions regarding pedal technique.[14] Though changing approaches to organ performance open onto a rich field

---

[13] Hermann Harrassowitz, "Geschichte der Kirchenmusik an St. Lorenz in Nürnberg," *Mitteilung des Vereins der Stadt Nürnberg*, 60 (1973), 1–151, at 7–11. A facsimile of the verse from the Rosenplüt poem is found on p. 9.

[14] The most often posed of these questions asks whether Bach used his heels, or just his toes. My answer is that he did use his heels though not nearly as often as in modern pedal technique. There are many

of inquiry, my main concern in this study is the cultural significance of the use of the feet across several hundred years from Arnolt Schlick to J. S. Bach some two centuries later, and then to his disciples, who would spread the German approach to making music at the organ throughout the world.

Chapter 1 begins in the fifteenth century and illuminates the mythic importance of the purported inventor of the pedal and his role in the construction of German uniqueness in its version of organ history; I trace the lasting relevance of this mythology and show how it continued to buttress historical claims for German technological and musical primacy at the instrument into the twentieth century. This historiographical inquiry provides a frame for appreciating the oldest contrapuntal genre requiring hands and feet: the trio. Chapter 2 also encompasses a broad chronological period in examining the largest polyphonic arrays that engage the feet and hands and test the physical and intellectual limits of the player. The organ's singular capabilities as a contrapuntal instrument are expressed in these formidable polyphonic genres, which in turn contributed to the status of the organ as the ultimate expression of German musical erudition and self-sufficiency. Chapter 3 traverses the northern half of Germany in the company of the greatest of walkers and organists, J. S. Bach, as it follows his progress across the land and the steps of his feet in virtuosic pedal solos and the dogged, though often liberating, cyclic patterns of the ground bass. I try to place these pedal achievements geographically and ethically in the topography of German culture of the eighteenth century. In Chapter 4 we journey beyond Germany's borders to see what travelers thought of the organs of other traditions that they encountered on their Grand Tours. We then return to Bach's region of Germany to examine the ways in which his music bolstered the position of the organ in an increasingly cosmopolitan Europe. Chapter 5 is even more concerned with Germans abroad as it follows representatives of the Bach tradition as they exported German pedals and pedaling in the nineteenth century. Chapter 6 attempts to imagine Bach at the organ in perhaps the most famous recital in the instrument's long history, offering a wider cultural context for the movements of Bach's performing body.

MY PEDAL PAST

As is the case for all modern organists, I am a product of the Bachian, pedal-based approach to organ-playing and its attendant pride in the musical

documented examples of the use of the heel in the eighteenth century in the Bach circle, especially in passages either directly transcribed from instrumental music or composed in imitation of it. Given this evidence, it would be hard to maintain that Bach involved his heels only in exceptional cases. See Quentin Faulkner, *J. S. Bach's Keyboard Technique: A Historical Introduction* (St. Louis: Concordia, 1984), pp. 45–47. See also Sandra Soderlund, *How Did They Play? How Did They Teach?: A History of Keyboard Technique* (Chapel Hill: Hinshaw Music, 2006), and Jon Laukvik, *Orgelschule zur historischen Aufführungspraxis*, trans. Brigitte and Michael Harris (Stuttgart: Carus, 1996).

capabilities of the feet. Like many, I came to the organ from the piano. To play the organ was to use the feet vigorously. My first teacher, Katherine S. Fowler (who had been the last student of the early-twentieth-century American virtuoso Lynwood Farnham), had me begin where Bach had started his students: with the short chorale preludes with obbligato pedal from the *Orgelbüchlein*. Two years later I found myself a finalist in the American Guild of Organists' Young Artists National Competition, held that year (1982) in Washington, DC on a large, electric action organ with four manuals and pedal. The competition's compulsory piece was, as in Musashino in 2008, a major Bach work: the Toccata, Adagio, and Fugue, BWV 564. The Toccata includes a long and difficult pedal solo (described in Chapter 3, p. 135); this test for the feet opens onto a concerto-like section with pedal trills and skeins of sixteenth-notes. The fugue is a lively and demanding gigue not unlike that of the A minor fugue, BWV 543 and also including a final pedal solo – one last obstacle that might trip up the feet before the end of some ten minutes of concerted organ-playing. In addition to the Toccata, Adagio, and Fugue, the competition's rules stipulated that two contrasting works be chosen by the competitor; these three pieces in total were to be played (and the registrations set up) within forty minutes of sitting down at the organ bench. My new teacher, Edward Hansen, one of the great American organ pedagogues of the late twentieth century, had laid out an ambitious program for his seventeen-year-old student: after the Bach would come Mozart's *Fantasie* in F minor, K. 608, originally for mechanical organ; to conclude I would play the *Final* from Louis Vierne's Sixth Symphony, op. 59 (1930) for organ.

In the transcription of the Mozart *Fantasie* (see Examples 3a and 3b) that I learned, the bassline is rather indiscriminately given to the feet, which are asked to play outlandishly difficult figures, from the rapid turns followed by leaps in the opening section, to the whirring sixteenth-note patterns in the coda. Although the *Fantasie* was written for mechanical organ, one doesn't doubt that Mozart himself could have tried his biggest organ piece himself on the large organs he encountered on his travels. But in the transcription I performed – quite foreign to eighteenth-century approaches to such music – the feet are asked not only to match the dexterity of human fingers, but to do so with the ease of a machine with its pinned barrel that perfectly churns out any and all figures, however thorny.

The *Final* of Vierne's Sixth Symphony ends with several pages of high-speed scales rushing up and down the pedalboard while the hands grab long-held full chords in the manuals above (see Example 4). Scales are among the hardest figures to play with the feet, and the Vierne movement – the last number of his last organ symphony – is the ultimate test of that facility; there are few things more difficult and depleting than playing a smooth legato at breakneck tempo, swiveling the body at the organ bench as the pedal line ascends and descends like a rollercoaster. As I

Example 3a   Mozart, *Fantasie* in F minor, K. 608, bars 1–9

sprinted towards the finish line on the last page of this piece, the proctor put his hand on my arm from behind and stopped me. I had run up against the forty-minute limit for the program within bars of the final chord. That experience probably helps explain why I have spent the last several years researching and pondering the ideological origins and development of the feet in organ performance. In Mozart's Austria instruments had limited pedalboards and organists there did little with their feet; Mozart thought of himself as an exception (see Chapter 3); a hundred years before Vierne published his sixth and last organ symphony the kind of pedaling he demanded of the player had been unimaginable. The pyrotechnics of these pages reflected the German influence, beginning in the middle of the nineteenth century, that had spawned the French virtuoso tradition and its often extravagant use of the feet, which in turn had me practicing Vierne's *Final* for the better part of a year as I prepared in Seattle in the northwest corner of the United States for the final round to be played in the country's capital. When I had set about learning the organ two years earlier I had simply assumed that organists always played with their feet: the more difficult the better.

Example 3b   Mozart, *Fantasie* in F minor, K. 608, bars 213–222

I am glad enough to have spent so many of my teenage hours exercising my feet at the pedalboard of the organ in the local church. I was unaware then that, viewed in the broadest historical frame, the organ with full pedals and the musical obsession with the feet they inspired were specific, and quite recent, developments within more than a millennium of European organ culture. From early on in my organ studies, I had played music without pedals by William Byrd, Girolamo Frescobaldi, and even Bach himself. But this wasn't "real" organ music; as a result of my early

Example 4   *Final* from Symphony No. 6 for Organ, Op. 59 by Louis Vierne, sprint to finish

training with excellent teachers and my own fascination with Bach's music, I had fully adopted a German attitude towards organ performance forcefully expressed by many writers during Bach's lifetime and long after it.

Example 4   (cont.)

THE ORGAN IN EXILE

Being stopped at a contest amid one of the most athletic and exacting pedal passages in the repertory is probably not unrelated to another motivation for writing this book, less nostalgic but not less personal: my broader subsequent awareness of the declining relevance of the organ in musical culture at large. Are the feet merely an oddity, a sideshow, a circus act, or is there something more complex and rewarding to this musical act than virtuosic display, however enlivening it may be? An awareness of the organ's changing cultural status is one of the larger motivations for writing this book. For even the most loyal subjects of the King of Instruments must now accept that he was long ago toppled from the throne he had occupied for centuries atop European music culture. The language of his court-in-exile embraces its own insularity: the organ's admirers speak of obscure repertories, mysteriously named stops, mathematically daunting pipe scalings, among other arcana. Expertise is the devotees' refuge; specialization assuages their isolation. On those occasions when the instrument does become the ostensible focus of wider attention, it usually serves merely as a prop for discussions of theory or for an inquiry into musical sources. The organ and its music are almost always absent.[15]

The great distance the organ has drifted from the mainstream can quickly be gauged by leafing through seminal publications from the seventeenth and eighteenth centuries; in many of these books the organ is a vast topic unto itself. In Mersenne's *Harmonie Universelle*, to cite just one of many examples, the organ is the only instrument allotted its own book, the longest in this encyclopedic work.[16] Closer to J. S. Bach's time and circle, Johann Jacob Adlung's *Anleitung zu der musikalischen Gelahrtheit*, like so many other treatises of its kind, begins the treatment of practical music with the organ, devoting to it 200 of the volume's 800 pages.[17]

Secularization, the displacement of the organ as the West's most complex technology, and other forces of modernity have conjoined increasingly to ignore this compendium of art and science, theory and practice, one endowed with the richest and longest repertory of any instrument. The organ also confronts many urgent themes of interest to musical scholarship and musical culture, among them the changing value of the symbols of European art music, the dynamic relationship between musical technology and the human body, and the mysterious connection between performer and audience, even when

---

[15] Like J. Peter Burkholder, who wrote the only article to address the organ and organ performance in the entire run of the *Journal of the American Musicological Society*, I lament the truth that "the organ repertory [is] so separate from the repertories that receive more attention from scholars and are better represented in our textbooks and teaching." (J. Peter Burkholder, "The Organist in Ives," *Journal of the American Musicological Society*, 55 [2002], 255–310.) That Burkholder feels obliged in his excellent article to explain aspects of the organ and of organ-playing in the most basic terms to the *JAMS* readership suggests the state of scholarly neglect into which the instrument and its music have fallen. And then, the listing of the *Festschrift* in honor of Harald Vogel, one of the most important organists of the last forty years, amongst the ethnomusicology books in the Publications Received section of a 2007 issue of the same journal might be taken as inadvertent, if accurate, confirmation of this state of affairs. The organ is marooned on a desert island waiting for the anthropologist to arrive. (*Journal of the American Musicological Society*, 60 [2007], 262.) See Cleveland Johnson (ed.), *Orphei organi antiqui: Essays in Honor of Harald Vogel* (Orcas, Washington: Westfield Center, 2006).

[16] Marin Mersenne, *Harmonie Universelle*, 3 vols. (Paris: Sebastian Cramoisy, 1636–37; reprint, Éditions du Centre National de la Recherche Scientifique, 1963), vol. III, pp. 307–412; English trans. Robert E. Chapman, *Harmonie Universelle: The Books on Instruments* (The Hague: Martinus Nijhoff, 1957), esp. pp. 391–393.

[17] Jakob Adlung, *Anleitung zu der musikalischen Gelahrtheit* (Erfurt: Jungnicol, 1758; reprint, Kassel: Bärenreiter, 1953), pp. 337–550.

the player is hidden from view behind his or her massive instrument.[18] Given the organ's unmatched wealth as a potential object of study, it may seem eccentric to concentrate my attention on the pedal. For reasons that I hope will emerge in the course of this book, the pedal symbolized the unique ways in which German organists played: the feet were the foundation of four-limbed performance because they controlled the largest pipes, conduits of an awesome profundity, crucial to the German conception of the organ and of the solo performance of polyphony. It is no accident that the rapturous contemporary accounts of Bach's organ-playing concentrate on his pedaling. Although I want to recapture these reports' excitement, my larger aim is to describe the cultural work done by this enthusiasm for what was once a specifically German musical practice. If we can better appreciate the significance of Bach's approach to performance, we can begin to understand again why the organ has so inspired experts and amateurs alike. It was not stature alone that made the organ king, but the manifold ways the instrument allowed, indeed demanded, a unique physical involvement in music-making, both intricate and flamboyant. All this is not to argue that music without pedal is less worthwhile: that the repertories of seventeenth-century Italy, Spain, England, and the Low Countries make only slight use of the feet does not diminish their musical value. Jan Pieterszoon Sweelinck was a great organist, yet his music seems to involve his feet rarely and his organs had only a few stops for the pedal. In Amsterdam he trained many north German students from that leading organ center of Hamburg in the art of counterpoint and probably performance, too, so that he became known as the "Maker of Hamburg Organists."[19] Nonetheless, playing with hands and feet in fully independent fashion is indeed something unique in Western music; I hope that my investigations of the cultural and musical value accorded this mode of performance might interest more than only faithful organists and devotees, and might also help others to appreciate the potential of this great instrument and its history. The organ is ready for a comeback. Let's see if Bach's feet can help lead the way.

[18] For a pathbreaking engagement with issues of embodiment and performance, see Elisabeth Le Guin, *Boccherini's Body: an Essay in Carnal Musicology* (Berkeley: University of California Press, 2005).
[19] Johann Mattheson, *Grundlage einer Ehren-Pforte* (Hamburg: the author, 1740; modern edn., ed. Max Schneider, Berlin: Liepmannsohn, 1910; reprint, Kassel: Bärenreiter, 1969), p. 332.

CHAPTER I

Inventing the organist's feet

THE MYTHOLOGY OF THE PEDALS

The desire to identify and honor inventors is itself inseparable from the restless, relentless human drive to invent. The Western obsession with technological innovation focuses on the individual, who, sparked by unique insight, is the engine of progress. Even in our own age, as human "advances" become ever more rapid and technological developments are disseminated with startling global efficiency, the credit for discoveries is more than simply a matter of staking out patents in the pursuit of personal riches. Aside from the utility and wealth-generating potential of their inventions, inventors also make people proud, especially *their* people – their village, their city, their country. Robert Friedel and Paul Israel have shown in their account of the development of the light bulb, that some twenty inventors devised successful solutions to the problem of incandescent illumination before Thomas Edison did, even if these other approaches were less efficient than that of the man ultimately credited with the invention itself.[1] The idea that there was a single inventor of the light bulb is simplistic, indeed inaccurate. Still, Edison was accorded that honor by history, just as he was enriched by the market. That an American was the inventor of the light bulb carries enormous symbolic value: the light bulb is a literal and figurative beacon of Yankee ingenuity, a global metaphor for bright ideas, indeed for invention itself.

The veneration of inventors was a practice cultivated by the Greeks, and in turn revived in early modern Europe, where the humanistic study of invention reflected a growing cultural emphasis on innovation and recognition for it. The central contribution to this revival was *De inventoribus rerum* ("On the inventors of all things") by the Italian humanist Polydore Vergil (1470–1555); first published in Venice in 1499, the study was expanded from three to eight books in 1521. This encyclopedic work was subsequently reprinted many times and translated into all major European languages; it was one of the most influential and widely disseminated books

---

[1] Robert Friedel and Paul Israel, *Edison's Electric Light: Biography of an Invention* (New Brunswick, New Jersey: Rutgers University Press, 1987), pp. 115–117.

of the sixteenth century. As Catherine Atkinson has shown in her study of
Vergil, his conception of invention was an expansive one; it included not
only the fabrication of objects such as musical instruments, and concepts
such as the calendar, but encompassed a vast range of things we now think
of separately under "discovery" (e.g., medical remedies, geometry), as well as
topics such as the founding of cultural institutions and practices such as
marriage and religion.[2] Fundamental to Vergil's project and its governing
rhetorical methods, however, was praise of individual inventors, mostly
from antiquity, as useful examples of what human striving and genius could
achieve.

In the domain of music, no technological achievement held the promise
to award more honor to its putative inventor than the organ, which boasted
a history longer than that of any other instrument, resounded in the pages of
the Bible and upheld a vital role in divine worship. The organ was one of the
most sophisticated and costliest of contrivances, complicated to construct
and difficult to operate, dazzling to the ear and to the eye. But even the
assiduous and imaginative Vergil had to consign the organ to the forlorn list
of inventions whose inventors remained unknown, alongside such inventions as important to the age of world discovery as the compass: denied their
due praise by the vagaries of the historical record, these anonymous figures
occupy what amounts to an appendix to the volume, the very last chapter of
the original three books of the 1499 edition of *De inventoribus*, which
follows directly on the author's treatment of prostitution and barbers. Vergil
lamented that "however worthy of admiration and praise" the organ was, no
individual could be accorded the honor of having devised and built the first
one. While Vergil acknowledged that the same uncertainty obtained for the
other keyboard instruments – the harpsichord and clavichord – failure to
establish an inventor was all the more acute in the case of the organ, given its
historical and cultural significance.[3]

Michael Praetorius, one of the leading organ experts and finest practical
musicians of the later sixteenth and early seventeenth centuries, had duti-
fully read *De inventoribus* in preparation for his treatise on instruments, *De
organographia* of 1619, the third part of which constitutes the seminal

---

[2] Catherine Atkinson, *Inventing Inventors in Renaissance Europe: Polydore Vergil's "De inventoribus
rerum" (1499 and 1521)* (Tübingen: Mohr Siebeck, 2007), pp. 1–66, 123–171. For a modern
English edition, see Polydore Vergil, *On Discovery*, ed. and trans. Brian P. Copenhaver (Cambridge,
Massachusetts: Harvard University Press, 2002). See also Polydore Vergil, *De inventoribus rerum*
(Venice: De Pensis, 1499).

[3] Praetorius offers his own translation of Vergil's short discussion of the organ in the *Syntagma musicum
III: De organographia* (Wolfenbüttel: Elias Holwein, 1619; reprint Kassel: Bärenreiter, 1985), p. 89;
Praetorius did not use the German translation of c. 1550, but one of the Latin editions. See Polydore
Vergil, *Eigentlicher Bericht, der Erfinder aller Ding*, trans. Marcus Tatius Alpinus (Frankfurt: Weygand
Han [between 1550 and 1552]), p. 212. In fact, the invention of the organ in its earliest form as the
hydraulis (water organ) can be attributed to Ctesibus, an Alexandrian engineer of the third century
BCE. See Peter Williams and Barbara Owen, *The New Grove Organ* (London: Macmillan, 1998),
pp. 42–43.

history of the organ. The book begins by following the course laid out by Vergil – with a search for origins. Copies of Vergil's *De inventoribus rerum* were plentiful north of the Alps, both in the original Latin and in German translation, and Praetorius would likely have consulted an exemplar in the impressive library of the Duke of Braunschweig-Wolfenbüttel, Heinrich Julius, one of the great patrons of the organ in its long history, and Praetorius's employer. Because of Vergil's critical, historically framed views of many religious practices, among them sacerdotal celibacy and papal indulgences, his book was censored in Catholic countries during the years of the Counter-Reformation of the sixteenth century, and accordingly all the more popular among Protestant humanists such as Praetorius.[4]

After an opening discourse on the organ's unparalleled perfection, lauding it as "a king above all other instruments," Praetorius's historical account proper begins by referring to *De inventoribus rerum* in acknowledging that the organ's inventor will indeed never be discovered. Praetorius shares Vergil's pessimism on the subject, but by the end of the chapter he is rejoicing in the incomparable effort and artifice that went into developing the organ, arguing that "although it is surely to be bemoaned that we know nothing actual or certain about the beginning and invention of the first [organ]," the evidence of the ingenuity and skill of so many "dear ancestors" [*liebe Vorfahren*], dead several centuries, could be seen in surviving instruments such as the 1361 console then still in the Halberstadt Cathedral in Praetorius's region of central Germany (Figure 1.1). These diverse, if mostly unattributed, efforts paved the way for the advances of Praetorius's own "glorious age" [*herrliche zeit*]: "To tell the truth, no art is so highly developed as that of the organ: for the subtle inventiveness and assiduous reflection of humans has brought it to such a point that it can now remain as it is without the slightest change, since its perfection and completeness lacks nothing and requires not the slightest addition or augmentation."[5] Praetorius moves from the thwarted search for a single, primordial father of the organ, to a collective, if utopian, view of technological progress.

In the midst of this progression from the instrument's uncertain inception to a spirited encomium to all those who, over centuries, have contributed to its advancement, Praetorius alights on a watershed invention that is crucial to the identity of the modern organ of which he is so proud: the pedal. Now a seminal figure in the organ's technological progress can be named, even if little is known about him: Bernhard the German. Praetorius moves this fifteenth-century monk from obscurity to the center of organ history and the instrument's path towards perfection. Bernhard makes his first appearance in Praetorius's chapter entitled "Approximately when and by whom the old organs were invented" [*Zu welcher zeit ohngefehr/und von weme die Alten Orgeln erfunden worden*], which, drawing partly on Vergil's

---

[4] Atkinson, *Inventing Inventors*, pp. 246–266.   [5] Praetorius, *De organographia*, p. 85.

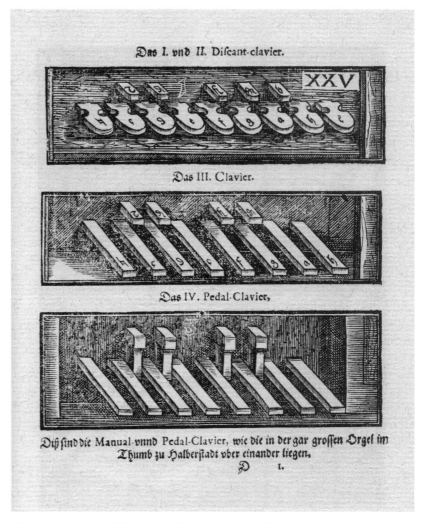

Figure 1.1   Console of Halberstadt Cathedral organ, 1361, from *De Organographia* (1619)

work, surveys the Old Testament, Classical sources, and the first Christian millennium before jumping forward 500 years to introduce the pedal's inventor. The chapter's title suggests what Bernhard's appearance confirms: that, unlike the undifferentiated continuum connecting antiquity with Vergil's present, Praetorius and subsequent writers following in his path draw a vital distinction between "ancient" and "modern," thus bringing what Praetorius calls "our" organs into the utopian glow of the present. However admirable and important the ancient instruments were, they were fundamentally different from their modern descendants: the introduction of full pedal, along with the invention of separable stops, is precisely what gave the organ its modern form, and it is Bernhard the German, Praetorius tells us, who not only improved and expanded the organ more generally, but made it possible to play ambitiously with the feet. Bernhard then went on to introduce pedals to the organ in St. Mark's in Venice in the year 1470, a landmark achievement and one that, according to Praetorius, gained great honor for the Germans beyond their borders.[6]

Praetorius's source for Bernhard's activities in Venice was the *Enneades*, a massive world history, written by the fifteenth-century Venetian scholar Marcus (Antonius Coccius) Sabellicus, whose own work on inventors had helped to inspire Vergil's project.[7] In a section of the volume devoted to the great artists of his native city, Sabellicus honors Bernhard as one of the city's illustrious men (*viri illustres*), placing him in the company of the Venetian luminaries Andrea Mantegna, and his brothers-in-law Giovanni and Gentile Bellini, who had made the paintings on the wings of the San Marco organ. For Sabellicus, Bernhard is one of Venice's greatest artists:

Of all men of the musical art who ever were, there can be no disagreement that for many years Venice held the most outstanding, a certain Bernard, known also as "the Teuton," on account of his birthrace. He played all musical instruments with the greatest skill. He was the first, to increase the harmonies under the control of organs, as even his feet also assisted [in playing] through the drawing of cables (i.e., trackers). His skill at the art was amazing in this respect, and the sound was fitted to all the harmonies [i.e., extended to the overtones, that is, to the mixtures]. By divine providence he was born for this: that the most beautiful art might enjoy all his talents.[8]

The expansion of the harmonic possibilities of the organ are tied to the German's feet in a development seemingly ordained by God for the enrichment of music in general. Bernhard is practically canonized for his virtuosity. He not only invents the technology, but seemingly, too, the way to use it: in Sabellicus's account, the skill of Bernhard's feet at the pedals has gone down in the annals of the city.

Yet neither Sabellicus nor Praetorius cites Bernhard as the inventor of the pedal. After all, Praetorius gives examples of earlier pedalboards: in his chapter on the invention of the pedal, he again praises "our dear old ancestors" [*unsere lieben alten Vorfahren*] for inventing "the method of producing musical sound through pedaling" some four centuries before his own time – that is long before Bernhard. Praetorius considers the 1361 Halberstadt Cathedral console with its pedalboard, knee levers and two-manual keyboard; the woodcut of this arrangement in Praetorius's treatise

---

[6] *Ibid*, p. 92. Praetorius cites Marcus Antonius Coccius Sabellicus, one-time librarian of St. Mark's in Venice. J. C. Printz names 1472 as the year of Bernhard's introduction of the pedal to Venice.

[7] Atkinson, *Inventing Inventors*, pp. 32, 42–43.

[8] Antonius Coccius Sabellicus, *Enneade* X, book VIII in *Operibus omnibus*, 4 vols. (Basel: Johannes Hervagius, 1560), vol. II, p. 999. How Praetorius found this obscure reference will itself remain obscure, though there are multiple copies of Sabellicus's book in the Wolfenbüttel library. The 1560 Basel edition of Sabellicus was acquired by Duke Julius in 1565. See shelf-mark: H: T 459⁰Helmst.

Figure 1.2   Console of Walcker Organ in Stiftskirche, Stuttgart, 1845

suggests a gymnastic apparatus as much as a musical instrument (see Figure 1.1 above). Five centuries later, Germany's Walcker organ company would make massive instruments with two sets of pedals with many more keys and stops, reflecting a similar multitasking attitude (see Figure 1.2). In *De organographia*, Praetorius also cites the one-octave compass of the pedalboard in San Salvatore in Venice from much earlier in the fifteenth century and predating Bernhard's work in the city.[9]

Praetorius's claims for Bernhard are at the same time more circumscribed and more expansive than that he simply invented the pedalboard. What Bernhard had done was to introduce the mechanical improvements that allowed for a decisive expansion of the pedal's potential; by developing trackers [*stricklein*] for the pedal, Bernhard made it possible for the feet "to help towards greater euphony [*wollautung*] and fuller textures [*vollstimmigkeit*]."[10] In this vestigial historical account, Bernhard's contributions allowed for a larger pedal range and for the independence of the feet from the manuals, freeing the feet from the subservient, supporting role in which they simply sustained a few long-held notes. Praetorius apparently believed that, thanks to Bernhard, the feet could play an indispensable role in music-making as they never had before. Operated by the four limbs of a single organist, the organ keyboards could now match the complexity of an ensemble of musicians performing polyphonic music. In Bernhard, Praetorius had found a German "ancestor" responsible for a decisive technological advance that vaulted the organ towards the modern age. Bernhard had not "invented" the pedal altogether, but he had refined and expanded the technology. Further, he had made it possible for the conception of a new music-making body: the organist playing with hands and feet in near equal participation.

That Bernhard was installed in so important a reference work as Sabellicus's book ensured that, as Praetorius put it, "we will not forget [Bernhard]."[11] But Sabellicus was also a local informant, probably even an eyewitness, to the transformation of the organ in St. Mark's; this perspective also allowed Praetorius to judge just how impressive the use of the feet was outside German-speaking Europe.[12] Through this source it could be seen that the innovation was important enough to be coveted in foreign lands and then enshrined in a cultural center of Venice's standing by its leading historian. That this level of sophistication had been taken up by the Italians and that Bernhard had been placed in the same exalted category as the greatest artists of the Venetian Republic, reflected back on the sophistication of the Germans and confirmed their leading role in the organ arts across Europe. Ironically then, it was an Italian source, recited in a German treatise, that gave birth to the myth of Bernhard as the inventor of the pedal. It is the German's introduction of the pedal to Venice and his ability to use it that are stressed in

---

[9] For a survey of organological sources for pedal keys, and for musical manuscripts from the late fourteenth century and the first half of the fifteenth century containing pedal indications, see Kimberly Marshall (ed.), *Historical Organ Techniques and Repertoire*, vol. III: *Late-Medieval Before 1460* (Colfax, North Carolina: Wayne Leupold Editions, 2000), pp. 4–21.

[10] Praetorius, *De organographia*, p. 93.   [11] *Ibid.*, p. 92.

[12] Renato Lunelli, *Der Orgelbau in Italien in seinen Meisterwerken*, trans. Carl Elis and Paul Smets (Mainz: Rheingold, 1956), p. 187.

Sabellicus and paraphrased by Praetorius. For both authors it was technical and technological skill at making and playing that launched the Bernhard myth, which then figured hugely in building up the status of his fellow countrymen as innovators and masters of the organ, especially when these contributions were viewed from beyond German borders.

While this crucial advance towards modernity supposedly ushered in by Bernhard had led to a vibrant, ever richer, mode of four-limbed performance at the organ, Praetorius notes that since Bernhard's time pedal-playing had been badly neglected in Italy; indeed, as Praetorius probably already knew through his contact with musicians such as Hans Leo Hassler of Nuremberg, who had studied in Venice and had with Praetorius been a participant in the 1596 Gröningen Congress (see Introduction), little sign of Bernhard's renovations at St. Mark's survived. Across Italy and indeed the rest of Europe, the art of making and playing the pedals along German lines would have to be introduced yet again by the foot-proud Germans. So crucial are the feet to Praetorius, that however real his appreciation of other organ traditions, his attitude towards other approaches is not without condescension: "Although the pedal is little and very rarely used in Italy, England and other places as well, the organ art of the present day still flourishes and excels."[13] In spite of Praetorius's gracious attitude, one not shared by later German writers, we see clearly in this passage the notion that "real" organists play fully with their feet. The contributions of other organ-playing countries come only in spite of their lack of footwork. Italian pedals with a single-octave compass and no independent stops were therefore not modern at all, but revenants, or perhaps atavistic eruptions, of the "old" organs built before Bernhard the German.

These other organ traditions did not allow the feet to participate with vigor and creativity, physical power and grace. Like those numerous writers who based their work on his seminal tract, Praetorius makes it clear that German organ pride was built from the bottom up: the Germans believed it was they who had developed the technological skill to make towering pedal pipes and the musical facility to activate them with their feet in the most virtuosic ways. Of the many formulations of this article of faith, that of Bach's first biographer, Johann Nikolaus Forkel, was one of the most virulent. Writing in the introduction to his list of Bach's organ works at the end of his 1802 biography of the composer, Forkel put it categorically: "The pedals are an essential part of the organ: by them alone is it exalted above all other instruments, for its magnificence, grandeur, and majesty depend upon them."[14] Forkel certainly knew of Bernhard the German, and his defense of the pedal assumes a long history of German dominance with the feet.

Forkel is only one of many writers whose works reflect the way in which the myth of Bernhard became central to the narrative of German organ

---

[13] Praetorius, *De organographia*, p. 96.   [14] *NBR*, 470.

modernity. The *Organopoeia* of 1690 by the influential central-German builder Johann Philipp Bendeler asserts flatly that Bernhard invented the pedal in Germany and then brought this invention to Italy.[15] In the *Historische Beschreibung der edelen Sing- und Kling-Kunst* of the same year, Wolfgang Caspar Printz also names Bernhard as not only the chief exporter, but also the inventor, of the pedals, "through which," writes Printz, stating the obvious for rhetorical effect, "one can contribute to the musical harmony with the feet."[16] However compelling the invention itself is, its musical exploitation is what is decisive; for the Germans the feet are essential for contrapuntal breadth at the instrument and for broader cultural standing. Bernhard's invention "brought the Germans not a little honor" Printz continues, by way of smug understatement.[17] Similarly, Bernhard is given sole credit for the invention of the pedals, and for their prompt export to Italy, in virtually all eighteenth-century treatises on the organ, as in Jakob Adlung's *Musica mechanica organoedi*, a book edited by J. S. Bach's student J. F. Agricola.[18] By Bach's time all organists must have been inculcated in the myth that a single German had devised the pedal and played it to the astonishment of foreigners.

Bernhard's presence can also be heard in accounts of the pedal heroics of the eighteenth century, as in Johann Samuel Petri's *Anleitung zur praktischen Musik*, first published in 1767, and then in a second edition of 1782, in Leipzig.[19] Petri deploys the well-worn rhetorical conceits that the organ is the most important and complete of instruments. His opening incantation of the ritual praise of organ perfection cites two of J. S. Bach's students, his son Wilhelm Friedemann (with whom Petri had studied) and David Nicolai, both virtuosos who had harnessed the instrument's sublimity, not least its "roaring, thundering bass."[20] After extolling the glories of the living masters of the organ, Petri rehearses the Bernhard myth: in 1470 Bernhard invented the pedal and brought these advances to Venice. In this view of history, the achievements of contemporary organ culture, embodied by J. S. Bach's students, are built on the seminal innovations of a German living three centuries earlier. Bach must also have known of the Bernhard myth and have recognized that his own abilities with hands and feet took their place in a long, proud history. As a renowned pedal-player and one

---

[15] Johann Philipp Bendeler, *Organopoeia* (Frankfurt and Leipzig: Calvisius, 1690; reprint, Amsterdam: Knuf, 1972), dedication, unpaginated.

[16] *Ibid.*, p. 113. Wolfgang Caspar Printz, *Historische Beschreibung der edelen Sing- und Kling-Kunst* (Dresden: Johann Georg, 1690; reprint, Graz: Akademische Druck- und Verlagsanstalt, 1964), p. 113. Presumably taking his cue from Praetorius, Printz also cites Sabellicus as his source.

[17] *Ibid.*, p. 114.

[18] Jakob Adlung, *Musica mechanica organoedi*, 2 vols. (Berlin: Friedrich Wilhelm Birnstiel, 1768; reprint, Kassel: Bärenreiter, 1931), vol. II, p. 94.

[19] The author had studied in Leipzig in the 1750s.

[20] Johann Samuel Petri, *Anleitung zur praktischen Musik*, 2nd edn. (Leipzig: Breitkopf, 1782; reprint, Munich: Katzbichler, 1999), pp. 285–286.

steeped in the history of his instrument, J. S. Bach must have thought that he was building not only on the efforts of his more immediate predecessors Buxtehude and Reincken, but on the long traditions of German pedaling, going back to the origins of making music with the feet in a modern, fully independent way.

In France, the encyclopedic study of organ-building by Dom Bédos de Celles, *L'art du facteur d'orgues*, accepted without contention the German claims for Bernhard, and acknowledged that the pedal was a German development, and that the pedalboard was necessary for the instrument to reach its modern state. The German translator of Dom Bédos's book adds a footnote emphasizing that with the introduction of the pedal the manual compass was extended using smaller keys more suitable for counterpoint and passagework, and that this in turn allowed for a proliferation of the pipes and distinct stops. The pedal was now essential, insists the editor Johann Christoph Vollbeding: "With time it became increasingly untenable to make an organ without pedal."[21]

Bernhard's name and deeds continued to echo long after Bach's time on the organ bench. The enduring vibrancy of the myth can be seen clearly in the first book on organ history published for a general audience, Johann Ulrich Sponsel's *Orgelhistorie* of 1771. Sponsel's opinions tend to be more fervent than those of professional organists or builders, and therefore provide a clearer barometer of the way German pride was elevated when talk turned to the organ and its pedals. For Sponsel, as for Praetorius, the pedal and the proliferation of manuals and independent registers are crucial to the "modern" organ. In tracing the path towards the modern, Sponsel tramples across the centuries of the organ's past, crushing earlier contributions and different attitudes with a confident modernity very different from Vergil's view of the ancients.[22] Along the way, though, Sponsel is especially attentive to clues about the use of the feet. He tells us that Guido of Arezzo claimed the organ given by the Byzantine Emperor Constantine V to Frankish King Pippin, in 759 was "played with feet and hands" ("*manum pedumque digitis pulsatur*"). Even if this were true, however, Sponsel finds it self-evident that "this cannot describe the kind of organ that is ours of the present day," for the Praetorian distinction between ancient and modern remains in place. Moving on, the ninth century is discarded because it brought no new developments to the organ: during this period the instrument remained merely a princely pleasure-machine, and had not yet taken up its devout presence in churches. "Our organ did not yet exist," argues Sponsel, because it would still be a few hundred years until the pedal was

---

[21] Johann Christoph Vollbeding (trans.), *Kurzgefaßte Geschichte der Orgel aus dem französischen des Dom Bédos de Celles nebst Herons Beschreibung der Wasserorgel* (Berlin: Ernst Felisch, 1793), p. 25.

[22] Sponsel cites Vergil in German translation in his book; see Johann Ulrich Sponsel, *Orgelhistorie* (Nuremberg: G. P. Monath, 1771; reprint, Hilversum: Knuf, 1968), p. 8.

invented.[23] Slashing his way through the epochs, Sponsel dismisses the tenth century as empty of "inventive minds" ("erfunderische Köpfe") and therefore unable to produce the modern organ: "The people were too stupid, because their teachers were yokels."[24] The eleventh and twelfth centuries don't fare much better: "No one thought about the organ. All were much more concerned with sewing a cross on their frocks and making for the holy lands, so they could earn a place in heaven through rape, robbery and murder."[25]

In his search for a modern organ fundamentally different from its primitive origins, Sponsel eventually comes to the dawning of a new age: "it was the fourteenth century after the birth of Christ that first brought the fortuitous period for the invention of our organs," though these are just the beginnings of that development towards the perfections assumed by Praetorius. An impressive researcher, Sponsel follows a far-flung bibliographic path which leads him to the seventeenth-century English cleric Henry Wharton's appendix to William Cave's *Scriptorum ecclesiasticorum historia literaria*, a massive bibliographic enterprise covering more than a millennium of ecclesiastical books annotated with information on the authors: "Marius Sanutus, with the family name Torsellus, a Patrician of Venice drew on the works of a certain German craftsman, and was the first to introduce into the Church pneumatic organs. [Sanutus] was famous in 1312."[26] Sponsel uses this source to buttress his claim that, long before even Bernhard, Germans were bringing the latest organ technologies to Italy, and to Venice in particular: "It seems to me highly likely," writes Sponsel, "that the honor of inventing our organs is due to a German. Even if Torcellus [sic] had the first organ erected in Italy, it was done by a German." But adopting Praetorius's distinction between old and new, Sponsel asserts that this is not yet the modern organ, which requires the use of the feet. Here again, Sponsel proclaims that the Germans will be pivotal: "As I will prove later, when the pedal was invented it was also certainly by a German."[27] Both the early fourteenth-century organ in Venice and Bernhard's invention of the pedal and introduction of it in Italy are landmark events in the long tradition of German innovation and export.

---

[23] Sponsel, *Orgelhistorie*, p. 56. Sponsel did not know that little more than a century after the supposed reintroduction of the organ into Western Europe, German craftsmen were already in demand in the South; in the late ninth century, Pope John VII wrote to Anno, Bishop of Freising, asking for Bavarian experts to "bring or send . . . a very good organum with a craftsman who can both play it and achieve all success in modulation." The translation is by Peter Williams, who has treated this document with his usual and always useful skepticism. See Williams, "Early Reference to the Organ in Presentday Southern Germany" in Kay Johannsen, Georg Koch and Stephan Rommelspacher (eds.), *Musicus Doctus: Festschrift für Hans Musch zum 65. Geburtstag* (Freiburg: Verlag Freiburger Musik, 2000), pp. 71–86, at pp. 73–74.

[24] Sponsel, *ibid.*, p. 59.   [25] *Ibid.*, p. 60.

[26] William Cave, *Scriptorum ecclesiasticorum historia literaria* (London: Chiswell, 1688–1698). For Sponsel to have found this reference in Wharton's addendum to Cave's monumental work is a very impressive piece of research indeed.

[27] Sponsel, *Orgelhistorie*, p. 64.

As for Bernhard himself, to whom Sponsel devotes an entire chapter, our author concedes that "the German" is a shadowy figure. While not directly admitting that his only primary source is Sabellicus, Sponsel does allow that no one knows Bernhard's last name nor where he came from. But he clings tenaciously to the myth that Bernhard invented the pedals, a development that made it possible that "our organs could attain that perfection, expressivity, and gravity which they now have truly achieved."[28] Sponsel holds these crucial qualities to be uniquely German. Sponsel's relentlessly progressive vision of organ history pleased enlightened reviewers, chief among them the music-lover and much-admired musical and literary critic Friedrich Nicolai, a friend and devotee of C. P. E. Bach. Nicolai praised the book for showing that "the organ, which was very imperfect in its earliest stages, was steadily improved, mostly by the Germans."[29] Nicolai agrees with Sponsel that the pedal marked the first major advance toward the organ's modernity; the Germans were responsible for the invention, and then had generously offered their knowledge to the outside world.

Bernhard's deeds loomed so large in Germans' own history of the organ – of *their* organ – that it was not until late in the nineteenth century that the first comprehensive study of the instrument's repertoire before J. S. Bach dared confront the myth. One of the greatest German organists of the nineteenth century, August Ritter, raised questions about the status that had accrued to Bernhard over the centuries. Published in 1884, Ritter's *Zur Geschichte des Orgelspiels, vornehmlich des deutschen, im 14. bis zum Anfange des 18. Jahrhunderts* (*Towards the History of Organ-playing, chiefly in Germany, from the 14th to the beginning of the 18th century*) embraces the notion of German preeminence at the instrument. But for the first time in written accounts of Bernhard the shadow of skepticism troubles the Bernhard myth. Ritter begins his account of the rise of organ-playing in the fifteenth century by celebrating the trio of seminal German organists of the period, all of them blind – Conrad Paumann, Arnolt Schlick, and Paul Hofhaimer. Conrad Paumann had traveled through Italy in 1470 and had declined lucrative offers from the courts at Milan and Naples; in Mantua he was knighted for his prowess on the organ and other instruments. He was a European celebrity, perhaps the first instrumentalist (he also played the lute and sang) to achieve that status. Ritter credits Paumann, Schlick, and Hofhaimer with founding the German tradition. He goes on as if in faithful subservience to received wisdom: "One could perhaps expect to see a fourth in this company, namely the oft-mentioned Bernhard the German."[30] But in contrast to these three organists, whose biographies are far better known

[28] *Ibid.*, p. 76.

[29] Friedrich Nicolai, review of Sponsel's *Orgelhistorie* in *Allgemeine deutsche Bibliothek*, 24/11 (1775), 114–116.

[30] A. G. Ritter, *Zur Geschichte des Orgelspiels* (Leipzig: Hesse, 1884), p. 89.

and from whom music of high quality survives, Bernhard remains a complete enigma: "Aside from the fact that we know as good as nothing with certainty about him as an organist, so is his proprietary right to the invention of the pedal, which Praetorius had ascribed to him, as doubtful [*zweifelhaft*] as his person."[31] Though Praetorius ascribed no such right to Bernhard, he had unwittingly inspired a myth that Ritter now refused to feed. Nonetheless, Ritter harbored little doubt about the preeminence of the ancient and still-flourishing art of pedaling in Germany; even without Bernhard as the founder of the pedal, the hugely demanding pedal parts by Arnolt Schlick from the beginning of the sixteenth century are proof for Ritter of wide-ranging German skill.[32]

It was not only the desire for a wider array of corroborating historical sources for Bernhard that led to Ritter's skepticism. Another contender, though one with hardly more unimpeachable bonafides than Bernhard, had emerged. The critic, organist, musicologist, and director of the Royal Conservatory in Brussels, François-Joseph Fétis, had pointed to a fourteenth-century source which he interpreted as proof that a Flemish musician, Louis Van Vaelbeke, had already been playing with his feet in the middle of the fourteenth century. The debate about the pedal's origins now took on a wider nationalistic color: Fétis was doubtless proud to offer evidence of his own country's importance in the history of organ-playing, and especially of pedaling, though, of course, that country had not existed as a modern state in the fourteenth century. For Ritter, too, writing after the establishment of the German nation in 1871, the designation of the "inventor of the organ pedals" had a much different meaning than it did for Praetorius nearly three centuries earlier. Fétis questioned Bernhard's mythic status in the entry on him in the first edition of his *Biographie universelle des musiciens et bibliographie générale de la musique* of 1837.[33] That Fétis would dedicate an entire page to a figure of whom the only historical record was to be found in the fifteenth-century humanist Sabellicus's world history speaks to the importance still accorded the invention of the pedals; verses from a Flemish chronicle unearthed by Fétis prompted his counter claim that a "Belgian" from Flanders should more rightly be accorded the honor:

> Hy was d'eerste die vant
> van stampien die manieren
> die man noch hoert antieren

---

[31] *Ibid.*, p. 89. [32] *Ibid.*, p. 102.

[33] François-Joseph Fétis, *Biographie universelle des musiciens et bibliographie générale de la musique*, 8 vols. (Brussels: Melines, Cans et Compagnie, 1837–1844), vol. I, pp. 374–375. See also Edmond van der Straeten, *La Musique aux Pays-Bas avant le XIXe Siècle* (Brussels: Van Trigt, 1878), pp. 154–155. Also a contender for inventor of the pedal was Albert Van Loos, thanks to his work around 1120 on the cathedral organ in Utrecht. See Henry Charles Lahee, *The Organ and Its Masters* (Boston: L. C. Page, 1903), p. 5.

The passage in question is ambiguous, and has been interpreted in many ways already by a host of nineteenth-century Belgian scholars; I offer this tentative translation:

> He was the first who discovered
> the manner of stamping
> which one still hears

While Fétis claims his intention is not "to take away glory from Bernhard," the implications are clear. Even allowing, as Fétis does, for the fact that Bernhard could not have known of Louis Van Vaelbeke's invention, and had devised the pedals without prior knowledge, the Flemish were there first. Unassailable as inventors of the pedal since Praetorius's time, if not before, the Germans were driven onto the defensive: "Now it appears," writes Ritter, "and it cannot readily be contradicted, that the Belgians claim the honor of inventing the pedal for their countryman Ludwig von Valbeck."[34] For all its pretense towards objectivity, music historiography of the nineteenth century served nationalist inclination and it did so nowhere more clearly than in writings about the organ and the role of the feet.

The first comprehensive study of organ-playing across Europe, Gotthold Frotscher's *Geschichte des Orgelspiels*, which appeared in 1935, was originally commissioned by the publisher as a revised edition of Ritter; but Frotscher, whose reputation would be badly tainted by his arguments for the uses of the organ in Nazi political celebrations,[35] extended the book to two volumes, far beyond the scope of his predecessor's more modest study. Frotscher makes the usual references to Praetorius, and to the organs in Halberstadt and San Salvatore. The late fourteenth-century organ in Norrlanda had been discovered, thus predating Bernhard by as much as a century, though again, its pedals were not viewed as modern in the sense understood from Praetorius to Sponsel. The Norrlanda organ's pedal keys, delicately carved as lovely florettes, comprise a diatonic scale and have a compass of one octave; the physical appearance of these keys speaks to their use for long notes – drones or slow-moving plainchant melodies (see Figure 1.3). It was for these or similar musical requirements that pedalboards were probably first constructed; and for the most part, this remained their purpose outside Germany, into the nineteenth century. Frotscher had also found other German literary sources citing pedal-playing in the late fourteenth century and in the earlier part of the fifteenth century,[36] but he still accepted it as "relatively certain" that Van Vaelbeke had indeed invented the pedal. For Frotscher, Bernhard the German had been

---

[34] Ritter, *Zur Geschichte des Orgelspiels*, p. 90.

[35] Gotthold Frotscher, "Die Orgel in der politischen Feier" in *Die Orgel in der Gegenwart* (Wolfenbüttel and Berlin: Georg Kallmeyer, 1939), pp. 5–8.

[36] Gottfried Frotscher, *Geschichte des Orgelspiels und der Orgelkomposition*, 2 vols. (Berlin: Max Hesse, 1935), vol. I, p. 40.

Figure 1.3   Organ Pedals, Norrlanda, c. 1400, Historiska Museet, Stockholm

demoted to what he had already been for Sabellicus and Praetorius – the importer of the pedal to Italy; his exalted status continued to fade.

In a nasty codicil to the reception history of Bernhard the German, a revival of his mythic image was already underway thanks to Hans Joachim Moser, the one-time liberal, who served in the music division (Reichstelle für Musikbearbeitungen) of the Nazi propaganda ministry, beginning in 1940. In his important 1929 book on Paul Hofhaimer, the celebrated blind Innsbruck organist, Moser seemed ready to accept that the "Brabanter Louis van Valbeke" had indeed devised the modern pedals.[37] But Moser continued to investigate the matter, and by the time of Frotscher's *Geschichte des Orgelspiels* of 1935, he had identified Bernhard as a German active in Venice around 1460, with the last name Murer, though later scholars have cast doubt on this finding.[38] In 1950, another eminent German organ historian, Ernst Flade, countered that the carillon pedals developed in Brabant in the thirteenth

---

[37] Hans Joachim Moser, *Paul Hofhaimer: Ein Lied- und Orgelmeister des deutschen Humanismus* (Stuttgart: J. G. Cotta'sche Buchhandlung Nachfolger, 1929), p. 107.

[38] Frotscher, *Geschichte des Orgelspiels*, vol. I, p. 102. See also Lunelli, *Der Orgelbau in Italien*, pp. 186–187. Fétis had made the same identification already in the 1837 article on Bernhard in the *Biographie*.

and fourteenth centuries gave rise to the practice of playing with the feet,[39] but Moser continued to pursue the matter, in spite of its increasingly questionable value to scholarship; in a paper presented at the International Musicological Society Congress held in Utrecht in 1952, the denazified Moser took a moment to question the meaning of the poem praising Van Vaelbeke as the inventor of the pedals; Moser argued that the passage more likely meant that Van Vaelbeke had simply been the first to play variations on the dance-form of the *Estampie*.[40] Reactions to this bit of rearguard revisionism go unrecorded at the conference. But in retrospect it is clear that Moser was hanging on to a debate whose time had come and gone: individual invention and the nationality of such a putative inventor seemed to belong to another era. In any case, this was a dangerous avenue to march down for an ex-Nazi bureaucrat in the aftermath of World War II, at an international gathering held in a country recently occupied by Germany. In his *Musik der deutschen Stämme* (*Music of the German Tribes*), a notorious book published in 1957, Moser would write confidently that he had taken care of the legend of Van Vaelbeke in his Utrecht congress paper; Moser dismissed the Flemish musician as a mere *Glockenspieler* (*carilloneur*), that is, not a true organist in the German sense. And even if the pedals had been invented by Van Vaelbeke, the Flemish people in any case constituted one of the Low German tribes described by Moser in his dubious, not to say nefarious, taxonomy;[41] Van Vaelbeke was still of Germanic origins and so too was the idea of involving the feet in organ-playing.

In 1967, ten years after Moser's book, Bernhard was nowhere to be found in the monumental *History of Keyboard Music* by Willi Apel, a German emigrant to the United States.[42] The idea of attributing to a single actor in the early history of the organ essential technological advances seemed obsolete, even ridiculous, in light of the diverse and complicated organological and literary sources. Now the music and the surviving instruments must speak louder than those of one mythic individual who had for so long been canonized by the Germans, ensconced so firmly in the history they had written of "their" instrument.

THE BIRTH OF PEDAL INDEPENDENCE: THE ORGAN TRIO

An invention becomes valuable to the extent that its potential is realized. Throughout the four centuries of German pedal dominance, from the

[39] Ernst Flade, "Literarische Zeugnisse zur Empfindung der 'Farbe' und 'Farbigkeit' bei der Orgel," *Acta Musicologica*, 22 (1950), 97–127, at 115.

[40] Hans Joachim Moser, "Die Niederlande in der Musikgeographie Europas," International Society for Musical Research, Fifth Congress, Utrecht, 3–7 July 1952, *Report* (Amsterdam: Alsbach, 1953), pp. 296–309, at p. 300.

[41] Hans Joachim Moser, *Die Musik der deutschen Stämme* (Vienna and Stuttgart: Wancura, 1957), pp. 36–39.

[42] Willi Apel, *The History of Keyboard Music to 1700*, trans. and rev. Hans Tischler (Bloomington, Indiana: Indiana University Press, 1972).

fifteenth century through to the second half of the nineteenth, Germans not only believed they had invented the pedal, but also that only they had set about fully exploiting it in diverse and ingenious ways. While Bernhard's status waned in the nineteenth century, Germans could still claim that they had written the book on the organ, or at least had published the first one. *Spiegel der Orgelmacher und Organisten* (*Mirror of Organ-builders and Organists*) by the blind organist Arnolt Schlick appeared in Mainz in 1511. Besides offering concise and compelling advice about organ design and maintenance, Schlick's book provides glimpses of his towering technical ambitions. The most astonishing of these have to do with the feet, as if right from the beginning of pedaling the full potential of the apparatus was to be exploited by German organists. Many of the astounding techniques have left hardly a trace in the surviving repertory from the early modern period, nor were many of them taken up – at least in written form – by succeeding generations. They include two- or three-voice polyphony with the feet alone, pedal runs and other passagework, a technique in which two-voice textures are played in the pedal then echoed by the manuals, and pedal solos of ample dimensions. Schlick's footwork is exuberantly, Germanically virtuosic.

Schlick, too, seems to take as tautological the notion that the Germans invented the pedals:

Playing only the manuals has been standard practice outside the German countries up to now, but now they are studying the pedals as well, and not without reason, for with the hands alone it is impossible to play every piece containing many parts correctly and with the parts in proper relation. But if one has the pedal to help, taking two or three voices, and also four in the manual, this makes seven parts altogether, which is impossible on the manuals without the pedal.[43]

What the pedal does, aside from astounding with runs and flourishes, is most fundamentally to contribute to the breadth and complexity of the polyphony [*Vollstimmigkeit*], giving shape, gravity and grandeur through contrapuntal detail. Though perhaps not as fast and flashy as pedal runs and leaps, such arrays of independent voices nonetheless represented their own form of bravura display, both physical and mental. The bold pretensions of Schlick's polyphony – sometimes decorated, sometimes austere, and always correct – were recognized in the fourth book of Andreas Ornithoparchus's *Musicae activae micrologus* of 1517: the book is devoted to counterpoint and the dedication lauds Schlick as *musicus consummatissimus ac organista probatissimus* – the most consummate musician and most excellent organist.[44] With this phrase, Ornithoparchus links together musical mastery, the organ, and counterpoint.

[43] Arnolt Schlick, *Spiegel der Orgel-macher und Organisten* (Mainz: Peter Schöffer the Younger, 1511), parallel trans. Elizabeth Berry Barber (Buren: Knuf, 1980), p. 29.

[44] Andreas Ornithoparchus, *Musicae activae micrologus* (Leipzig: Schumann, 1517; reprint, New York: Dover, 1973), unpaginated (p. 90 in facsimile edition). See also Douglas E. Bush, "Musicus Consummatissimus: the Biography and Organ Music of Arnolt Schlick," *Organ Yearbook*, 16 (1985), 26–46.

In Schlick's music, as is also made clear in the *Spiegel*, the conception and execution of counterpoint at the organ demands abundant and skillful use of the pedal. More than that, a single organist skilled in four-limbed performance can undertake the project of polyphony with a complexity greater than can any other soloist.

At stake in the assertion that Bernhard invented the pedal, and in Schlick's musical and literary statements of German pedal authority, were the bragging rights at having sponsored a development seen by Germans to be so central to the history of the organ. But the revolutionary importance of the pedal, according to German writers, lay in enlisting the feet as equal partners in music-making, for along with this physical mode of performance, the pedals spawned a unique way of conceptualizing music polyphonically. Ever since Schlick, ubiquitous has been the German assertion that under the feet and hands of their organists polyphony flourished.[45] Michael Praetorius had suggested that the German polyphonic approach had been spawned by the first primitive pedals developed even before the time of Bernhard the German; it was the primordial pedal that allowed organists "at last, with practice, to perform a trio."[46] Now each hand could deliver an independent, if rudimentary, contrapuntal line while the feet did the same below. Praetorius seems even to suggest that early development of polyphony took place at the organ: first came the two-fisted *bicinium* and the hard-won discovery of contrapuntally convincing cadences; the next step was the *tricinium* made possible through the involvement of the feet, with which the organist could explore many-voiced florid counterpoint alone at his instrument.[47] The separation of the organ into divisions associated with distinct manuals, and the development of stops, not only provided for increasing sonic variety, but also led to a kind of music-making in which discrete polyphonic parts were given to distinct limbs of a single player: the organist's body itself became a polyphonic mechanism, an animated extension of the organ, the glorious machine that was itself one of the most magnificent and complicated pieces of technology of pre-industrial Europe. The trio literally embodied the modern organist's ambitions: it was the first polyphonic genre to involve both hands and feet, and would remain the touchstone ever after.

A physical and contrapuntal ideal for the organist, the trio is by far the most prevalent texture in Schlick's *Tabulaturen Etlicher lobgesang*, an elegant volume so diminutive (measuring only about 6 × 8 inches) that it seems a miracle that it can contain so much music of inexhaustible beauty; as in Bach's *Orgelbüchlein*, the art of composition for the biggest instruments finds perfection in the smallest of formats. Schlick published the *Tabulaturen*

---

[45] Just one example, directly related to the question of pedals in Italy and the addition of manuals in the north, is Ernst Flade's assertion that "Because of the 'embryonic' pedal the Italian organs [of the fifteenth century] were unsuited to the exposition of polyphonic lines." Flade, "Literarische Zeugnisse," 124.

[46] Praetorius, *De organographia*, p. 97.   [47] *Ibid.*, p. 101.

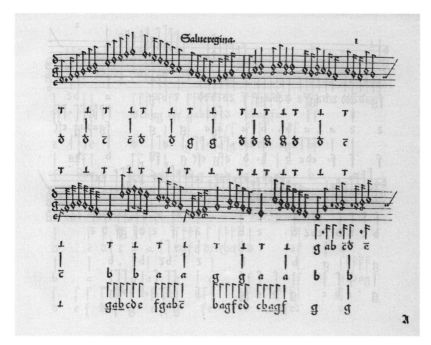

Figure 1.4   Arnolt Schlick, *Salve Regina* from *Tabulaturen Etlicher lobgesang* (Mainz, 1512)

in 1512, a year after the *Spiegel*,[48] and presented it as a unique contribution to the art of organ-playing, offering pieces that were "new and never heard before." In contrast to the pedagogical *Fundamenta* of the fifteenth-century organist Conrad Paumann, where two-part textures predominate, eight of the fourteen movements in Schlick's *Tabulaturen* are trios. It is true that Schlick is not specific about how the pieces are to be performed. He uses the so-called Old German tablature in which the soprano is represented on a six-line staff and the lower voices are printed in gothic letters without barlines; this is akin to open-score in which each polyphonic voice is given its own line (see Figure 1.4). These lines are not assigned specifically to manuals or pedals, as they would be in the case of Bach's trios with their performance indication, taken from his French models, "à 2 Clav. et Pedal."[49] Given the notation's clear separation of voices on their own staves, Schlick's *Tabulaturen* allows,

---

[48] Arnolt Schlick, *Tabulaturen Etlicher lobgesang und lidlein uff die orgeln und lauten* (Mainz: Peter Schöffern, 1512; reprint, Leipzig: Zentralantiquariat, 1979).

[49] That the soprano part is in staff notation can give the impression that the upper voice is somehow more important or at least more florid than the others; this is sometimes the case, but by no means always. Often one of the lower parts, especially that which would be taken by the left hand, is as highly decorated as the soprano. (In the New German tablature adopted later in the sixteenth century, the upper voice was written in tablature, too, perhaps an acknowledgment that all voices could be complicated, and that the soprano no longer held the primacy partly implied by the notation.)

indeed encourages, flexibility in the realization of the music. But Schlick stresses that integrity of the voices is the ideal, and to achieve it the pedal remains crucial:

Not only polyphony, but also many smaller songs and other pieces with three or four parts, cannot be played perfectly on the manuals, as is the case when parts go too far from each other, so that one voice must give way to another or be silent at times altogether because one cannot reach it with the hands. Also sometimes the voices come too close together, so that they coincide, as at a cadence. This may be done perfectly, and each part may better have its own tone and be heard, if the pedal and manual are used together.[50]

We must, then, assume that Schlick had the pedal in mind for the optimal performance of his trios, since by his standards a realization of the music without the feet obscures the polyphony. A further clue to the deployment of the pedal is that the lowest part of the tablature always fits on the compass of Schlick's pedal F–c1 – a range of an octave-and-a-half – and the inner parts often extend beyond it. Further, at several points the lowest part purposefully traverses exactly the full range of the pedal, as in *Pete quid vis* (see Example 1.1). These are all indications that for Schlick, the true organist commands counterpoint with manuals and pedal.[51]

Praetorius's description of the pre-modern trio suggests that these were relatively sedentary, groping affairs of limited melodic range and contrapuntal sweep. The trio becomes modern only after the organ becomes modern. Schlick's ideal instrument has two manuals and pedal, without a large number of stops, but replete with separate registers for both hands and feet that can be combined in effective and pleasing ways; Schlick's model organ outlined in the *Spiegel* was not an outsized creature meant to overwhelm and awe, but a modest musical tool.[52] Such a refined instrument would not only be beautiful, but would allow for polyphonic clarity, which

Example 1.1   Arnolt Schlick, *Pete quid vis* from *Tabulaturen Etlicher lobgesang* (1512), bars 46–48

---

[50] Schlick, *Spiegel*, pp. 29–31.

[51] Various less obvious solutions are also possible, when one plays one or the other of the lower parts at different pitch levels, using either 4′ or 16′ stops. See also Arnfried Edler, "Arnolt Schlick – Musicus consummatissimus ac organista probatissimus" in Frank Heidlberger, Wolfgang Osthoff, and Reinhard Wiesend (eds.), *Von Isaac bis Bach: Festschrift Martin Just zum 60. Geburstag* (Kassel: Bärenreiter, 1991), pp. 115–126, at p. 124.

[52] Schlick, *Spiegel*, p. 59.

necessarily required independent stops in the pedal.[53] Although Schlick also refers to massive polyphonic structures (see Chapter 2) and dazzling solo conceits, his ideal organ is, not surprisingly, ideally suited to trios like those of the *Tabulaturen*.

Schlick was concerned that the keyboards for hands and feet be positioned so as to allow enough space for the human body to move comfortably across the demanding landscape of the music. He recommends not only that the distances between the pedals and the manuals and between the manuals themselves should be "workable and convenient," but also that the relationships should be standardized, and the keyboards should be centered over one another rather than displaced to the right or left.[54] One can imagine the difficulties the blind Schlick complains of when encountering instruments that departed from more familiar and logical arrangements.[55] Schlick had argued already, at the beginning of the sixteenth century, that the pedal anchored the organist and gave him his bearings.

Given the independence of the limbs required by Schlick's polyphony, and most clearly represented in his trios, ergonomic considerations are paramount; the organist should be able to "sit as freely as possible, and not need to twist himself around to perform or seek an advantageous position, or make do."[56] As Schlick cautions in the *Spiegel*, the keys must be long enough "so that the feet can be used behind one another and may cross in running passages or scales in the pedal." The bench must be high enough to allow the feet to hover and fly over the keys.[57] The proportions and relative position of the manuals and pedalboard must be laid out so that hands and feet can pursue both free-flowing counterpoint and virtuosic flourishes. The human triumph of the early modern organ, as recognized by Praetorius's history and exploited by Schlick, was to allow the organist full range of motion and a balanced posture so that the body parts could deliver their contrapuntal lines unencumbered: at a well-designed console built according to Schlick's suggestions, the organist could swivel at the waist, and the arms move in different directions from each other and from the legs. These ergonomic considerations are much less critical at other keyboard instruments where both feet are planted on the floor. At the organ, especially when the demanding polyphony of a Schlick is pulling the player in all directions, the music and the performer

---

[53] *Ibid.*, p. 63.

[54] Schlick's pleas for standardization had to wait for implementation 366 years from the publication of the *Spiegel*; on October 3, 1876 the Royal Prussian Ministry of Religious, Educational, and Medical Affairs (Königliches Preußiches Ministerium der geistlichen-, Unterrichts- und Medizinalangelegenheiten) declared that the middle C of the manuals and tenor C of the pedal should be aligned; this had in fact long been the case, and remains the most common placement of the pedal. See Walter Edmund Ehrenhofer, *Taschenbuch des Orgelbau-Revisors* (Graz: Universitäts-Buchdruckerei, 1908; reprint, Buren, The Netherlands: Fritz Knuf, 1980), p. 51.

[55] Historic organs in which the pedalboards are displaced significantly from their more typical alignment with the manuals are massively disorienting; the seventeenth-century instrument in Westerhusen, Ostfriesland in north Germany, is one surviving example.

[56] Schlick, *Spiegel*, p. 53.   [57] *Ibid.*, pp. 49–50.

Example 1.2   Arnolt Schlick, "O dulcis Maria", verse 5 of *Salve Regina* from *Tabulaturen Etlicher lobgesang*, bars 1–9, long notes in pedal

hang in the balance. This new form of musical movement allowed for modern trio playing.

Of the eight trios in the *Tabulaturen* only one has the pedal deliver a simple *cantus firmus* in long, held notes; this is the final verse of *Salve Regina*, in which the upper voices engage in imitative dialogue above the resounding pedal notes (see Example 1.2), a texture cultivated through the seventeenth century into Bach's time and ever since. Aside from the last verse of *Salve Regina*, all of Schlick's other trios have active bass parts that confront a range of contrapuntal and technical problems. Before attaining its three-voice texture, the *Benedictus* begins with the opening motive heard alone in the pedal; delegating this line to the feet seems to be the most logical and effective performance option, and results in this short pedal solo (see Example 1.3).[58] The bass is not given the kind of figuration found in the upper parts, but in terms of rhythmical and contrapuntal independence the pedal remains fully involved with its manual interlocutors. The celebrated *Maria zart* starts off as a *bicinium* between right hand and pedal (if the feet take the lowest line, as seems the best option), with the parts moving in counterpoint that escapes its own inertia through the melodic decorations Schlick introduces into the *cantus firmus*. After three bars the pedal bursts free of its slowly rising long notes and into full-fledged interaction with the soprano, with the middle voice entering just as the feet become more animated (see Example 1.4).

The touchstone nature of the trio in Schlick's organ art is nowhere clearer than in the dramatic three-part texture that dominates the very first page of

---

[58] The first *Da pacem* in *Tabulaturen Etlicher lobgesang* also begins with a solo bass entrance, surely also played with the feet.

Example 1.3 Arnolt Schlick, *Benedictus* from *Tabulaturen Etlicher lobgesang*
(with pedal opening), bars 1–6

Example 1.4 Arnolt Schlick, *Maria zart* from *Tabulaturen Etlicher lobgesang*, bars 1–5

the *Tabulaturen* (see Example 1.5). This setting of the *Salve Regina* begins
as an austere *bicinium*, then adds a third voice in the pedal, and soon after
that another one in the manuals to achieve four real parts; it is as if right
from the opening of this seminal publication, Schlick is tracing the trajectory of the development of organ polyphony from two- to three- and then to
four-part florid counterpoint, a kind of polyphonic cataloging that also
tests the scope of the instrument and its player. The rhythmic acceleration
of the six-note *semifusa* flourish (transcribed as eighth-notes in Example 1.5)
in the uppermost part anticipates the pedal entrance on G, the second-
lowest key on Schlick's pedalboard, and imbues the moment with self-
conscious theatricality – like a curtain swiftly raised to reveal the modern
organist's feet. The arrival of the pedal comes after the ancient art of
decorating a *cantus firmus* with a free contrapuntal voice has been author-
itatively demonstrated – two-part counterpoint is the most venerable form
of polyphonic elaboration and the genre of the *bicinium* can stand on its
own. Indeed, the two-part polyphony prevails more than long enough at the
opening of this setting to convince one that this texture could have obtained

Example 1.5   Arnolt Schlick, *Salve regina* from *Tabulaturen Etlicher lobgesang*,
first verse, bars 1–13

throughout the verse; as a result we hear the introduction of the third voice as a sudden shift.

But the anchoring quality of the pedal immediately converts the surprise at its entry into respect: the unexpected is transformed into the self-evident. After entering, the feet assert their presence by moving with even, assured steps, rising against the unshakeable tenor upwards an eleventh – like a prayer rising to Mary.[59] The two free outer parts – one in the right hand, the other in the feet – revolve in parallel, then in contrary motion, around the central axis of the *cantus firmus*, gracefully articulating contrapuntal and physical space while the left hand anchors the body and the counterpoint. The pedal ascends all the way to the very top of the pedalboard, to the highest c, which it holds for twice the duration of the preceding scale, as if rejoicing at having conquered this summit. Relinquishing these heights, the feet then traverse the entirety of Schlick's pedal keyboard down to the

---

[59] One could conceivably play the *cantus firmus* in the pedal at 4′ pitch and the bassline in the left hand, but the fact that the opening measures of the bass part perfectly cover the pedal compass would suggest that part's performance by the feet.

Example 1.6   J. S. Bach, Prelude in D, BWV 532/1, bars 1–5

low F. The fourth voice enters (in bar 13) only after the pedal has taken full and authoritative measure of its dominion, establishing the breadth and majesty of its compass and sonorous gravity, and made its claim to fully equal and independent status. At the pedal's introduction in the *Tabulaturen*, the organist is required to execute one of Schlick's scales, immediately testing not only his own skill, but also making sure that the pedalboard is constructed properly.

Schlick's opening pedal scale is slower than those which bolt from the gate in Bach's D Major Prelude, BWV 532/1 (see Example 1.6) and which tax the organist in the final sprint of Vierne's Sixth Symphony (see Introduction, Example 4). While these later scales are more athletic than the pedal entry of *Salve regina*, Schlick implied in the *Spiegel* that flashing runs were also in his technical arsenal and playable by the best of his contemporaries. Even if separated by several centuries, the scales of Schlick, Bach, and Vierne all share the same motivating ambition: to command musical space with the feet independent of the manuals – to match the hands in technical and contrapuntal range. Schlick's opening scale could well have been one of those things "new and never heard before" trumpeted in the volume's preface. From its outset the *Tabulaturen* enacts the proud claims of the *Spiegel*: Germans play the organ with their feet, with great facility and unstinting independence, ingenuity, and control. If the trio distills the organist's art to its purest form, then Schlick is that form's purest master. Chances to use double pedal as well as to present rhythmically and melodically more complicated passages in the bassline will follow in the *Tabulaturen*, but the importance of the feet to contrapuntal integrity has been set forth at the outset of this seminal volume in the history of polyphonic pedal-playing.

VIRTUOSIC INDEPENDENCE OF HANDS AND FEET:
BACH'S TRIOS

When, as some have claimed, J. S. Bach "invented" the organ trio in the eighteenth century, he was in fact articulating an ideal that was as old as German pedal dominance at the organ. The trio was the most obvious test of organ proficiency; it was both the oldest and most unforgiving format in which to demonstrate independence of the feet from the hands. The prolific German writer on music in the first half of the eighteenth century, Johann Mattheson, himself an organist who had heard and admired both Bach and Handel, scornfully referred in 1731 to the widespread habit of simply doubling the lowest note of the manuals with the pedal: for him and many others this violates the precepts of authentic organ-playing.[60] As he wrote in his *Grosse General-Bass Schule*, professionals should maintain a higher standard than slovenly village organists; yet, according to Mattheson, even in urban centers the commitment to pedal independence was slipping. The practice of shadowing the left hand with the pedal was becoming more widespread and harder to suppress even in the trials for organists' posts in Hamburg, long home to a large number of the finest organs and organists in Europe. These auditions were not only necessary for finding the best candidate (though Mattheson also complained that in Hamburg this was impossible because of rampant simony), but for judging the health of organ-playing in northern Germany, heartland of the independent pedal.

The trio remained the most effective diagnostic measure of that health. For the 1725 organists' trial for the position at the Hamburg Cathedral, where he was then Director of Music, Johann Mattheson must have played a crucial role in setting the tasks for the applicants. In his description of the requirements for the audition, Mattheson stresses the importance of the trio in demonstrating the fundamental skills of the applicants: after devising a modulating prelude on the spot, the organist then had to improvise a chorale prelude, "specifically using two manuals with pedal in a pure three-part harmony, without doubling the bass."[61] Not only must the feet be independent, but the left hand must also be fully developed and not merely fill in gaps in the harmony: "the middle voice must also move [*moduliren*] nicely."[62] It is as if each part of the body must have a mind of its own. These distinct prerogatives are conveyed most clearly in the trio texture, where errors become glaringly obvious; anyone who has played a trio at the organ, or perhaps even tried to devise one on the spot like the 1725 applicants in Hamburg had to do, knows what thinking this way feels like in the body.

---

[60] Mattheson, *Grosse General-Bass Schule* (Hamburg: Johann Christoph Kißner, 1731; reprint, Hildesheim: Olms Verlag, 1968), pp. 34, 37.
[61] *Ibid.*, p. 34.   [62] *Ibid.*

When J. S. Bach played the organ in Hamburg in 1720 for Mattheson and for the other musical and civic leaders of that flourishing city – he was apparently offered the position at the Jacobikirche, but refused, it seems, to pay the traditional fee required to take it up – he likely played a trio as outlined by Mattheson. It is against this level of sophistication that Mattheson inevitably measured the trios improvised by the Hamburg Cathedral applicants of 1725.

That Bach was very much in Mattheson's mind at the 1725 Hamburg auditions is clear from the next task laid out for the candidates – a fugue to be "four minutes long," but more important that it be "good rather than long" says Mattheson. The subject was the same as that of Bach's G minor Fugue, BWV 542/2, a piece Mattheson and other Hamburg organists knew and admired. This sprawling, frenetic four-voice fugue demonstrates its contrapuntal integrity with greatest intensity in trio sections where the three voices are often widely spaced and given their own rhythmic profiles, all of which serve to amplify their independence and the rigor of the polyphony. The trio between hands and feet begins with highly delineated counterpoint (see Example 1.7a): the fugue subject enters in the bass to commence the three-part texture with the left hand issuing against-the-grain syncopations in bar 56 along with various other unexpected rhythmic moves in the right hand; vibrant echoes between the hands follow midway through in bar 57 against a newly energized bassline. The texture is constantly shifting, exercising the player in a variety of ways. Bach then highlights the overriding independence between the voices by suddenly pursuing the opposite strategy, allowing the three parts suddenly to spiral down together in parallel motion for two-and-a-half bars of almost brazenly unindependent counterpoint beginning in bar 61: at this point a challenging, high-speed trio in vigorously florid counterpoint gives way to a long skein of *fauxbourdon*, the simplest of descending parallel chords in first inversion – a stretch of uninterrupted similar motion unexampled in Bach's organ works. At the beginning of this passage, the organist is high up in the range of the manuals and the pedal and clings to a precarious perch, performing the devilish reiterations of the first four-sixteenth-note pattern. After swiveling the body down from the highest part of the pedals and manuals towards the comforts of the middle register, the feet and left hand continue their downward trajectory and the right hand splits off from the *fauxbourdon* freight-train and climbs upward as the pedal descends to the deep end of its compass and the pedal-point at bar 65 that provides some relief from these exertions.

Another trio section with hands and feet follows nine bars later at bar 73 (see Example 1.7b), and here the pedal is given the syncopated line of sixteenth-notes and tied eighths, before it arrives at a pedal-point on G on which the left foot stays while the right foot climbs upward until it reaches b-natural – a yawning interval, a tenth away from the left foot; as if the disparate duties of each voice weren't enough, Bach now threatens to pull

Example 1.7a   J. S. Bach, Fugue in G minor, BWV 542/2, bars 54–65

the organist from the bench by splaying the legs. Bach then navigates his way out of this awkward physical predicament by having the highest voice abstain from the counterpoint and remain on the high g2, while the lower voices continue to churn away. But the highest voice can hardly relax, as Bach gives it a long trill that must be maintained against the activity below. These passages of exposed, perilous polyphony are the technical crux of

Example 1.7b   J. S. Bach, Fugue in G minor, BWV 542/2, bars 73–79

Example 1.8   Georg Böhm, *Herr Jesu Christ, dich zu uns wend*, bars 1–5

Bach's fugue and demonstrate how the trio and all its animated demands are introduced across Bach's oeuvre.

The type of trio lauded by Mattheson seems to be relatively rare in surviving musical sources from the period, though a good match for his description would be a setting of *Herr Jesu Christ, dich zu uns wend*, by Bach's teacher, Georg Böhm (see Example 1.8). Böhm had lived in Hamburg in the 1690s; he had probably provided his young student, Bach, with connections to the great Hamburg organists, including J. A. Reincken. Böhm certainly gave Bach access to copies of north-German organ works. As Mattheson suggests in his account of the distinct modes of chorale variation that organists had to demonstrate at auditions, Böhm's trio makes up one verse in a set of five. During Bach's schooldays in Lüneburg from 1700 to 1702, Böhm was organist in the city's Johanniskirche, with its large Hendrik Niehoff organ of the mid-sixteenth century; the impressive pedal towers, which now frame the central case, were added in 1712. Böhm's *Herr Jesu Christ, dich zu uns wend* was transmitted in a manuscript copied by Bach's student in Weimar, J. T. Krebs and his Weimar colleague and relative, Johann Gottfried Walther. The piece is French in its flowing style and rhythmic nuance; also like the French approach to the genre, the pedal is independent but simple, following its own course but not an equal to the manuals in difficulty and energy (though Böhm could demand much of the feet when he wanted to in other genres). The left hand in this trio is a capable and articulate participant in the three-way conversation, evincing what Mattheson called proper "modulation" – that is, independence. Bach must also have copied and played the piece, and was also surely the conduit for conveying the manuscript to the copyists from his circle whose efforts ultimately led to its survival.

According to Bach's Obituary – written by his second son, Carl Philipp Emanuel and his former student, Johann Friedrich Agricola – Bach wrote most of his organ works while employed in Weimar between 1708 and 1717; in the ducal chapel he had what amounted to a private organ studio. It was at this time that Bach was studying French and north-German models and developing his own novel paradigm of the trio. One of his earliest treats the same melody set by Böhm, *Herr Jesu Christ, dich zu uns wend*, BWV 655a (see Example 1.9). With this setting Bach has produced

Example 1.9a   J. S. Bach, *Trio super: Herr Jesu Christ, dich zu uns wend*, BWV 655a, bars 1–6

Example 1.9b   J. S. Bach, *Trio super: Herr Jesu Christ, dich zu uns wend*, BWV 655a, bars 52–55

something far longer, more complex, more technically demanding and formally expansive than his teacher's modest variation. Bach's trio freely elaborates on material thematically derived from the chorale; it is only in the final third of the piece that Bach introduces what was at the time a more typical type of trio, one with the *cantus firmus* at last being presented in longer note values in the bass, while the upper parts continue their conversational interplay and serpentine figuration.

Bach revised *Herr Jesu Christ, dich zu uns wend*, and his other earliest trios, for inclusion in the so-called "Leipzig" Chorales (BWV 651–668, also known as the "Great Eighteen") assembled some three decades later. These early sources and the later autograph versions stress the uniqueness of the genre by giving each piece the heading "Trio super" followed by the name of the chorale.[63] These trios set a new eighteenth-century standard for left-hand "modulation" and pedal independence. The other trios found in the Leipzig Chorales and the still-later Schübler Chorales are equally difficult and diverse. The *Trio Super: Nun komm, der Heiden Heiland*, BWV 660 has the left hand and pedal perform the accompanimental lines as if they were two gambists, while the right hand delivers an ornamented version of the chorale – a fiendishly difficult part to execute gracefully against the awkward passagework below (see Example 1.10). The ritornello of this extended exercise in balance is a full-blown *bicinium* replete with motivic dialogue and interlocking sequences between the left hand and pedal; during these statements of the ritornello the right hand is allowed to grab onto the bench to aid stability. But that equilibrium is tested every time the right hand has to release its grip and deliver the long, artfully decorated *cantus firmus* that must somehow remain elegant and easy, as if unconcerned with the

---

[63] The only other generic designation Bach uses in the manuscript is "Fantasia" (BWV 651).

Example 1.10   J. S. Bach, *Trio super: Nun komm der Heiden Heiland*, BWV 660, bars 1–14

unrelenting exertions ongoing in the lower parts: to paraphrase Mattheson, the right hand must not know what either the left hand or the pedal are doing.

Bach's trios push the feet to new levels of adaptability. In the print of his last published trio, included as one of the so-called Schübler chorales (issued

Example 1.11   J. S. Bach, *Kommst du nun Jesu, vom Himmel herunter*, BWV 650, bars 1–17

c. 1748), Bach does not indicate the deployment of hands or feet. The chorale prelude on *Kommst du nun, Jesu, vom Himmel herunter* (BWV 650) is a transcription of a cantata movement (BWV 137) and Bach does not specify that the chorale melody should be played in the pedal – he could as easily have decided to give the vigorous bassline to the feet (see Example 1.11). In his personal copy, however, Bach tinkered with the arrangement, and specified that the *cantus firmus* (placed on the middle staff in the print) be played at 4′ pitch by the pedal. Clearly, among eighteenth-century owners of the print, or of manuscript copies, either solution was available; perhaps Bach played it both ways, too. Each mode of performance offers distinct challenges. Making the feet play the music of the lowest staff sends them bounding all over the pedalboard; charged with the *cantus firmus*, the feet must deliver graces and difficult trills, which Bach added to his personal copy while

Example 1.11   (cont.)

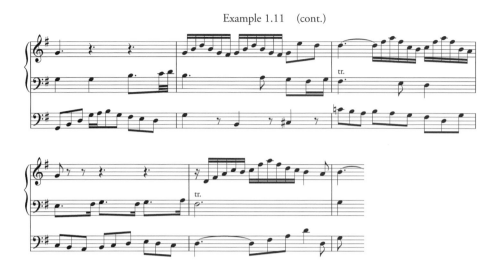

specifying that this line be taken by the feet. The performance possibilities of *Kommst du nun Jesu* demonstrate how German feet had to be adaptable in ways Boyvin and other French masters of the trio (see Introduction, p. 9) would never have imagined. It is not only that the pedalboard and the technical prowess of the player must be up to the task, so must the German organ with its rich allotment of pedal stops: in his personal exemplar, Bach asks for a 4′ stop, which could be a flue or a reed, or combinations that can be heard in the manuals. Only the German organs allowed for this kind of diversity of approach, and only German organists could execute these diverse solutions.

The modular approach to treatment of the chorale in which any of the three parts can deliver the *cantus firmus*, even in decorated form, finds its most seamlessly elegant expression in Bach's *Trio super: Allein Gott in der Höh' sei Ehr'*, BWV 676, from the *Clavierübung III* of 1739, Bach's first published volume of organ music. As in many of his other chorale trios, in *Allein Gott* Bach derives the opening ritornello from the hymn tune. But as always, he imbues the figure with an effervescent quality that seems to escape its sense of obligation to the well-known *cantus firmus*, before the chorale melody emerges gracefully from the sixteenth-note ritornello (see Example 1.12a). The chorale comes into rhythmic relief because of its somewhat longer note values, but it is much more of a piece with its surroundings than the more obvious statements of the chorale in Bach's earlier trios; the ritornello often saunters directly into the chorale statement, and then returns to the sixteenth-notes without clear demarcation between these elements. Only once (at bar 33) does a rest follow the statement of a line of the chorale. Even cadences are often elided or simply avoided. After being played by the left hand in the initial pass through its first two phrases, the chorale then migrates to the right hand for the reprise of the *Stollen* (the

Example 1.12a   J. S. Bach, *Trio super: Allein Gott in der Höh' sei Ehr'*, BWV 676, bars 1–17

A of the melody's AAB structure in the so-called German bar-form). The alternation of the *cantus firmus* between the hands then proceeds line by line through the course of the piece, as decorated echoes between the manuals integrate the chorale melody ever more thoroughly into the free elaboration of it.

Example 1.12b   J. S. Bach, *Trio super: Allein Gott in der Höh' sei Ehr'*, BWV 676, bars 78–91

With the transition to the *Abgesang* (the B element in the chorale melody), Bach increases the complexity. The feet take up the chorale in canonic imitation of the hands, first the right (at bar 78) and then the left (bar 87) (see Example 1.12b). The canonic voices provide a platform for the rippling figuration that continues above, and indeed, never abates over the course of this longest of Bach's trios. The rather schematic introduction of the *cantus firmus* in the pedal of the earlier trios has given way to a fully equal participation of the feet in which the longer pedal notes are propelled forward by the sixteenth-notes, while at the same time operating in canonic tandem with the other manual voices. In these placid moments in which the prevailing harmonic rhythm of the trio seems to slow down, the *Kenner*, to whom Bach specifically directed the *Clavierübung III*, would have recognized that this deceptively simple texture upholds absolute independence between left hand and pedal, artfully integrating canonic artifice into the bubbling trio. What sound like the simplest moments in the piece are in fact highly contrived, yet supremely elegant; when the feet slow down they are at their most contrapuntally rigorous. This trio is an exquisite example of Mattheson's description of the trio with fully independent pedal as a *wohlklingende Gemeinschaft* ("harmonious cooperation") extending to six minutes, that is, to the length of the entire chorale variation set demanded of the 1725 Hamburg Cathedral candidates.[64] Migrating from hands to feet, the *cantus firmus* of Bach's trio on *Allein Gott* traces a path back to the origins of the trio and obbligato pedal-playing.

DANCING TO THE IDEAL

Although Bach seems to have developed his approach to the organ trio first in the chorale settings discussed above, his most concerted confrontation with the genre came with his Six Sonatas, BWV 525–530, whose main sources are two manuscripts stemming from the Bach family: an autograph copy probably made c. 1727, and another manuscript in the hand of Anna Magdalena Bach, later divided and the missing section recopied by Wilhelm Friedemann Bach. The origins of these manuscripts suggest just how important the trios were in the musical life of the Bachs, and probably to the formation of one of the greatest organists of the next generation – Bach's first son, Wilhelm Friedemann. After J. S. Bach's death, the organ trios were held up as the ultimate test of true organ-playing.

In the list of organ works in Forkel's biography, which relied on information from Bach's sons Carl Philipp Emanuel and Wilhelm Friedemann, the trios "for two claviers and obbligato pedals" are the final entry, and the prime carrier of Bach's musical and familial legacy: "Bach composed [the trios] for his eldest son, Wilhelm Friedemann, who, by practicing them, had to prepare himself to become the great performer on the organ that he afterward was. It is impossible to say enough of their beauty. They were composed when the author was in his most mature age and may be considered as his chief work of this description."[65] A later eighteenth-century history of the Thomasschule praises Bach as the greatest organist

---

[64] Mattheson, *Grosse General-Bass Schule*, p. 34.
[65] Johann Nikolaus Forkel, *Ueber Johann Sebastian Bachs Leben, Kunst und Kunstwerke* (Leipzig: Hoffmeister und Kühnel, 1802; reprint, Kassel: Bärenreiter, 1999), pp. 471–472.

of his day and describes Wilhelm Friedemann as the son who inherited the organ art most directly. The account goes on to make grand claims for Bach's organ music, "that it surpassed all that had previously been written for the instrument."[66] The trios were again the clearest expression of a technique that demanded utter independence: "the left hand had to be as capable as the right, and he treated the pedal as its own voice." Other Bach devotees praised the timeless modernity of the trios; Carl Philipp Emanuel wrote that they "are written in such *galant* style that they still sound very good, and never grow old, but on the contrary will outlive all revolutions of fashion in music."[67] He also cites the collection as the crowning illustration of the importance of the pedals in organ-playing and Bach's mastery of them: the trios are stylistically timeless, and so technically ambitious that their difficulty will not be surpassed even by flashier "modern" pieces. But for all their conversational refinement and gallant finesse, the relentlessness of the pitfalls is unmatched, the slightest hitch is noticed, the disturbance of the flow marked by the player's body and the listener's ear. Things can go wrong immediately and irrevocably as in no other genre: it is impossible to fake your way through a trio sonata movement.

The dialogue between right hand and pedal at the opening of Bach's E flat sonata, BWV 525/1, is enriched when the left hand enters, joining in thematically but expanding the range of internal references and technical difficulties. The first bar's sixteenth-note *figura corta* interjections are delivered easily by alternating feet, as if a conventional organ pattern might predominate (Example 1.13a). What follows, however, is clearly indebted to the typical shape of instrumental continuo lines: with scalar motion beginning at the end of bar 2 and then broken triads, which fit less easily under the feet, as in Schlick. The allusion of bar 6 to the main theme requires a sensitive cantabile phrasing across the rather awkward leaps: some organists use heels, some just toes. The sometime student of Wilhelm Friedemann Bach, Johann Samuel Petri, criticized those organists who played the upper octave of the pedals with the right foot and the lower octave with their left: such lazy deficiency inflicted serious injury on the music, since as Petri put it, the continuo line would no longer be continuous, thus violating its most basic premise.[68] In the second edition of his treatise, *Anleitung zur praktischen Musik* (*Introduction to Practical Music*) of 1782, Petri urges the organist to learn how to play both conjunct and leaping lines fluently, and the exercises he lays out are designed to improve these skills. As can be seen in Figure 1.5, these make some use of the heel (in Petri's system 1 indicates the right toe; 2 the left toe; 3 the right heel; and 4 the left heel). In mimicking the trio, the feet must do what the cello or bassoon does, without disrupting the flow of even rapid lines in awkward keys.

---

[66] *BD*, 3: 313.   [67] *NBR*, 406; *BD*, 3: 441.
[68] Johann Samuel Petri, *Anleitung zur praktischen Musik* (Leipzig: Johann Gottlob Immanuel Breitkopf, 1782; reprint, Munich: Katzbichler, 1999), pp. 323–324. This exercise also appears in the first edition of 1767.

Example 1.13a   J. S. Bach, Sonata No. 1 in E flat, BWV 525, first movement, bars 1–10

The final pedal entrance (Example 1.13b) of the theme in BWV 525/1 comes low on the pedalboard (only the second time the theme appears in the bass in the entire movement); this forces the organist to turn his or her body and slide it down the bench to execute the figure with the care and shape its thematic importance requires. Only two previous passages in the movement have required this close attention to the lower register, and at the close of the piece it is especially contorting physically – Bach saves the hardest part for late in the piece, the octave shift downward requiring a major reapportioning of weight, balance, orientation. This low bass entry is dramatically important, but technically it must seem as easy as all that preceded it. The pair of downward-leaping sevenths in bars 52 and 53 that

Example 1.13b   J. S. Bach, Sonata No. 1 in E flat, BWV 525, first movement, bars 50–58

Figure 5   J. S. Petri, *Anleitung zur praktischen Musik*, p. 322

follow the theme are perilous too. The closing three bars have the feet hopping across mostly thirds and working their way quickly from c1 in bar 56 down nearly two octaves to E flat. The feet have to cross this distance while each hand busily elaborates the same central e flat1–e flat2 octave; against this manual material, the pedal must negotiate a mix of flats and naturals to bring the piece to an elegant close.

Example 1.14 J. S. Bach, Sonata No. 1 in E flat, BWV 525, final movement, bars 1–37

The final movement of the first Trio Sonata is a flamboyant exercise in see-sawing between ever-decreasing intervals. In the opening half of the binary form, the lower part of each hand moves upward towards a fixed pitch in the upper part of the hand. In the bassline, the figure measures the pedalboard, with one foot moving against the fixed reference point of the other (see Example 1.14). (In the second half, beginning at bar 33, Bach

Example 1.14   (cont.)

inverts the subject, and the measuring process accordingly proceeds in the opposite direction.) At bar 10 the feet finish off their ascent of the scale but at the arrival in bar 11 they do not race forward with the sixteenth-note figures as the manuals had done. Bach does not ask the pedal to do every-thing the manuals can: there are limits to its velocity. After a few bars of slower bass notes, the feet confront an exercise in eighth-notes beginning in bar 17 that recalls the rhythm of the opening theme: but rather than pacing off close intervals up the scale, the pedal now bounces between thirds and their inversion, tenths, repeating each of these three times in alternation. Musically, this conveys an arch humor: the more conventional approach of using all thirds would be easier physically, but less buoyant musically. This exercise in spreading and narrowing the legs must be conducted against the feather-light elaboration of the sequence in the manuals above.

The closing gesture beginning at bar 28 combines a sixteenth-note figure related to the opening theme, while the eighth-notes above flatten out the rocking pattern to the compact interval of the major second. The harmony remains static above the pedal-point B flat as the manuals answer each other in invertible counterpoint at bars 28 and 29. In spite of the continued whir of sixteenth-note motion there is a sense of repose here. In all three parts in succession (right hand, left hand, then pedal) the eighth-notes are meant to be easy, elegant. The relaxation of the cadence is one of physical relief and musical contrast: the intervallic closeness and technical ease come in humorous contrast to the bawdy back and forth so prevalent up to this point. The rustic stomping at either end of the pedalboard has given way to the refinements of polite conversation, as if to say it could have all been made this easy, but, of course, was not. Not even the typical octave leap is asked for in the pedal when the actual cadence finally comes: all is contained and controlled, knees together, grin suppressed. Starting as an ebullient extrovert, the music retires more mindful of its manners. As so often in Bach's music, this change of character signals a humorous turn. The rest in bar 31 is the wink that caps the joke. The sudden disappearance of the non-stop Bachian sixteenth-note motion with the eighth-notes at the beginning of the measure is already a kind of cessation, a coy withdrawal. The puncturing witticism that is the eighth-note rest in all parts seems to hold within it all the insouciant energy of the movement – a split second of repose, just to bring into relief how hard the exercise has been up to that point. The repeat magnifies the joke: the cadence and the run up to it are funnier, more enjoyable the second time around because we know what to expect, and are better prepared to appreciate the comic diction.

Bach's humor proves a more fundamental point, however: musical expression and technique are inseparable. The eighth-note rest is about not only musical poise, but physical poise, too. If one is not balanced with hands and feet in equilibrium on the bench, one will stumble, ruining the moment with a clumsy shudder. If one is pressing too hard on the keys and clinging on, one could lurch in one direction or another when suddenly there is no resistance, and nothing to grab onto. Such a loss of balance would disturb the music with some obvious mistakes or hesitations. The eighth-note rest is the punchline of the piece, heard four times, and distilling in its fleet silence the Trio Sonatas' essence of musical and physical interplay. Only an organist juggling three polyphonic parts on three distinct keyboards – each hand with its own line, the feet with the bass – can understand the thrill of keeping these balls in the air, and when they suddenly seem to hang motionless over that eighth-note rest, one can only smile and wait. Playing such a piece and waiting through such a moment is a pleasure deriving not only from the cooperation and independence of hands and feet, but from the way the division of labor across the limbs allows for the player to understand polyphony as a physical act involving the whole body.

BACH AND BERNHARD

Whether Bach knew of the pedigree of the organ trio whose earliest beginnings were outlined by Praetorius and whose potential was first demonstrated by Schlick is beside the point; like Mattheson and many others, Bach recognized the genre as the truest measure of independence between the limbs, in which such sometimes striking, often reserved, insights came to life through physical grace. While the trio for hands and feet seems first to have been developed to a high musical art by Schlick, it was Bach who cast it anew with a vitality drawn from eighteenth-century virtuosity. Bach's trios became the truest test of German organ-playing – of left-hand modulation and pedal independence. Paradoxically perhaps, the trio was both the foundation of German organ-playing and its most demanding expression. More voices could add to the tasks of hands and feet, but there was no clearer manifestation of what independence of the limbs meant at its highest level of ambition; that the trio was the most transparent four-limbed texture also meant that each voice could be clearly heard and the moments when the organist faltered most easily noticed. An article with "Suggestions for Beginning Organists" published in an 1844 edition of *Urania*, a German periodical for professional and amateur organists, drew on an essential German attitude extending back to Schlick and forward to our own time in claiming that the trio was "the true foundation of organ-playing," with Bach's essays in the genre as the reference point of both difficulty and excellence.[69]

Still, the august historical dimension of the trio and of vigorously independent pedal was certainly crucial to eighteenth-century Germans' awareness of, and pride in, their mode of organ performance. Forkel devoted many of the later pages of his 1801 *Allgemeine Geschichte der Musik* (*General History of Music*) to the organ.[70] The instrument is introduced into Forkel's narrative emerging in modern form in the midst of a discussion of figural music and

---

[69] *Urania*, 1 (1844), 11.
[70] J. N. Forkel, *Allgemeine Geschichte der Musik* (Leipzig: Schwickert, 1788–1801; reprint, Graz: Akademische Druck- u. Verlagsanstalt, 1967), vol. II, pp. 668–670.

polyphony: Forkel cites "our compatriot" [*unser Landsmann*] Bernhard the German as the inventor of the pedal in Venice at the end of the fifteenth century;[71] while this development had made the organ an instrument rich in harmony ("harmoniereiches Instrument"), there is no evidence that the Italians produced any contrapuntal music to take advantage of this advance. Not so the Germans. As Forkel goes on to argue, Bernhard must have known what the pedal would mean for augmenting harmonic possibility and for the creation of larger contrapuntal structures, otherwise he wouldn't have invented it in the first place. While the origins of polyphony lay in the Netherlands, the Germans were quick to take it up, and indeed they led the way in counterpoint by transferring these practices to the organ: "Such a splendid instrument as the organ, to whose perfection the Germans contributed so much, flourished there from very early on."[72] Forkel concludes that by the sixteenth century, the German organ art – a polyphonic art to be sure – had risen to unimagined heights.[73] While his account of Bernhard was then the most scholarly, if still flawed, treatment of this figure, his praise reflects the enduring value accorded Bernhard as an emblem of German technological and musical innovation. Forkel's respect for J. S. Bach's trios, and for Bach's pedaling more generally, can be seen in the context of the historian's awareness of the pedal's origins.

Bach, too, was likely steeped in the myth of Bernhard, if one considers his ubiquitous position in music treatises touching on the history of the organ and of polyphony. For Schlick, who articulated counterpoint through the human form with such austere elegance and who might even have known the mythical Bernhard, the organ with manuals and pedal became a means for the single organist to play music that normally demanded many musicians. From the most obvious perspective Bach's emulation of the trio sonata for two treble instruments above a bassline demonstrated the wide-ranging capabilities of that single organist: he managed alone to do what three players on separate instruments could do. That the organist could pull stops such as the Violon Bass, Viola da Gamba, Hautbois, and other registers found on central-German organs of Bach's period, only heightened the associations between the sound brought to life by a single organist and the lively music-making of a group of individual players. The remarkable independence of German organists' limbs and their assignment to the individual lines of demanding ensemble pieces comes into clearer relief when we picture Nicolaus Bruhns's stunt, recounted by Mattheson, of playing the violin while seated at the organ bench and producing the bassline at the organ pedals; aside from its novelty, this shows how adept organists were at dealing with discrete contrapuntal lines and disparate physical tasks. Bruhns's duo becomes Bach's trio: the pedal

---

[71] Forkel uses two different dates, the usual 1470, as well as 1480, the latter possibly a typographical error. See *Allgemeine Geschichte*, vol. II, pp. 668, 724.
[72] Forkel, *Allgemeine Geschichte*, vol. II, p. 725.   [73] *Ibid.*, p. 729.

in both plays the part of the cello in an ensemble trio sonata, and instead of a single treble line in the Bruhns trick, Bach's hands each take on the role of an individual violin.[74]

The organ fugue typically had more voices, but the trio's allocation of parts to three individual keyboards and three discrete sounds made all the more vivid and impressive the multitasking of the single organist, the soloist as ensemble. One of the most obvious ways for the organist Bach to appear modern was to emulate the prevailing chamber music genres of the time; Bach did this with an ear for the up-to-date such that his followers held his trios to be fashionable decades after the composer's death. That Bach knew nothing of Arnolt Schlick's music is irrelevant. The tradition mythically embodied in Bernhard and crystallized in the *Tabulaturen* was what made possible, however indirectly, Bach's own demanding physical interactions with the organ. To claim that the Germans had invented the pedal and that they had then exploited its true potential was to argue that at the "instrument of instruments" the organist was the "musician of musicians." What the Germans had developed was not just a technology for allowing the feet to join the hands in making music. They had also invented a new musical body: that of the organist, the universal musician at that universal instrument. Long before Bach's trios, German feet had carried the organist over the threshold into musical modernity.

---

[74] Johann Mattheson, *Grundlage einer Ehren-Pforte* (Hamburg, 1740; modern edn. ed. Max Schneider, Berlin: Liepmannsohn, 1910), p. 26.

CHAPTER 2

Harmonies of the feet, visions of the body

COMPREHENDING THE ORGAN'S DIMENSIONS

As no other musician, the organist is dwarfed by his, or her, instrument. That is doubtless one reason many are drawn to play it – to have at the tips of the fingers and the soles of the feet control over such monumental musical means. The largest pipes of the great instruments of Bach's day were six times his height. Even mid-sized organs like that favored by Schlick were too much for the player to take in visually from the console. The largest instruments that filled the west-end galleries of churches from the fifteenth century on towered over the organist. Often these organs had a division on the gallery rail behind the organist, the *Rückpositiv*; it was typically designed as a smaller version of the main case, and had the effect of enclosing the player so that he could not be seen from down below in the church. Large organs made it difficult, even impossible, for the player to sense exactly where the boundaries of the instrument lay. What other musical instrument can you not take full measure of as you play it? Almost all others can be carried, moved, or even destroyed with one decisive blow. Even the harpsichord – or a modern grand piano on wheels – can be pushed or pulled across the floor. Not so the King of Instruments. Dismantling it is a job for a small army. The organ is itself a piece of architecture and cannot be carried from the church in case of fire. Massive in stature and anchored to their surroundings, too many of the great organs of the European tradition could not be spirited to safety but instead went down in flames when the bombs of World War II fell. In that catastrophe the organ's size was its greatest enemy.

The sheer scope of the instrument and the timbral range of the thousands of pipes housed within its magnificent case suggested infinite power and possibility. The perceived perfection of the organ derived from its technological complexity, a sophistication that allowed it to rise several stories from the gallery which was itself already high above the church floor. The organ was also likened to the human form, itself perfectly constructed by God: the organ's keys were teeth; the pipes were throats; and the openings where the sound was generated were mouths.[1] Many instruments of Praetorius's time

---

[1] Praetorius, *Syntagma musicum III: De organographia* (Wolfenbüttel: Elias Holwein, 1619; reprint, Kassel: Bärenreiter, 1985), pp. 85–88. Praetorius took this comparison between the human body and the organ from Girolamo Diruta, *Il Transilvano*, 2 vols. (Venice, 1593–1607), vol. I, preface, unpaginated.

and into Bach's had a division of the organ just above the organist's head in the middle of the case: this was called the *Brustwerk* ("division in the breast"), since it nestled in the living, breathing chest of the anthropomorphized instrument. Continuing the analogy, the bellows were lungs so long as they continued to be filled by the hidden calcant – the bellows-treader. One of the most awe-inspiring capabilities of the organ was its unique power to sustain sound without interruption: such unwavering sonorities resounded as a simulacrum of the eternal chord, the harmony of the spheres. The diverse stops placed a compendium of musical sonorities at the organist's disposal, sounds imitating the human voice (likened often to the basic Principal stop or more explicitly mimicked by the Vox humana) and all instruments – from strings and flutes, to crumhorns and trumpets. Jakob Adlung was one of the many writers who made the calculation for purposes of impressing on his readers the endless store of sonic permutations that the organ offered: an instrument with 40 registers could generate 1,201,911,627,775 combinations; even allowing for the fact that not all of these were usable according to the dictates of either tradition or common sense, the possibilities were in effect endless.[2] At the organ a single musician commanded a symphony: many instruments in one were at the disposal of many musicians in one.

The apparatus of the keyboard allowed the highly trained movements of the organist to be conveyed far from the body and into the organ's architecture, onto its arrangement of pipes set on wind chests in distinct parts of the instrument. The keys, trackers, and rollers (the mechanisms connecting the console to the wind chests on which the pipes were arrayed) were like the nerves, tendons and muscles of the organ's body, which propelled the musical figures – giant gestures or slender arabesques, complicated webs of polyphony or single clarion blasts – out into reverberant churches with a sound that seemed bigger than life. Minuscule physical movements could produce massive musical shapes in architectural space. These unique means to create a whole world of sound from a console built into the largest and most heavenly of instruments was surely what inspired Athanasius Kircher's allegory of creation in which God is an organist, who begins his task of inventing the world first with the lowest pipes of the pedal and then proceeds upward through the registers.[3]

---

[2] Jakob Adlung, *Anleitung zur der musikalischen Gelahrtheit* (Erfurt: J. D. Jungnicol, 1758; reprint, Kassel: Bärenreiter, 1953), pp. 496–503. Adlung calculated the combinations using the algorhythm 2^n-1, where n is the number of stops. When he got to a rather large organ with 40 stops his calculations, demanding in an age before calculators, seem to have gone slightly askew. The correct number of combinations for a 40-stop instrument is in fact 1,099,511,627,775, so he was wide of the mark by a mere hundred billion or so.

[3] For an account of this creation story with God as organist, see Athanasius Kircher, *Musurgia universalis* (Rome, 1650; facsimile reprint, Kassel: Bärenreiter, 1988), p. 115; see also the German translation, *Germaniæ redonatus: sive Artis Magnæ de Consono et Dißono Ars Minor: Das ist, Philosophischer Extract und Auszug aus … Musurgia universalis*, trans. Andreas Hirsch (Schwäbisch Hall: Hans Reinhold Laidigen and Johann Christoph Gräter, 1662; reprint, Kassel: Bärenreiter, 2006), pp. 252–258.

Although the organist cannot visually take in the expanse of his instrument from the console, he can hear the extent of its sound and therefore aurally gauge the dimensions of the organ from which it emanates. This is not to say that his is the best position from which to appreciate the musical effect of the sound: given the size of the instrument, that location is almost always down in the church. But while playing, the organist takes a kind of sounding of the musical means at his disposal. If he cannot see his instrument, he can hear it: one could even say that the diverse registers, alone and in combination, drawn from different parts of the organ allow him to imagine – to see an image – of the giant construction looming around him, from the pedal roaring on either flank to the angelic pipings high above in the *Oberpositiv* atop the main case. Conversely, the listeners down in the church gazing up at the organ's façade are prompted to imagine the motion of the organist hidden above. The elegant transparency of the trio, the rumbling of a pedal solo, or the sublime arrays of many-voiced counterpoint – all could inspire a picture of the organist's movements in the listener's mind.

On the one hand, the size of the organ was far greater than that of other instruments, but on the other, its resources allowed organists unique means to understand musical space – and by this I mean the disposition, contour, and cooperation of discreet polyphonic voices. The player may not have been able to see, or perhaps even to grasp the totality of his instrument while playing it, but he could use it to parse counterpoint with his limbs in ways impossible for other musicians. Praetorius's historical account of the trio describes the crucial first move towards the allocation of polyphonic parts between hands and feet. The "invention" of four-limbed performance massively expanded the range of musical possibilities of a single person; still, a lone organist could do no more than his fingers and feet were capable of. Though he could match a choir of voices and instruments – according to Kircher's organ allegory, God had created the angels by pulling the 16′ pedal stop – the organist could not, for example, perform alone Kircher's famed thousand-voice canon of angels singing an enormous *Sanctus*, a piece meant to evoke the heavenly concert.[4] However redolent of the eternal, the organ was still on earth, and the organist had only two hands and two feet. Samuel Scheidt, in his seminal *Tabulatura nova* of 1624, cautioned organists not to try to span more than an octave between the feet when using both simultaneously in large contrapuntal textures since they simply couldn't reach it, and further, one imagines, the player might even be pulled from the bench in attempting still wider stretches.[5] Scheidt closes the volume with double pedal that stretches beyond this rule twice, once in the third bar, while otherwise

[4] Kircher, *Musurgia*, frontispiece. See also David Yearsley, *Bach and the Meanings of Counterpoint* (Cambridge University Press, 2002), pp. 21–22.

[5] Scheidt, Samuel, *Tabulatura nova* (1624) in *Denkmäler deutscher Tonkunst*, ed. Max Seiffert (Leipzig: Breitkopf & Härtel, 1892), vol. I, p. 223.

Example 2.1   Samuel Scheidt, *Modus ludendi* from *Tabulatura nova*
(Halle, 1624), bars 1–3

demonstrating elegant voice-leading – the counterpoint and organist in perfect balance. By exceeding the octave Scheidt was making the point still more loudly that this was outsized music, both polyphonically and physically (see Example 2.1).

Scheidt's advice acknowledges the physical limits of the human body at the organ. One of the most remarkable aspects of the early history of organ pedaling, and in particular of Arnolt Schlick's unmatched contribution to it, is how vigorously Schlick tested those limits in polyphonic music that exceeded even Scheidt's six contrapuntal voices played by one organist. Schlick's reference in the *Spiegel* to "polyphonic solos with the feet alone" suggests that already at the beginning of the sixteenth century, playing multiple voices in the feet was an advanced, but essential technique, and not a particularly rare one.[6] At the outset of writing for and about the organ, Schlick had almost matter-of-factly described a mode of playing that must have been astonishing to all who witnessed it. Only a single towering example of Schlick's pedal polyphony survives: *Ascendo ad patrem meum*, a piece rediscovered by Renato Lunelli in the City Library in Trent in northern Italy in 1949.[7] Composed around 1520, this massive ten-part setting has four real parts in the pedal alone, exceeding even the claims of the *Spiegel* (where only three-part pedaling is described), and demonstrating just how ambitious Schlick was when it came to exploiting the full potential of the feet and hands. This unparalleled polyphonic achievement is the last of ten pieces found in the Trent manuscript: eight canonic settings of *Gaude Dei genetrix* and a *bicinium* on the melody of *Ascendo ad patrem meum* that precede the final ten-part setting, the most physically difficult in the manuscript, and one of the most demanding pieces ever conceived for the organ, requiring great flexibility of ankle and leg, good balance, poise and

---

[6] Arnolt Schlick, *Spiegel der Orgel-macher und Organisten* (Mainz: Peter Schöffer the Younger, 1511); parallel trans. Elizabeth Berry Barber (Buren: Knuf, 1980), p. 29.

[7] Renato Lunelli, "Contributi trentini alle relazioni musicali fra l'Italia e la Germania nel Rinascimento," *Acta Musicologica*, 21 (1949), 41–70. The Trent manuscript shows the influence of the Hofhaimer tradition (Ms. 1947 from Biblioteca Civica di Trento). See also Hans Joachim Moser, "Eine Trienter Orgeltabulatur aus Hofhaimers Zeit" in *Studien zur Musikgeschichte: Festschrift für Guido Adler, zum 75. Geburtstag* (Vienna: Universal-Edition, 1930), pp. 84–86.

precision. This polyphonic array taxes the mind, too, which must manage the amassed parts, directing the feet to grab chords with heel and toe together while the hands pursue their own parts. Polyphonic playing of this kind fostered, indeed demanded, a physical engagement with complex musical textures in which contrapuntal parts are assigned to the limbs with even greater specificity than they were in the trio. Right from the start of the organ's modernity its full potential was already recognized, and these experiments allowed the blind Schlick and, two centuries later, Bach, himself blind in old age, to see beyond their instrument's dimensions and into musical space – and, so they thought, into heaven.

THE ASCENT OF ORGAN POLYPHONY

The greatest example of early modern German pedal ambition survives not in Germany but in an Italian library; it is a testament to the cultural value of such music that it could be accorded the status of priceless, international gift. A crossroads of organ cultures at the permeable border between German- and Italian-speaking Europe, Trent was the first Italian city to be encountered after leaving South Tyrol, which since World War I has belonged to Italy, but was long part of the Austro-Hungarian Empire.[8] The glories of the German organ art would have been known in northern Italy before Schlick sent his set of unique pieces to the Italian Prince Bishop of Trent, Cardinal Bernardo Clesio sometime after 1520. German organ-builders were active on the Italian peninsula across the fourteenth and fifteenth centuries; as in Venice, this period documents an organ in Trent that relied on German expertise for its construction.[9] During a 1508 visit of the Emperor Maximilian I to Trent, the celebrated imperial organist Paul Hofhaimer performed for the city's civic and ecclesiastical luminaries and for members of their musical establishments.[10] Hofhaimer and Schlick would have met at the Diet of Worms in 1495, and at least once again at Torgau in Saxony in 1516.[11] Hofhaimer had also trained the Italian Dionisio Memo, who served as organist in St. Mark's, Venice in the early sixteenth century – that is soon after Bernhard the German was said to have introduced "German" pedals to that instrument.[12]

---

[8] After Napoloen's defeat at the Battle of Leipzig, Trent was annexed to the province of South Tyrol by the Hapsburg Empire in 1814.

[9] Lunelli, "Contributi trentini," 46.

[10] *Ibid.*, 42–44. Hofhaimer could have played in San Pietro with its important organ; an organ for the cathedral was then under construction.

[11] Hans Joachim Moser, *Paul Hofhaimer* (Stuttgart and Berlin: Cotta, 1929), pp. 44, 46.

[12] *Ibid.*, pp. 40–41. Memo later made his career in England. Interestingly, one of the dedicatory poems by Fantinus Memmus, a relative of Memo, for Hofhaimer's *Harmoniae poeticae* (Nuremberg, 1539), praises Hofhaimer for his general mastery of music, his heavenly melody, and his magical hands, but never mentions the feet, as if this aspect of the German organ art did not indeed have purchase in Venice. Hofhaimer's scant surviving organ music does not require the kind of pedalwork of his contemporary Schlick; yet, the music of Hofhaimer's student Hans Buchner required impressive command of pedaling, making it almost certain that Hofhaimer had mastered and taught these techniques, too.

We can assume that Hofhaimer taught his Italian charge how to play like a German, and that he used Bernhard's Venetian pedals to their fullest. As an organ expert and virtuoso, Hofhaimer himself had been called over the Alps at least one other time, around 1486 to Bozen (Bolzano), just north of Trent in South Tyrol. With all the organists and organ-builders of German extraction or influence active in the region south of the Alps, it is not surprising that the Venetian Sabellicus specifically mentioned the national origins of the monk, Bernhard, in his account of the organ and its pedals in St. Mark's.

Though Schlick apparently never crossed the Alps himself, he did send his own music as an emissary of "true" organ-playing to Trent. In his dedicatory letter, Schlick alluded to the coronation of Charles V as Emperor; this took place in Aachen in 1520, and it is quite possible that Schlick had performed the music contained in the manuscript at the imperial festivities. If Schlick did appear there, he would have had the opportunity to display his incomparable abilities before an international audience of eminent musical and political personages. In the preface to the *Tabulaturen Etlicher lobgesang* of 1512, Schlick's son had written that his father had often performed before "emperors and kings, electors, princes, both temporal and ecclesiastical."[13] Whether or not Schlick played at the coronation of Charles V, he was apparently accustomed to having his music appreciated by the powerful and discerning. Clesio had himself been lavishly installed as bishop in Trent in 1514, with organ music provided by one Giorgio the "German Musician" [*Alemanno Musico*].[14] When Schlick sent his music to Trent, he knew that German organ-playing was already valued in that city, and he would also have believed that his extraordinary musical gift would not go unappreciated: Schlick's dedicatory letter expresses his hope that the music he has sent will please Clesio, and thus "honor an exceptional music-lover [*liephaber*]."[15]

When Clesio received Schlick's precious manuscript, the bishop had already begun overseeing his great architectural project: the construction of Santa Maria Maggiore, site of the Council of Trent, which Clesio brought to his city, and which began its work a few years after his death in 1539. One of the great patrons of the arts in northern Italy in the sixteenth century, Clesio would from the start have been thinking about an organ for the new church. In the event, he endowed Santa Maria Maggiore with one of the most spectacular instruments ever made. The elaborate marble balcony completed in 1534 remains a tourist attraction to this day. The carver of the case, itself provided with painted doors and magnificent statuary, lauded

---

[13] Letter reprinted in Arnolt Schlick, *Orgelkompositionen*, ed. Rudolf Walter (Mainz: Schott, 1969), foreword, unpaginated.

[14] Lunelli, "Contributi trentini," 46. This musician is conjectured by Lunelli to have been Jörg Schapff from the Hofhaimer circle. See also Moser, *Paul Hofhaimer*, p. 33.

[15] Foreword, Schlick, *Orgelkompositionen*, unpaginated [2–3].

the instrument as "one of the world's most beautiful creations."[16] (An engraving made nearly 150 years later provides a glimpse of the organ façade and is shown in Figure 2.1.) Clesio had the instrument built by a German, Caspar Zimmermann, who completed the legendary project between 1532 and 1536; it was prized for its unusual reed stops and its large, independent pedal. Clesio then diligently searched for an organist who could play it, and found a blind Tyrolean, whose name goes unrecorded, but who was known to be a German as that designation was understood in the sixteenth century.[17] Repaired, rebuilt, and refurbished over the next three centuries, but always retaining its original glory if not its exact sonority and specification, the organ remained a destination for admiring tourists from across Europe into the nineteenth century. No vestige now remains of the original instrument. The church was hit three times by lightning over the course of the eighteenth century and then again in 1819, when the organ was completely destroyed. These successive lightning strikes gave rise to myths that the organ had been built with supernatural aid, and that the people of Trent had blinded the organ-builder so that he could not make another instrument to compare with theirs.[18]

The intricacy and grandeur of Schlick's manuscript, culminating in the ten-part *Ascendo ad patrem meum*, was a musical gift to Trent's Prince Bishop that anticipated the opulence of the extraordinary organ he had commissioned for Santa Maria Maggiore. It is even possible that Clesio's plans for the organ inspired Schlick, who died sometime after 1521, to send to Trent his most experimental, expansive, and self-aggrandizing new compositions, which Schlick claimed would produce something utterly "new, enlivening, unusual, artistic" [*Etwas news lustigs Seltzsams Kunstreichs*]. Sent to northern Italy a decade after the publication of the *Spiegel*, this music pushes far beyond the already impressive richness and complexity of organ-playing laid out in that treatise and in Schlick's *Tabulaturen*. Each of the settings of *Gaude Dei genetrix* forms a *canon sine pausis* between one pair or (in one case) two pairs of voices. As in the *Tabulaturen*, the application of the pedal is not specified, but it is clear that its use was again crucial to the integrity of the counterpoint. In these canons the feet are either synchronized with the left or the right hand: the alignment of fixed contrapuntal parts is an exercise in polyphonic and technical precision. As in the *Tabulaturen*, the trio is crucial

---

[16] Bartolomeo Otello to the Parish of Salò in 1547. Cited in Renato Lunelli, *Der Orgelbau in Italien in seinen Meisterwerken*, trans. Carl Elis and Paul Smets (Mainz: Rheingold, 1956), pp. 169–170.

[17] Lunelli, *Der Orgelbau in Italien*, p. 170.

[18] Renato Lunelli and Antenore Lulli, *I "bellissimi organi" della Basilica di S. Maria Maggiore in Trento* (Trent: Comitato per le Manifestazioni Inaugurali, 1945), pp. 10–12. Johann Nepomuk Ritter von Alpenburg, *Deutsche Alpensagen* (Vienna: Wilhelm Braumüller, 1861), p. 369. Another version of the legend has it that after the organ-builder was blinded he found his way to the organ and destroyed the vox humana stop, apparently held by the story to be the most beautiful of the organ's registers. See Ignaz Vincenz Zingerle, *Sagen, Märchen und Gebräuche aus Tirol* (Innsbruck: Wagner, 1859), pp. 382–383.

Figure 2.1   Detail of the organ in Santa Maria Maggiore. From Michele Angelo Mariani,
Trento, con il sacro Concilio, et altri notabili (Trent, 1673)

in the Trent collection, making up three of the eight verses. The opening
verse gives a sense of the exactitude of contrapuntal thought and execution
(see Example 2.2). In this verse the *cantus firmus* is heard in the alto while the
outer voices move in staggered counterpoint against it, remaining aligned
with one another. The kind of free-flowing independence of the trios of the
Tabulaturen is set aside in favor of an even more self-conscious polyphonic
scheme, "in which," as Schlick noted in his letter, "no composition resembles

Example 2.2   Arnolt Schlick, *Gaude dei Genetrix*, verse 1, bars 1–6

another, and each setting is made with a different counterpoint and with its own rule."[19] The strange beauty of these pieces derives from the unrelenting precision, and the masterful demonstration of inventiveness against self-imposed limitation. In contrast to the outbursts of florid figuration in the *Tabulaturen*, the Trent settings of *Gaude Dei genetrix* abjure the distraction of ornament, leaving the contrapuntal essence of the composition unobscured.

Concluding the Trent manuscript are two settings of *Ascendo ad patrem meum*; the second is Schlick's crowning achievement, one that takes the contrapuntal precision of the canons of *Gaude Dei genetrix* to its physical and cognitive extreme. Considered together, Schlick's dual elaborations of *Ascendo ad patrem meum* present his most modest and his most massive organ pieces side by side. First comes Schlick's only surviving *bicinium* – counterpoint at its most minimal, with no feet involved (see Example 2.3). After this rises the ten-part setting – three more voices than what Schlick described in the *Spiegel* as polyphony at its most extravagant (see Example 2.4). The text of the antiphon to the *Benedictus* for Ascension is from John 20:17:

Ascendo ad Patrem meum, et Patrem vestrum, Deum meum, et Deum vestrum.
I ascend to my Father and to your Father, to my God and to your God.

The metaphor of ascent operates on many levels in Schlick's setting: to the imperial throne for Charles V; to heaven for Jesus; and to the heights of the organ art, to the limits of human comprehension and anatomical possibility in music-making.

In his dedicatory letter to Clesio, Schlick describes the ten-part setting first as a choral piece.[20] But Schlick proudly informs his patron that the piece can also be played by a single organist, and in this instance the composer does specify the deployment of the voices between manuals and pedal. The manuscript is notated not in score, but in the choirbook format typical of the period; the six parts are placed on the *verso* side (four discants and two tenors to be played in the organ version with the hands), and the four parts on the *recto* side (Bassus I through IV, to be played with feet) (see Figure 2.2). Modern editions transcribe this choirbook layout into

---

[19] Schlick to Clesio in Schlick, *Orgelkompositionen*, ed. Walter, unpaginated [2–3].
[20] Stephen Keyl, *Arnolt Schlick and Instrumental Music circa 1500* (PhD thesis, Duke University, 1989), pp. 381–382.

Example 2.3   Arnolt Schlick, *Ascendo ad patrem meum, bicinium*

Figure 2.2   Arnolt Schlick, *Ascendo ad patrem meum*, ten-part setting

Example 2.4   Arnolt Schlick, *Ascendo ad patrem meum*, ten-part setting

organ score on three staves: the feet on one staff, the hands divided between two. In performing the piece at the organ, ten fingers are charged with six of the voices, and the four useable elements of the feet (two heels, two toes) are fully occupied with the remaining four parts. If capable of this extraordinary polyphonic technique, the lone performer becomes an entire ten-voiced choir. Indeed, the organist's body is itself divided like a choir, one voice

Example 2.4   (cont.)

heard in the left toe, another in the left heel, and on upward to the little
finger of the right hand.

Even though Schlick first described the ten-part setting of *Ascendo ad
patrem meum* as a choir piece, it is surely significant that each of the four bass
voices fits into the octave-and-a-half pedal compass of the south-German
organs of his time. A further clue as to the piece's relationship with the organ
can be seen – and felt – in the way the pedal part lies in the feet. Two-note
pairs played in one foot never exceed the span of a third: there are no
intervals of a fourth or fifth between the heel and toe of the same foot. If
Schlick had been unconstrained by such physical considerations then wider
voicings of the chords would certainly have resulted from the free flow of
four contrapuntal parts; these would have required significant rewriting to
be playable by the feet. Only in four spots do unreachable intervals occur,
but these happen as a result of oblique motion on the weak parts of the beat,
and simply require that a consonant note be let go a bit early, a practice that
was probably normal even in smaller-scale polyphony and which in any case
does not damage the contrapuntal integrity of the individual voices. Such
a thinning of the texture was a prudent way to play polyphony especially in
massively reverberant churches such as Santa Maria Maggiore; further,
continuous legato was probably not part of Schlick's performance practice.
In another passage (bar 3), the organist can restrike the tenor d as it moves
from one foot to the other over the course of its duration, or merely let it
resound through to the end of the bar without attempting to depress the
key again. In sum, the four bass parts can be played throughout as thirds in
one foot or the other, or in both simultaneously. That the organist is not

asked to adapt or to approximate the "choral" version of *Ascendo ad patrem meum* seems to confirm that the piece must have been "composed" for or at the organ, even if Schlick had choral performance in mind for it: this must be why these ten parts fit so well under the limbs.

With what seems to be at least a touch of false modesty, Schlick's letter accompanying the Trent manuscript presents his most massive piece as an attempt merely "to do something further and more artistic in the practice of music." Yet this setting can hardly be construed as an ambassadorial gesture intended to make good Schlick's claim in the *Spiegel* that Germans were then exporting pedal know-how to other countries, including Italy. The ten-part setting of *Ascendo ad patrem meum* is more than just an attempt, as Schlick rather disingenuously claims, to offer the dedicatee (and presumably his organist, for he would have to be the one to play it) the chance "to learn something of further use." The work presents German pedal accomplishment as an object of veneration rather than of emulation. Clesio's organist was a German presumably willing to answer the challenge presented by the large setting of *Ascendo ad patrem*. But especially for organists of other traditions, this was an unreachable ideal: the real limit of counterpoint has been reached; there is nowhere further to go, no more body parts to call on, except perhaps the nose or the knees, as in the levers of the old organ in Halberstadt described by Praetorius. It is no wonder that when confronted with virtuosity of this magnitude, Italians did not develop their own pedal tradition until the nineteenth century.

That the angles and positions of the limbs and their parts (the individual fingers, heels, and toes) are difficult to find with complete accuracy, certainly helps explain why Schlick argued in the *Spiegel* for rationalization and standardization of the dimensions and placement of manuals and pedalboards. The lower four parts of *Ascendo ad patrem meum* require the involvement of both heels and both toes, with each foot acting as a kind of caliper or compass measuring out the span of intervals in various angles across the pedalboard; Schlick's masterpiece amounts to a musical anatomy lesson, a dissection of the physical possibility of the foot, as the pedal keys become the template for measuring the precise motions and range of positions of which the feet are capable. This examination of the body in performance is not unlike the investigations into human form by Schlick's south-German contemporary Albrecht Dürer, who might well have met Schlick at Charles V's coronation in Aachen.[21] Both Schlick and Dürer investigate in their work the potential of the body – its proportions, its reach and range of motion, its flexibility, its center of balance. The ten polyphonic parts laid out in the pages of *Ascendo ad patrem meum* are the equivalent

---

[21] Anja Eichler, *Albrecht Dürer, 1471–1528*, trans. Fiona Hulse (Cologne: Könemann, 1999), p. 112.

of a dynamic drawing – a motion-picture if you like – of the movements of the organist's hands and feet. These contemporary investigations of human form share a common goal: Dürer's depictions of feet in his *Four Books on Human Proportion* of 1528 are more than the representation of the body according to numerical ratios,[22] just as Schlick's ten-part polyphony is not just an extreme exercise in counterpoint for a single organist (see Figures 2.3a and 2.3b). In precise and unprecedented ways both artists tried to understand the nature and possibilities of the human body with the means at their disposal: Dürer on paper, Schlick at the organ.

Viewed in the choirbook format in which it was presented to Clesio, *Ascendo ad patrem meum* verges on abstraction, pushing the faculties of the human mind to, or perhaps beyond, their limits. For individual singers performing a single line, there is nothing particularly demanding about this music. But an organist must necessarily be aware, as he or she tries to make sense of this tapestry of voices, of how the parts cross and tangle, leap upward by large intervals and then fall back down. The *cantus firmus* of the ten-part setting alone provides the exception to the unpredictable paths taken by the other polyphonic voices; this plainchant melody is heard in the second tenor voice and remains relatively untroubled by the complicated choreography of voices around it. The plainsong melody ascends the octave and then slowly makes its way back down, relatively free from incursions by the other parts. This melody spans only an octave and stays mostly in the lower fifth of that range from c1 to g1. The gravitational center of the piece, the *cantus firmus* is the reference-point fixed amongst the dynamic motions of the nine other polyphonic parts, nearly equal in number above and below.

The mass of voices on paper must be parsed by the performer's body to be rendered as sound. Given the way the feet naturally splay to reach these four-part chords at the pedalboard, the left toe will play the pitch that is at any given time the lowest of the four pedal notes, while the right toe will take the highest. But because of the wide-ranging nature of each of the pedal voices, there is no way to connect individual lines with any consistency to one heel or one toe. The polyphonic parts move across body parts, and this fluidity is especially apparent in the voices allocated by Schlick to the feet. If we follow the Bassus IV over the first three bars of the setting we see it leap up an octave, over the three other bass parts (see Example 2.4 and Figure 2.2): this voice begins in the toe of the right foot, then moves to the heel of the left for the first three pitches of bar 2, before leaping up the octave and to the toe of the right foot again on the second beat of bar 3. With ten voices loaded onto

---

[22] Albrecht Dürer, *Hierinn sind begriffen vier Bücher von menschlicher Proportion* (Nuremberg: Albrecht Dürer's Widow, 1528); the images in Figure 3 are found on pp. 29 and 52.

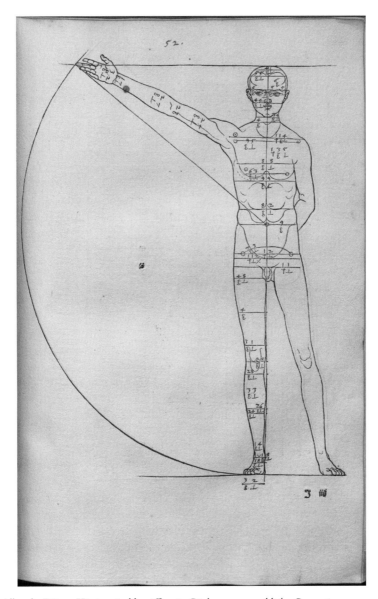

Figure 2.3a   Albrecht Dürer, *Hierinn sind begriffen vier Bücher von menschlicher Proportion*, Nuremberg, 1528

four limbs and crowded into one-and-a-half octaves of pedal compass and little more than three octaves on the manual, this kind of polyphonic intertwining is inevitable, especially if individual lines are to have any dynamic quality to them.

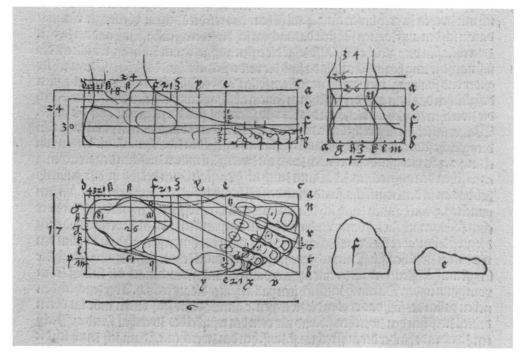

Figure 2.3b   Albrecht Dürer, *Hierinn sind begriffen vier Bücher von menschlicher Proportion*, Nuremberg, 1528, diagrams of the feet

Schlick's *Ascendo ad patrem meum* pushes the boundaries of what can be fitted into the manual and pedal compasses and what can be executed by hands and feet, not to mention what can be dealt with by the brain. For the Trent gift of 1520 a pinnacle of the organ art had been climbed, by Schlick and by Clesio's first organist (himself a blind German), the accomplishment to be marveled at by the organ-loving Bishop, his German organist, and us. In the region where Bernhard the German had been credited with importing his pedal "invention" fifty years earlier, the limits of the feet's potential, and therefore of the organ's contrapuntal scope, had been reached by a blind virtuoso.

PEDALING IN SOUTH GERMANY AFTER SCHLICK

Neither the experiments of *Ascendo ad patrem meum* nor the other less strenuous modes of pedal performance pursued by the Germans were taken up in Italy. Schlick would perhaps not have been overly surprised by this apparent reluctance, even though in the *Spiegel* he had predicted that the Italians would begin to use their feet in imitation of the German example. But he would have found it extremely puzzling, and probably disappointing, to discover posthumously that over the course of the sixteenth

Example 2.5   Hans Buchner, *Agnus Dei primum: in resurrectione Domini, pedaliter,*
bars 1–9

century vigorous pedal also disappeared from his native south Germany. Paul Hofhaimer's student, Hans Buchner (1483–1538), a somewhat younger contemporary of Schlick, compiled his own *Fundamentum* around 1520. His organ music, the majority of it explicitly *pedaliter*, offers ample chances to play with double pedal and on occasion demands figuration in the pedal as well (see Example 2.5); that a copy survives from the middle of the sixteenth century indicates the work's continued pedagogical relevance for the contrapuntal treatment of plainsong at the organ.[23] The larger historical trajectory, however, was that the Italian style of organ-playing apparently encroached to the region north of the Alps, exactly the opposite trend than the one optimistically forecast by Schlick. While it would be wrong to claim that pedal-playing vanished altogether from southern Germany, by the seventeenth century complicated music for the feet seems largely to have disappeared from the region. The Stuttgart organist, Johann Ulrich Steigleder, published forty settings of *Vater unser im Himmelreich* in 1627 in which he allowed for the option of playing a tenor cantus firmus on a "special" [*absonderlich*] pedal stop.[24] In 1645 the Nuremberg organist, Johann Erasmus Kindermann, seems to have been the first to publish an organ fugue specifying a pedal entry, which comes at the close of the piece and counts as easy for the feet, unless one implausibly takes the sixteenth-note run in the bassline with the feet in the antepenultimate bar (see Example 2.6). Johann Mattheson also reports on a

[23] *Abschrift M. Hansen von Constanz*, Basel University Library, F. I. 8. Buchner was active around Lake Constanz, though his career was disrupted by the Reformation; his students and at least one of his sons must have carried on the practices that had made south Germany a leader in pedal mastery.

[24] Johann Ulrich Steigleder, *Tabulatur Buch, darinnen dass Vatter Unser auf 2, 3, und 4, Stimmen Componiert, und Viertzig mal Varirt würdt* (Strassburg: Marx von der Heiden, 1627); modern edn., Johann Ulrich Steigleder, *Compositions for Keyboard I: Corpus of Early Keyboard Music*, vol. XIII, ed. Willi Apel *et al.* (American Institute of Musicology, 1968), p. 83. See variation 36.

Example 2.6   Johann Erasmus Kindermann, *Intonatio super: Gib frid zu unser zeit*,
bars 24–33

famous improvisation at the coronation of Leopold I in Frankfurt in 1658, in which Johann Kaspar Kerll, a Saxon by birth who studied in Rome and worked in Brussels, Munich, and Vienna, concluded a fugue on a subject submitted by Leopold himself by introducing the theme in the pedal at the end of the piece to augment the texture to five voices.[25] But in spite of these demonstrations of pedal independence in the service of polyphony, such accomplishments did not compare to northern prowess, and in general marked a much less ambitious approach than that of Schlick. For the most part, the feet became ancillary in south Germany, providing tonal support at cadences, holding pedal-points, but relinquishing, for reasons that perhaps deserve particular study, their status as equal partners in polyphonic textures.

The historical record with regard to pedaling in south Germany in the eighteenth century makes for a similar, if more ambiguous, picture. The important south-German organist and pedagogue Justin Heinrich Knecht (1752–1817) published in 1795 his *Vollständige Orgelschule für Anfänger und Geübtere* (*Complete Organ School for Beginners and More Advanced Players*), in which he asserted the importance of the pedal, whose mastery requires "patience and toil." Knecht seems to hold to the view that takes pedaling not as the basis of organ playing – as it was in the north – but as something of an oddity, even if one that was required of professionals: "the main difficulty of pedal-playing consists in that the feet must play many passages which appear to require more than two feet."[26] This strikes a defensive pose; a northern organist would be unlikely to apologize for what seems difficult for the feet, even more to suggest what they can't do. While Knecht

---

[25] Johann Mattheson, *Grundlage einer Ehren-Pforte* (Hamburg, 1740); modern edn. ed. Max Schneider (Berlin: Liepmannssohn, 1910), p. 136.

[26] Justin Heinrich Knecht, *Vollständige Orgelschule für Anfänger und Geübetere* (Leipzig: Breitkopf, 1795; reprint, Wiesbaden: Breitkopf & Härtel), p. 10.

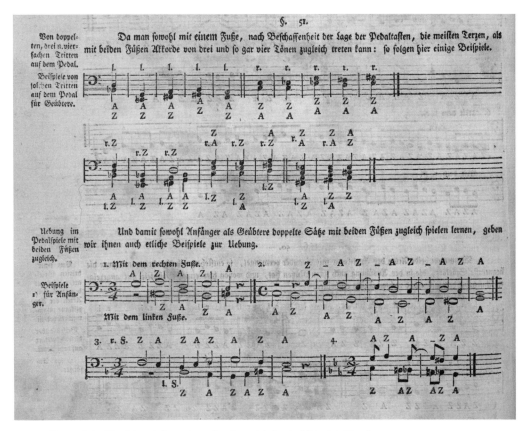

Figure 2.4   Double, triple, and quadruple pedal. Justin Heinrich Knecht,
Vollständige Orgelschule, Pt. 1, p. 52 (1795)

writes many exercises for the feet in his organ method, including a demonstration of two-part polyphony for the pedals, the volume's example pieces, as in Knecht's other works for organ, rarely introduce independent pedal: a few moderate trios, an occasional pedal outburst, are about as demanding as it gets. It seems likely that grandiose playing with the feet did have a role in improvisation at the organ, or else Knecht wouldn't have bothered to include this material in his tutor. But pedaling seems primarily to have been a matter of attention-getting trickery rather than rigorous polyphony. A striking example is Knecht's demonstration of the way to grab the four notes of a diminished-seventh chord with the feet alone (see Figure 2.4); this sounds impressive but is actually quite easy, given the way these chords fit comfortably under the heels and toes. Such effects were a long way from the varied chords in thoroughgoing polyphony of Schlick's *Ascendo ad patrem meum*.

The different attitude towards pedaling in north and south Germany frames Mozart's 1789 competition with the organist Johann Wilhelm

Häßler, a student of a student of Bach. In a letter describing the encounter, Mozart wrote that many in attendance had assumed that because he was from Vienna he could not play the pedals. Boasting that he quickly disabused the audience of this prejudice, Mozart dismissed his opponent as a mere footman: "This Hässler's chief excellence on the organ consists in his foot-work."[27] This grudging, and somewhat backhanded, compliment seems to admit that Häßler was more proficient with his feet than was Mozart, a difference in technical accomplishment that would accord with their respective backgrounds. Mozart's seemingly defensive claim that his own skill transcends regional difference, and his disparagement of Häßler as a mere pedal-proficient, takes for granted the much less ambitious approach of the south while stressing the centrality of the feet in the northern tradition.

NORTHERN FEET IN POLYPHONIC MUSIC

While Schlick's legacy seems to have withered in the south, vigorous polyphonic pedal-playing thrived in the north. Double pedal had been an important topic for the seventeenth-century north Germans: impressive examples survive from Hieronymus Praetorius, Samuel Scheidt, Matthias Weckman, Franz Tunder, and Dieterich Buxtehude.[28] This tradition demanded not only the pedal pyrotechnics heard in the free *praeludia* (see Chapter 3), but also the stricter allocation of contrapuntal parts among the hands and feet. Weckman was organist at the Jacobikirche in Hamburg in the middle of the seventeenth century, and the final verse of his cycle on *Es ist das Heil uns kommen her* is, like Scheidt's *Modus ludendi*, in six parts, two of which are in the pedal; slight by comparison with the massive *Ascendo ad patrem meum*, Weckman's inspiring essay in double pedal demonstrates that massive polyphonic frameworks can be constructed with dynamic, roving counterpoint. At the opening (Example 2.7), the three upper parts enter in descending order while melodically ascending. The *cantus firmus* enters in bar 2 in the right foot and provides a reference-point akin to that of the plainsong in Schlick's ten-part setting. The left foot then initiates a melodically inverted treatment of the free counterpoint introduced in the manual; the lower of the two pedal lines is followed in its contrary course by the lowest manual voice taken by the lower fingers of the left hand. In contrast to the decidedly varied melodic motion of *Ascendo ad patrem meum*, the almost exclusively conjunct nature of Weckman's contrapuntal

---

[27] W. A. Mozart to Leopold Mozart, 16 April 1789, in *The Letters of Mozart and His Family*, ed. and trans. Emily Anderson, 3rd edn. (London: Norton, 1985), pp. 923–924. See also Katalin Komlós, "Mozart and the Organ: Piping Time," *The Musical Times*, 143 (2002), 59–61.

[28] Michael Belotti, "Buxtehude und die norddeutsche Doppelpedaltradition" in Arnfried Edler and Friedhelm Krummacher (eds.), *Dietrich Buxtehude und die europäische Musik seiner Zeit* (Kassel: Bärenreiter, 1990), pp. 235–244.

Example 2.7   Matthias Weckman, *Es ist das Heil uns kommen her*, verse 7, bars 1–9

parts can be easily followed, their contours drawing the ear with them; rarely do the parts cross, and in the instances when they do, any confusion resulting from these superimpositions is quickly neutralized by the melodic momentum of the stepwise movement. Rationally divided between the limbs, these scalar patterns stay on course, ascending or descending, for a bar or more at a time before changing direction. Driven by this strong linear motion, the voices spread apart and then seek greater proximity to one another: as the distance between the voices increases and decreases, the texture seems to swell and contract. Weckman's music is transmitted in the letter-system of north-German organ tablature, where the counterpoint is clearly delineated and can be felt and followed in the feet and fingers. To look down at your hands and feet playing this music is to see the counterpoint spread out before you.

While J. S. Bach probably did not know Weckman's music, his own approach to full contrapuntal schemes at the organ continues the tradition of *Es ist das Heil uns kommen her*. The young Bach had heard and studied the music of Johann Adam Reincken, Dieterich Buxtehude, and other masters of double pedal and organ counterpoint. One of the most impressive and demanding examples of multiple part-writing for the pedal from the later seventeenth century is the first fugue from Nicolaus Bruhns's *Praeludium* in G, a piece transmitted in the Bach circle, indeed probably brought back from north Germany by Bach himself.[29] The short-lived Bruhns (1665–1697) had been a student of Buxtehude and was organist

---

[29] Staatsbibliothek zu Berlin, Mus. ms. 40644 ("Möller" Manuscript).

Example 2.8   Nicolaus Bruhns, six-voice fugue from *Praeludium* in G, bars 56–62

in Husum in Schleswig-Holstein. Like Weckman's chorale setting, Bruhns's fugue is in six real parts, divided rationally between the limbs: each hand takes two voices, without any crossing or confusion, and each foot is likewise charged with a separate polyphonic line (see Example 2.8). Not as dense as *Ascendo ad patrem meum*, the music is faster, far more athletic than Schlick's or Weckman's chorale settings. When all six voices are in action in the Bruhns fugue the effect is as glorious as it is difficult. The superimposed layers of Schlick's ten parts, with individual polyphonic voices crossing from one body part to another, are thinned and separated from one another; the organist becomes an ensemble of distinct musicians, one voice to each foot, two to each hand, with the contrapuntal parts given unambiguous and unchanging anatomical assignment. As in Weckman's six-part *cantus firmus* setting, Bruhns's fugue allows a much clearer sense of both the vertical and horizontal nature of polyphony than was possible in the contrapuntal thicket of *Ascendo ad patrem meum*; in Bruhns's lively six-voice polyphony the player can follow the linear progress of individual voices in the hands and feet. The hand itself becomes divided, with the right and left side of each become a region where the polyphony of a particular voice lies, though the middle fingers can go either way to discharge their polyphonic duty, either towards the thumb or little finger. Without double pedal the fugue would risk becoming a nonsense musically and technically, with voices often on top of one another vying for the very same keys. It is the upper pedal voice that most often overlaps with the manuals, but the organist can keep these lines distinct in his or her mind even though they often occupy the same range, because these parts are being played on a manual and pedal-board respectively and by different limbs. In the north-German tradition, the

Example 2.9   J. G. Walther, Toccata and Fugue in C, bars 70–76

pedalboard is independent from the manuals – it is not coupled (as in Italian organs), and the pedal division has its own separate stops that allow the polyphonic lines to overlap in range without interfering with one another. It is the nature of the north-German organ and its organists' skill with the pedal that allows these six parts to be played cogently.

Bach's contemporaries also explored the possibilities and pitfalls of double pedal. His Weimar colleague and relative, J. G. Walther, was also a collector of northern music, and left the only example I know of a polyphonic pedal solo, which comes in the midst of a fugue, where the counterpoint is maintained with the feet alone.[30] Solo statements of the single-line subject in fugues are virtually unheard of in eighteenth-century organ music. The one exception that comes to mind is from the Toccata and Fugue in D minor, BWV 565; so rare is such a solo statement in the feet, that it might confirm suspicions, harbored by many scholars, that the piece was originally conceived not for organ at all, but more likely for violin.[31] Walther's solo is therefore doubly surprising since it is fully polyphonic – a *bicinium* for the feet alone in florid counterpoint (see Example 2.9). At the outset of the fugue the two hands treat an analogous two-part texture comprised of the subject and its countersubject; midway through this insouciant fugue, the feet do the same, while the hands suddenly, and unexpectedly, fall silent for these two-and-a-half bars of solo polyphony.

---

[30] This kind of pedal solo is also mentioned by Schlick, *Spiegel der Orgel-macher und Organisten*, trans. Barber, p. 29.

[31] Peter Williams, "BWV 565: A Toccata in D Minor for Organ by J. S. Bach," *Early Music*, 9 (1981), 330–337.

This counterpoint using double pedal is akin to that in the Bruhns *Praeludium*, except that the hands are inactive during the display. This is the only passage of double pedal specified by Walther for this fugue in the autograph manuscript transmitting the piece. While not a long solo, it demonstrates that the feet can do what the hands do, that they, too, can manage not only the physical difficulties of brisk and artful two-part writing, but they can carry forward fugal discourse on their own.[32] This unique passage confirms again that long after Schlick, the north-German organists of the seventeenth century had become the leading proponents of obbligato pedal-playing. They were then emulated by their central-German admirers, Walther and Bach, both of whom made crucial contributions to this tradition through their collecting, teaching, composing and playing.

PRAISING THE PAST WITH TWO FEET

Double pedal was a retrospective pursuit, an attempt to measure up to, and perhaps surpass, a history rich with contrapuntal marvels stemming from Weckman, Buxtehude, and many others. Bach's two greatest essays in double pedal are the chorale preludes on *An Wasserflüssen Babylon*, BWV 653b and *Aus tieffer Noth schrey ich zu dir*, BWV 686. The first of these is an early five-part version of the four-part revision included by Bach in his "Leipzig" Chorales collected late in his career; appearing in the *Clavierübung III* of 1739, the six-part setting of *Aus tieffer Noth* was the only double-pedal piece published by Bach in his lifetime. In both pieces the feet and left hand are charged with two parts respectively: the right hand contributes its own two contrapuntal parts to *Aus tieffer Noth*, while it plays the single line of the *cantus firmus* in *An Wasserflüssen Babylon*. Both are unique textures in Bach's surviving oeuvre.

The most ambitious chorale fantasy of the great Hamburg organist Johann Adam Reincken, whom Bach had first heard when a schoolboy in the nearby city of Lüneburg from 1700 to 1703, was also based on the melody *An Wasserflüssen Babylon*. The teenage Bach copied Reincken's fantasia, which extended to more than 300 bars, in organ tablature sometime around 1700 in a manuscript rediscovered in 2006.[33] According to his Obituary, Bach improvised on *An Wasserflüssen Babylon* for half an hour at his famous 1720 recital on the large organ in Hamburg's Katharinenkirche, where Reincken had been organist for some sixty years. Bach's choice of this chorale as a

---

[32] Staatsbibliothek zu Berlin, Mus. ms. 2251/4, pp. 6–10. See Johann Gottfried Walther, *Sämtliche Orgelwerke*, ed. Klaus Beckmann, 4 vols. (Wiesbaden: Breitkopf & Härtel, 1998–1999), vol. I, p. 156; and Kirsten Beißwenger, "Zur Chronologie der Notenhandschriften Johann Gottfried Walthers" in *Acht kleine Präludien und Studien über BACH: Georg von Dadelsen zum 70. Geburtstag*, ed. Collegium of the Bach Institute, Göttingen (Wiesbaden: Breitkopf & Härtel, 1992), pp. 11–39.

[33] Michael Maul and Peter Wollny (eds.), *Weimarer Orgeltabulatur: Die frühesten Notenhandschriften Johann Sebastian Bachs* (Kassel: Bärenreiter, 2007).

vehicle to demonstrate his skill was meant to pay homage to Reincken, who attended the concert and was then nearly a hundred years old: "I thought that this art was dead," the ancient Reincken reportedly said to the middle-aged Bach after the recital, "but I see that in you it still lives."[34] Among the most famous stories in organ lore, this account must have been passed on from J. S. Bach to C. P. E. Bach, one of the authors of the Obituary. Had he wanted to impress Reincken, Bach would likely, at some point over that legendary half hour, have demonstrated his skill at double pedal, a venerable and important technique for north-German organists. I do not want to claim that Bach's double-pedal version of *An Wasserflüssen Babylon* is necessarily associated with that 1720 Hamburg performance, but, as others have suggested, the work could be partly based on the music he improvised before Reincken and the other dignitaries assembled in the Katharinenkirche.

Like the German organists before him, Bach's treatment of *An Wasserflüssen Babylon* translates disembodied counterpoint into a well-apportioned physical act involving both hands and feet. The opening, and the interludes which echo it, retain the polyphonic integrity of the German trio, but expand the number of voices to four – that is, one per limb (see Example 2.10). When the chorale melody is being delivered by the right hand, the left hand and pedal are engaged in much the same kind of physical task as in the Bruhns fugue, though at a slower tempo and without the spirited repetitions of Bruhns's subject. The leaps, suspensions, and decorated resolutions of the accompaniment of *An Wasserflüssen Babylon* are a tour de force of florid counterpoint in four parts. Double pedal brings clarity to the texture; if it had been burdened with three parts, the left hand could not have projected the dynamic quality of the part-writing with its passing-tones and the frequent leaps of wide intervals such as fifths. Much like Bach's four-part chorales from the cantatas, the four-part writing of the accompanimental voices of *An Wasserflüssen Babylon* is without rests, consistent throughout, elaborating the constant harmonic rhythm with carefully conceived counterpoint, each part made up predominantly of quarter-notes and eighths. The four-part accompaniment flows along like the river it is meant to evoke, while the plaintive chorale, lightly decorated with elegiac ornament, sings above the contrapuntal motion below. The individual parts are not vigorous, but they move as they mourn; each shifting maneuver of left hand and feet is a test of poise and placement.

This physical motion conveys to the organist a sense of the polyphonic action of the voices in a way that is not possible at any other instrument. One might get an idea of what the body tells an organist about this polyphony by imagining a similar performance of Bach's four-part setting of the same chorale, BWV 267, using double pedal (see Example 2.11). By playing the four-part chorale setting with the soprano in the right hand, the alto in the left, the tenor in the right foot, and the bass in the left,

---

[34] *NBR*, 302.

Example 2.10   J. S. Bach, *An Wasserflüssen Babylon*, organ chorale prelude,
BWV 653b, bars 1–15

Example 2.11   J. S. Bach, *An Wasserflüssen Babylon*, four-part chorale, BWV 267

one gains a much greater sense of the motion of the individual voices without losing a sense of the harmony. A double-pedal version of the piece makes the organist enact more demonstratively than at any other instrument what C. P. E. Bach, in his preface to the first edition of his father's chorales printed in 1765, called "the quite special arrangement of the harmony and the natural flow of the inner voices and the bass."[35] Contrary and parallel

[35] *Ibid.*, 379.

motion, adjacent intervals and leaps, spacing between the voices – all of these become more tangible, less abstract, when the legs and hands each move independently. Just to cite one example, the right foot's leap up a fifth in the tenor in the first bar expresses the motion of the part-writing more visibly than if both parts are taken by the left hand which would play a fifth on the second beat then move out to an octave: this is an easier and smaller physical gesture less vividly expressed by the body. With each limb proceeding independently, yet in concert, a fundamentally clearer picture of the polyphony emerges than when it is played on a single manual by the hands. The erudition and elegance of the polyphony can be seen in the keyboard format, and more shiningly in the open score often favored by students of Bach's four-part chorales. But these modes of knowledge offer something quite different than that learned when the body moves through this music at the organ bench. In parting out the voices between the limbs, each hand and foot becomes a moving entity, like four individual musicians, four embodied voices. As in this experiment, the four-part interludes of Bach's *An Wasserflüssen Babylon* fully engage the polyphonic quartet that is the human form at the organ, and in so doing project the calmly perfect polyphony of his four-part chorale style.

The organ stops used for these accompanimental parts in the five-part setting of *An Wasserflüssen Babylon* also figure in our understanding of the piece, and the message its polyphony imparts to both player and listener. Received opinion suggests 8′ in both pedals and manuals, since 16′ in the lower two parts would be too dense and thereby muddy the texture; because of the crossing of the middle parts, one cannot simply couple the manual stop to the pedal, since this would obstruct the counterpoint. It would be essentially pointless to play this piece without independent pedal stops, not only because of the redundancy this causes between the middle two accompanying voices, but because the couplers on the organs of Bach's time actually pull down the manual keys, creating potholes in the polyphony as the right foot depresses its notes and interferes with the lower manual voice. In contrast to central-German instruments, the organs of the north admired by Bach usually did not have couplers connecting manuals to pedal, another indication of the premium placed on independence of the feet. A matching registration, but with a discernible differentiation between hands and feet, seems the best solution: the sound chosen for pedal parts should be similar to those of the manual but not indistinguishable from them. For the aged Reincken down below on the floor of the Katharinenkirche, such a registration would have allowed him to recognize that Bach was indeed playing double pedal, that venerable technique of the north-German masters. Other knowledgeable listeners would have heard this, too, and in the sounds emanating from the organ they would have been able to imagine the organist's body in motion even though they could not see it. It is not only the disembodied sound that is meant to move the listeners, but the physical feat that brings this polyphony to life.

Bach's six-part setting of *Aus tieffer Noth schrey ich zu dir*, BWV 686 is his valedictory statement on double pedal. Adopting the *stile antico* that he explored beginning in the early 1730s, this chorale prelude has the look and feel of massive organ polyphony as cultivated by Weckman, Scheidt, Hieronymus Praetorius (a predecessor of Weckman as organist at the Jacobikirche, Hamburg) and indeed, going still farther back in time, Schlick. Both the ancient Phrygian mode of the *cantus firmus* and the text provided by Martin Luther's translation of Psalm 130 add a patina of timelessness to this monument; the six real parts, Bach's fullest organ texture, provide a foundation of enormous gravity. Depth of sound parallels the profundity of the counterpoint and the urgency of the message:

> Aus tiefer Not schrei ich zu dir,
> Herr Gott, erhör mein Rufen.
> Dein gnädig Ohren kehr zu mir
> und meiner Bitt sie öffen:
> denn so du willst das sehen an,
> was Sünd und Unrecht ist getan,
> wer kann, Herr, vor dir bleiben?

> Out of deep distress I cry to you,
> Lord God, hear my call.
> Turn your merciful ears to me
> and open them to my plea:
> for if you will look upon
> what sin and wrong is done,
> who can abide you, Lord?

The manual parts enter first, treating the chorale melody contrapuntally with note values halved (see Figure 2.5). After each of the four manual voices enters, the lower pedal adds a fifth part to the texture, plumbing depths by drawing on the *Gravitas* Bach found so essential to the German organ sound.[36] The title in the original print – "a 6. In Organo pleno con Pedal doppio" – announces the grandeur of the enterprise: full organ for the fullest polyphony Bach ever undertook at the keyboard. At the entry of the first pedal part at bar 7 Bach alerts the organist yet again that there are two pedal voices: the marking "ped. dopp." somewhat redundantly reminds the player that his right foot will soon be called upon to deliver the final voice, the *cantus firmus* itself, in the upper octave of the pedalboard.[37] These double-pedal indications count as warnings, and help prevent the player from making the mistake of, for example, playing the quarter-note A just prior to the entrance of the *cantus firmus* with the right foot. These cues in the score confirm that

---

[36] See Jakob Adlung, *Musica mechanica organoedi* (Berlin: Johann Lorenz Albrecht, 1768), Pt 1, p. 288.

[37] For a wider discussion of Bach's use of the designation "Ped." in his organ works, see Robert L. Marshall, "Organ or 'Klavier'? Instrumental Prescriptions in the Sources of Bach's Keyboard Works" in George Stauffer and Ernest May (eds.), *J. S. Bach as Organist: His Instruments, Music, and Performance Practices* (London: B. T. Batsford, 1986), pp. 212–240, esp. pp. 221–224.

Figure 2.5   J. S. Bach, chorale prelude on *Aus tieffer Noth schrey ich zu dir*, BWV 686, *Clavierübung III*, 1739

this is an extraordinary technique in 1739, a tribute to the past and a statement of Bach's awareness of his own confrontation with history.

In order to make the polyphony clearer on the page, Bach abandons the two-stave format he generally uses for *organo pleno* pieces, one that was typical for this texture throughout the eighteenth century.[38] Instead he adopts a layout that is unique in his oeuvre, amounting to a kind of semi-open score, with two voices on each staff. Occasionally the upper voice of the lower staff migrates to the upper staff, but the four upper parts are consistently divided between the two hands: two voices in the left and two in the right, with virtually no crossing. The notation conveys the physical delineation of the parts: as if cleaving to his vocal model of the *stile antico* motet, Bach ensures that each voice remains in a distinct range. The feet are similarly deployed, the left foot holding forth over a wide range to pursue its free counterpoint in the bass; adopting the approach of the north-German organist Weckman and others, Bach charges the right foot with the *cantus*

---

[38]   Compare, for example, the five-part *Kyrie*, BWV 671, also from the *Clavierübung III*, printed on two staves.

firmus. In Bach's *Aus tieffer Noth* the lower voice of the left hand often crosses the chorale, but because of their differing rhythmic and musical responsibilities (free counterpoint versus *cantus firmus*) they, too, retain their independence. This polyphony is as clearly laid out as in Bruhns's G Major fugue. The two pedal parts themselves form an unfailingly correct *bicinium*, whose contrapuntal credentials emerge clearly even when heard in the full six-part structure. This setting of *Aus tieffer Noth* is one of Bach's clearest examples of complex music divided rationally over the body.

The clarity that the organist's body brings to the polyphony in *Aus tieffer Noth* can be gauged by comparing it with Bach's autograph copy of his other exercise in six-part keyboard polyphony, the second *Ricercar* from the *Musical Offering*, BWV 1079 where the six voices are all taken by the hands, though nothing prevents the piece from being played on the organ. Bach published the *Ricercar* in open score, but wrote it out in keyboard format as well. Needless to say, there is no question about the purity of the counterpoint in the *Ricercar*, but often the wash of voices makes the polyphony nearly impossible to parse physically. One can see the masterful counterpoint, and recognize its integrity in the open score; but in such tangled spots as that seen in Example 2.12, the body can no longer fulfill the mechanical function of expressing the progress of the individual parts. As sometimes occurs in the six manual parts of Schlick's *Ascendo ad patrem meum*, the extent of the voice-crossing obscures the individuality of the polyphonic lines still further. By contrast, the two voices in each of the manual staves of the *Clavierübung* print are allocated to either side of the hands; double pedal allows Bach to enact the independence of counterpoint by dividing it between the limbs. It is this physicality that connects German organists from Schlick to Bach. The apparent timelessness of Bach's double-pedal chorales is not only to be heard as a demonstration of its self-consciously venerable style. In addition, this music aspires to perfection in the complete and rational way it exploits the possibilities of the human form. In these works counterpoint stands for part against part, both contrapuntal and physical, both on the page and in the body.

Example 2.12   J. S. Bach, six-part *ricercar* from *A Musical Offering*, BWV 1079, bars 50–51, based on autograph manuscript in two-stave keyboard format, Staatsbibliothek zu Berlin, Mus. ms. Bach P 226

BLIND ORGANISTS

Just as he cannot see all the far-flung parts of a large organ, the organist must also imagine its sound in the space, often vast, beyond the console and out in the church. Even if an organist can see, he is in many ways blind to his instrument. The musician, essayist and translator Christian Friedrich Michaelis (1770–1834) seems to have been one of the first writers to point out that the organ had long encouraged the "development and demonstration of the great musical talent of persons robbed of their sight." Noticing that many leading figures in the early history of the organ, beginning in the sixteenth century, were blind, Michaelis observed that "they appear to have gained more with regard to the art than they lost because of their misfortune."[39] Indeed, none of the greatest early modern organists could see: Paumann, Schlick, Hofhaimer, Antonio de Cabezón; later there were Francisco Correa de Arauxo, the Dutch organist and *carilloneur* named Pothoff (whom Burney heard in Amsterdam and whose sweaty performance he so memorably described), John Stanley, and Johann Jacob de Graaf (who played his transcriptions of Vivaldi concertos in the New Church in Amsterdam in the early eighteenth century and indirectly inspired Bach to do the same).[40] There is also the great tradition of blind French organists continuing into the twentieth century with such musicians as Louis Vierne and Jean Langlais, among so many others.[41] Handel and Bach could even be added to the list, although they became blind late in life, and did not learn to play without the aid of sight.

This is not the place to investigate blindness at the organ as the significant cultural and cognitive phenomenon it was and continues to be. Blind musicians excelled at other instruments, too; Paumann, for one, was himself a famous singer and lutenist, besides being an organist. But what I want to suggest in connection with the unique status of polyphonic performance such as we have seen in *Aus tieffer Noth* and *Ascendo ad patrem meum*, is that the framework provided by the organ with independent pedals allowed blind German organists to conceptualize complicated contrapuntal structures in ways impossible at other instruments. I believe that the physical act of organ performance made it possible for these blind musicians to keep track of individual lines while molding them into polyphonic wholes; it was this corporeal engagement with relatively abstract musical configurations that must have allowed Schlick, to turn to the most celebrated example of such

---

[39] *Caecilia*, 2 (1825), 218.

[40] The Young Duke Johann Ernst of Weimar may have heard de Graaf play; it was he who brought back copies of Vivaldi's concertos to Weimar; these copies sparked Bach's crucial confrontation with Vivaldi's music and the transformation of Bach's style. This according to Bach's pupil Philipp David Kräuter, *BD*, 3: 649 and *NBR*, 319.

[41] Most of these organists were trained at the National Institute for Blind Youth [*Institution nationale des jeunes aveugles*].

compositional mastery by a blind man, to draw from the organ his still unsurpassed polyphonic elaborations.

Clearly Schlick relied on a sighted scribe to produce the manuscript that he sent to Trent (see Figure 2.2 above). But the matter-of-fact notes on the page arrayed across a mind-boggling ten voices immediately raise the question: how could a blind musician compose the unique work that is *Ascendo ad patrem meum*? In her study of musical composition in the period from 1450 to 1600 Jessie Ann Owens has shown how the use of full score for composing and presenting music became common practice only towards the end of the sixteenth century.[42] Even sighted musicians among Schlick's contemporaries did not afford themselves what seem to us the obvious advantages of a score. There are instances, especially involving the education of beginning composers, of the use of score; one of the earliest examples comes from Ornithoparchus's *Micrologus* of 1517, indeed from the very fourth book of the treatise dedicated to Schlick. Ornithoparchus illustrates a ten-line staff, mentioned by other treatises as well, with an array of clefs; this format is advised to allow the student to see the contrapuntal relationships of the voices.[43] As Owens points out, however, composers were also adept at composing complicated polyphonic music in their heads before writing it down, as hard as this may be for us to imagine now, given the extent to which the arts of memory have atrophied in our own time. Master composers often had conceived the piece in their minds before commencing to set it down in notation.

Owens also claims that there is no evidence before the end of the sixteenth century that composers heard music in their heads when they examined its notational representation on paper, especially in choirbook format. Rather, getting a sense for how a piece sounded by looking at the score was a later development. The most common way for a composer to judge his work was to have it performed by singers, who were, of course, each responsible for only one of the polyphonic parts; the composer used his ears to judge the success of the music and to listen for errors and infelicities. There is also evidence that some composers used instruments – especially lutes or keyboard instruments – to compose with as well as to check their work. The best sixteenth-century organists were even capable of reading from choirbooks and producing at the keyboard the polyphony from the disparate parts set down on different parts of the page; this counts as another astonishing feat when seen from a modern perspective. Like reading from

---

[42] Jessie Ann Owens, *Composers at Work: the Craft of Musical Composition, 1450–1600* (Oxford University Press, 1997), pp. 42–45. For a fascinating treatment of the projection of sound into space at the organ, and especially among blind women in nineteenth-century France, see Ingrid Sykes, *Women, Science and Sound in Nineteenth-Century France* (Frankfurt: Peter Lang, 2007), pp. 123–146.

[43] Andreas Ornithoparchus, *Musicae activae micrologus* (Leipzig: Schumann, 1517; reprint edn. New York: Dover, 1973), unpaginated (p. 99 in reprint edn.).

open score, it was also a skill obviously irrelevant to the blind Schlick but crucial to his sighted contemporaries, especially those brave enough to attempt the ten parts of *Ascendo ad patrem meum*.[44] Still, to read ten polyphonic parts in choirbook format would seem to be beyond the cognitive powers of even some of the most gifted sixteenth-century organists.

Needless to say, blind musicians need impressive powers of memory simply in order to play a piece that they may have learned by ear or, in modern times, by Braille. The blind twentieth-century German organist Helmut Walcha is said to have learned Bach fugues by having each voice played individually; from these disparate contrapuntal lines he could then assemble the piece in his mind and play it in its entirety.[45] Clearly Schlick must have had similar mental abilities, having memorized the corpus of liturgical melodies he set and improvised on. He could well have improvised pieces like those in the *Tabulaturen* or even have conceived them in his mind, then dictated them by letter name, or sung or played them, to the scribe. While the large setting of *Ascendo ad patrem meum* tests the limits of memory and cognition, a similar procedure would still have been possible. Thus Schlick could have tested his magnum opus for errors without having to assemble a choir, though he may well have had the chance to hear the piece sung as well. I doubt that he would have forgone such a pleasure after the labor he must have expended to produce the work. But the fact – and it can hardly be a coincidence – that the four bass parts fit so conveniently on heels and toes, and the upper parts in the fingers, at least suggests that the piece could have been composed at the organ. In this scenario, rather than follow the continuous flow of individual lines, Schlick heard the piece mainly as a succession of many-voiced sonorities corresponding to precisely choreographed postures. Each new position of hands and feet provided him with a physical image of the entire sonic fabric at a given instant, the state of sound at each moment of change. The organ allowed the blind man to gain a global picture of massive harmonic structures erected through perfect counterpoint. What the organist enacts is a series of physical positions proceeding through time, and he does so while trying not to lose all sense of the diachronic movement of counterpoint without which the music will become inert. The polyphonic propriety of this massive complex is assured not so much by the player's aural faculties but by tactile sense and physical positioning.

The musicological debate about simultaneous versus successive composition is a long and contentious one.[46] Perhaps Schlick followed the approach outlined by Owens, and the one recommended by most theoretical sources (intended as instructional manuals, not descriptions of the practice of great

[44] Owens, *Composers at Work*, pp. 49–55.
[45] Joseph Coppy and Jean Willy Kunts, *Helmut Walcha: Nuit de lumière* (Paris: Broché, 2007), p. 19.
[46] Outlined in Owens, *Composers at Work*, pp. 3–7.

composers) in which, in the case of a *cantus firmus* setting, one contrapuntal line is added in its entirety and then the next. These would be the two extremes: composing one complete part before proceeding to the next or conceiving the piece as a succession of chords. But given the rational allocation of the parts to the organist's body, it is clear that the organ provided a powerful conceptual means for constructing this expansive polyphonic edifice, without writing it down, seeing it in the mind and hearing it in space before having it committed to paper. Perhaps Schlick's son Arnolt Schlick the Younger, who was his assistant for the publication of the *Tabulaturen*, was his scribe and assistant in this process.

The concept of "seeing" music with the body informs the preface to Schlick's *Tabulaturen* written by Schlick the Younger when he claimed that although his father had been robbed of his "external eyes" [*eusserliche augen*], God had heaped musical gifts on the blind organist, "sharpening his inner eyes of reason and sense."[47] Articulating these abstract structures with feet and hands at the German organ allowed Schlick the Elder to make sense of polyphonic space: he could see with his reason because he enacted the movement of the individual voices with independent limbs. It seems likely that Clesio's blind Tyrolian organist learned Schlick's piece and performed it for his patron; as a German he would likely have been trained in the multivoiced and multilimbed polyphony practiced by Schlick. These blind, early modern organists accomplished the task physically and with the ears, rather than by following the mass of individual parts on paper. To play from memory and to improvise in the dark as blind organists do, is, in the words of the modern blind organist David Liddle, "to be freed from the tyranny of clefs" and the constrictions of notation that inevitably give rise to conceptual boundaries.[48] With the help of his body a blind organist could conceptualize ten-part polyphony even if, or perhaps precisely because, he could not see its notational representation with his eyes, with his "external" vision. The organ provided an optimal tool for checking a complex contra-puntal composition alone, playing it for personal pleasure and to the glory of God, hearing it in acoustic space and feeling it in the body. Only the organist seated at the organ using all four limbs had the luxury, indeed the ability, to extend the ambition of solo polyphony to ten real parts.

These same modes of making intricate, yet massive, configurations of sound concrete in performance were also crucial to sighted players in devel-oping their own profound knowledge of counterpoint. The Germans claimed that they were the masters of this art, and it is not coincidence that for several centuries the leading German contrapuntists were predominantly organists as

---

[47] Arnolt Schlick the Younger, preface to Arnolt Schlick, *Tabulaturen Etlicher lobgesang und lidlein uff die orgeln und lauten* (Mainz: Peter Schöffern, 1512; reprint, Leipzig: Zentralantiquariat, 1979), unpaginated; see also Schlick, *Orgelkompositionen*, ed. Walter, unpaginated.

[48] David Liddle, private communication, November 4, 2008.

well. Certainly Bruhns could have written a six-part fugue for instrumental ensemble as lively and persuasive as the one he produced for the organ. But he would not have been able to exalt in the sheer joy of doing himself what would otherwise be the work of a six-member ensemble, enjoying a comprehensive picture of all the melodic lines and their interaction. The knowledge and accomplishment that come with actually playing all of these six parts should not mask the fact that while most organists are lucky enough to be able see this polyphony on the page, a parallel, still deeper, understanding is fostered by the body.

In his celebrated *Letter on the Blind* of 1749, Denis Diderot argued that the blind know the shape of things through touch; therefore, he concluded, they think of "'vision' as a kind of touch that extends to distant objects."[49] I would argue that musical touch is also a way of seeing sound with the body, but not just for the blind. Touching the keyboard not only allows organists a way to measure the dimensions of the large instrument around them that exceed their ability to see it; to depress the keys of different divisions with hands and feet is to take a sounding of the layout of the organ above and around the player. Beginning in the early modern period, the manuals and pedals also made it possible for the organist literally to grasp intangible music – especially abstract counterpoint – with his limbs. Molyneaux's famous question, which exercised Diderot and so many others, asked whether a blind person, having held a cube, would be able to recognize it as such if he were suddenly cured and could see. The organ allowed the organist, blind or sighted, to hold polyphony in his body, so that he could see it with his "inner eye."[50]

In the projection of polyphony onto the human form a new way of thinking about music was born with the early modern German organ. Often claimed as the most "abstract" of music, counterpoint became palpable in the organist's body. The transparency of the trio, from Schlick to Bach, laid out this concept at its barest; the massive textures of *Aus tieffer Noth* and *Ascendo ad patrem meum* made the art of multilimbed performance one of measuring the exact progress of still more voices on fingertips, toes and heels; feeling the trajectory of individual lines and the ever-shifting distances between them became an essential mode of musical knowledge. The contrapuntal designs of *An*

---

[49] Denis Diderot, "Letter on the Blind" (1749), trans. in Michael J. Morgan, *Molyneux's Question: Vision, Touch, and the Philosophy of Perception* (Cambridge University Press, 1977), p. 33.

[50] In support of my interpretation of Schlick's "inner-sight," I might refer to psychological studies that have shown that parts of the brain are significantly reorganized as a result of congenital blindness, so that, for example, the visual cortex of the blind is engaged when reading Braille, but is not active when the sighted do the same thing. Morton A. Heller (ed.), *Touch, Representation, and Blindness* (Oxford University Press, 2000), p. 3. One could also mention reports from blind organists that dividing the parts between the body conveys to them a clearer sense of the polyphony, even when the voices – and limbs – cross (private communication from David Liddle (November 4, 2008). These considerations deserve their own study if we are to appreciate more fully the accomplishment and pivotal contributions of the blind to the history of the organ.

Wasserflüssen Babylon and *Aus tieffer Noth* demonstrate clearly that the organist's art, practiced at its most demanding in large polyphonic works, is fundamentally an epistemology of the body. To execute such rich polyphonic structures – four parts in continuous motion even below a plaintive *cantus firmus* – is to know how counterpoint feels. The pedal was required for this physical engagement with massive polyphonic structures. As Carl Friedrich Zelter, director of the Berlin Singakademie, wrote to his friend Goethe in 1831, the feet might be considered the foundation of contrapuntal thinking: "One might say of old Bach, that the pedals were the ground-element of the development of his unfathomable intellect, and that without feet, he could never have attained his intellectual *height*."[51] According to Zelter the body was, for Bach, crucial in the conceptualization of elaborate contrapuntal structures: the organist thinks with his feet. This physical knowledge was held in common by those who could see and those who could not.

If the Obituary is to be believed, Bach lay blind on his deathbed in the summer of 1750 dictating his final chorale, *Vor deinen Thron tret' ich hiermit*, BWV 668, printed in open score as an addendum to the posthumous edition of the *Art of Fugue*.[52] How did he make these refinements to the complex counterpoint while blind and confined to his bed? A lifelong organist, he could have felt the polyphonic voices in his limbs: the bass in his feet, the two inner voices in the left hand, the *cantus firmus* in the right. Like the blind visionary Schlick before him, Bach would have been able to keep straight in his own mind the course of the individual polyphonic parts and to express these musical thoughts to his scribe by imagining for the last time how it felt to play the organ with all limbs in motion. To invent, to augment and to exploit the pedal was to play compositionally on a scale and a level of conceptual complexity that could not be matched by other musicians. To be an organist was to claim a kind of knowledge of polyphony that was not only cerebral, but was also articulated on the whole human form.

---

[51] Zelter to Goethe, May 7, 1831 in *Goethe's Letters to Zelter: with Extracts from those of Zelter to Goethe*, ed. A. D. Coleridge (London: George Bell and Sons, 1892), pp. 451–452. See Russell Stinson, *The Reception of Bach's Organ Works* (Oxford University Press, 2006), p. 18.

[52] See David Yearsley, *Bach and the Meanings of Counterpoint*, pp. 1–41.

CHAPTER 3

Walking towards perfection: pedal solos and cycles

A WALKING BASS

In the idiom most typical of pedal-playing, the feet progress as if they are walking. They alternate left and right, moving through their music in much the same way that they move through life. Nearly ubiquitous in the seventeenth and eighteenth centuries, this peripatetic musical figure remains the standard to this day. At the organ, the "walking bass" operates at both the literal and metaphorical level: organists' feet walk or run over the pedalboard, one foot and then the other, mimicking ambulatory motion in the act of conveying a musical sense of distance covered. In feverishly practicing Bach organ works for eight straight days in preparation for his 1840 recital at the Thomaskirche in Leipzig to raise money for a monument to J. S. Bach, Felix Mendelssohn wrote to his mother that "he walked nothing but pedal passages in the streets"; Bach's music was in Mendelssohn's legs even as he patrolled the city where Bach himself had once hurried between his many tasks.[1] This kinship between walking and pedaling is something all organists know in their bodies. Walking is (or, at least, was) as crucial to everyday life as pedaling was to organ-playing in the Bachian tradition: in the daunting pedal solos of the Prelude and Fugue in A minor, BWV 543, which Mendelssohn played at that Leipzig concert of 1840, the pedestrian becomes sublime (see Introduction, Example 1). As Mendelssohn's letter makes clear, the back-and-forth of walking and pedaling are kindred forms of movement that rely on and celebrate the feet as means of transport, be it musical or geographic.

Bach's *Wir glauben all an einen Gott*, BWV 680, published in the *Clavierübung III* of 1739, provides one of the clearest evocations of a walker's attitude, both physical and mental – his movements and his goals (see Example 3.1). The setting treats a paraphrase of the chorale melody's first two phrases fugally in the manuals. This energetic, syncopated counterpoint is elaborated above a recurring two-bar theme in the pedal that acts

[1] Felix Mendelssohn to Lea Mendelssohn, August 19, 1840, in Paul Mendelssohn Bartholdy and Carl Mendelssohn Bartholdy (eds.), *Letters of Felix Mendelssohn Bartholdy from 1833 to 1847*, trans. Lady Wallace (London: Longman, Green, Longman, Roberts, & Green, 1863), p. 192; see also R. Larry Todd, *Mendelssohn: a Life in Music* (Oxford University Press, 2003), p. 401.

Example 3.1   J. S. Bach, *Wir glauben all an einen Gott*, BWV 680, bars 1–20

like a ritornello whose continual reappearances are separated by lengthy rests. The ostinato remains constant through the various key-changes that present it in both major and minor mode; the figure is transposed four times between the opening statement and the final, sixth iteration that closes out the journey back in the tonic of D minor. The shape of the pedal line suggests an archetypal narrative of ascent and descent in perfect symmetry.

The first half of the ostinato's journey climbs upwards in eager eighth-notes moving by the melodic intervals of fourths alternating with thirds. This combination of intervals is the most common path towards higher ground in the pedal; in its regularity and the distance marked out by its steps, the figure is as natural as walking, deriving its contour from the same physical knowledge. The figure forcefully projects the movements of the feet into the church; heard on full organ (*In Organo pleno*, according to Bach's own performance direction) with a registration of all due *Gravitas*, the feet move with real purpose. The ostinato can be heard to derive from the pace and practice of the walker: this association between musical pattern and human locomotion is not in play when a figure like this is heard on the violone or bassoon, or other bassline instruments. *Wir glauben all* is truly a walker's piece at the organ.

After the upward-stepping figure covers the octave to d1, the return journey quickens the pace, moving back home to the tonic d in double-time sixteenths, with seconds and thirds in alternation: this is the complement to the ostinato's rising figure and is the most common method for moving flowingly downward. As in life, the homeward leg of any trip inevitably seems faster; the first half striving towards the summit, the second half tumbling back down, like going up and over the Harz mountains Bach had to cross on his way from Arnstadt to Lübeck in the late Fall of 1705 and again on his return in the winter of 1706 four months later. The *Wir glauben all* ostinato's ascending and descending elaborations of the scale are basic pedal figures. The straightforward scale in direct motion is a primary mode of progress for the hands, but is much more awkward for the feet – it is not as obvious or easy a motion as that of *Wir Glauben all*, either in ascent or descent. The pedal line of *Wir Glauben all* seems to play itself because the body of the organist recognizes, enjoys, walking movements.

The reappearance of the ostinato in different keys throughout the piece also creates a sense of progress and return as it visits new harmonic areas which open onto new vistas – each individual statement regaining its more local goal of rest (the tonic of the given ritornello) before the final long-range return home. This is a walking tour of D minor and its related tonalities, proceeding from the tonic to the keys of the surrounding tonal landscape, always arrived at with confidence and an unflagging sense of direction. To be sure, one could interpret the workaday, forward-stepping nature of the ostinato in any number of ways: the basic musical material mirrors the foundational tenets of the creed. That these patterns are thematically unified, not to say standardized, supports the notion of "one" God; the unwavering profile of the ostinato might also represent unflagging belief.[2] These and other hermeneutic angles, with their promises and pitfalls, offer

---

[2] Robin A. Leaver, "Bach's 'Clavierübung III': Some Historial and Theological Considerations," *Organ Yearbook*, 6 (1975), 17–32.

vistas onto the geography of the piece. But the physicality of this pedal line evokes something that is not merely a willful exercise in interpretation of musical figures: the ostinato's relation to the body is not metaphorical. Play the piece and you will feel as if you are walking. It is an uplifting, invigorating feeling.

THE LONG WALK

Bach was both one of history's greatest organists and one of its most famous walkers. Walking mapped out his early life. He was poor and walking was the only way to get where he wanted to be, both geographically and artistically. Orphaned at ten, he likely walked the twenty-five miles from Eisenach to his brother's house in Ohrdruf. The journey of 1700 that took him to Lüneburg – to Georg Böhm and the St. Michael's school – some five years later was one of about two hundred miles. His repeated trips to Hamburg were the Lüneburg Bach's youthful visits to hear the famed organist of the Katherinenkirche, Johann Adam Reincken, and reflected his eagerness to learn from his elders; the journey was a forty-mile round trip, probably lasting two days in each direction.[3] Bach's longest journey is one of the most famous outings in the annals of German walking. The Obituary of 1754 relates that "while [Bach] was in Arnstadt, he was once moved by the particularly strong desire to hear as many good organists as he could, so he undertook a journey, indeed on foot, to Lübeck, in order to listen to the famous organist of St. Mary's Church there, Dieterich Buxtehude."[4] The writer of this passage, Bach's son Carl Philipp Emanuel, stresses the mode of transport as physical proof of Bach's commitment to learning, one so strong that he made a journey of some two-hundred-and-fifty miles to Lübeck and then covered that same distance again on his return to Arnstadt. Bach set out in the late Fall of 1705 and must have encountered cold, rain, and perhaps even snow, especially on the walk south, four months later, in the ensuing winter. On his return Bach would face angry questioning from his employers for his extended absence, one that had exceeded by some three months the modest leave of a few weeks originally granted; the young organist had even remained away from his post for the Christmas season.[5] That Bach was not summarily sacked on his return was a testament to his skill, a prowess only augmented by what he had learned in the north.

Whether the youthful *Praeludium* in C, BWV 531, was written before or after the trip to Lübeck, it sets off on its own opening ramble with the avidity of the champion walker: the back-and-forth arpeggio of the opening

---

[3] Klaus Eidam, *The True Life of Johann Sebastian Bach*, ed. Hoyt Rogers (Basic Books: New York, 2001), p. 21. In my discussion here I am trying to distance myself from the folksy, man-of-the-people account offered in this whimsical, largely spurious, book.

[4] *NBR*, 300.   [5] Kerala Snyder, "Arnstadt to Lübeck," *Musical Times*, 127 (1986), 672–677.

Example 3.2   J. S. Bach, *Praeludium* in C, BWV 531, bars 1–14

takes big, confident steps and continues without a break, over varied leaps and through minor deviations, with the goal of C Major always in view on the musical horizon (see Example 3.2). The skips and jumps could make one think of leaping over puddles or skirting ruts in the road. Bach allows the organist no time to consider the next step; the feet lead on their own.

The trill that closes out the solo might be heard and felt in the organist's body as the hurried excitement that carries the adventurer to the destination in a last burst of energy. In contrast to the carefully planned and laid out itinerary of *Wir glauben all*, the *Praeludium* in C rejoices in the freedom and exuberance of youth: the feet find their way seemingly without a map.

Bach's decision to continue his schooling not in Ohrdruf or elsewhere in Thuringia but in Lüneburg allowed him to pursue more fully the organ as his main path towards musical and professional advancement. An important part of that decision must have been that Lüneburg was not only home to the school at St. Michael's, but also to the Thuringian transplant, Georg Böhm, who presided over the ancient organ in the Johanniskirche built in the middle of the 16th century by the great Brabanter, Hendrik Niehoff. Typical of the Brabant organs, that in the Johanniskirche had virtually no independent pedal division, and Böhm complained that the single 16′ stop for the feet meant that the instrument "was without all gravity." The expansion of the organ to include a full and independent pedal was long desired by Böhm and was finally realized within a decade of Bach's studies with him. Arp Schnitger's student Matthias Dropa added two pedal towers and a rich assortment of independent pedal stops, including two 32′ registers, as in the great organs of Hamburg.[6]

Böhm had lived and studied in Hamburg and had connections to Reincken; he likely encouraged Bach to make his trips there. The large organs of Hamburg, with their fully developed pedals, surpassed most of those of Thuringia in *Gravitas* and overall magnificence. All four of the organs in the principal churches of Hamburg had two massive full-length 32′ registers, one the broad, substantial Principal – the intrinsic "organ sound," the oldest style of pipe and the one not conceived of to imitate other instruments – and the other a more brazen reed, the deep trombone [*Posaune*]. This kind of gravity, admired by Bach in his surviving organ reports and pronouncements, was to be experienced in all its earth-shaking profundity only in the north. Equally as outstanding were the greatest organists of the north, chief among them Buxtehude and Reincken. Böhm would have helped Bach prepare himself to understand what he would hear during his visits to Hamburg. As the two recently resurfaced tablatures in Bach's youthful hand establish, Bach not only had access to northern music before his matriculation in Lüneburg, but he also studied ambitious *pedaliter* works of the north-German school while there. It was in Böhm's home that Bach copied Reincken's masterpiece, the vast chorale fantasia on *An Wasserflüssen Babylon*.[7]

---

[6] Gustav Fock, *Arp Schnitger und seine Schule* (Kassel: Bärenreiter, 1974), pp. 104–105.
[7] *Weimarer Orgeltabulatur*, ed. Michael Maul and Peter Wollny (Kassel: Bärenreiter, 2007). On the final page of the manuscript, the young Bach noted that he had made the copy in Böhm's house. See p. I/8. See also preface, xxix.

Instead of walking north to Lübeck, the young Bach might rather have chosen to study with Johann Pachelbel in Nuremberg, only half as far as Lübeck was from Ohrdruf.[8] Johann Christoph Bach, the elder brother with whom Bach had gone to live after the death of their parents in 1695, had been a student of Pachelbel, who had occupied several important organist posts in central Germany in the 1680s and 1690s. But at the organ Pachelbel could not offer what Buxtehude could. Bach's nineteenth-century biographer, Philipp Spitta, made the point with characteristic bluntness: because Pachelbel and other southerners made little use of the pedal, Bach had nothing more to learn from them. Spitta clinches the point by turning farther south to the Salzburg organist Georg Muffat and his beautifully engraved print from 1690, *Apparatus musico-organisticus*; one of the volume's most arduous toccatas concludes with the epigram *Dii laboribus omnia vendunt*: "Heaven concedes all to the industrious." But because there was no independent pedaling in any of the pieces in the collection, Spitta asserts that even a piece Muffat boasted required much practice "would doubtless have been played straight off by men like Buxtehude and Bruhns."[9] However, partial though this claim is, it does, I think, accurately represent Bach's view that as a man of twenty, having already studied the works of the south Germans under the aegis of his older brother and perhaps, too, the available organ works of the northern masters (for example Buxtehude's *Nun freut euch lieben Christen g'mein*), his future adventures in the organ arts lay to the north. A return to the organs themselves also must have been an alluring prospect for Bach when he set off on the great walk of 1705–6 from Arnstadt to Lübeck.

Anecdotal and source evidence confirms that Bach was an insatiable musical omnivore. He copied music with real dedication. But his walking also represents the prerequisite for acquiring further knowledge that manuscripts alone cannot provide: to hear from the master himself, to meet him, to watch and to listen, to learn the final aspects of the art not available at home. There were excellent organists in Bach's native Thuringia, but they were not Buxtehude, Reincken, or Böhm. The young Bach could write out Reincken's sprawling chorale fantasy on *An Wasserflüssen Babylon* and learn its lessons in a way only copying a manuscript can provide. He could then play it, make it part of the vocabulary of his body. Finally, he could walk and hear Reincken himself. Long-distance, virtual learning could not substitute for the real thing: the great organist in person, the music in performance.

---

[8] Peter F. Williams, *J. S. Bach: a Life in Music* (Cambridge University Press, 2007), p. 46.
[9] Philipp Spitta, *J. S. Bach*, trans. Clara Bell and J. A. Fuller-Maitland, 3 vols. (London: Novello, 1889), vol. I, p. 268.

WHAT WALKING MEANS

Walking is about more than movement, the attainment of a geographical destination, whether nearby or far away. As a form of leisure and recreation, and as a public display of social standing, it became increasingly important in the later eighteenth century. That it was already a significant aspect of civic life is evident from the riverside promenades of Bach's Leipzig, where the more refined elements of society could see and be seen.[10] To cover territory with a goal in mind is something different. The definition of walking [*Wandern*] and related words in Johann Heinrich Zedler's *Universal-Lexicon*, which began to appear in 1732, little less than a decade after Bach moved to Leipzig, is much longer than that on the more pleasurable, not to say idle, *Promenade* or *Spaziergang* also defined in Zedler.[11] Reading the Obituary's account of the long walk against the Zedler article concerning *Wandern* provides a wider cultural context for evaluating the longstanding claim that Bach embarked on his journey not for adventure alone but to improve himself. The Obituary stresses that the young man went on foot, and it refers to the trip as a *Reise*; Zedler informs us that for craftsmen, *Reisen* is a synonym for *Wandern*, and the *Lexicon* identifies these explicitly with the search for knowledge.[12] Zedler's entry on *Wandern* links the word with *Wanderschafft* [peregrination] and *Wanderjahre* [years of travel] and documents the centrality of walking for those in search of personal and professional betterment. "Wandern" does not mean wandering randomly or simply hiking for physical exercise through a revivifying natural world, as it has since the nineteenth century; rather, the verb denotes setting off on foot after completing one's apprenticeship with a master craftsman. The article claims that this is a quintessentially German activity, one not practiced in other countries of Europe. When apprentices [*Handwerksgesellen*] are fully trained but still not completely matured in their professional breadth, they go off on foot in search of aspects of their art not known by the local craft traditions where they have studied, usually for a number of years. The roaming of a young man bent on self-improvement is not "aimless or idle":

It is not that this setting off leads the travelers to spend their time in the street, or in taverns, or even in barns, but instead with other masters, working in irreproachable workshops, in order to gain knowledge not acquired during their years of study, or to achieve practice, experience and perfection of that which they previously only understood partially.

---

[10] Sabine Krebber, *Der Spaziergang in der Kunst* (Frankfurt: Peter Lang, 2002), p. 22.
[11] J. H. Zedler, *Grosses vollständiges Universal-Lexicon*, 64 vols. (Leipzig: Zelder and Ludovici, 1732–1754; reprint, Graz: Akademische Druck- und Verlagsanstalt, 1961–1964), vol. xxix, col. 792.
[12] *Ibid.*, vol. xxxi, col. 385. The lengthy article on "Reisen" that precedes the just-cited entry linking "Reisen" and "Wandern" with handworkers is concerned mostly with aristocratic travel and the Grand Tour; see vol. xxxi, cols. 365–380. See also vol. xxix, col. 792.

Zedler's article describes how the young craftsman often sets out without knowing exactly where he is headed, hoping nonetheless to find a master from whom further secrets can be learned. These peregrinations are imbued with moral purpose. "To become ready to journey [*Wanderfertig werden*]," as Zedler puts it, means more than simply being physically prepared and logistically provisioned for the trip; one has also to be ethically disposed to search for what is needed to attain greater mastery, whether making shoes, as the example in Zedler's *Lexicon* would have it, or playing the organ.[13] In his quest for perfection the journeyman faces the perils of all travelers: highwaymen, lack of accommodation and food, blisters on the feet, and inclement weather. But graver still was the danger of losing ethical and professional direction; one could lose the way geographically, but still more serious was straying morally. Traveling could bring with it the dissipation of the desire for knowledge, a weakening of commitment to one's craft wrought by drink and indolence. According to the Zedler article, these wanderers sometimes ended up unable to support themselves, and had to turn to begging, thus becoming nuisances to the local communities where they found themselves.

In spite of these risks and potential social strains, Germans welcomed the wandering craftsmen; according to Zedler, the culture of hospitality that allowed journeymen to travel ultimately resulted in the superior skills of German craftsmen: the search for knowledge was abetted by a willing population. The Zedler article on hospitality [*Gastfrey seyn*] stresses the importance of kindness to traveling strangers shown in biblical stories and in Antiquity. Although taking in unanticipated visitors is one of the most basic human virtues, this is presented most emphatically as something Germanic, since the German forebears cultivated hospitality more assiduously even than the Romans: "The old Germans placed more value on [hospitality], and it was viewed as a grave crime [*Injurie*] when a stranger was not taken in."[14] According to Zedler, Germany produced better craftsmen than elsewhere in Europe, because Germans were willing to support this kind of itinerant travel and the exchange of ideas and passing on of knowledge it furthered.

This wider cultural support for the traveling craftsmen bent on self-improvement colors the anecdote found in Friedrich Wilhelm Marpurg's *Legende einiger Musikheiligen* (*Legends of some Musician-Saints*) about a young and hungry Bach on the road. Still in the midst of his apprentice years with Böhm, Bach has been to Hamburg to hear Reincken and is on the long walk back to Lüneburg. The young wayfarer happens on an inn and salivates at the smells emanating from the kitchen. As the complaints of his stomach inspire melancholy thoughts, a window is flung open and a pair

---

[13] *Ibid.*, vol. LII, col. 1964.   [14] *Ibid.*, vol. X, col. 390.

of herring heads thrown onto the garbage heap. Marpurg is careful to make it clear that Bach does not beg, and that he is not a lowly scavenger: herring heads are a delicacy for Thuringians and cannot be wasted. The surprise is that a kindly, anonymous gentleman has left in each head a Danish ducat that allows Bach not only to add meat to his meal, but provides a stipend to support further travels to Hamburg. The young orphaned and impoverished boy, rich only in talent and desire to learn, relies on the good offices of an unknown patron for encouragement of the *Wandern* that will one day pay unimagined dividends not only to those with whom he comes into contact, but for a vast posterity. It is this communitarian attitude which nourishes the wandering organist as he moves through his country. The herrings are a classic example of German support for a hungry journeyman in search of knowledge: it is not hospitality itself that is uniquely German, but the support of craftsmen who sometimes find themselves down on their luck during their wander-years, claims Zedler. Organ-playing is also to be thought of as a craft, nurtured by the Germans, who support wandering because it enriches everyone. The kindness of the gift of herring heads and ducats mirrors Bach's own moral bearing symbolized by his walking, proof of his commitment to his art and ultimately to others. He becomes a great organist because he is a great walker, because he goes out on his two feet in search of what he needs to do to improve his art.

FEET ALONE (IN BUXTEHUDE'S FOOTSTEPS)

Probably the main reason Bach went to Lübeck in 1705 was to learn from Buxtehude's concerted vocal music heard at the famous Vespers *Abendmusik* held each Advent season. But no less important was the fact that Buxtehude was himself one of the finest practitioners of the pedal-based organ art of the northern masters. One item that Bach must have had in his satchel on the home journey back to Arnstadt in early 1706 during the shortest and probably the coldest days of the year, was a copy of Buxtehude's *Praeludium* in C, BuxWV 137 (see Figure 3.1). The only substantive source for this rightly celebrated work is the so-called Andreas Bach Book, a manuscript collection compiled and largely copied by Bach's older brother Johann Christoph, who was apparently also eager to benefit from the fruits of his younger sibling's sojourns in the north;[15] the most likely route for J. C. Bach's access to BuxWV 137 was through J. S. Bach.

---

[15] Andreas Bach Book, Leipzig, Musikbibliothek der Stadt Leipzig, III.8.4; Buxtehude's *Praeludium* comes very near the end of the manuscript, on pp. 234–237. See Robert Hill's Introduction to *Keyboard Music from the Andreas Bach Book and the Möller Manuscript*, ed. Robert Hill (Cambridge, Massachusetts: Harvard University Press, 1991), pp. xv–xlvii. There are two other complete manuscript copies and one fragmentary copy, all deriving directly or indirectly from the Andreas Bach Book. See *Dieterich Buxtehude: Collected Works*, vol. xv, Pt. 1, ed. Michael Belotti (New York: Broude Trust, 1998), p. 30.

Figure 3.1   Dieterich Buxtehude, *Praeludium* in C, BuxWV 137

This free work, with its alternation between contrapuntal and improvisatory sections typical of northern *praeludia*, would have been an appropriate commemoration of Bach's long walk, for the first question an improviser conjuring the magic of the *stylus phantasticus* must answer is:

Figure 3.1   (cont.)

how to begin? The answer: with the feet. Buxtehude's *Praeludium* begins
with a pedal solo, among the most flamboyant of the north-German
organists' modes of amazement and display. The feet fly into action and
through the complex mechanism of the organ, that technological wonder of

Example 3.3   Dieterich Buxtehude, *Praeludium* in C, BuxWV 137, bars 1–2

the pre-industrial world, convert the potential energy of filled bellows
and silent pipes into rushing kinetic sound. The first eight notes are disarm-
ingly simple, but they have an incontrovertible quality, for who can argue
with a C Major triad answered by a descending octave on the dominant and
then an emphatic resolution to a tonic octave ending on the lowest key of the
pedalboard, the deepest note possible on the large organ of the Marienkirche
in Lübeck (see Example 3.3). Here again the choreography of these figures is
that of the walker. An exordium like that of Buxtehude's *Praeludium* and
those it inspired must provoke amazement, both in the listeners below and in
the organist himself: amazement at the skill of the feet; amazement at the
audacity of beginning only with them; amazement at the sheer power of the
sound they can by themselves send soaring through the interior of the
Marienkirche in the 17th century, to resound down the centuries and to
us. That Buxtehude could use his feet with such conviction meant that many
others would emulate his example.

How lucky we are that Buxtehude's *Praeludium* survives at all, that it was
saved for history by the traveling Bach, whose journeys depended on the
help of many strangers. Bach surely had Buxtehude's solo in his ears and in
his legs when he composed his own Toccata in C, BWV 564. Unlike the
Praeludium in C, BWV 531, mentioned above, and BuxWV 137, the
Toccata does not begin with a pedal solo, but with a section of fantastical
monophony given to the hands. The first gesture of the pedal solo that
ensues after these virtuosic flourishes echoes that of BuxWV 137, and both
strive for the same goal: to clear out enough sonic space for an imposing
pedal solo to ensue.[16] J. S. Bach's teacher, Böhm, was also an admirer of
Buxtehude and might well have drawn inspiration from this same piece.
After a full C Major chord heard in both pedal and manuals, Böhm's own

---

[16] Christoph Wolff has pointed out that the first bar of an early chorale by J. S. Bach, *Herzlich lieb hab
ich dich, o Herr*, BWV 1115 contains the opening figure of BuxWV 137, as does a chorale on the
same melody by Bach's Weimar colleague, J. G. Walther. Wolff sees these figures as allusions to
Buxtehude's *Praeludium*. Both of these chorale preludes are *manualiter* pieces, and do not aspire to
the rhetorical force of any of the pedal solos cited here. See Wolff's Introduction to his facsimile
edition, *The Neumeister Collection of Chorale Preludes from the Bach Circle (Yale University Manuscript
LM 4708)* (New Haven: Yale University Press, 1986), p. 9, n. 55. See also Russell Stinson, "Some
Thoughts on Bach's Neumeister Chorales," *Journal of Musicology*, 11 (1993), 455–477, at 468.

Example 3.4a   Georg Böhm, *Praeludium* in C, bars 1–2

Example 3.4b   J. S. Bach, Toccata in C, BWV 564, bars 13–14

Example 3.4c   J. L. Krebs, *Praeludium* in C, bars 11–12

Example 3.4d   William Albright, *Jig for the Feet* (*Totentanz*), from *Organbook III* (1980), bars 1–3

C Major *Praeludium* takes the opening three-note anacrusis – what Johann Gottfried Walther and other theorists would call *suspirans* – of the Buxtehude *Praeludium* and uses it to generate an entire solo, closer in dimension to Bach's.[17] Indeed, Böhm's opening gambit is an audacious extension of Buxtehude's initial motto; Böhm's feet run with the figure over nearly two full bars before pausing after those same falling octave Gs that come after only three notes in the Buxtehude solo (see Example 3.4a). It

[17] J. G. Walther, *Musicalisches Lexicon* (Leipzig: Wolffgang Deer, 1732; reprint, Kassel: Bärenreiter, 1953), p. 244. See also Wolffgang Caspar Printz, *Phrynis Mitylenaeus, oder Satyrischer Componist* (Dresden and Leipzig: Johann Christoph Mieth and Johann Christoph Zimmermann, 1696), Pt. 2, p. 60.

could even have been Böhm who made a copy of BuxWV 137 available to Bach, his young student from Thuringia; Bach's own most famous C Major pedal solo begins in the same vein as did Buxtehude's (see Example 3.4b). The C Major pedal solo of Bach's student J. L. Krebs, written in the middle of the eighteenth century, follows as if in apostolic succession (see Example 3.4c). Even the demonic pedal solo of William Albright's *Totentanz* (1980), raises the specter of Bach and, in turn, of Buxtehude's definitive essay on pedal rhetoric (see Example 3.4d).

The pedal solo is always a special case, though Schlick had alluded to the practice already at the beginning of the sixteenth century: for a keyboard-player to make music without his hands is often thought of as counter-intuitive not to say downright bizarre. At the opening of Buxtehude's *Praeludium* the far more nimble fingers, expert at grabbing massive chords and ripping off lightning runs, are given the seemingly menial task of clinging to the bench to prevent the organist from falling from his perch. The hands, these champions of speed and finesse capable of so much more than the club-like appendages below, are themselves bystanders to the grandiose opening statement. But however facile these fingers are, what they cannot do is power the organ's largest pipes. Those giant columns belong to the feet.

Walking involves the whole body, but the legs and feet are the engines, moving the person along, even as the arms swing freely, or plant the walking stick. In this regard, too, the pedal solo summons associations with walking, of letting the feet carry the body forward. The legs stomp away at a wide keyboard of limited compass (two octaves and two notes, C to d1) on large keys to be depressed against the resistance of a heavy action by the feet clad in bulky buckled shoes. How unlikely it might now seem to the uninitiated that this opening declaration achieves its authority when the mode of performance itself seems to flirt with the comic. To those unfamiliar with the north-German organ art the image might bring to mind a peasant dancing and tromping around the barnyard rather than a learned musician starting into a sublime musical oration. However odd this way of making music may seem to some, for the north Germans, and for Bach, there is nothing more exalted.

The plenum – the full organ – is deployed for a large-scale *praeludium* like this one. In the pedal, stops ranging from the 32′ Principal up to the multi-rank Mixture are pulled out, and when the organist's left foot strikes the lowest C of the pedalboard, as it does to conclude the opening motto of this pedal solo, it sends out into the church a phalanx of pitches seven octaves wide stretching over a span equal to that of the entire compass of the modern piano: the 32′ Principal sounds two octaves below the depressed C; the tiny pipes of the Mixture extend upward over five octaves. When a battery of reeds, including the powerful and deep 24′ Posaune, is added into the ensemble, the organ produces an apocalyptic rumble accompanied by the stratospheric singing of angels, like those effigies hovering above the pedal pipes in the Marienkirche.[18] The construction of the largest organ pipes was a performance in itself, requiring from the organ-builder a virtuosic command of the tools of casting, and of smelting alloys that would allow columns 32′ high with thin walls a quarter-inch thick to withstand the inexorable pull of gravity over several centuries.

Indeed, for the Nuremberg organist Johann Erasmus Kindermann, not coincidentally the first to publish a fugue with independent pedal in 1645 (see Chapter 2, p. 87), it was in these high mixtures that "one recognizes the choir of the heavenly congregation."[19] There is no other sound in the seventeenth-century world that approaches this: undergirded by the lowest pipes, which Athanasius Kircher also believed evoked the "innumerable angels and blessed spirits" [*unzählbare Engel und selige Geister*] of heaven, this array of pitches produces a mightily stacked sonority.[20] When wrestled with by the feet alone this sonority seems to tilt and teeter, exhilarating to the point of terror – the sound likened often to thunder or even to God's wrath.[21]

Rising two stories above the console was the distinctive Gothic facade of the large organ of the Marienkirche, unchanged from the time of its construction in 1518 (see Figure 3.2). With its long row of pipe mouths as flat as the Baltic shoreline by Lübeck it proclaimed its ancient origins. In the outer and central fields of the main case rose the 32′ open Principal – the lowest and largest pipes. Out in the church this façade sent the visual message to listeners below that the instrument had vast pedal riches over which the organist ruled with his feet and imagination. Even the more ancient organ in the *Totentanz* side-chapel in the Marienkirche had a massive pedal division: of the forty stops of this "smaller" instrument, no less than fifteen belonged to the feet (see Figure 3.3). These were the two instruments – the larger was removed in 1851, the smaller destroyed by Allied bombs in 1942 – "presided over by the world-famous organist and composer Dieterich Buxtehude," as a 1697 guidebook to Lübeck put it.[22] Both organs would certainly have been available to Bach during his stay.

The visual presentation of the pedal of the large organ on the west wall extended to that part of the instrument that hangs on the gallery rail behind

---

[18] As Peter Williams has put it with regard to the famous organ in Görlitz known to Bach, the angel-trumpeters "assured an apocalyptic effect every time they played, *via* the organist's feet, *Vom Himmel hoch* or *Wachet auf!*" *The European Organ* (Bloomington, Indiana: Indiana University Press, 1966), p. 136.

[19] See H. H. Eggebrecht, "Zwei Nürnberger Orgel-Allegorien des 17. Jahrhunderts," *Musik und Kirche*, 27 (1957), 170–181, at 176.

[20] Athanasius Kircher, *Germaniae redonatus: sive artis magnae de consono et dissono ars minor*, trans. Andreas Hirsch (Schwäbisch Hall: Hans Reinhold Laidigen and Johann Christoph Gräter, 1662), p. 253.

[21] Johann Samuel Petri, *Anleitung zur praktischen Musik* (Leipzig: Breitkopf, 1782), p. 285.

[22] *Die Beglückte und Geschmückte Stadt Lübeck* (Lübeck: Johann Gerhard Krüger, 1697), p. 114; quoted in Snyder, *Dieterich Buxtehude: Organist in Lübeck* (New York: Schirmer, 1987), p. 57. For accounts of the two organs see Snyder, "Buxtehude's Organs: Helsingør, Helsingborg, Lübeck". Part 2: "The Lübeck Organs," *Musical Times*, 126 (1985), 427–434, and *Dieterich Buxtehude: Organist in Lübeck*, 2nd edn. (University of Rochester Press, 2007), pp. 78–87.

Figure 3.2   Large organ, Marienkirche, Lübeck

the organist. The pedal's 16′ Principal occupied two small towers to either side of this *Rückpositiv*. To the expert eye and even to the not-so-expert ear the facade of both the main case (the *Hauptwerk*) and the *Rückpositiv* brought the pedal sonically and visually forward. At the console the organist was surrounded by the pedal's architectural and aural presence. The 24′ foot

Figure 3.3   *Totentanz* organ, Marienkirche, Lübeck

Posaune (a deep reed stop that extended only to FF rather than to the CC of the Principal) was at the back of the case.

Given the pedal resources found on these two organs it cannot surprise us that a musician of Buxtehude's ability and ambition should leave behind the greatest collection of *pedaliter* pieces of the seventeenth century, admired by later organists from Bach to Brahms and beyond.[23] During Buxtehude's own lifetime organists from at least two subsequent generations made their

---

[23] On becoming acquainted with Buxtehude's *Ciacona* in D minor, Brahms wrote, "I can hardly resist sharing it with a publisher, simply for the purpose of creating joy for others." Brahms to Philipp

pilgrimages to the Marienkirche. There was Nicolaus Bruhns (see Chapter 2, p. 91), whose few surviving organ works are rich with pedal difficulties including flamboyant pedal solos inspired by those of his teacher.[24] Another student, Georg Leyding (1664–1710), began his own C Major *Praeludium* with a long perpetual-motion pedal solo.[25] Still younger lions – Bach, and two years before him Handel and his sometime friend Johann Mattheson from Hamburg – came later, partly to consider their prospects of becoming Buxtehude's successor, but just as crucially to hear the "venerable" [*wohlgedachter*] organist on the instruments of his genius.[26]

As essentially improvised genres, the toccatas and *praeludia* of the north-German *stylus phantasticus* lived and died in the moment of their creation. Largely for this reason one searches the not inconsiderable repertoire of north-German free works before Buxtehude and can find only the faintest trace of a pedal solo. Still, we know from as far back as Schlick that the idea of the pedal solo was not new when Buxtehude brought the technique to new heights. North-German organists had long demanded much of their feet, and the surviving sources document a robust tradition of double pedaling in works from across the seventeenth century (see Chapter 2). Yet in the same period passages for the feet alone are nearly non-existent. The main reason for this might be that counterpoint in double pedal was more the stuff of careful consideration than was fantastical monophony, and therefore more likely to be written down. The lack of solo pedaling in this earlier repertoire may also have something to do with the apparently more limited scope and less flamboyant nature of the notated *praeludium* before Buxtehude and his generation expanded both its dimensions and its dramatic intensity. The fortuitous survival of the opening movement of Tunder's multi-verse setting of *Jesus Christus, unser Heiland* gives us a tantalizing glimpse of solo footwork before Buxtehude. Here the feet deliver the sort of figure that so often leads to the first note of the *cantus firmus* in the soprano in seventeenth-century north-German chorale settings (see Example 3.5a). Buxtehude does something quite similar in the pedal in one of the verses of his setting of the *Te Deum laudamus*, BuxWV 218, though the shape of the line is closer to that of the opening of BuxWV 137 (see Example 3.5b). However rhetorically bold these one-bar passages may be, they are on a different scale and have a different intent than the full-blown pedal solo. Each chorale prelude opening offers a single gesture rather than a series of gestures, a flourish rather than an argument, a burst of

Spitta, January 19, 1874. *Johannes Brahms im Briefwechsel mit Philipp Spitta*, ed. Carl Krebs (Berlin: Verlag der Deutschen Brahms-Gesellschaft, 1920), p. 53; quoted in Snyder, *Dieterich Buxtehude*, p. 235.

[24] Johann Mattheson, *Grundlage einer Ehren-Pforte* (Hamburg, 1740; modern edn. ed. Max Schneider, Berlin: Liepmannsohn, 1910), p. 26.

[25] Georg Leyding, *Sämtliche Orgelwerke*, ed. Klaus Beckmann (Breitkopf & Härtel, 1984), p. 4.

[26] Johann Mattheson, *Grundlage einer Ehren-Pforte*, p. 94.

Example 3.5a   Franz Tunder, *Jesus Christus, unser Heiland*, verse 1, bars 1–2

Example 3.5b   Dieterich Buxtehude, *Te Deum laudamus*, BuxWV 218, verse 3, bars 203–204

energy not a series of questions and declarations that together build an argument as they build momentum. What Buxtehude does in his pedal solos – perhaps for the first time in music history – and what he is asking later organists to do, is not merely to impress with solo feet, but to persuade.

Just how extraordinary Buxtehude's pedaling was, even in his own day, can be seen more clearly by pulling back from the organ loft of the Marienkirche to take a broader European perspective. In 1699 Johann Pachelbel, then organist in St. Sebald's church in Nuremberg 400 miles to the south of Lübeck, published a small set of keyboard variations (without pedal) entitled *Hexachordum Apollinis* and dedicated them to Buxtehude and the Imperial organist in Vienna, Tobias Richter.[27] The two dedicatees represent vastly different approaches to the organ art. As in the organ music of his south-German and Austrian predecessors and contemporaries, Richter's surviving work makes no explicit use of the pedal, instead leaving the few interventions the feet do make to the discretion of the organist. The feet are never crucial, and are never used for elaborate display.

As for the composer of the *Hexachordum Apollinis* himself, Pachelbel's surviving organ works duly reflect his southern orientation. His larger free works are mostly organ-point toccatas, with only long drones to occupy a single stationary foot. This was the approach to pedaling characteristic of

---

[27] For a modern edition of Richter's works, see *Denkmäler der Tonkunst in Österreich*, vol. XXVII, ed. Hugo Botsbiber (Graz: Akademische Druck- und Verlagsanstalt, 1959); see also *Orgel- und Claviermusik der kaiserlichen Hofkapelle, Wien, 1500–1700*, ed. Siegbert Rampe (Kassel: Bärenreiter, 2006).

Example 3.6   Johann Pachelbel, *Praeludium* in D minor, bars 1–5

south Germany and indeed of Italy. A south German by birth and training, Pachelbel also spent several years in Thuringia in central Germany before returning to Nuremberg. His single surviving pedal solo (see Example 3.6) found in a source of central-German origins and likely composed during his time in the region, relies on the same sort of alternate pedaling found in Buxtehude's C Major *Praeludium*.[28] Although Pachelbel's is quite a long solo by seventeenth-century standards, it is a pedantic affair, lacking the rhetorical energy – the big leaps, the shocking rests, and the fantastical mixture of the predictable and the unexpected – that sets Buxtehude's pedal work apart. One could even float the hypothesis that Pachelbel's pedal solo is indebted directly to the tradition represented by Buxtehude, since he might well have never ventured such a thing had he not traveled north and come into contact with organists who knew Buxtehude's music. It seems hard to imagine that Pachelbel's praise for Buxtehude found in the *Hexachordum* dedication is based merely on reputation and not also on concrete knowledge of the worthy Lübeck organist's most ambitious free works.

BUXTEHUDE'S PEDAL SOLOS

Sadly, we do not have any rapturous accounts of Buxtehude's pedaling in action, as we do of Bach's (see Chapter 6). Nonetheless, both organists and non-organists alike must have been astonished by what this famous musician could do with his feet. And in any case, the *Praeludium* is enough evidence to tell us that the feet were as important a part of Buxtehude's arsenal as they were of Bach's. Within Buxtehude's oeuvre the opening solo is a rare thing, although we must be careful about the inferences to be drawn

---

[28] The single source for the piece is of central-German provenance (Staatsbibliothek zu Berlin, Mus. ms. P 247).

Example 3.7   Dieterich Buxtehude, Toccata in D minor, BuxWV 155, bars 114–115

Example 3.8   Dieterich Buxtehude, Toccata in F, BuxWV 156, bars 121–122

from the extant manuscripts; these represent probably only a small remnant of the music he made at the Marienkirche organs, and also only a portion of those pieces he committed to paper, since so much must be considered lost. Nonetheless, I would claim for this solo a special status. Of the 22 or 23 large-scale *pedaliter praeludia* and toccatas that survive only three begin with pedal solos: the *Praeludia* in C, BuxWV 137, in E minor, BuxWV 143, and in G, BuxWV 147.

To be sure, nearly all of Buxtehude's free works have at least one section designed to demonstrate pedal prowess, and often these passages are accompanied by the manuals. One unusually long example of six bars comes from the large Toccata in D minor, BuxWV 155, which has a sequence of ascending broken chords in the pedal marked by chords above (Example 3.7). Then there is the glorious moment in the F Major Toccata, BuxWV 156, which takes the generic pedal figure of alternating thirds and displaces them by an octave: the run-of-the-mill thirds become earth-shaking tenths encouraged onward by the manual overlay (Example 3.8). Whether accompanied or unaccompanied, interior pedal "highlights" such as these are usually just one bar long, occasionally two.

Although impressive and well-placed, the moments of pedal display in the course of many of Buxtehude's free works do not hog the spotlight in the way that the three opening solos do. The effect of the solo will necessarily be far different if it emerges from an ongoing fantastical discourse than if it is the starting point for that discourse. The positioning of pedal solos at the outset of the oration encourages, perhaps demands, expansiveness. But these solos are not only longer; they are both richer and riskier – for sustaining the interest of the distant auditors for 15 or 20 slow seconds, and doing so at the very beginning of a piece with only the feet, is a daunting task.

THE RHETORIC OF MOTION

Almost all the fantastical free works open with much longer *manualiter* flourishes than the opening motto of BuxWV 137. Only the Toccata in D minor, BuxWV 155, with its fiery succession of decorated D minor chords punctuated by rests, approaches its urgent declamation.[29] The pedal solo at the start of BuxWV 137 contains the most exhortatory utterances with which Buxtehude began any of his surviving musical orations. The first steps in the walking motion of this journey are bold, the leap down an octave bolder still. After the plunge to the low C in the pedal solo of BuxWV 137 the subsequent dotted quarter-note rest not only allows the blast to ring down the church, but it also gives the organist time to swivel his body hard to the right and to the high reaches of the pedalboard; when measured against the pedal compass and the small frame of the organist himself, two octaves traverse a huge expanse. Safely rotated to the top of the pedalboard, the highest note of that compass is reached at the beginning of the third bar. From these heights the feet busy themselves again, but their antic motion seems at first without direction or purpose other than to demonstrate how nimble they can be. Nonetheless, a general descent emerges from the whir of notes; this descent uses a figure called *superjectio* by J. G. Walther, who was himself an avid collector and copyist of Buxtehude's music and played a vital role in its survival. Again, *superjectio* is one of the most common of pedal figures since before Buxtehude's time because it provides a ready way to decorate a scale with alternating feet. This is the purposeful walking figure we have already seen in Bach's *Wir glauben all*. Melodic descent does not mean return to an opening position at the middle of the compass or lower than it, but rather forward movement. Buxtehude is going somewhere now: the footsteps cover musical ground and evoke real spatial movement.

[29] The exordium of Buxtehude's C Major *Praeludium* is as much about silence as it is about sound, even when the border between these two categories would have been made magnificently unclear in the echoing acoustic of the Marienkirche. Mattheson tells us that fantastical passages such as this are free from the constraints of meter; but however approximate the notated rests may be with respect to the actual fantastical performance of this passage, their main job is to make the declaration more emphatic. Mattheson's frequently cited description of the *stylus phantasticus* is found in his *Vollkommener Capellmeister* (Hamburg: Christian Herold, 1739; reprint, Kassel: Bärenreiter, 1954), pp. 87–88. For an English translation, from which my translations sometimes depart, see *Johann Mattheson's Der vollkommene Capellmeister: a revised translation with critical commentary*, trans. Ernest C. Harriss (Ann Arbor, Michigan: UMI Research Press, 1981), pp. 216–219. See also David Yearsley, "*Stylus Phantasticus* and the New Musical Imagination" in Sverker Jullander (ed.), *GOArt Research Report*s, vol. II (University of Gothenburg, 2000), pp. 91–105.

As soon as a general direction for the argument seems to have been found, the equally idiomatic rocking thirds of the last beat of bar 4 reverse direction and climb back upwards. Only the slight alteration over the last beat of bar 3 – the hardest part of this unbroken string of sixteenth-notes because it cannot be played with alternating feet – changes this pattern so as to arrive on a provisional imperfect cadence whose octave volley echoes that of the falling octaves heard twice in bar 1. This bounding/ricocheting sixteenth-note octave then generates a proto-sequence punctured by abrupt rests and driven by three upbeat thirds, a version of that same *suspirans* figure; here the figure is modified from its more typical scalar form to a variant more easily played by alternating feet. Gathering momentum, the line abandons the expansive rhetoric of the opening for a hurried succession of *suspirans* flourishes as it hurtles through bar 5 and towards another imperfect cadence, at which the manuals unexpectedly intervene for the first time. The snatched G Major triad that jolts the lower G of the falling pedal octave tells us that the hands cannot be held off for long. Indeed, the feet deliver a final passage of *superjectio* – the longest in the solo – before the manuals enter again for good, bringing us for a third time to the imperfect cadence on G and the end of the pedal solo, though the long, low notes of the pedal heard beneath the ensuing manual flourishes play a crucial role in bringing the opening exordium section to a cadence on C Major at bar 11.

Describing this solo largely in terms of individual figures cannot capture its dramatic impact. Rather, such an account illuminates the interplay between ready-made component parts and the uplifting rhetoric they achieve. Consider again the skein of sixteenth-notes beginning in the middle of bar 2 and extending until bar 4. If this were the bass of a continuo aria, it would fail to convince: it is too repetitive, too obvious, too predictable. I do not mean to confuse the generic differences between more syntactically driven modes of seventeenth-century music-making and the freedom of the *stylus phantasticus*. My intent is rather to emphasize the pre-learnt nature of these patterns, the assemblage of which was a prerequisite of improvisatory competence, even brilliance. Buxtehude defeats our expectations with sudden rests, slight but crucial alterations in a pattern, the unexpected manual chord. Even with these fantastical touches, however, we cannot be swayed simply by the notes on the page. Away from the organ, or better, away from the pedals, this music fails. Thus Ferruccio Busoni's reading of Bach's Toccata at the piano falters only during the pedal solo.

For the pedal solo to succeed, the listener must know that the feet are making the music; they must convince as much by physical force as by rhetorical power. The barlines of chorale preludes and fantasias, passages in double pedal and even trios could as well be music for instruments or voices. But in pedal solos it is not just because the lowest pipes of the organ are heard that we know the feet are at work. The profile of the line – its idiom – signifies to the listener that this is a pedal solo and therefore

Example 3.9   Dieterich Buxtehude, *Praeludium* in E minor, BuxWV 143, bars 1–3

warrants, demands even, the suspension of at least some of the standard rules of musical discourse so that the listener can be allowed to be astonished at what is being accomplished. In this sense a pedal solo is truly a show-stopper: while the rules of musical syntax are by no means completely ignored, the imperatives of forward motion give way to repetition, circulating patterns, the sometimes obsessive working out of a given figure and its variants, as in the opening solo of the E minor *Praeludium*, BuxWV 143 (Example 3.9). A gripping pedal solo like this one succeeds by coming dangerously close to imploding under the solipsistic tendencies of virtuosic display; indeed, such repetitions often give modern ears the impression that a pedal solo sounds like an exercise rather than a piece of music. But this is to misunderstand the rhetorical mode of the pedal solo, one that dramatizes the organist's movements and projects them across large architectural distances. This is why the scribe did not deem it necessary to indicate "Ped." at the opening of BuxWV 137, though this indication is often used in many other pieces in the manuscript (see Figure 3.1 above). Propelled by the lowest stops on the organ, the back-and-forth, walking pattern is the clearest signal that the music belongs to the feet.

Buxtehude turns to a *ciacona* as the last of the three large sections of his *Praeludium*, BuxWV 137; it is this structure that gave the piece the popular name it is often known by – the Prelude, Fugue, and Chaconne. The thematic material for both the *ciacona* and the fugue is related to that of the pedal solo (see Example 3.10). The opening motive of the chaconne – the leap up the octave from the low C, the *superjectio* descent to the dominant – reminds us that the feet began the journey which will now culminate with them hammering away again and again at this theme. All these variants of the opening motto are also to be played with alternating feet.

The *ciacona* is a crucial genre of the north-German organ art, described and lauded by theorists whose accounts suggest how often it was requested at organists' auditions and practiced by improvising organists.[30] Although

---

[30] Johann Mattheson, *Grosse General-Bass Schule* (Hamburg: J. C. Kißner, 1731; reprint, Hildesheim: Olms Verlag, 1968), p. 35.

Example 3.10a   Dieterich Buxtehude, *Praeludium* in C, BuxWV 137, bars 1–2

Example 3.10b   Dieterich Buxtehude, *Praeludium* in C, BuxWV 137, bars 37–38

Example 3.10c   Dieterich Buxtehude, *Praeludium* in C, BuxWV 137, bars 75–77

ostinatos are prominent in Buxtehude's vocal and chamber music, they are even rarer in his surviving free organ works than an opening pedal solo.[31] In these organ ground basses the pedal cycles back through the ostinato pattern, refusing to yield its harmonic or motivic dominion. The fantastical solo and the ground bass seemingly occupy opposite ends of the musical spectrum when it comes to freedom: the former is unbounded by meter and melody, the latter binds itself to the regularity of the ostinato. If the feet do take a break for one or more passes through the ostinato, their return only confirms their power. The hands are left to comment – often in the most exhilarating and unexpected ways – on what the feet inexorably present and re-present as a given. Both the ostinato and the pedal solo defy the normal progression of musical time, but in very different ways: where the pedal solo often risks becoming trapped in a phantasm of technical bravura, the ostinato indulges in a surfeit of short-range teleology which ultimately threatens the very idea of a larger goal.

In the midst of his discussion of chaconnes, Friedrich Erhard Niedt, the Copenhagen organist and influential theorist, suddenly veers away from his topic to rail against organists who constantly pull the low, powerful pedal stops when playing thorough-bass. Such overbearing accompaniments played by self-indulgent organists, Niedt complains, spoil pieces of delicate affect: "A bad habit has been gaining ground with several organists, i.e., they

---

[31] Buxtehude's only surviving freestanding ostinato works are the two *Ciaconas*, BuxWV 159 and 160 and the Passacaglia, BuxWV 161. Only two ground basses appear within Buxtehude's other *pedaliter* works – in the *Praeludia*, BuxWV 137 and BuxWV 148. There is also a ground bass in the *manualiter* Toccata, BuxWV 165.

Example 3.11   Dieterich Buxtehude, *Praeludium* in C, BuxWV 137, bars 74–76

can neither live nor play ... unless the sixteen-foot pedal always drones along. [The] pedal is tortured ... and trodden upon incessantly, to make it buzz and boom."[32] Why does Niedt indulge in one of his characteristic diatribes just here, when he admits that it is not directly related to the topic under consideration? Perhaps because he knows from experience that the *ciacona* offers the perfect medium for the expression of the pedal's power – a simple pattern made lofty by the full tonal resources of the north-German organ. In the case of an affecting aria, this impulse should be suppressed in the name of taste and expression; but in the *ciacona* for solo organ it can be indulged without restraint.

Nowhere is this controlling influence of the feet insisted on more jubilantly than in the *ciacona* of BuxWV 137. The central fugue is separated from the *ciacona* by a few bars of long-held chords which provide a platform for showy runs; only a rumble of sixteenth-notes in the pedal disturbs the long pedal point on A, and inevitably the progression of sonorities gravitates towards C Major. Out of the cadence to the home key at bar 75 bursts the *ciacona* theme, the feet throwing off the shackles of harmonic stasis with a vigor only they can supply (see Example 3.11). Whether the "Presto" marking for the *ciacona* goes back to Buxtehude cannot be known for sure; but this indication confirms the exuberance inherent in the octave leap and subsequent *superjectio* figure, both of which refer back to the opening pedal solo. One could imagine, even have expected, a second fugue with the same theme as the ostinato; as Niedt – among others – shows, such themes were generically polymorphous, readily put to various purposes at the hands and feet of a skilful organist.[33] The fact that we hear the feet alone for the rest of bar 75 suggests a ground bass, though for a moment the possibility remains that this will be a fugue built from the bottom up.[34] The ostinato is then confirmed in the

[32] F. E. Niedt, *Musicalischer Handleitung dritter und letzter Theil* (Hamburg: Benjamin Schiller's heirs, 1717); English trans., *The Musical Guide*, trans. Pamela Poulin and Irmgard Taylor (Oxford: Clarendon Press, 1989), p. 158.

[33] *Ibid.*, pp. 155–163.

[34] The second fugue of the *Praeludium* in G minor, BuxWV 150, begins (at bar 90) with a pedal statement of the subject, which could just as easily have been an ostinato bassline.

Example 3.12   Dieterich Buxtehude, *Praeludium* in C, BuxWV 137, bars 95–97

next bar when the hands join in with chords rather than in imitation of the pedal material. That this motive begins the *ciacona* alone brings the long-term, call it formal, association into relief; this mini-solo is heard twice more at regular intervals in the course of the *ciacona* (bars 87 and 96), each time after four passes through the cycle. At these moments the manuals defer to the ostinato, the hands brusquely silenced by the feet, most dramatically when the upward arcing flourish of sixteenth-notes at bar 96 disappears as if dispersed into the winds by the thunder below (see Example 3.12). The opening pedal solo echoes through this glorious piece just as it echoes through so many pedal solos written after it. All who want to call themselves organists must follow in these footsteps.

FRUITS OF THE JOURNEY

Bach's eagerness to pursue even more adventurously the path marked out by Buxtehude is clear from the technical perils of the direct descendant of BuxWV 137: Bach's fabled pedal solo in his Toccata in C, BWV 564 took its inspiration from Buxtehude's signal C Major exordium. Bach's exploration of pedal technique must have seemed extraordinary in its time, beginning well within eighteenth-century borders then bursting through them with a breathtaking flamboyance. The thirds between alternating feet are the most familiar engine of pedal motion. The arpeggios in the first half of the solo are technically demanding, but not uncommon in the great north-German *praeludia* of the seventeenth century (see Example 3.13). Coming close on the heels of the broken arpeggios at bar 23 are the thirty-second-note triplets leading to a rare pedal trill in bar 24. Bach then quickly increases the precision required: the three triplets become a sixteenth followed by two thirty-seconds, this time ascending. The snapping dactyls of bars 24 through 26 are, I believe, unprecedented in the north-German pedal solo, and require either the use of the heel or, if the organist opts to use only the toes, crossing of the feet.

   With these difficulties now overcome, the crux of the piece still lies ahead. It begins at bar 28 with a fiendish run based on the triplet figure first tested ten bars earlier; this final terrifying plunge starts from c1 – the

Example 3.13   J. S. Bach, pedal solo from Toccata in C, BWV 564, bars 13–32

highest note on many eighteenth-century pedalboards – and falls an octave-and-a-half, the precipitous descent finally halted by a turn (which includes sixteenth to thirty-second note dactylic rhythms) back up to the dominant G. Midway through bar 30 a leap up a seventh after the dotted eighth on the dominant (this dotted eighth seems longer than it is, coming directly after such exertions) begins a trill that accelerates into the double termination of the group of eight (!) thirty-seconds before the series of rhythmically and melodically jagged leaps down the octave to low G at the end of bar 31. As the hands enter to make the cadence to the tonic, the left foot stretches down to the low C, the lowest note on the organ, not heard since the pedal-point rumbling intermittently below the manual flourishes which open the Toccata. The final sprint to the finish of the solo, which begins with a long

Example 3.14   Openings of Dieterich Buxtehude, Ciacona in C minor, BuxWV 159 and
J. S. Bach, Passacaglia in C minor, BWV 582

(a) BuxWV 159, bars 1–4

(b) BWV 582, bars 1–15

stretch of falling triplets at bar 29 and concludes with the low C in bar 32, spans two octaves, covering the entire range of most eighteenth-century German pedalboards – it is strenuous stuff.

Bach's long walk had brought back with it not only new lessons in the art of the pedal solo, but in the ostinato as well. Perhaps like Mendelssohn "walking pedal passages" around Leipzig, Bach was similarly engaged over some of the more than 200 miles home, his feet improvising solos and chaconnes as they carried him across the countryside. A long walk gives one lots of time to think and to practice in novel ways what one has learned. In addition to the pedal-oriented elements of solo and ground bass that frame BuxWV 137, the "Andreas Bach Buch" contains two Buxtehude Chaconnes (BuxWV 159 and 160) and a Passacaglia (BuxWV 161) by him; the first of these is in C minor and has a theme not so unlike that of Bach's only essay in the genre, also in that key, and perhaps the last piece copied into the manuscript (see Examples 3.14a and 3.14b). Of course, Buxtehude's theme is half the length of Bach's. These Buxtehude ground basses were probably among the treasures with which the traveler, Bach, traipsed back from Lübeck.[35] Bach's own Passacaglia takes its place fittingly in his brother's manuscript volume, where the ostinato works by Buxtehude are collected.[36] If source-critical information is to be believed, Bach's Passacaglia could have been composed very soon after his return from Lübeck – as early as 1706 – though perhaps some years later;[37] the earlier dating would be a remarkable testament to the power with which the young Bach, only three years into his professional career as an organist, explodes the generic guidelines he brought back with him from Lübeck, and, indeed, those he had already internalized through earlier study of keyboard ostinatos.

In Buxtehude's ground basses the feet almost always stay their course without significant detour; there can be modulations to other key areas, and the manuals sometimes take over the ground bass theme, giving the pedal a rest and providing a change of texture. But the feet do not elaborate the theme; they are dependable, if seemingly uncreative. Bach's Passacaglia sets itself free from these constraints. Indeed, a new role for the feet is announced with the unlikely solo that begins the piece: just the theme alone, without the manual harmonizations that mark the opening of Buxtehude's ground basses. The unaccompanied opening is unexampled in organ ground basses of the period: it is only because of the definitive status of Bach's Passacaglia that we are so used to the exposed ostinato statement. If rewritten to accord with Buxtehude's approach, Bach's Passacaglia would begin on the third beat of bar 8; in Buxtehude's chamber vocal works the ground bass can be delivered alone at the outset of a section of a piece, but always with continuo accompaniment filling out the harmonies above. To add chords to Bach's opening pedal exposition of the passacaglia theme would be ridiculous; the point of this provocatively naked solo statement is not only to draw attention to the ensuing welter of invention, but also to emphasize the controlling presence of the pedal: heard alone for eight long bars, the feet set out the rules of the game. This is not a bravura pedal solo like those that begin Bach's Toccata in C, BWV 564 or his Prelude in C, BWV 531, but rather a statement about pedal authority and independence, which will be expressed in startling ways over the course of the piece.

But to provide the foundation is also confining; ruling in this rigid way is to limit possibility and Bach's feet will not be content with a role that is

---

[35] BWV 582 is entered upside down in the middle of the manuscript, MB Lpz III.8. For a list of contents of the manuscript see Robert Hill, *Keyboard Music from the Andreas Bach Book and the Möller Manuscript* (Cambridge, Massachusetts: Harvard University Press, 1991), pp. xxxvii–xlvi. The theme of BWV 582 shows a still closer resemblance to that of the *Christe* from the second mass of André Raison's *Premier Livre d'Orgue* (Paris, 1688).

[36] A *ciacona* in D by Pachelbel is also in the Andreas Bach Book. See Hill, *Keyboard Music from the Andreas Bach Book and the Möller Manuscript*, p. xlii.

[37] Hans-Joachim Schulze, *Studien zu Bach-Überlieferung im 18. Jahrhundert* (Leipzig: Peters, 1984), p. 50. Schulze favors the dating between 1706 and 1712, Robert Hill posits the timeframe of 1708 to 1713; see his *Keyboard Music from the Andreas Bach Book and the Möller Manuscript*, p. xxii.

Example 3.15   J. S. Bach Passacaglia in C minor, BWV 582, bars 39–46

Example 3.16   Dieterich Buxtehude, *Ciacona* in E minor, BuxWV 160, bars 101–104

in one sense foundational, but in another subordinate. After only three variations involving the manuals, the feet begin to decorate the ostinato line by picking up on the invention floated first in the soprano in bar 40 in the bridge from the fourth to the fifth variation (see Example 3.15). Increasingly, the pedal asserts its right to become more active in the elaboration of the theme. Buxtehude himself had done this sort of thing in organ ostinatos, as in the pedal solo from the E minor *Ciacona* (Example 3.16). After three more literal restatements in Bach's Passacaglia, the pedal again joins in with the hands, this time with a *figura corta*, rather than the dactyls of the feet's previous intervention.

When Bach has the theme itself migrate to the upper voice, first in a transparent *bicinium* with a running left hand and no pedal, one could well suspect on hearing the piece for the first time that the passacaglia format will be subject to considerable experiment, even fundamental transformation

Example 3.17   J. S. Bach, Passacaglia in C minor, BWV 582, bars 88–100

(see Example 3.17). The transfer of the ostinato to another voice confirms that the ground bass is being treated as a *cantus firmus*, an abstract and independent entity no longer confined to the lowest voice of the harmonic texture. Freed from its role as guardian of the ostinato, the pedal then jumps into this *bicinium* as an accompanimental voice, with the back-and-forth descending figure of *Wir Glauben all*, while the theme is heard unadorned in the soprano. This inversion of the harmonic structure is also something new in the history of organ ostinatos with independent pedal; more active than ever before after their eight-bar silence, the feet threaten to stride off into another piece and pull the passacaglia with them. As if to quell this fear – though as always one immediately suspects an ulterior motive – Bach gives the next three variations to the hands alone, concluding this group with wispy arpeggios, monophonically outlining the harmony in the least-cluttered figurative fashion. When the pedal comes in again at bar 128 it resumes its original, undecorated form, and remains faithful to the barest ostinato for the duration of the passacaglia, as if to make us believe that the centrifugal tendencies of Bach's invention had been quieted – that the piece will end as a passacaglia should, with the feet moving inexorably on their predetermined course at the lowest tier of the harmony according to the plan laid out at the beginning (see Example 3.18).

This apparent return to decorum and tradition proves illusory; in retrospect it seems almost like a decoy – a cover for the unexpected fugue, unsanctioned by the dictates of the genre of the passacaglia, that breaks out after the massive cadence in bars 167–168 following the final pass through the ostinato in the pedal (see Example 3.19). Yet the two-part invertible counterpoint that begins at the point marked "Thema fugatum" does not unambiguously signal a fugue right away, since the passacaglia theme is present in the home key in the upper voice, an inverting maneuver Bach has previously demonstrated. Even if the energetic countersubject implies a new level of polyphonic propulsion and intent, the first three bars of this fugal half of the piece are still just an elaboration of the theme (Example 3.19, bars 180–185). It is only with the iteration of the theme as a fugal answer in the soprano transposed to G minor at bars 173–174 and with the same countersubject with which the fugue began that we can no longer mistake Bach's intention to renovate the genre of the passacaglia. When the feet enter they do so again with the stately ostinato theme, perhaps making one more gesture towards cyclic stability – another feint towards safety with the passacaglia bass still in its traditional role. But then the pedal vaults forward with the countersubject on the way to a cadence in G minor. After an intervening rest of one-and-a-half bars, the feet take off with a rollicking back-and-forth, using the typical patterns found in Buxtehude's pedal solos, Bach's *Wir glauben all* and so many other striding figures. Although they will take up the subject twice more – once in G minor, once in F minor – the feet will not allow themselves to be reined in. They are off and running.

This destabilizing of the ostinato's grip in favor of the democracy of fugue in which all voices are equal gives rise to some exhilarating moments of pure freedom. The feet reach a furious pitch below the parallel manual trills in right and left hands at bars 259–260, a passage which seems to open up a fissure in the landscape of the piece, as the pedal surges up, then down, the manuals holding on above but shaking frantically (see Example 3.20). Emerging from this turmoil, the pedal runs for the finish in a breathless contrapuntal climax predominantly made up of sixteenth-notes with many wide leaps and right-left alternating patterns, topped off with a

Example 3.18   J. S. Bach, Passacaglia in C minor, BWV 582, bars 120–135

touch of double pedal at the last of the series of confirmatory plagal cadences in bars 277 to the end following the shattering Neapolitan chord in bar 275 and the quickly discharged perfect cadence from bars 276 to 277. The toppling of the Passacaglia's regime by the revolutionary outbreak of the

Example 3.19   End of Passacaglia and first section of Fugue from J. S. Bach,
Passacaglia in C minor, BWV 582, bars 161–196

fugue is a declaration of the rights of the pedal as an equal in the discourse of
polyphony, pursuing the permutations of subject and countersubject with the
rigor and energy of the manuals. As a consequence, when the feet are asked to
do what the hands do, the music becomes richer, bigger, more difficult.

Example 3.19 (cont.)

After a geographical journey undertaken, as the Obituary stressed, by foot, it seems entirely fitting that Bach's feet would transform the genre of the passacaglia; BWV 582 began as a contained, even constrained opening with feet alone seeming to accept their supporting role, a harmonic

Example 3.20   Trills and tumultuous rush to finish of J. S. Bach, Passacaglia in C minor,
BWV 582, bars 258–282

foundation for manual variation. But the fugue turns the piece into a manifesto of pedal independence. While we admire the genre-busting intelligence, the contrapuntal acumen, the endless capacity for variation and invention above an ostinato pattern, the player experiences the piece as

Example 3.20   (cont.)

a long crescendo of the body, pursuing greater rates of speed and higher levels of physical activity. Both the epochal pedal solo of the Toccata in C and the fugal insurrection of the Passacaglia demonstrate that Bach would – to continue our metaphor of the walk – venture farther and perhaps faster than his predecessor, Buxtehude, across limitless fields. That both pieces walk, even run, towards their new musical goals is more than just a fitting tribute to Bach's journeys: had Bach not walked to Lübeck this music would never have been written in this way. The modern organist recreates the movement of Bach the walker each time he plays, marveling at where those feet take him, to places that were still unmapped in the early eighteenth century.

A MORAL QUEST

Bach brought back from his months of apprenticeship in Lübeck more than a renewed understanding of virtuosic display for feet alone and of the potential of the ground bass. Another stop on the itinerary of the long walk was a confrontation with the chorale prelude. While this fundamental organ genre could take a wide array of shapes, it was not, according to most commentators, concerned with individual glory and personal display but rather was directed towards shared religious devotion and the greater good. The chorale prelude required "modesty" [*Bescheidenheit*], as Mattheson put it, for without this the organist would be unable to inspire the congregation to pious, heartfelt singing.[38] The chorale was the genre most associated with the devout, circumspect attitudes of everyday people; it was held to be the essence of the organist's art, the core of his craft.

The long walk apparently changed Bach's service-playing; when he returned from Lübeck his chorale preludes and hymn accompaniments, so crucial to the Arnstadt liturgy, were different. At a February 21, 1706 meeting of the Arnstadt Consistory, the body that oversaw religious life in the town, Bach was both rebuked for his long absence and for musical developments in his style that, according to the most obvious inference to be made from the coincidence of the two reprimands, had been a result of the trip that had kept him away so long. The Consistory noted that it had reproved the young organist, "for having made many curious variations in the chorale, and mingled many strange tones in it, and for the fact that the congregation has been confused by it."[39] Chided for having given too free a rein to his imagination, Bach then adopted a sullen and defensive musical posture: "The organist Bach had previously played rather too long, but after his attention had been called to it by the Superintendent, he had at once fallen into the other extreme and made it too short." While Bach's employers and members of his congregation were apparently not overjoyed with the fruits of his travels, the young organist had come back initially emboldened, before becoming resentful that this knowledge gained from his "wandering" had been thought unhelpful, even intrusive. The Arnstadt Consistory and congregation did not initially perceive Bach's expanded musical vision as an enrichment, and it seems clear the willful Bach was not terribly subtle in exhibiting the new facets of his art.

In spite of the apparently rocky public reception of these experiments, his first students began coming to study with Bach within a few years of his return from Lübeck. The starting point of Bach's pedagogical program in teaching, both the chorale prelude and the art of organ playing, is the *Orgelbüchlein*, which may have been begun as early as 1708, but was largely assembled in 1712 and 1713.[40] The title-page of the autograph promises to help the beginner learn to develop a chorale in "diverse ways" and "to acquire facility in the study of the pedal since in the chorales [in the collection] the pedal is treated as wholly obbligato."[41] Indebted to the Ninth Commandment, the rhymed couplet with which Bach concludes his *Orgelbüchlein* dedication is close in spirit and practical effect to the notion of hospitality so crucial to the traveler:

---

[38] Mattheson, *Der vollkommene Capellmeister*, p. 473.
[39] Translation based on *NBR*, 46; *BD*, 2: 19–21.
[40] Russell Stinson, *Bach: The Orgelbüchlein* (Oxford University Press, 1999), pp. 15–17.
[41] " . . . anbey auch sich im *Pedal studio* zu *habilitiren*, indem in solchen darinne befindlichen Choralen das Pedal gantz obligat tractiret wird." *BD*, 1: 214. *NBR*, 80.

> Dem höchsten Gott allein zu Ehren,
> dem Nächsten, draus sich zu belehren.
>
> In Praise of the Almighty's will
> and for my neighbor's greater skill.[42]

This language echoes through the article in Zedler's *Lexicon* on "Being useful and of service to your neighbor" [*Förderlich und dienstlich seyn dem Nächsten*],[43] which, citing the usual biblical passages, retails the core values of not coveting your neighbor's wealth (nor, presumably, his wife), and helping him to prosper materially and ethically. Bach's injunction to the user of the *Orgelbüchlein* partakes of the same altruistic impulse, offering knowledge to those willing to make the effort to learn from it: it is a little book that can fit easily in the rucksack, and whose viaticum can sustain one through an entire lifetime of musical journeys. The individual acts of hospitality – the herring and other kindnesses not taken up by organ lore – that allowed Bach to make it through his many walks then made it possible for him in turn to contribute to the musical and moral health of his friends and neighbors, and especially his students and family. The *Orgelbüchlein* dedication can be read as a reflection on the ideal of hospitality towards the traveling craftsman, as the youthful wanderer Bach repays with great profits the initial, anonymous donations that made his musical journeys and growth possible.

In her influential and illuminating literary studies of the Bible, Mary Ellen Chase traces recurring metaphors of the feet in the Old Testament.[44] She hypothesizes that their special significance derives from the importance of movement to a nomadic people, most famously in the escape from Egypt. The feet literally moved them, and then became symbols of spiritual aspiration, of the religious journey towards the Promised Land and towards God. The Old Testament, which Bach read scrupulously, is filled with walking. Bach owned a copy of Heinrich Bünting's widely reprinted and translated *Itinerarium Sacrae Scripturae*, the first part of which detailed "the travels of patriarchs, judges, kings, prophets, princes, etc. reckoned according to German miles."[45] Judging from this book alone, biblical walking could well have been an important topic of study for Bach. The beginning of Bünting's chapter on "The Travels of Abraham" gives a good sense of the author's approach:

---

[42] The rhymed translation comes from *NBR*, 80.
[43] Zedler, *Universal-Lexicon*, vol. IX, cols. 1409–1410.
[44] Mary Ellen Chase, *Life and Language in the Old Testament* (New York: Norton, 1955), pp. 122–134.
[45] Heinrich Bünting, *Itinerarium Sacrae Scripturae* (Magdeburg: Ambrosius Kirchner, 1589), p. 73. English trans. taken from *The Travels of the Holy Patriarchs, Prophets, Judges, Kings, Our Saviour Christ and his Apostles* (London: Basset, 1682), pp. 56–57. See Robin A. Leaver, *Bach's Theological Library* (Neuhausen-Stuttgart: Hänssler-Verlag, 1983), p. 79. After its original publication in 1582, the book appeared in many subsequent editions from the late sixteenth to the early eighteenth centuries.

1. Abraham went out of his own Country of *Ur* in *Cheldea*, to the City of *Haran* in *Mesopotamia*, which is 376 miles.
2. From *Haran*, by God's commandment he went to *Sichem* which is 400 miles.
3. From *Sichem* he went to the Plain and Wood of *Mamre*, to the Hill between *Bethel* and *Hay*, which is 28 miles.

The chapter lists all fifteen of Abraham's journeys referred to in Genesis, and concludes "that all the Travels of the Patriach *Abraham* were 1794 miles." These were trips over great distances that must have had particular resonance for the champion walker Bach. Bünting places all towns and important sites geographically according to their distance in miles from Jerusalem. As Chase also points out, the most pervasive and enduring images of the Old Testament depict Jerusalem as the eternal city and the ultimate goal of the journey towards God. She cites the Second Isaiah, for whom Zion, the easternmost hill of Jerusalem, is the place where God's feet are. One walks on one's own feet to the feet of God, and sings their praises: "How beautiful upon the mountains/Are the feet of him that bringeth good tidings." (Isaiah 52:7)

The penultimate setting from the *Orgelbüchlein*, a project never completed by Bach, treats the chorale *Alle Menschen müssen sterben* (*All men must die*), a funeral hymn associated in Bach's time with texts about the "Heavenly Jerusalem."[46] It is a piece that embodies the idea of a journey, and does so using a pedal motion akin to walking – a *figura corta* of three sixteenth-notes alternating between the feet (in the pattern right-left-right), and followed by two eighth-notes which stride across wider intervals; except for the last two pedal notes in bar 1, these are always played with the left foot and then the right (see Example 3.21). In the sixth of the seven verses the chorale describes eternal life as the gleaming heavenly city one travels towards, a vision encapsulated in the image of Jerusalem. The sixth verse runs:

> O Jerusalem, du Schöne,
> ach, wie hell glänzest du!
> Ach, wie lieblich Lobgetöne
> hört man da in sanfter Ruh'!
> O der großen Freud' und Wonne!
> Jetzund gehet auf die Sonne,
> jetzund gehet an der Tag,
> der kein Ende nehmen mag.
>
> Jerusalem, you fair one,
> oh, how brightly you shine!

[46] Johann Anastasius Freylinghausen, *Geistreiches Gesang-Buch* (Halle: Verlegung des Waysenhauses, 1741), pp. 968–990. *Alle Menschen müssen sterben* is the first chorale in this section of the chorale book.

Example 3.21   Pedal figure, J. S. Bach, *Alle Menschen müssen sterben*, BWV 643, bars 1–4

> Oh, how sweet the sounds of praise
> that one hears in gentle peace!
> Now rises the sun,
> now begins the day,
> that will have no end.

In the chorale's opening verse, the transitory nature of earthly existence and the decay of the flesh give way to a vision of a transfigured body among the saved after the travels are over, and Jerusalem is eventually reached in the penultimate strophe just cited:

> Alle Menschen müßen sterben,
> alles Fleisch vergeht wie Heu;
> was da lebet, muß verderben,
> soll es anders werden neu.
> Dieser Leibe, der muß verwesen,
> zu der großen Herrlichkeit
> die den Frommen ist bereit.

> All men must die,
> all flesh flies away like hay;
> what now lives, must rot,
> if it is to be renewed.
> This body must decompose,
> to the great glory,
> which awaits the blessed.

Modern players and listeners may find incongruous the apparent disjunction between the fatalistic assertion of human mortality in the chorale's first line and the buoyant affect of Bach's setting. The chorale melody itself exudes triumph, and the joyful acceptance of death as the final leg of the journey towards redemption is amplified by Bach's condensed, energetic figuration; the *cantus firmus*, unadorned in the soprano except for the final flourish of ornament in the last bar, is carried forward by the pressing elaboration below. The direction of earthly life is towards heaven. The familiar *suspirans* sixteenth-notes followed by two eighths alternating between the feet are the most utilitarian of pedal gestures and are shared with the opening of the C Major pedal solos by Buxtehude and Bach and by the most exuberant passages from Bach's Passacaglia. The pedal carries the piece towards its destination, the heavenly Jerusalem, without hesitation or doubt. But this chorale prelude is undeniably an earthly piece as well; the pedal motive behaves as if undertaking that most earthbound of activities, walking. The music literally embodies a fundamental paradox: a physical gesture so familiar in the limbs is meant to describe the demise of the body that plays it.[47] Musical walking becomes an exercise in spiritual recreation; to master this piece is to sense what the new limbs in heaven will feel like after life's final walk and the transformation of the depleted body. Whether Bach thought of the piece in these figurative terms or not, he surely enjoyed its physicality. In irrepressible counterpoint to its mortal text, *Alle Menschen müssen sterben* exudes youth and energy. That the piece is part of the *Orgelbüchlein*, a collection whose dedication advertises its higher moral purpose, helps confirm the relevance of walking to its practices and purpose: Bach's own commitment to his craft, one fueled by his determination and by the goodwill of others along his far-flung musical and geographic route, results in a piece that extols the very commitment to the organ that was reflected in his walking; the *Orgelbüchlein* pays back the investment made in the organist by others with an embodiment of the ultimate rewards of heaven. The value of learning to play and to devise obbligato lines for the feet comes not only in the related disciplines of performance and composition, but in preparing the organist and his listeners for death.

In later life Bach could not have walked as much as he had as a young man. Biographical documents relate that when Bach tried to meet Handel in Halle in 1719 he took the coach there; he also went by coach to Berlin in 1747 when in his sixties to play for Frederick the Great. That he availed himself of this mode of transportation, one he was unable to afford in his youth, demonstrated that he had arrived materially and professionally; he was a success. For his engagements as organist and organ expert he did not walk, as he had done when he was learning the art and science of his profession. The metaphorical journey on foot and the real one with the pedaling feet at the organ continued to the end. The pedal solos of his youthful *praeludia*

---

[47] For a discussion of eighteenth-century Lutheran views of instrumental music in heaven used by the transfigured body, see David Yearsley, *Bach and the Meanings of Counterpoint*, pp. 28–32.

disappear from his mature works: unbounded fantasy and physical freedom give way to tight formal constructions and demonstrations of large-scale organization. The seemingly inexorable repetition and variation of the Passacaglia – devoid of self-serving pedal solos – and the spontaneous eruption of its fugue might be taken to signal brilliant youth, or perhaps the departure from it. The carefully planned schemes of the later years forsake the improvisational quality of the road trip; the physical spontaneity of the detour yields to the carefully planned itinerary. The coach follows the road, rather than cutting directly across the field. In 1713 or so, when Bach composed *Alle Menschen müssen sterben*, his years of apprenticeship were over. The long walk became part of family lore and his historical legacy; it remained in his limbs when he played the organ, not only recalling the past, but also bringing to mind encouraging thoughts of the final journey still ahead.

CHAPTER 4

The pedal in the cosmopolitan age of travel

A GERMAN ORGAN ON THE GRAND TOUR

An abiding sense of inferiority pervaded German music culture in the seventeenth and eighteenth centuries: nearly ubiquitous was the fear that foreign music was better. This self-doubt spawned affronted defenses of native musical values,[1] even as it colored the adventurousness that sent countless musicians to France and especially to Italy in search of that which could not be found at home: the latest musical fashions of composition and performance heard in the richness of their native environments. The dominance of the French language and of French fashion at German courts in the seventeenth and eighteenth centuries, the taste for French dancing, the rise of Italian opera and instrumental genres such as the sonata and concerto, and the influx of foreign virtuosos all produced a cultural trade deficit between Germany and the European south. Constantly confronted with the bald truth that theirs was a debtor nation in the marketplace of musical ideas, German musicians reflexively measured their worth against foreign standards.

No account of German inadequacy is as unstinting as that found in Johann Joachim Quantz's *Versuch einer Anweisung, die Flöte traversiere zu spielen* (*Essay on Playing the Flute*) published simultaneously in 1752 in German and in French, the latter being the language of the Berlin court where Quantz was employed. His education and travels funded by the cosmopolitan Saxon court rich in foreign music and musicians, Quantz had made a grand musical tour between 1724 and 1727, with the longest part of his stay spent in Italy and shorter periods in France and England. In Quantz's seminal treatise the Italians and French lead, the Germans follow. The Italian music is "unrestrained, sublime, lively, expressive, profound, and majestic"; the French are "lively, expressive, natural, pleasing and comprehensible."[2] Yes, Quantz lists some of the national faults to which

---

[1] See, for example, F. W. Marpurg, *Critischer Musikus an der Spree* (Berlin: Haude and Spener, 1749–1750; reprint, New York: Olms Verlag, 1970), p. 354.

[2] J. J. Quantz, *Versuch einer Anweisung, die Flöte traversiere zu spielen* (Berlin: Voss, 1752; reprint, Leipzig: Deutscher Verlag für Musik, 1983), p. 323; trans. as *On Playing the Flute*, trans. Edward R. Reilly, 2nd edn. (New York: Schirmer, 1985), p. 334.

the French and Italians had been prone and the tendencies toward stagnation and decline to be witnessed in both nations in the eighteenth century. But these petty foibles in no way compare with the abuse Quantz dishes out to his fellow Germans, whose traditional style he describes as "flat, dry, meager, and paltry."[3] Obsessed with rules and slavishly correct in their compositions, Germans needed to go to Italy to break free from all that, just as Quantz himself had done. In Quantz's telling, the Italians would seem entirely justified in having once thought of all Germans as practitioners of the *gusto barbaro* – the barbarous style.[4]

But there is one area of European culture where, according to Quantz, Germany has long reigned supreme: in everything to do with the organ. The famed flutist, who encouraged his collection of flute duets to be played on the organ,[5] argues that as early as the middle of the seventeenth century, organist-composers Froberger, Pachelbel, Reincken, Buxtehude, and Bruhns "wrote almost the first very tasteful pieces for their instruments," and they did so without relying on foreign influences from the south.[6] The German organ art was then brought "to its greatest perfection" by the "admirable [*bewundernswürdig*] Johann Sebastian Bach," whom Quantz himself had seen perform at the Potsdam Palace in 1747 when he improvised on the Royal Theme in front of Frederick the Great and his stable of star musicians. The next day Quantz was certainly among the large audience that heard Bach play the organ at the nearby Heiliggeistkirche.[7] Among the few German musicians Quantz mentions in his long treatise, organists are held up as the greatest indigenous musical heroes. In his account of the German organ tradition, Quantz is expressing an article of faith: only at the King of Instruments did Germany hold sway over its European musical counterparts.

While Germany's cultural trade deficit extended far beyond music, pride in their organs armed Germans for their confrontation with the other European arts, both at home and on the Grand Tour. One of the most popular German travel guides of the mid-eighteenth century was Johann Georg Keyßler's *Neueste Reisen durch Deutschland, Böhmen, Ungarn, die Schweiz, Italien und Lothringen* (*Latest Trips through Germany, Bohemia, Hungary, Switzerland, Italy, and Lorraine*), which appeared first in 1740 but was subsequently reprinted several times both in German and in English translation; this thick book gives a good impression of Germans' own view of their standing in the cultural geography of Europe. On his visit to Naples, the usual southern terminus of the Grand Tour, Keyßler catalogs the city's immense cultural riches. At Monte Oliveto, for example, the church elicits a

[3] *Ibid.*, p. 325; trans., p. 335.   [4] *Ibid.*, p. 331; trans., p. 340.
[5] See David Yearsley, *Bach and the Meanings of Counterpoint* (Cambridge University Press, 2002), p. 101.
[6] Quantz, *Versuch*, p. 329; trans., p. 339.   [7] *Ibid.*

rapturous account of its altars, ornate Bibles, and family chapels filled to overflowing with beautiful objects. But when Keyßler's attention turns to the organ he is conspicuously underwhelmed, an attitude that is all the more marked coming so soon after the unrestrained praise of the church's other artworks: "The organ of the church cost 3,000 scudi and people here make a big deal out of it."[8] After blithely dismissing the Monte Oliveto organ as merely a decorative object, Keyßler then proceeds to a grand statement about Germany's dominance at the instrument: "The outstanding organs alone, which one finds in Germany, surpass all the foreign ones, and this has attained for Germany – both for the makers of this musical instrument, as well as for the artists who know truly how to play it – a great advantage over all other nations."[9] It is the organ that puts Germany on the cultural map.

Likewise, the preface of Joachim Christoph Nemeitz's *Nachlese besonderer Nachrichten von Italien* (*Selection of Special Reports from Italy*), first published in Leipzig in 1726, acknowledges that Italy triumphs over all other nations in architecture, painting, and music; birthplace of the great sculptors and painters, Italy is also the "storehouse" [*Magazin*] which has supplied "the whole of Europe with Capellmeisters, Castrati, female singers, and other virtuosi."[10] While Nemeitz readily grants Italy overall superiority in the musical arts, he assures his readers that "our nation surpasses all others when it comes to the organ."[11] The organists of the Italian peninsula are belittled as light and frivolous: Italian organs are commented on only for the lavish decorations and cute toy stops, such as nightingales and cuckoos.[12] The organ bolstered those preparing themselves for the Grand Tour or otherwise trying to get a vicarious sense of it through the travel literature. In the context of Germany's collective inferiority complex with respect to Italian art and music, the organ alone provided Germans with the joys of smugness.

We see these attitudes reflected in the travel diary of J. S. Bach's sometime employer Prince Leopold of Cöthen, who visited several organs in villas (and in their surrounding gardens) on his tour of Italy in 1712.[13] These small instruments were equipped with the typical bird sounds of Italian organs; prompted by the travel literature he used to guide him through Italy, Leopold saw these organs more as novelty items than as

---

[8] Johann Georg Keyßler, *Neueste Reisen durch Deutschland, Böhmen, Ungarn, die Schweiz, Italien und Lothringen*, 2nd revised edn., 2 vols. (Hanover: Heirs of Nicolai Förster and Son, 1751), vol. II, p. 826. Several editions in Germany, and in translation in French and English.

[9] *Ibid.*

[10] Joachim Christoph Nemeitz, *Nachlese besonderer Nachrichten von Italien, als ein Supplement von Misson, Burnet, Addisson, und Andern* (Leipzig: Johann Friedrich Gleditsch, 1726), preface and p. 427.

[11] *Ibid.*, p. 428.   [12] *Ibid.*, p. 14.

[13] *Reise des Erb-Prinzen Leopold zu Anhalt-Cöthen nach Holland vom Jahre 1710* (Köthen: Historisches Museum, Register 1734, Inventar-Nr. VS 462), pp. 132, 140, 161–162. The diary was written by Leopold's Page, Emanuel Leberecht von Zehmen. See Günther Hoppe, "Bach-Gedenkstätte Schloss Köthen: Kleiner Führer durch die Ausstellung", (Cöthener Bach-Heft, Nr. 9), 27 (viewed through Herzog August Bibliothek Digital Library at http://diglib.hab.de/wdb.php?dir=mss/ed000004).

instruments fit for proper music-making. Only one church organ is remarked on in the diary: that in Santa Maria Maggiore in Trent, praised by Leopold as a "beautiful and large organ" [*schöne und grosse Orgel*].[14] Trent was the first Italian city encountered by tourists after coming over the Alps from Innsbruck, and the lavishly decorated organ in the city's Santa Maria Maggiore was an important destination for tourists, an artistic triumph visually and sonically, as it had been from its completion in the 1530s by a German builder (see Chapter 2). Prince Leopold duly visited this organ with a travel guide – probably Maximilien Misson's *Noveau voyage d'Italie* – in hand; the Santa Maria Maggiore organ was an important sight to be seen according to this popular book, reprinted many times in several languages after it was first published in 1691.[15]

A few decades before Prince Leopold's visit, this same organ had made a showy appearance in Wolfgang Caspar Printz's *Satyrischer Componist*, first published in the 1670s. In the last chapter of the book's two volumes the narrator, Phrynis Mitilenaeus, resumes his picaresque adventures when he is called away from Germany to Italy, indeed to Trent. Finding himself with a day to kill, Phrynis is shown around the city by a German who lives there, and they make their way to Santa Maria Maggiore. The organ astonishes Phrynis, who had not expected to find an instrument so beautifully decorated or boasting such big pedal pipes in the facade. Phrynis learns from his German guide that the early sixteenth-century instrument had recently been restored and enlarged with ten new stops by a builder with the distinctly Italian-sounding name Eugenio Casparini.[16] "My usual curiosity made me ask him who this Casparini was," says Phrynis. "To this [the guide] answered in the following way: He is a German by nationality. Indeed he was born in Sora in Nieder-Lausitz."[17] Printz's pride speaks through the German expatriate character, who, standing on foreign soil,

---

[14] *Ibid.*, 162.

[15] Francois Maximilien Misson, *Nouveau voyage d'Italia, fait en l'année* ... (The Hague: Bulderen, 1691). Misson says that the "organs" in Santa Maria Maggiore are "extraordinarily large," and that they "counterfeited the cries of a great many Animals." Travelers always seemed to comment on the toy stops. Misson takes a dim view of organists' fondness for trickery, as being "unsuitable to the gravity of the place." Quoted from Misson, *A New Voyage to Italy*, 4 vols. (London: Bonwicke *et al.*, 1714), vol. I, p. 181. Nemeitz saw his book as a supplement to Misson and says much the same thing about the organ in Trent. For more on the organ itself, see Renato Lunelli, *Der Orgelbau in Italien*, trans. Carl Elis and Paul Smets (Mainz: Rheingold, 1956), pp. 168–182.

[16] Wolffgang Caspar Printz, *Phrynis Mitylenaeus, oder Satyrischer Componist*, 2 vols. (Dresden, Leipzig: Johann Christoph Mieth und Johann Christoph Zimmermann, 1696), vol. II, p. 224. The *Satyrischer Componist* was first published in three separate volumes in Quedlinburg. (Printz says the organ had thirty-two stops before Casparini added another ten. This massively exaggerates the number of stops on the organ, betraying his Germanic orientation in which forty-stop organs were not unusually large; this would have been more than any other organ on the Italian peninsula.) F. X. Mathias and Joseph Wörsching, *Die Orgelbauer-Familie Silbermann in Straßburg*, ed. Paul Smets (Mainz: Rheingold Verlag, 1960), p. 18. For Printz's own Italian journey see Johann Mattheson, *Grundlage einer Ehren-Pforte* (Hamburg, 1740; modern edn. ed. Max Schneider, Berlin: Liepmannsohn, 1910), p. 267.

[17] Printz, *Satyrischer Componist*, vol. II, p. 224.

extols a fellow countryman, a boy from Brandenburg, who had come to Italy and – in his view – become its best organ builder. In his *Historische Beschreibung der edelen Sing- und Kling-Kunst* of 1690 Printz had praised Bernhard the German, in similar tones of adulation to those he sung in Casparini's name: Bernhard's innovations were not only important musically, but his introduction of the pedal to Italy had also "brought the Germans not a little honor."[18] Bernhard's improvements to the fifteenth-century organ in San Marco were at the time unique in Italy; by the end of the seventeenth century Casparini's instrument in Santa Maria Maggiore was seen to be exceptional because of its independent pedal division. With five stops, one of them a five-rank mixture and two of them reeds, the pedal division was relatively small by north-German standards, but large when compared with "native" Italian instruments with their typical "pulldowns" – the pedal keys perpetually coupled to the manual. Like all the best international exchanges, Eugenio Casparini's engagement with organ-building on the Italian peninsula was mutually enriching. When Casparini returned home to Germany in 1697 to make his most famous organ in Görlitz after more than a half century in Italy, his work was inflected by southern elements; for example, at Görlitz he built an Italian Fiffaro, a detuned, undulating stop. The contract for the Görlitz organ included several stops to be made "as at Trent"; the renown of Casparini's famed Italian organ extended to Silesia and beyond.[19] Large, independent pedal divisions remained a northern ideal, and the massive pedal at Görlitz had twenty stops. While the Trent organ was smaller, its fame was even greater, and its appeal to German tourists easily as intense. The entire exchange between Phrynis and his German guide staged in Printz's *Satyrischer Componist* sounds like the script for a real-life German tourist's visit to the city (Printz had himself been to Santa Maria Maggiore in Trent in the early 1660s, before the Casparini rebuild of 1686–1687;[20] for an image of the Trent organ in the state Printz saw it in in the 1660s, see Figure 2.1). Printz begins his treatise by admitting that he was spurred to write the book because Italy was so much richer in musical treatises than Germany.[21] He ends it with a set-piece of German self-congratulation: in the first Italian city encountered by travelers after coming down from the Brenner Pass stood one of the great monuments to German artistic achievement.[22] For Germans, the Grand Tour in Italy began with a trip to a German organ.

---

[18] Wolfgang Caspar Printz, *Historische Beschreibung der edelen Sing- und Kling-Kunst* (Dresden: Johann Georg, 1690; reprint, Graz: Akademische Druck- und Verlagsanstalt, 1964), p. 114. Presumably taking his cue from Praetorius, Printz also cites Sabellicus as his source.

[19] Peter Williams, *The European Organ 1450–1850* (Bloomington: Indiana University Press, 1966), pp. 142–143.

[20] See Johann Mattheson, *Grundlage einer Ehren-Pforte*, p. 266.

[21] Printz, *Satyrischer Componist*, vol. I, p. 2.

[22] Casparini had also been active in German-speaking Bozen in South Tyrol.

THE PEDAL AND THE LITTLE FINGER

Italy remained the engine of musical fashion in eighteenth-century Europe, but it also offered proof of German dominance at the organ. At numerous places in his voluminous writings, Johann Mattheson would invoke the longstanding notion that it was mastery of the organ that set Germans apart. Musician, critic, and secretary to the British consul in Hamburg, Mattheson was another one of those cosmopolitans who stayed at home. Although he never made it to France or Italy, he was adept in ancient and modern languages, and kept abreast of musical, political, and literary developments across Europe. Among his diverse talents nurtured by an enviable education, Mattheson was also an organist and expert on the organ's history, construction, and literature. His widely disseminated views on musical internationalism and the merits of German contributions to European culture must have been well-known to Quantz, whose own account of national styles shares much with that of his elder Hamburg colleague. In a book published in 1752, the same year as Quantz's *Essay on playing the Flute*, Mattheson repeated views he had first aired in print more than three decades earlier: that all northerners – Germans, Danes, and Swedes – as well as the French, are influenced by the Italians, who lead the way. But he insists that he is not one of those "stiff Germans" who "out of blind prejudice" praise all that is foreign.[23] While he admired the foreign, he could claim that the organ provided the ballast preventing the listing German ship from capsizing under the weight of its ever-growing Italian cargo. Throughout his long life, Mattheson argued for what he called a musical patriotism that recognized the value of foreign influence but defended native values as well.

The organ lay at the center of Mattheson's pride in German culture. While acknowledging the centrality of Italy in other areas of musical life, he contrasted the decline of the Italian organ arts with a literally bold-faced assertion of Germany's preeminence at the King of Instruments:

Concerning finally the best-known and greatest masters of the organ, one can certainly say that **Germany produces the most famous organists**. The fame of Frescobaldi and Pasquini climbed in earlier times over the Alps, but from other Italians one has heard no miracles on the organ. It is indeed curious, that Italy has been and will be at all times a high (lofty) school of music. One sees, however, in the construction [and playing] of their organs, that they do not strive for as much as the Germans.[24] [Mattheson's emphasis]

---

[23] Johann Mattheson, *Philologisches Tresespiel* (Hamburg: Johann Adolph Martin, 1752), p. 98.

[24] Johann Mattheson, *Der vollkommene Capellmeister* (Hamburg: Herold, 1739; reprint, Kassel: Bärenreiter, 1954), p. 479. See also Ernest C. Harriss, *Johann Mattheson's Der vollkommene Capellmeister: a revised translation with critical commentary* (Ann Arbor, Michigan: UMI Research Press, 1981), pp. 860–861. Mattheson also believed that the pedals had been invented at the end of the fifteenth century. *Der vollkommene Capellmeister*, p. 466.

The bold type hammers home the point for anyone harboring the slightest doubt about what all in Germany already knew to be true.

Mattheson goes on to comment condescendingly on the pull-down pedals of Italian organs with their smaller keys and more limited compass. He reminds his readers that Bernhard had once been praised in Venice as the greatest of musicians because he introduced organs with pedal; yet, the current instrument in San Marco had lapsed into a weak and unpleasing state.[25] The attitudes of German superiority reflected in the travel literature are here given powerful formulation in the major work of German music theory of the first half of the eighteenth century. Never having enjoyed a Grand Tour, Mattheson nonetheless makes an armchair visit to the famous organ in Trent in *Der vollkommene Capellmeister*, claiming that "a big deal is made of it."[26] He turns to the instrument directly after claiming that German organists surpassed the Italians. Mattheson then tells his readers how Handel ("Signor Sassone") played the Casparini instrument to the amazement of the organist of Santa Maria Maggiore. Only when one of the two greatest living German organists visited Trent's famous organ could the true potential of that instrument at last be heard.

While Italian and French organs did not provide full opportunities for the German organists, one can be assured that Germans got what they could out of these instruments' smaller pedalboards. When northern virtuosos, chief among them Handel, came to an instrument such as Casparini's with a distinctly German pedal, they doubtless exploited as far as they could the opportunity to demonstrate the German way of playing. Given the assumed German superiority at the organ, the contest between Handel and Scarlatti in Rome in 1708 or 1709 could not have ended otherwise, though its outcome was reported at the end of Handel's life to his biographer John Mainwaring. According to this account Handel was proclaimed the master at the organ, Scarlatti perhaps gaining the edge at the harpsichord. Mainwaring reports that Scarlatti then followed Handel around Italy, learning from his skill at the organ.[27] One of the instruments they may have visited together could have been in Santa Maria Maggiore in Trent. On the Grand Tour of the organ the Saxon was King.

After disparaging Italian organs and organists and then extolling Handel's exploits in Trent, Mattheson produces an alphabetical list of the German organists in his hall of fame. Atop that list – and explicitly placed there out of alphabetical order – stand the famed contemporaries Handel

---

[25] *Ibid.*

[26] "Von der eintzigen Tridentinischen Orgel wird groß Wesen gemacht." This is almost exactly the same phrase Nemeitz uses in his description, which might suggest that, since Mattheson had never been to Trent, he could have had Nemeitz at hand. Mattheson, *Der vollkommene Capellmeister*, p. 479. The "Tridentinische Orgel" referred to by Mattheson must be the one in Santa Maria Maggiore.

[27] John Mainwaring, *Memoirs of the Life of the Late George Frederic Handel* (London, 1760; reprint, Amsterdam, 1964), pp. 59–62.

and Bach: the one had conquered Italian organs and organists (including Scarlatti), while the other had never left German lands, but was a true musical cosmopolitan whose music drew on and transformed influences from France and Italy. That Johann Sebastian Bach never ventured beyond Germany strangely added to his prestige as a German organist, for it was in precisely this role that he was held up by contemporaries as a bulwark against the threatening brilliance of foreign virtuosos. In 1751 Georg Philipp Telemann – who had enjoyed a year in Paris, but had never been to Italy – wrote a poem in honor of his recently deceased friend, J. S. Bach, in which this greatest of organists becomes Germany's answer to long-held Italian superiority in all other realms of instrumental music-making:

> Let Italy go on her virtuosi vaunting
>> Who through the sounding art have there achieved great fame –
> On German soil they also will not be found wanting,
>> Nor can they here be held less worthy of the name.
> Departed Bach! Long since your splendid organ-playing
>> Alone brought you the noble cognomen "the Great."
> And what your pen had writ, the highest art displaying,
>> Did some with joy and some with envy contemplate.[28]

However important Bach's contributions as a composer of vocal and instrumental music may have been for Telemann and others, the largest part of his fame and posthumous legacy rested on his achievements as an organist; it was in this capacity that he came chiefly to exemplify native German values as against foreign imports.

Telemann's poetic opposition between Italian virtuosity and German mastery at the organ is embodied in Bach's concerto transcriptions of Vivaldi concertos (BWV 592–596), where the hands and feet of a lone organist become an orchestra ripping-off speeding passages given in the originals to unencumbered soloists (Examples 4.1a and 4.1b). Bach fills out harmonies and enlivens the bassline, even taking general rests in the third movement (Examples 4.1c and 4.1d) to introduce showy pedal flourishes. Throughout, Bach's emulation of, or perhaps competition with, racing Italian strings involves the entire body in ways that produce full sonorities previously reserved at the organ for grand polyphonic designs: the A minor concerto (BWV 593) divides layered orchestral textures across the limbs. The left foot nonchalantly plucks the bass note on each downbeat and projects the larger, unhurried, harmonic rhythm (see Example 4.2). By contrast, the incessant right foot is edgy and eager, tapping out repeated notes; the passage begins with twelve measures of e1 that could not be

---

[28] *Neu-eröffnete Historische Correspondenz von Curiosis Saxonicis* (Dresden: P. G. Mohrenthalen, 1751), pp. 13–14. Reprinted in F. W. Marpurg (ed.), *Historisch-Kritische Beyträge zu Aufnahme der Musik*, 5 vols. (Berlin: G. A. Lange, 1754–1758), vol. II, p. 561. See *BD*, 3: 6–7. English translation taken from *NBR*, 373–374.

Example 4.1a   Antonio Vivaldi, Concerto in A minor for Two Violins, Op. 3, No. 8, RV 522, first movement, bars 1–7

Example 4.1b   Antonio Vivaldi, Concerto in A minor for Two Violins, Op. 3, No. 8, RV 522, first movement; transcription for organ, J. S. Bach, BWV 593/1, bars 1–7

farther from the independent polyphony of historic German double-pedal writing. The canzona subject of the Bruhns *Praeludium* (see Example 2.8) has here escaped the decorum of polyphonic purpose and become a knocking, textural effect. Bach expands the palette of double pedal to the realm of percussion: drums were found on many Italian organs, and some central-German ones as well. The German organist was capable of discharging the duties of many individual participants in polyphonic concert; but his feet could also spur on the directed frenzy of the eighteenth-century Italian concerto. Above this galloping drone, the left hand provides the energy of high-voltage Italian violin playing, heard in the Vivaldi original in the second violin. The cantabile melody of the first violin is taken by the right hand, which rides above this fast rocking accompaniment, as if concerned not in the least with speed, but only with singing as beautifully as it can. The organist manages to do what the entire group of soloists and continuo did in Vivaldi's Venice; the northern body at the organ bench discharges four discrete but cumulative effects. This division of labor could

Example 4.1c   Antonio Vivaldi, Concerto in A minor for Two Violins, Op. 3, No. 8,
RV 522, third movement, bars 58–63

Example 4.1d   Vivaldi, Op. 3, No. 8, third movement; transcription for organ, J. S. Bach,
BWV 593/3, bars 58–62

only be achieved by organists with vigorously independent feet and hands. While Schlick had sent a gleaming, if unapproachable, demonstration of his unmatched skill to Trent in written form, the influence in Bach's Vivaldi transcription migrates in the other direction: the latest Italian style is

Example 4.2   Bach/Vivaldi, BWV 593/3, bars 85–91

performed with venerable German double pedaling, each of the four limbs doing something quite different.

The competition and cooperation between foreign and native in Bach's Germany might help us reflect anew on the significance of Bach's celebrated organ recitals, reported in the press and crucial to his fame both during his lifetime and after it. Why did these events warrant this kind of coverage and adulation, not only among experts and devotees, but also among the larger populace? Many of Bach's greatest triumphs came in the Saxon capital of Dresden, one of the great international music centers of eighteenth-century Europe. A city glittering with stars, Dresden was also racked by tensions arising between immigrants and natives, foreign musical forms and indigenous ones. In 1720 the Elector, August the Strong, sacked the entire Italian opera ensemble for an insult issuing from the haughty lips of the castrato Senesino aimed at the German Director of Music, Bach's friend Johann David Heinichen. Unwilling to break its expensive addiction to *opera seria* and parallel forms of cultural expression, the court slowly renewed its support for Italian musicians and music over the next decade.

A more harmonious relationship between the foreign and the domestic was sealed in the marriage between another of Bach's Dresden friends, the German Johann Adolph Hasse, and the Italian diva Faustina Bordoni. The pair took up triumphant residence in Dresden in 1731 as Kapellmeister and *prima donna* with the opera *Cleofide*, composed by Hasse and starring Faustina. *Cleofide*, not to mention the more than thirty Dresden operas to follow from Hasse, was a vast spectacle of Italian origin taking place for the benefit of the Catholic court; like the Saxon Electors, who converted from Lutheranism to be able to rule simultaneously as Polish kings, Hasse had become a Roman Catholic in Italy. Bach was in the audience for this epoch-making premiere; he played a concert on the famous Silbermann organ in the Sophienkirche the very next afternoon of September 14, 1731. The opera premiere was not just a fortuitous moment to bring Germany's greatest organist to town; more than that, Bach's concert must have been received by some as an answer to foreign imports, not to say, domination: after a sumptuous Italian opera, Dresden was treated to an indigenous German organ recital. As in Telemann's poem, Bach becomes Germany's answer to Italian opulence; ravishing but superficial, Italian music consisted not of profound and learned fugues, but of light "ditties" [*Liederchen*], as Bach is said to have called the arias he and Wilhelm Friedemann heard in the Dresden opera house – including those of *Cleofide*.[29] Bach's organ works, even his fugues, were crucially influenced by Italian music; but at the organ he was unambiguously German in the way he played the instrument and in the kinds of complicated and demanding music he brought forth from it.

Whereas Vivaldi was a virtual visitor to Germany through his music, other tourists came in the flesh. Bach's preemptive knockout of the touring Louis Marchand in Dresden in 1717 can be read as the triumph of a German organist over a French one: Bach let the competition come to him, then duly vanquished it. According to a story later told by Bach's partisans, Marchand left town under cover of darkness. Although the play-off never happened, Bach's Obituary, written largely by C. P. E. Bach and J. F. Agricola and published in 1754, renders a lasting critical judgment of the respective abilities of the native German and the visiting Frenchman; the authors make a less-than-flattering comparison between Marchand's pandering organ musettes – another kind of "ditty" for Christmas – and Bach's multi-voiced fugues.[30]

Bach's exposure in Germany to the brisk traffic in Vivaldi's music was one example of what could happen when a geographically parochial German organist got hold of the latest imports. But the introduction of new ideas and the changes they encouraged could also threaten to erode dearly held values. The rejection of insipid effects of foreign genres such as Marchand's musettes might well have masked a deeper fear harbored by self-appointed keepers of German standards. Chief among the potential casualties to the onslaught of Italian idioms were not only the stern affect

---

[29] Johann Nikolaus Forkel, *Ueber Johann Sebastian Bachs Leben, Kunst und Kunstwerke* (Leipzig: Hoffmeister & Kühnel, 1802; reprint, Kassel: Bärenreiter, 1999), p. 48; *NBR*, 461.

[30] *NBR*, 301. In fact, Bach seems to have respected Marchand, perhaps not least because of his use of the pedal in his organ works – particularly impressive for a Frenchman. The opening movement, the *Plein jeu* of Marchand's first suite published in 1699 involves the use of double pedal, an almost unexampled technique in France, and by no means easy on the pedalboards of French baroque organs. Bach also learned much from French organ trios. See George Stauffer, "Boyvin, Grigny, D'Anglebert, and Bach's Assimilation of French Classical Organ Music," *Early Music*, 21 (1993), 83–96.

and grave style in German organ-playing, but, more generally, contrapuntal integrity in composition, which at the organ was founded on, and secured by, independent pedal. For the Germans, the organ and organ-playing had the farthest to fall with the catastrophic weakening of its true foundation. One of Bach's greatest admirers, Friedrich Wilhelm Marpurg, argued that the decline of fugue coincided with the rising popularity and influence of fashionable Italian music, which saps the "manly element that should prevail in music." In its place spreads the "rubbish of womanly song," as he put it in his preface to the 1753 edition of the *Art of Fugue*.[31] Accordingly, Marpurg decries the erosion of the strong and independent values of counterpoint, itself most typically associated with the organ. That is not to say that other keyboard instruments are less suited to the *Art of Fugue* or polyphony more generally, but that the organ stands at the pinnacle of contrapuntal accomplishment crowned by Bach's collection.

Mattheson, too, praised the *Art of Fugue* by making this connection between fugal mastery and the organ more explicitly; after stating that the *Art of Fugue* "will astound all French and Italian makers of fugue," Mattheson deploys one of his beloved commercial metaphors in touting the value of Bach's collection: "How would it be if every foreigner and native ventured a Louis d'or on this rarity?" He then moves quickly to what is for him an ineluctable statement of fact: "Germany remains for certain the true land of the organ and fugue."[32] Fugue and the organ are inextricably linked for the Germans and both are international markers of German greatness. This emphatic statement of the obvious comes in the context of a comparison between Italian, French, and German music. While recognizing the dominance of Italian styles, and the lessons in suavity to be learned from the French, Mattheson is clear about what the Germans have to offer: "To be sure, the Italians and French can learn from German composers about pure polyphony, the best way to play thorough bass, firmness of tempo, and sound organ-playing."[33] The Germans are praised again by Mattheson for their "rigorous fugal art" [*arbeitsame Fugenkunst*] and "thorough organ-playing" [*gründliches Orgelspiel*], which were built, as Mattheson so often stressed, on independent pedal-playing and the integrity of the polyphonic parts so timelessly reflected in the *Art of Fugue* and apostrophized by Mattheson. In an increasingly cosmopolitan European scene to which few musicians were indifferent, organists kept German pride and ambition stoked. This is why Quantz goes out of his way to stress the point in a treatise on playing the flute: when comparing themselves against the Italians and the French, the Germans relied on the organ for self-esteem.

The well-traveled musical cosmopolitan Quantz could also decry the decline in the national standards, since he believed Germans could claim a

---

[31] *NBR*, 377.   [32] Mattheson, *Philologisches Tresespiel*, p. 97. See also *BD*, 3: 13–14; *NBR*, 377.
[33] Mattheson, *Ibid.*

particular mastery of the organ on the basis of the impressive application of the pedal: "Of the manner in which the pedals should be used, many have not heard a thing. Among them, the left foot and the little finger of the left hand are so closely connected with one another that one is not trusted to strike a note without the fore-knowledge and agreement of the other."[34] Shadowing the fundamental tones of the left hand with the left foot is a fair description of Italian pedaling and was a hacker's approach not worthy of real German organists; while Quantz does not draw a direct connection between the dominance of the Italian style and the slovenly tendencies in German organ-playing, it is clear from the critical discourse of mid-century Germany that this is precisely what was thought to be happening by those disposed to lament the decline of standards. To be a legitimate organist, as Quantz and so many others understood it, was to be master of physical counterpoint; independence of polyphonic parts required the independence of parts of the body, especially the feet from hands. Indeed, the feet secured the organ's position as a German cultural icon, and without this integrity that, too, would be lost. Mattheson also castigates those who simply doubled the lowest note of the manuals with the pedal: for him and many others this did not constitute real organ-playing. The untrained village organists of Germany shared this simplistic, and ultimately demeaning, approach to the pedal with the Italians.[35]

For Mattheson, the best organists, those approaching the caliber of Bach and Handel, were those who "could pull from their sleeves all the art and science that belongs to manual and pedal."[36] The organ drew its power from its "incomparable" strength and vast compass, from the tiny pipes of the mixtures to the massive pedal pipes; because one could – and should – play with both hands and feet, the organist had the ability to produce the fullest harmonies and the richest polyphonic textures.[37] As Mattheson's accounts of organists' trials in Hamburg make clear (see Chapter 1), demonstration of pedal mastery was an essential part of the audition process for selecting organists in one of Europe's greatest organ cities; crucial to this mastery was the ability to pedal without doubling the bass, "so that," wrote Mattheson, as if he were repeating an organist's motto, "the feet don't know what the hands are doing."[38]

The tethering of the little finger to the pedal line was a perennial target of scorn in the Bach organ tradition throughout the eighteenth century and into the nineteenth. In a letter to Abt Vogler, whose playing was famous – infamous for many – for its storm scenes and other pictorialisms that departed drastically from the august traditions of the Bachists, the writer

---

[34] Quantz, *Versuch einer Anweisung*, p. 329; Reilly trans., p. 339.
[35] Mattheson, *Grosse General-Bass Schule* (Hamburg: J. C. Kißner, 1731; reprint, Hildesheim: Olms Verlag, 1968), p. 34.
[36] *Ibid.*, p. 32.　[37] Mattheson, *Der vollkommene Capellmeister*, p. 471.
[38] Mattheson, *Grosse General-Bass Schule*, p. 34.

and talented organist Christian Friedrich Daniel Schubart cautioned against letting "the pedal always play along with the left hand as small-town schoolmasters do." Instead the true organist should "with the help of this mighty pedestal of the pedal make his playing as polyphonic as possible."[39] Schubart enjoined Vogler to use his travels to demonstrate the true art rather than the superficially pleasing in order to illustrate the true greatness of what Schubart called the "German Organ Ideal." Johann Nikolaus Forkel, whose Bach biography appeared in 1802, described the gulf between the dependent limbs of the inept and the magnificent independence of Bach, "[who] produced with the pedal not only the fundamental notes, or those for which common organists use the little finger of the left hand, but he played a real bass melody with his feet."[40]

It was not just large-scale free works that required independence of the feet; as Mattheson, Quantz and many other writers confirmed, the foundation of service-playing was the chorale, both the prelude to it and the accompaniment of the singing congregation. Independent pedal was essential for this most Lutheran music, even in its simplest four-part form. The flash and dash of Bach in solo recital in Dresden, or Handel astonishing the Italians on their home turf, were one thing, but for Mattheson and so many other Germans, the essence of the organ's power came in religious sentiment and especially corporate singing. For this reason Germans were so often scandalized by the operatic music that despoiled services in Italy. Proper harmony required the use of the pedal, and this in turn was necessary for the sponsoring of true feeling, as the laments of Mattheson, Quantz and others about the declining abilities of village organists make clear. For the good of the religious community, and in turn therefore, civic life, these organists were crucial and in extreme cases could represent not only fundamental dedication to the art of organ-playing but also to religious feeling. As one mid-eighteenth-century writer near Berlin put it: "If the cold in winter is so great that the fingers cannot hold out through an entire hymn, why can one not play the bass with the pedal while the hands warm themselves?"[41] The image of the local organist firing devotion with his feet even in frigid

---

[39] C. F. D. Schubart, *Vermischte Schriften*, ed. Ludwig Schubart, Sohn, 2 vols. (Zürich: Gessner, 1812), vol. I, pp. 71–79, at p. 76. When Charles Burney met Schubart in 1772 he was organist in the Lutheran church in Württemburg, and Burney praised him as "formed on the Bach school" and "original in genius" before enumerating his outstanding merits as a keyboard-player. Burney, *The Present State of Music in Germany, the Netherlands, and United Provinces*, 2nd edn., 2 vols. (London: Becket, Robson, and Robinson, 1775), vol. I, pp. 108–109. Schubart's defense of independence between pedal and left hand was often cited in the nineteenth century with respect to service-playing and the maintenance of standards among Protestant organists, especially in villages. See B. C. Natorp, *Ueber Rinck's Präludien* (Essen: Bädeker, 1834), reprinted in *Johann Christian Heinrich Rinck: Dokumente zu Leben und Werk*, ed. Christoph Dohr (Cologne: Verlag Dohr, 2003), p. 95; J. H. Häuser, *Geschichte der christlichen, insbesondere des evangelischen Kirchengesange und der Kirchenmusik* (Quedlinburg and Leipzig: Basse, 1834), p. 264; *Euterpe*, 11 (1845), 190; F. C. Anthes, *Die Tonkunst im evangelischen Cultus* (Wiesbaden: Friedrich, 1845), p. 142.

[40] Forkel, *Ueber Johann Sebastian Bachs Leben, Kunst und Kunstwerke*, p. 20; *NBR*, 438.

[41] F. W. Marpurg, *Historisch-Kritische Beyträge*, vol. II, pp. 194–195.

conditions was one that in turn warmed the collective German heart. From the highest pinnacles of art in celebrated urban churches to the sturdiest Lutheran hymns in simple rural chapels, the feet buttressed musical and religious life against moral decline. Pedal independence was a bulwark of national pride and a rare sign of German musical integrity.

Just how important the feet were not only in the villages but in the cosmopolitan capital of Dresden is also to be seen in the controversy surrounding the appointment of the organist at the Frauenkirche in 1742; the church had been built between 1726 and 1743 as a soaring architectural assertion of the continued vitality of Lutheranism in the heartland of the Reformation as against the Catholicism of the court. When the Dresden City Council awarded the organist post at the Frauenkirche to J. S. Bach's student Gottfried Homilius in 1742, mastery of the pedal proved to be the decisive issue. In 1736 Bach had played one of his most famous recitals on the just-finished instrument, the masterpiece of the Saxon organ-builder Gottfried Silbermann.[42] As always, Bach's pedal technique had been on display, just as it would have been when Homilius sat down on that bench six years later. Homilius began his audition by playing a Prelude and Fugue – it is unclear if this was an improvisation, but the use of the word *gespielt* suggests that it was not, in contrast to the improvised fugue on a given theme with which the program concluded. Such a prelude, and likely the fugue as well, would certainly have contained flashy pedalwork, perhaps even a pedal solo.

Some time after Homilius's successful audition, however, Count Heinrich von Brühl, the Saxon Prime Minister, attempted to procure the position for his own candidate, the *Musicum instrumentaler* Krause. This is precisely what Brühl had been able to do in Leipzig, where he successfully installed his own man, Gottlob Harrer, as the successor to J. S. Bach, even having the power, not to say the gall, to stage Harrer's audition for the Directorship of Music in that city before the proud Bach had had the courtesy to die. Facing political pressure from Brühl in the Saxon capital where he lived, the Dresden City Council nonetheless rejected the Prime Minister's candidate because he "did not make use of the pedal at all, which meant that the Gravity [of the instrument] was completely lost."[43] In sustaining Homilius's appointment, the City Council was not only asserting its prerogatives against monarchic incursions, but also defending the august traditions of Lutheran organ-playing in the city's new and magnificent Lutheran church. When it came to choosing an organist for the landmark Lutheran church in the leading cultural center in Germany,

---

[42] *NBR*, 188.
[43] Hans John, *Der Dresdner Kreuzkantor und Bach-Schüller Gottfried August Homilius* (Tutzing: Hans Schneider, 1980), p. 19.

mastery of the pedals proved decisive in sweeping aside the wishes of even the most powerful official in Saxony.

The technological sophistication and size of German organs made them tourist destinations of Europe-wide appeal, just as the German organists were themselves famous attractions. Bach as organist was not only viewed as an insular corrective to, or even defense against, foreign influence (as in Telemann's panegyric of 1751), but as a beacon that shone into foreign countries. The Obituary calls him a "world-famous organist" [*der im Orgelspielen Weltberühmte HochEdle Herr Johann Sebastian Bach*]; foreign musicians knew of his music, and visitors – other than Marchand – must have heard him play in major musical centers. His recitals across Germany – Hamburg, Dresden, Berlin – were reported in the press, and his music disseminated in prints and manuscript. Jakob Adlung's *Anleitung zu der musikalischen Gelahrtheit* (*Introduction to Musical Learning*) of 1758 is explicit about Bach's international reach as a keyboardist, and especially as an organist and composer of difficult, elaborate chorale preludes: "It would be futile to explain in depth here, how he astonished not only Germany but all of Europe with his strengths."[44] In the retrospect of the nineteenth century, Adlung's description of Bach's international celebrity bolstered the notion that eighteenth-century German organists had counterbalanced massive foreign influence.[45]

After Bach's death, his students became tourist attractions. One of his final pupils, Johann Kittel, carried on the Bach legacy and demonstrated it to foreigners in the important central-German organ center of Erfurt. Kittel's own student, Rinck, one of the most important Bachists of the early nineteenth century, reports on one such international encounter between his teacher and a visiting Italian organist. In Rinck's retelling of the story, an Erfurt gentleman brought the foreign virtuoso to see Kittel on a Sunday, presumably to the divine service at the Predigerkirche, where Johann Pachelbel had been one of Kittel's predecessors as organist in the 1680s. Kittel asked for a subject for improvisation from the visitors, who both demurred, until at last:

the Italian chose as a theme, b, a, c, h. –"I will combine this theme with another subject," said Kittel. And out of this developed a double fugue, which astonished and amazed all present. After the conclusion of this masterful performance, he was given the highest possible praise, and the Italian said: "I will never play the organ again, since I've now heard the greatest master of this sublime and godly instrument."[46]

[44] Jakob Adlung, *Anleitung zu der musikalischen Gelahrtheit* (Erfurt: J. D. Jungnicol, 1758; reprint, Kassel: Bärenreiter, 1953), p. 690. See also *BD*, 2: 122.

[45] See B. Widmann, "M. Jacob Adlung über Johann Sebastian Bach," *Euterpe*, 14 (1854), 103–105.

[46] J. C. H. Rinck, *Selbstbiographie* (Breslau: G. P. Aderholz, 1833), reprinted in *Johann Christian Heinrich Rink: Dokumente zu Leben und Werk*, ed. Christoph Dohr (Cologne: Dohr, 2003), pp. 17–42, at p. 25.

The revelatory power of German organs and organists effects the conversion of the pilgrim to the German way. That the theme for this sermon in sound, this improvised miracle, is the musical version of Bach's name only heightens the epiphany.

A MUSICAL TOURIST COMES TO GERMANY

Between the years 1770 and 1772 the English musician and author Charles Burney made two lengthy trips across continental Europe to collect material for what would become his *General History of Music*, the first of its four volumes appearing in 1776. In contrast to most musical travelers of our own time, the traveler Burney, who was himself an organist, always visited the notable organs of a city as one of his first orders of business: from St. Gervais in Paris, traditional post of the Couperin family, to the huge organ in St. John Lateran in Rome, to the even larger instrument in St. Bavo in Haarlem, to the Jacobikirche in Hamburg, to name but a few of the magnificent monuments to European music he marveled at. Already in Paris, near the outset of his continental tour of 1770, Burney had visited Claude Balbastre at his home, in his large music room, which housed many instruments including "a very large organ, with pedals which it may be necessary for a French organist to have for practice."[47] Having come directly from a country without pedals, Burney is fascinated by the novelty of Balbastre's house-organ. Burney also saw impressive footwork in the Netherlands, but as is clear from Joachim Hess's collection of organ dispositions published two years after Burney's tour of the region, most of the Dutch organs then still had, from the German point of view, stunted pedals; most notable among the scarce counterexamples is the instrument, of fifty-nine stops, fifteen of them in the pedal, in Haarlem's St. Bavo, built in 1735–1738 by the German Christian Müller. The organ at the Oude Kerk in Amsterdam when Sweelinck had held the post in the seventeenth century had had only two pedal stops; when Burney visited in 1772 and was treated to a memorable pedal display by the blind organist Pothoff, the instrument he heard, with its full pedalboard and complete assortment of independent stops, was the work of another German, Christian Vater, from 1724 (rebuilt in 1738 by Christian Müller). Hess ends his book with the specification for a model large organ, which proposed a substantial and independent pedal on the German pattern.[48]

As at Balbastre's home, Burney again focuses on the pedals at St. John Lateran in Rome, and reports that the "organist [Colista] is very dextrous"

---

[47] Charles Burney, *The Present State of Music in France and Italy* (London: T. Becket and Co., 1771), pp. 38–39.
[48] Joachim Hess, *Dispositien der merkwaardigste Kerk-Orgelen* (Gouda: Johannes Vander Klos, 1774), p. 167.

with the feet.[49] But these remarks seem pallid indeed when compared to the response elicited when Burney found himself in north and central Germany two years later.

When Burney reached Saxony in the organ territory of J. S. Bach and his students, the pedals became the center of his descriptions. Burney spied Bach's legacy everywhere: "All the present organ-players in Germany," wrote Burney, "are formed upon his school."[50] Burney's account of Christlieb Siegmund Binder, the Saxon court organist, at the Silbermann organ in the Hofkapelle in Dresden in September of 1772 concentrates on the fleet and powerful feet of an old man: "[Binder] played three or four fugues in a very full and masterly manner, making great use of the pedals … To use the pedals of these huge instruments much, at the same time as two hands are fully employed on the stiff and heavy manuals, is a very laborious business."[51] Like Bach's biographer Forkel, who called Binder "a genuine organ-player" [*ein echter Orgelspieler*],[52] Burney was impressed by the Dresden court organist's performance not only on account of its erudition, but also for the sheer physical power and determination that allowed him to play this behemoth with both hands and feet, a struggle conducted in the organ loft far from the rest of the listeners three stories below in the church.[53]

A few weeks after his uplifting encounter with the Silbermann instruments of Dresden, Burney traveled to Hamburg, where he devoted an entire morning to the city's organs, noting that no less than five of them had ranks of thirty-two-foot-long pedal pipes which played two octaves below the notated pitch; on four of them these largest of pipes were visible in the pedal towers, visually framing the main case and rising up to the vaulted heights of the ceiling. At the Petrikirche, Burney heard Johann Ernst Bernhard Pfeiffer, an organist who had likely witnessed J. S. Bach play in Hamburg way back in 1720. The aged Pfeiffer provided a direct link back to the era of Mattheson and Bach; he had been one of the unsuccessful candidates for the organist post at the Hamburg cathedral in 1725, when Mattheson had submitted the theme from J. S. Bach's G minor fugue, BWV 542, for the candidates to improvise on (see Chapter 1, p. 51). Many of these organists would have known where the theme came from; Pfeiffer could well have heard Bach play a fugue on the same subject in his Hamburg recital in 1720; Pfeiffer also made a manuscript copy of BWV 542.[54] By the time of

---

[49] Burney (see n. 47), p. 374.
[50] Charles Burney, *The Present State of Music in Germany, the Netherlands, and United Provinces*, vol. II, p. 83.
[51] *Ibid.*, p. 55.
[52] J. N. Forkel, *Musikalischer Almanach für Deutschland auf das Jahr 1782* (Leipzig: Schwickert, 1782; reprint, Hildesheim: Olms Verlag, 1974), p. 120.
[53] Burney, *The Present State of Music in Germany, the Netherlands, and United Provinces*, vol. II, p. 56.
[54] Pfeiffer had perhaps gained access to the piece through Mattheson. See Jürgen Neubacher, "Johann Ernst Bernhard Pfeiffer und die Organistenproben" in Nicole Ristow, Wolfgang Sandberger, and Dorothea Schröder (eds.), *Critica musica: Studien zum 17. und 18. Jahrhundert: Festschrift Hans*

Burney's Hamburg visit Pfeiffer had been at the Petrikirche for nearly four decades. One might speculate that Pfeiffer could even have played Bach's G minor fugue for Burney, a sometime admirer of Bach's organ works, and, indeed, of Pfeiffer's playing: "M. Pfiffer [sic] is in years, but must have been a very brilliant performer in his youth, and he still retains his powers of execution, both with hands and feet, beyond any one I ever heard, at his time of life."[55] Here was someone who had not studied directly with Bach but who carried on that tradition with all his limbs.

The fifth and biggest of Hamburg's organs, one which Burney mistakenly believed to be the largest in Europe, was the impressive instrument that filled the west gallery of the city's newest church, the Michaeliskirche (see Figure 4.1). The organ had been finished just two years before Burney's visit, and featured a more modern design, which focused attention on the largest pipes by bringing them to the center of the case, the scalar progression rising upward from either flank in a visual crescendo that culminated with the largest pipe of the open 32′ Principal, placed prominently on its own in the very middle of the case. This pipe was indeed thirty-two feet high, and more than two feet wide; it rose some eight feet above the rest of the pipework on either side. Built by Johann Gottfried Hildebrandt, whose father's instruments had been much admired by J. S. Bach, the Michaeliskirche organ had been donated to the church by Johann Mattheson, who had set aside upwards of 40,000 Marks Silver and then gave yet more for the addition of various extras and for a richly carved case appointed with lavish decorations. The organ had sixty-four stops, with a massive pedal division of fourteen stops, including three registers at 32′, two of them full length.[56] Above the largest central pipe was a painted portrait of Mattheson in his prime, held aloft by angels fluttering as if on updrafts billowing from the wind summoning the *Gravitas* of the biggest, deepest pedal pipe. Looking down from above the largest of Hamburg's organs was the proud, bewigged head of the leading literary defender of German organ prowess, himself an organist.[57] In this way the apotheosis of Germany's greatest music critic was enacted above the divinely perfect instrument he and so many others held to be both a symbol of Germany's musical achievement and its major contribution to European culture.

Joachim Marx zum 65. Geburtstag (Stuttgart: Metzler, 2001), pp. 221–232, at pp. 223–224. For a modern edition of two organ fugues by Pfeiffer, see Jürgen Neubacher (ed.), *Drei Orgelfugen aus dem Repertoire der Hamburger St. Petrikirche* (Sankt Augustin: Butz Musikverlag, 2001).

[55] Burney, *The Present State of Music in Germany, the Netherlands, and United Provinces*, vol. II, p. 221.

[56] With the addition of a stopper a pipe will sound an octave lower. In the Michaeliskirche pedal, the 32′ Subbaß is stopped, and thus its longest pipe is roughly half that length. The 32′ Principal was open and therefore full length. In contrast to the other great organs of Hamburg, which were pitched high, at *Hochchorton*, the organ in St. Michael's was a whole-tone lower, in *Kammerton*, so that all the pipes, especially the largest of these, were even longer than those giants in the other Hamburg churches.

[57] Ulrich Dähnert, *Der Orgel- und Instrumentenbauer Zacharias Hildebrandt* (Leipzig: Breitkopf & Härtel, 1960), pp. 141–148.

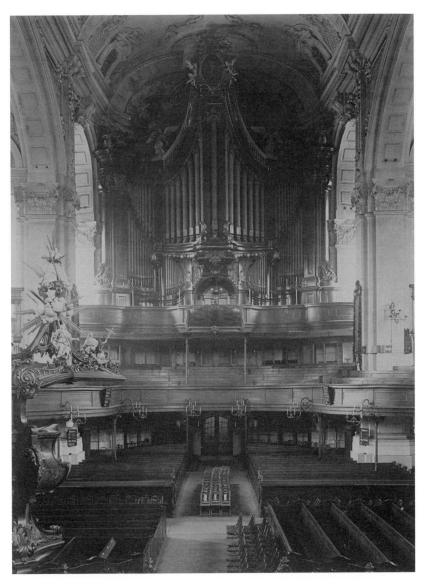

Figure 4.1   J. G. Hildebrandt organ (1767–1771), Michaeliskirche, Hamburg

When Burney came to Hamburg and marveled at its organs in 1772, C. P. E. Bach had been Director of Music in the city for nearly five years; his music-making at the clavichord would prove to be the highpoint of Burney's trip. Yet this second son of J. S. Bach did not – could not! – demonstrate any of the city's organs for his visitor as his father surely would have done with great relish. Indeed, according to Mattheson, J. S. Bach had "exhibited his playing on the most various and greatest organs, and aroused universal admiration for his ability" during his 1720 trip to Hamburg in what must have been the greatest organ crawl in history.[58] But fifty years on, Burney writes that for the visit to the Michaeliskirche, where C. P. E. Bach would later be buried, "M. Hartmann, a *dilettante*, was so obliging as to play on this instrument a considerable time, in order to let me hear all its powers. M. Bach has so long neglected organ-playing, that he says he has lost the use of the pedals, which are thought so essential throughout Germany, that no one can pass for a player worth hearing, who is unable to use them."[59]

One should not underestimate the irony and indignity of a Bach son finding himself in arguably the greatest organ city in Europe and not feeling himself able to do justice to its organs. Where J. S. Bach had, in C. P. E. Bach's words, regretted never having had a truly large and excellent organ at his disposal, his son was surrounded by an embarrassment of riches yet plagued by an embarrassing lack of ability to enjoy them. As the ardent admirer of C. P. E. Bach, the poet Matthias Claudius put it soon after Bach's arrival in Hamburg to take up his post: "Bach does not play the organ at all and must endure an array of criticisms, which must seem extraordinary to him."[60] So proud were Hamburgers of their organs, that some did not shy away from criticizing one of the most revered of contemporary German musicians for his admitted inadequacy at the instrument of instruments. By refusing to play for Burney, C. P. E. Bach was intent on safeguarding the standards of organ-playing inculcated in him by J. S. Bach, even if he could no longer put them into practice and demonstrate them for visitors who would have expected just such an exhibition. C. P. E. Bach would not debase himself or the organ by playing without using his feet. That would be too sad a sight and sound for a Bach son to endure, even if his guest from a country with pedal-less organs would not necessarily have minded.

Such feelings of inadequacy at the ultimate Bachian instrument must also color the "Comparison of Bach and Handel," a document almost certainly written by C. P. E. Bach in response to Charles Burney's account of the Handel commemorations of 1784 which praised Handel above Bach. In that publication Burney had had the audacity to claim that "In his full, masterly, and excellent, *organ-fugues*, upon the most natural and pleasing subjects, [Handel] surpassed Frescobaldi, and even Sebastian Bach."[61] Published in 1788, the last

---

[58] Johann Mattheson, *Der Musicalische Patriot* (Hamburg: the author, 1728), p. 316. English trans., *NBR*, 91.

[59] Burney, *The Present State of Music in Germany, the Netherlands, and United Provinces*, vol. II, p. 221.

[60] Matthias Claudius to Heinrich Wilhelm von Gerstenberg, October 1768, quoted in Hans-Günter Ottenberg (ed.), *Carl Philipp Emanuel Bach Spurensuche: Leben und Werk in Selbstzeugnissen und Dokumenten seiner Zeitgenossen*, (Leipzig: E. A. Seemann, 1994), pp. 67–68. See also Ernst Suchalla (ed.), *Carl Philipp Emanuel Bach: Briefe und Dokumente, Kritische Gesamtausgabe* (Göttingen: Vandenhoeck & Ruprecht, 1994), pp. 163–164.

[61] Charles Burney, *An Account of the Musical Performances in Westminster-Abbey, and the Pantheon, May 26th, 27th, 29th; and June the 3d, and 5th, 1785* (Dublin: Moncrieffe, Jenkin, White, H. Whitestone, Burton, and Byrne, 1785), p. 58.

year of C. P. E. Bach's life, the Comparison responds with a larger statement about the true nature of the organ: "the pedal is the most essential part of an organ, without which it would have little of that majesty, greatness, and power that belong to it alone above all other instruments. Anyone who knows at all what the word 'organ' means will grant that."[62] Taking it as a given that true organ-playing was German organ-playing, the Comparison then goes on to castigate Handel's neglect of the feet, the émigré having been "compelled, as an Englishman, to renounce his skill with the pedals that, as a German, he had possessed."[63] The feet are an unambiguous marker of national affiliation and of fundamental musical and cultural importance: Handel's cosmopolitanism comes at the expense of his native training and talent. Organs without pedals, such as those in England, are deemed for all intents and purposes worthless by C. P. E. Bach; in Germany even the small village organs were unlikely to be without them. Because German mastery of the pedal and therefore of the organ in its complete form extends back to the instrument's origins, "Good organists have from time immemorial been at home in Germany."[64] The pious, pedaling organist was an essential feature of Germany's patrimony and its present musical geography, despite there having been some erosion even within J. S. Bach's own family.

Burney's visit to the Michaeliskirche in Hamburg, where the amateur had played instead of C. P. E. Bach, is also related in the Comparison, but here turned against the Englishman: "When [C. P. E.] Bach told him that he could not play the pedal, he [Burney] is said to have laughed and said the pedals were not essential."[65] The author of the Comparison – C. P. E. Bach talking about himself in the third person – then goes on to describe the unmatched technical and compositional intricacies J. S. Bach demanded of organists' feet. Foreigners, and especially in this instance an Englishman like Burney, cannot understand or appreciate the musical and ethical value embodied in good organ-playing. In contrast to the English, who can have no idea of real organ performance, only a "German connoisseur" knows that the organist "plays the most difficult and most perfect of instruments, which requires uncommon talents, knowledge, and practice to do it full justice."[66]

---

[62] [C. P. E. Bach], "Auszug eines Schreibens aus – – – vom 27sten Febr. 1788," *Allgemeine deutsche Bibliothek*, ed. Friedrich Nicolai (Berlin and Stettin: Nicolai, 1788), vol. LXXXI, Pt. 1, pp. 295–303. English trans. based on *NBR*, 401–409. See also *BD*, 3: 437–445.

[63] [C. P. E. Bach], "Auszug," p. 298. Trans. based on *NBR*, 404.

[64] "Die guten Organisten [sind] in Deutschland von jeher zu Hause gewesen." [C. P. E. Bach], "Auszug," pp. 298–299; *NBR*, 405.

[65] [C. P. E. Bach], "Auszug," p. 298; trans. *NBR*, 404. C. P. E. Bach rehearses the same arguments about the relative merits of his father and Handel as organists, especially those having to do with the use of the pedal, in a letter of January 21, 1786 to Johann Joachim Eschenburg. The close parallels between these two documents confirm C. P. E. Bach's authorship of the "Comparison" and demonstrate also that the Hamburg organ tour with Burney and the Englishman's subsequent references to it made a deep impression on Bach. See Suchalla (ed.), *Carl Philipp Emanuel Bach: Briefe und Dokumente*, pp. 1133–1135.

[66] *NBR*, 405.

The inherent value of the organ and its players can truly be recognized only by Germans themselves, who set the standard of the organ art and uphold it in defiance of foreign influence and ignorance. It is in this context that we must understand C. P. E. Bach's refusal to dishonor the German organ tradition by playing the large organs of Hamburg as an Englishman might have done – without his feet. Doubtless still smarting from his failure to demonstrate the organs for his visitor, C. P. E. Bach must have found Burney's apparent lack of adequate respect for his father's fugues, especially those for the organ, as backhanded confirmation of Emanuel's own failings. If C. P. E. Bach had only been able to play his father's music on the great organs of Hamburg, would that not have been enough to confirm for his ignorant visitor Sebastian's unequaled contrapuntal and physical stature? So crucial to Bach's legacy are the pedals that they form the central and lengthiest part of the Comparison, which can be read as a parable of two German organists: the one who remained true to his national craft, the other who turned away from it, physically and morally. Having been born a hundred miles from one another in the same year, and having narrowly missed meeting one another in the flesh during their lives, the two greatest German organists of the eighteenth century – the men at the top of Mattheson's list, Johann Sebastian Bach and Georg Frideric Handel – are made to duel posthumously. C. P. E. Bach has the contest decided by the feet.

But C. P. E. Bach's "Comparison of Bach and Handel" gets it only partly right. It is true that very few organs in England had pedals, but Handel apparently did not neglect completely the exercise of his feet in organ-playing. Burney himself related in the same account of Handel's life in which he claimed Handel's organ fugues to be better than those of Bach, that Handel played the St. Paul's Cathedral organ because "of the exercise it afforded him, in the use of the pedals."[67] The pedal compass of the St. Paul's organ was one octave, so that only some of Handel's German skills could be deployed over its stunted range. Nonetheless, it is hard to imagine that when Handel came to the newly finished organ at Haarlem in the Netherlands in 1740 he did not deploy his feet on its massive pedal division; he can hardly have shied away from playing this magnificent instrument, built by the German Christian Müller and later visited by Burney, as C. P. E. Bach would later do during his years in Hamburg.

But it was not just on his trips to the continent that Handel might have demonstrated the resilience of his pedal technique, in spite of his years in England and the expansion of his waistline. German pedals and pedaling were not only a point of fascination for English travelers abroad, they could also be marketed by the shrewd musical entrepreneur. This would explain

---

[67] Charles Burney, *An Account of the Musical Performances . . . in Commemoration of Handel* (London: Payne and Son, 1785), p. 33.

why the first concerto in Handel's Op. 7 is a display piece for the feet;[68] the range of the pedal part exceeds the octave compass then known on but a few English organs, and accordingly questions about the organ in the theatre at Lincoln's Inn Fields, where the concerto was performed in the 1740 season, remain unanswered. Handel had introduced the concertos as an added attraction to his oratorio performances. Only Op. 7, No. 1 specifies use of the pedal, with a solo flourish in one of the first episodes and hardly letting up through the rest of the movement; the piece confirms that Handel retained a robust pedal technique and a certain amount of stamina (see Example 4.3). While this pedal part is not the most creative music ever conceived, it launches the feet at high speed, the right and left alternating as if in a full run. Rather than hidden up in the organ loft, this display would have been in full view on stage, and in a country where organs were almost universally without pedals, this showpiece must have counted as a stunning attraction. Far from renouncing this crucial aspect of his Germanness, that was as characteristic of his origins as his much-parodied accent, Handel capitalizes in this concerto on the novelty of his pedal skill. Though Handel became a British subject in 1727, he remained true to both his Lutheran faith and his pedal past. The "exercise" of his feet at the St. Paul's organ could not have been as vigorous as on German organs, given the smaller compass; but at Lincoln's Inn Fields he had an organ with what was apparently a bigger pedal range. Therefore one would have to adjust C. P. E. Bach's claims that Handel had, by virtue of his expatriate status, left behind an essential part of his Germanness; to the contrary, this concerto exploits precisely these abilities for the benefit of foreign spectators sure to be amazed by such four-limbed performance. This is virtual tourism, eighteenth-century style: Handel invites his London audience to peek into the organ loft to watch a German play the pedals as no Englishman could.

What was missing in the flashy Op. 7, No. 1, however, was the giant sound of the organs of Handel's native land. In the Lincoln's Inn Fields Theatre, his footwork has become aerobic spectacle denuded of its sublime resonance: the pedals become superficial rather than profound. It is fitting that the music should be so fleet: the piece is about movement, about showing off the feet in action. A real German organ would not have provided the visual confirmation of this pedal motion provided by the man mountain sprinting across the pedals on stage; in London, the figuration could have easily been played by the left hand, probably without any difference in the sound, given this anomalous English organ's lack of *Gravitas*. The concerto and the instrument on which it was played by Handel stand in

---

[68] The prejudice against Handel's organ-playing remained strong through the nineteenth century and colored many other comparisons of Bach and Handel, for example that of Philipp Spitta: "But with [Handel concertos] the organ is only a more powerful clavier; and of true organ style there is as good as none." Philipp Spitta, *J. S. Bach*, trans. Clara Bell and J. A. Fuller-Maitland (London: Novello, 1889; reprint, New York: Dover, 1951), vol. II, p. 137.

Example 4.3   Handel, Organ Concerto in B flat, Op. 7, No. 1, HWV 306, first movement, bars 7–12

relation to the "real" organs of "home" as an indoor climbing wall does to the Matterhorn, difficult but undaunting, thrilling but unthreatening, entertaining but not profound, and with nothing of the daring harmonic moves that are said to have characterized the organ improvisations of Handel's late, blind years.[69]

The volleys of nationalistic sentiment echoing between England and Germany over the relative merits of Bach and Handel got one more blast the year after the appearance of the Comparison in the fourth and final volume of Burney's *General History of Music*, for which his European tours were the research trips. The *History* is flush with praise for Handel's organ concertos and playing, but returns inevitably to the comparison with his illustrious contemporary, J. S. Bach. In a footnote, Burney boasts a deep knowledge of Bach's music, then lofts the old complaints about its artificiality, linking this to excessive devotion to full harmony and contrapuntal rigor: in contrast to the casual quality of Handel's organ fugues pilloried by C. P. E. Bach, J. S. Bach will, in Burney's outlandish vignette, go to ridiculous lengths not only to achieve expansive textures but also to maintain polyphonic integrity: "He was so fond of full harmony, that besides a constant and active use of the pedals, he is said to have put down such keys by a stick in his mouth, as neither hands nor feet could reach."[70] A stick in the mouth with limbs sprawling across many keyboards made for a visual caricature of the unnatural music such an act yields. The multitasking body is asked to do more than is musically valuable; the obsession with wide-ranging, exacting part-writing leads to the bizarre contortions of prosthetic polyphony. As if four limbs weren't enough, Bach wanted to sprout a fifth.

In the *General History of Music*, Burney respectfully repeats the lessons of his 1772 journey: "The organs of Germany in magnitude, and the organists in abilities, seem unrivalled in any other part of Europe, particularly in the use of the pedals."[71] In the *History*, Wilhelm Friedemann Bach, whom Burney never heard play, is likewise praised specifically for his pedalwork. But Burney takes Bach devotee Friedrich Wilhelm Marpurg, for one, to task by claiming that the German theorist included only two English organists, Keeble and Stanley, among his list of great players, and for making no mention whatever of "Handel's [sublime] manner of playing the organ."[72] Because Burney had not fully appreciated, or perhaps accepted, the pedal-centric conception of German organ-playing, he had seen nothing wrong with elevating Handel's organ fugues above Bach's. It was also for this

---

[69] John Hawkins, *History of the Science and Practice of Music*, 3 vols. (London: Payne, 1776), vol. III, p. 413.

[70] Burney, *A General History of Music*, 4 vols. (London: Becket, Robson, and Robinson, 1776–1789), vol. IV, p. 593.

[71] *Ibid.*

[72] *Ibid*, at p. 587. Burney cites Marpurg's *Abhandlung von der Fuge* as the source for his list, but the passage does not appear there.

reason that Burney did not understand why English organists were largely ignored by Marpurg. Though he had been deeply impressed by German organists' feet while on his continental tour, Burney did not advocate a transformation of English playing through an introduction of pedals and the necessary training of English feet, because he did not see them as crucial to organ-playing. However impressive, the feet were not essential.

NATIONALISM FROM THE BOTTOM UP

When Burney visited Hamburg in 1772, C. P. E. Bach was in a nostalgic mood: "You are come here," Burney reports the city's Director of Music saying to him, "fifty years too late."[73] This remark has often been taken to refer to the sorry state of church music and to the demise of the Hamburg opera, which had been founded in 1678 and closed in 1738. But surely Emanuel would also have had in mind the state of the organ arts, a decline he acutely felt and to which he must have believed he had contributed. Two years after Burney's visit, Emanuel wrote to Forkel a long letter in which he described his father's comprehensive knowledge of organ construction, adding in a marginal note, "these sciences perished with him."[74] The organ's past haunted C. P. E. Bach's Hamburg present: criticized by some of Hamburg's citizens and unable to demonstrate the organs for his English visitor, he must often have contemplated his father's legacy and his own path away from the instrument on which that legacy had been built. In the course of Emanuel's civic life and duties in Hamburg he had constantly had to listen to the city's organs, and to stand by as they were played by organists who could never approach J. S. Bach's mastery. As Emanuel's refusal to play for Burney suggests, the organ cast a shadow of anxiety over the Bach sons, none of whom left *pedaliter* works of any significance. Wilhelm Friedemann and the Bückeburg Bach, Johann Christoph Friedrich, remained powerful improvisers and players revered by their contemporaries,[75] but neither left behind any "real" organ music that would begin to approach the scope and complexity of the works in their father's corpus. The sons didn't – couldn't – even try to fill the shoes he'd left behind. Among J. S. Bach's many pupils only J. L. Krebs, whose father had also studied with Bach in Weimar, produced a substantial body of large-scale organ works; that many of these were based directly on those of J. S. Bach shows just how difficult it seems to have been to escape the anxiety of influence. Perhaps only in the ephemeral moment of improvisation could the art continue to flourish, dying away just as quickly as it was recalled, fantastical and unscrutinized.

[73] Burney, *The Present State of Music in Germany, the Netherlands, and United Provinces*, vol. II, p. 246.
[74] *NBR*, 396; *BD*, 3: 284.
[75] Forkel, *Musikalischer Almanach . . . auf das Jahr 1782*, pp. 119–120.

One of the things that comes through so strikingly from Burney along with his amazement at the large organs of Bach's regions of Germany, is the advanced age of the men who played them. In Dresden, Binder had been seemingly exhausted by his exertions at heavy keyboard actions. Emanuel Bach was nearly sixty, suffered from gout, and had given up the organ. While Burney noted the impact of J. S. Bach's enormous and influential pedagogical efforts over some four decades of teaching, many reported a decline in the organ traditions he had fostered. In the *Musikalischer Almanach für Deutschland auf das Jahr 1782*, it took Forkel seven pages to list the greatest German pianists/clavichordists; that catalog begins with three Bach sons – Wilhelm Friedemann, Carl Philipp Emanuel, and Johann Christoph Friedrich. Yet the organists filled only two pages, with C. P. E. Bach dropped and his brothers remaining. Forkel had to concede gloomily "that this catalog of the best organists in Germany turned out to be very short."[76] A rigid defender of the august Bachian standards of organ-playing, Forkel admitted to this select group only "those who know how to play the organ in its true manner," that is, with fundamental knowledge of four-part harmony and a command of the pedal.[77] If not exactly robust, however, the Bach tradition was at least being curated by the men on Forkel's list, two of whom were encountered by Burney on his travels. But by C. P. E. Bach's own admission Forkel had rightfully stricken him from the ranks of the organists in a musical magazine read across Germany.

It is difficult to know whether such jeremiads reflect the pessimism of traditionalists in the face of falling numbers and the seductive charms of foreign music. As Burney heard and noted, J. S. Bach's music retained its currency among his devotees; but even they spoke of the need for renewal. On the opening page of the first volume of his *Beginning Practical Organist* [*Der angehende praktische Organist*] of 1801, J. C. Kittel laments the sorry state of organ-playing "not only in the country but in cities as well"; Kittel then reassures his readers that his method is based on the principles he learned from Bach, and refined during fifty years of his own teaching.[78] In the foreword to a collection of chorales that appeared two years later, Kittel stressed again the old Bachian emphasis on obbligato pedal-playing, including in the performance of simple four-part harmonizations.[79]

In the same year that Kittel's treatise appeared, Forkel devoted many of the later pages of his *General History of Music* [*Allgemeine Geschichte der Musik*] to the organ.[80] The instrument emerges in modern form in the

---

[76] *Ibid.*, pp. 113–122.   [77] *Ibid.*, p. 122.

[78] J. C. Kittel, *Der angehende praktische Organist*, 3 vols. (Erfurt: Beyer and Maring, 1801–1808; reprint, Buren: Knuf, 1981), vol. I, [p. 1].

[79] J. C. Kittel, *Vierstimmige Choräle mit Vorspielen . . . für die Schleswig-Hollsteinischen Kirchen*, 2 vols. (Altona: J. F. Hammerich, 1803), vol. I, foreword.

[80] J. N. Forkel, *Allgemeine Geschichte der Musik*, 2 vols. (Leipzig: Schwickert, 1788–1801; reprint, Graz: Akademische Druck- u. Verlagsanstalt, 1967), vol. II, pp. 668–670.

midst of a discussion of figural music and polyphony: Forkel cites "our compatriot" [*unser Landsmann*] Bernhard the German as the inventor of the pedal in Venice at the end of the fifteenth century[81]; while this development had made the organ an instrument rich in harmony [*harmoniereiches Instrument*], there is no evidence that, in contrast to the Germans, the Italians had produced any contrapuntal music to take advantage of this advance. As Forkel goes on to argue, Bernhard must have known what the pedal would mean for augmenting harmonic possibility and for the creation of larger contrapuntal structures, otherwise he wouldn't have invented it in the first place. While the origins of polyphony lay in the Netherlands, the Germans were quick to take it up, and indeed led the way in counterpoint by transferring these practices to the organ: "Such a splendid instrument as the organ, to whose perfection the Germans contributed so much, flourished there from very early on."[82] Forkel concludes that by the sixteenth century, the German organ art – a polyphonic art to be sure – had risen to unimagined heights.[83]

This link between polyphony and pedaling solidified German preeminence at both: the connection is expressed more starkly still in Forkel's Bach biography, which appeared in 1802, a year after the second volume of his *General History* and Kittel's treatise. In Forkel's life of Bach, the organ derives its status from the largest pipes, whose expressive power can only be fully exploited by expert feet at the pedalboard. Forkel's account of Bach's organ music begins with a forceful assertion of this basic quality of the most German of instruments:

The pedals are an essential part of the organ: by them alone is it exalted above all other instruments, for its magnificence, grandeur, and majesty depend upon them. Without the pedals, this great instrument is no longer great: it approaches the little positives, which are of no value in the eyes of competent judges. But the great organ, provided with pedals, must be so managed that its whole compass is brought into action: in other words, the composer and the player must require from it all that it can perform. Nobody has ever done this more than J. S. Bach.[84]

These musical values reflect moral ones, for the organist's body enacts the contrapuntal creed of the pure German art of composition. Without independent pedal and pedal-playing, the sonic and conceptual profundity of organ polyphony cannot be respected, never mind further explorations. It was not by accident that the Burney/C. P. E. Bach exchange over Bach and Handel had taken place on the battleground of fugue, a genre that demonstrated most strikingly the differences between the "true" German conception of the organ and foreign attitudes less lofty than those cultivated by the

---

[81] Forkel uses two different dates, the usual 1470 and 1480, the latter possibly a typographical error. See *Allgemeine Geschichte*, vol. II, pp. 668, 724.
[82] *Ibid.*, p. 725.   [83] *Ibid.*, p. 729.
[84] Johann Nikolaus Forkel, *Ueber Johann Sebastian Bachs Leben, Kunst und Kunstwerke*, p. 59. *NBR*, 470.

Bach tradition.[85] Burney and C. P. E. Bach had not been the first to measure the two contemporaries on the yardstick of counterpoint. In the *Abhandlung von der Fuge* of 1753, Marpurg had claimed that Handel's fugues were generally free, while most of Bach's were stricter and more erudite; further, Marpurg insisted that Bach had treated the pedals with particular consideration for the nature of the human body and the properties of the organ.[86] All these factors made it clear that the greatest organ fugues were those of the incomparable Bach.

The memory of the Bach/Burney polemic hung in the air into the first decades of the nineteenth century; in the same letter to Vogler cautioning against frivolity and lax pedal-playing at the organ, Schubart complained of the *Schadenfreude* of the English traveler at the state of organ-playing in Germany, which "was once the homeland of masters of the organ, but now has entire provinces which are utterly barren . . . [so] that a Burney rejoices at how extremely rare true German organists have become, in a country otherwise so rich in great men."[87] In contrast to the cheap melodrama of the storms and frights favored by the likes of Vogler, the organ's true sublimity was to be displayed through high-minded polyphony. There is no more self-conscious a demonstration of this ideal than Bach's Fugue in C, BWV 547/2, an example of what Marpurg called a Bach "Art Fugue" [*Kunstfuge*] or "Master Fugue" [*Meisterfuge*]. Over the first two-thirds of this magisterial polyphonic oration, a piece rarely commented on in the scholarly literature, Bach subjects the one-bar theme to a host of complicated procedures in four-voice counterpoint; strikingly, this full texture is without any pedal, its absence all the more blatant because of the vigorous involvement of the feet in the preceding Prelude. After a lengthy treatment of the subject in *rectus* form in the first section (Example 4.4a), Bach undertakes an examination of his material in melodic inversion (Example 4.4b), before impressively combining the two forms in *stretto* (Example 4.4c), the three sections demonstrating these features of the theme stitched artfully together. Still the pedal is silent. The piece could well have ended after these lengthy and learned manual investigations; the drawn-out, two-bar pedal point (without the feet!) under broken chords that follows the combination of the subject with its melodic inversion would normally portend the end of a fugue. But for the lack of a pedal entrance, the harmonic intensity and contrapuntal density would have been sufficient to close out the fugue without loss of honor to the composer or disappointment to learned listeners. Indeed, if one were to truncate BWV 547/2 and come to a cadence after this

---

[85] For more on Burney on the notion of "Classic" German music, see Celia Applegate, *Bach in Berlin: Nation and Culture in Mendelssohn's Revival of the St. Matthew Passion* (Ithaca, New York: Cornell University Press, 2005), pp. 75–77.

[86] F. W. Marpurg, *Abhandlung von der Fuge*, 2 vols. (Berlin: Haube & Spener, 1753–1754; reprint, Hildesheim: Olms Verlag, 1970), vol. ɪ, p. xxvi, vol. ɪɪ, pp. 19–20. See also *NBR*, 359.

[87] C. F. D. Schubart, *Vermischte Schriften*, vol. ɪ, p. 74.

Example 4.4a   Contrapuntal combinations in manuals, J. S. Bach, Fugue in C, BWV 547/2, bars 1–8, *rectus*

Example 4.4b   Contrapuntal combinations in manuals, J. S. Bach, Fugue in C, BWV 547/2, bars 27–30, *inversus*

pedal-point and before the eventual entrance of the pedal itself, the fugue could already have taken its place among the most erudite examples from *The Well-Tempered Clavier*. But the epic silence of the pedal seems to get louder and louder as the artifice unfolds at great length in the hands.

Rather than a counterintuitive *manualiter* conclusion, the pedal-less pedal-point promises something far more dramatic than what has been

Example 4.4c   Contrapuntal combinations in manuals, J. S. Bach, Fugue in C, BWV 547/2,
                bars 34–38, *rectus* and *inversus*

Example 4.5   J. S. Bach, Fugue in C, BWV 547/2, "pedal-less" pedal point and
               pedal entrance in augmentation, bars 47–52

heard so far in this already eventful fugue (see Example 4.5). A flurry of
stretto at the close of the pedal-point in the manuals in bar 48 at last ushers
in the momentous pedal entrance, which, when it comes, does so in
augmentation, with the hands above treating the subject in *rectus* and
inversus. The pedal announces itself with a depth and regal pace that only
the organ, with its gravity and unlimited sustaining power, can attain: this
fifth voice is not music for the little finger, but for the proudest of feet. With

the arrival of the pedal Bach takes the already complicated argument to a new level of sonic and contrapuntal profundity, beyond and beneath the riches of the *manualiter* fugue that precedes the thunderous entry of the previously absent bass. The theatricality of this entry derives not only from the artfully planned staging of the crux to this contrapuntal tour-de-force, but from the larger philosophical statement the fugue makes about the pedals themselves and their defining contribution to the organ's unique status. A self-sufficient manual fugue is transformed by the arrival of the pedal into a demonstration of what lies at the true foundation of organ polyphony and what gives the instrument its distinctive rhetorical and contrapuntal power. This is what Zelter meant about Bach achieving his "intellectual height" through the use of the pedal (see Chapter 2, p. 106).

Such a representation of contrapuntal omnipotence founded on the feet and projected by the unwavering profundity and brilliance of the organ's sound are more than an evocation of the sublime. The unmatched gravity of thought, action, and sound transcended the theatrics of display and took on a symbolic power perhaps undreamt of by Bach. The incipit of this and other large preludes and fugues concluded Forkel's Bach biography, in which the organ reigns above all other instruments; Bach's legacy is based largely upon his dominance at it. Forkel begins his account of Bach's life and work by describing his own project as "a patriotic undertaking . . . to rouse the breast of every true German." Forkel concludes the book with the well-known, not to say infamous, declaration of patriotism made in the context of the Napoleonic Wars and French invasions of the German states: "And this man, the greatest musical poet and the greatest musical orator that ever existed, and probably ever will exist, was a German. Let his country be proud of him; let it be proud, but, at the same time, worthy of him!"[88] For Forkel, the organ is the prime purveyor of a distinctly Germany mastery of counterpoint and a crucial element in Protestant devotional life; the instrument assumes a vital role in supporting the proto-nationalistic aims of his seminal Bach biography, the hands and feet of a single musician figured as a holy vessel of communal devotion. From at least the time of Praetorius onward the organ had been an emblem of German musical advancement as its most important contribution to European culture. In this capacity the organ shone when German tourists visited foreign organs and when foreigners came to the German homeland to see and hear the instruments and players of the Bachian tradition. The C Major Fugue was proof that this had to be experienced in Germany with players using all four limbs on instruments of commensurate scope and gravity. The fullness of this kind of performance – its sight and its sound – could be had in no other country.

---

[88] Johann Nikolaus Forkel, *Ueber Johann Sebastian Bachs Leben, Kunst und Kunstwerke*, pp. v, 59. *NBR*, 419, 479.

That the pedal made German organs and organists unique, meant also that the feet played an important part in the construction of Bach as a nationalist hero. The German nation was some seventy years from its founding when Forkel published his Bach biography, but the organ and its players had long been a symbol of German musical legitimacy, from at least the time of the transalpine pedal missionary Bernhard the German. The refinements of culture; the glow of pride at native talent and technology; the comparison of musicians from various countries; and the set-piece encounters of the Grand Tour: all these had long been inflected by national feeling. I do not want to overstate the importance of the pedal; its symbolic power in the eighteenth century and earlier belongs to a larger, though still nascent, sense of cultural nationalism.[89] But neither should this power be discounted simply because it was one of several parallel developments in national sentiment. When evaluating the cultural standing of the German "nation," Mattheson, Marpurg, Quantz, C. P. E. Bach, and German tourists turned repeatedly to the organ as a bulwark against the fashionable imports from the European south and as a standard-bearer of German musical self-sufficiency and technological prowess. The organ was a mighty fortress. What has changed with Forkel's account of Bach is that the instrument of his mastery no longer simply bolsters collective self-worth in the cultural sphere, but requires allegiance from a people, which is itself to be unified behind that symbol. That this can lead to ugly places is obvious (see Chapter 6). Long a source of national pride, the organ pedal had become political.

As we have seen, the contemporary reception of Bach as an organist drafted him into national service. Mattheson places him and Handel at the top of the list of great German organists, who are the best in the world and far above those of other non-pedal-playing traditions, not least because they used their feet. Bach's music shows his keen interest in national styles, something he registered overtly in the famous 1730 memorandum to his employers in Leipzig, noting that "German musicians are expected to be capable of performing at once and *ex tempore* all kinds of music, whether it come from Italy or France, England or Poland."[90] From the central-German city of Leipzig he surveyed, and was invigorated by, a musical scene as diverse as the various European costumes seen in Figure 6.9. My reading of Schlick, Quantz and many others argues that the German organ art was an important reference point for German cultural identity beginning at least in the early modern period, and probably even earlier. I see no reason to think Bach would have strayed much from this line; while most of his

---

[89] See Ruth-Ellen Boetcher Joeres, "The German Enlightenment (1720–1790)" in Helen Watanabe-O'Kelly (ed.), *The Cambridge History of German Literature* (Cambridge University Press, 1997), pp. 147–201, esp. pp. 147–155.

[90] *NBR*, 150; *BD*, 1: 63.

celebrated German contemporaries ventured to Italy and France, he spent almost his entire life in a small region of central Germany whose boundaries are marked by the town of his birth, Eisenach in Thuringia, and the place of his death, Leipzig, one hundred miles to the east. Yet in his home provinces and on his occasional travels within Germany he would likely have embraced the unique status of the organ in German music. Given his oeuvre and what we know of his activities as a virtuoso, Bach must have been more committed than most to the primacy of German organ traditions, if only because he invested so much effort into learning from the past in his pursuit of the new.

CHAPTER 5

Treading the globe: the worldwide expansion of the German pedal ideal

IN BURNEY'S FOOTSTEPS

Praised and criticized by Burney and others, German organs remained tourist attractions into the nineteenth century, marveled at by visitors for their size, variety, and brilliance. Equally astonishing was the playing of German organists. In 1828 in London, Edward Holmes published his *Ramble Among the Musicians of Germany*, recounting a trip that passed through Cologne, Darmstadt, Munich, Vienna, and Prague, before arriving in Dresden. In the Saxon capital, the self-styled Professor of Music turned his attention from the start to the city's famous organs. Like Burney before him, Holmes enthuses about the legendary *Gravitas* of these German instruments, and once again it is the feet and the pedals over which they dance that light the visitor's enthusiasm: the organ and its acrobatic operator are incomparable to anything he has seen or heard in England. At the Sophienkirche, where Wilhelm Friedemann Bach had been organist and his father had played important recitals, Holmes encounters Johann Gottlob Schneider, one of the leading organists of his generation (see Figure 5.1). For his English readers, Holmes places the German organ art in its proper perspective: "We held a conversation on the German method of organ-playing, and agreed that the instrument was, out of all comparison, the most difficult of attainment, as it required that the performer should have all the command of the best pianoforte player, and afterwards that he should attain the organ touch, style, and a facility in the use of the pedals."[1] Both seeing and hearing are crucial to the tourist's experience:

For sheer organ-playing Schneider is, however, quite alone; the difficulties which he there masters make all ordinary attempts appear child's play in the comparison ... The enthusiastic pleasure with which Schneider plays, makes it tenfold pleasant to see and hear him; he is not like a coxcomb who works hard and affects ease, he is wrapt up in his subject, plays with care, but with no more appearance of effort than necessarily grows out of such attempts.[2]

---

[1] Edward Holmes, *A Ramble among the Musicians of Germany* (London: Hunt and Clarke, 1828), p. 196. For more on Holmes, see E. D. MacKerness, "Edward Holmes (1797–1859)," *Music & Letters*, 45 (1964), 213–237.

[2] Holmes, *ibid.*, p. 197.

Figure 5.1   Silbermann Organ (1720), Sophienkirche, Dresden, photo c. 1930

The exhausting labor of the aged Dresden organist Binder described by Burney (see Chapter 4, p. 171) contrasts with the ease with which the massive instrument is operated by his successor. Bach's body is conjured by his nineteenth-century epigone at an instrument he had once played:

One morning on which we visited the church, happening to be rather sultry, before beginning to play he whipped off his coat, saying to his company "*Verzeihen sie* [sic]*, mein* [sic] *Herrn*" (Your pardon, gentlemen), and in that pleasant state of informality plunged into the thick of the Kyries of Sebastian Bach, playing the whole of six and seven real parts with such a towering skill in the pedals as to make one think the old author returned from his grave.[3]

The number of voices is prone to exaggeration by the English traveler when confronted with German organs and organists.[4] No seven-voice organ pieces survive from Bach, nor do any of the Kyrie settings exceed five voices. Perhaps the piece Schneider played was Bach's six-part *Aus tieffer Noth*, BWV 686 (see Chapter 2, p. 98); this certainly would have been a well-chosen vehicle for impressing a musical tourist wanting to experience the full sonic and visual effect of double pedal. Schneider has an acute sense for the drama of the moment, seen in the casual way the sublime performance is set up with the throwing down of his coat, exposing the body of the player, especially the feet, for easier admiration. Schneider seems well aware that he is a tourist attraction.

But in his account Holmes makes a turn that the eighteenth-century traveler Burney does not: Holmes wants to take home concrete benefits from his experience and for his readers to do the same, for he tells them that much is to be learned from German organs, and imagines what benefits would result from "uniting Silbermann's magnificence with the sweet *cathedral* quality of tone for which the organs of the Temple and Westminster Abbey are noted." Holmes asks those back in England to use their

imaginations to fancy with what effect a piece of florid and artful counterpoint comes out of a German organ, where the player sits with a flood of sound ready to the touch of his fingers, and a store of thunder lying harmless at his feet. The thickness, depth, and independence of the pedals, here vindicate supremely the poetical ascendancy of the fugue over every other class of musical composition; and in slow subjects, when the bass rolls in its ponderousness – there is no disputing it – it is like the fiat of the Omnipotent.[5]

Once the ramble is over, new horizons open up back at home. Holmes's proposal for German enrichment of English traditions would indeed become a reality in his homeland over the next few decades, in no small measure thanks to his own proselytizing efforts.

The English conversion to pedal-playing was part of the universal adoption of German-style pedal performance across Europe that had been heralded by Arnolt Schlick in 1511, and then by Praetorius some one

---

[3] *Ibid.*, pp. 197–198.
[4] Frederick the Great would do the same when his memory expanded J. S. Bach's six-voice fugue improvised in Potsdam in 1747 on one of the Prussian King's Silbermann pianofortes to an incredible eight voices – without the use of the feet. *BD*, 3: 276; *NBR*, 366–367. See also Yearsley, *Bach and the Meanings of Counterpoint* (Cambridge University Press, 2002), p. 157.
[5] Holmes, *A Ramble*, pp. 192–193.

hundred years later. Yet the acceptance of German pedals and pedaling did not occur until the nineteenth century. It would hardly be risky to claim that ease of travel and increased communication allowed for the rapidity of the eventual transformation of European organs in the nineteenth century, but the results of industrialization do not alone account for the triumph of one performing tradition over another. German pedaling could as well have withered and dispersed, overwhelmed by the lazy feet of the rest of Europe. After all, as we've seen (Chapter 2, p. 86), in south Germany pedal skill seems to have receded in the seventeenth century rather than having effected the expansion Schlick had anticipated. To be convinced of the value of pedal independence the English – and others – needed more than simply reports from abroad. They had to witness the astonishing coordination of four-limbed performance in the service of Bach's music in its native environment and also in the British Isles. Fully aware of the power of German organ performance, virtuosos took to the road, and even though foreign instruments rarely made such displays easy, or even possible, the pages of German music periodicals extolled expansion of German organ-building and performance throughout Europe, from the large Walcker organ of three manuals and pedal built in 1840 for St. Petersburg to an even bigger one of three manuals and pedal for Valencia Cathedral by the Ibach firm, completed in 1860; its sixty stops, with fourteen in the pedal, made it "one of the largest and most beautiful organs in Spain."[6] According to Valencia's main newspaper, "Truly impressive above all else is the effect of the low pedal stops, whose tone penetrates into the farthest corners of the [vast] church."[7] The project was the initiative of the "prize-winning Professor and first Organist Don Pascual Perez" (y Gascon), founder of the school of music in Valencia; he was a Bachist and welcomed this full pedal as a crucial cultural import in a country lacking a pedal tradition to match that of Germany.

When we sense the evangelical enthusiasm of Holmes and Perez and so many others, it is easy to begin to believe that the transformation of organ culture was preordained – that the German ideal had always represented the proper way to play the organ. This is not a moral judgment claiming that obbligato pedaling is a higher good, musically and ethically. Rather, the English and others became convinced that organs should have full, independent pedals thanks in large part to the decisive role of German virtuosos playing Bach at the instrument. The technology alone could not bring about such a change, but the thrill of hearing and playing Bach's music as he had done, with hands and feet at an organ with full pedalboard, could. Once the contest in England was decided in favor of pedal independence over left-hand virtuosity, the emancipated English feet were freed to carry the

---

[6] *Euterpe*, 21 (1861), 48.
[7] *Diario Mercantil*, December 9, 1860; reprinted and translated into German in *Euterpe*, 21 (1861), 48.

message of the self-sufficient musician at the instrument of instruments to the far corners of their worldwide empire.

"INSULAR" LEFT HANDS VERSUS "GERMAN" FEET

There was resistance to this transformation. A few years before the publication of Holmes' book, the organist and conductor Sir George Smart had made his own continental tour, with the obligatory visit to the organs of Dresden. Smart could say quite flatly of the Hofkapelle organ, distilling more harshly sentiments similar to those expressed by Burney half a century earlier, that "It is large and may be celebrated in Germany but would not be in England."[8] A quarter-century later at the International Industrial Exhibition held in London in 1851, Smart was confronted with something he viewed as an unwelcome visitor to his country – a German organ with full pedals erected in the Crystal Palace. Asked to try out the instrument, Smart balked, responding defensively to the invitation by likening this essential feature of the German organ to something to cook sausages on: "My dear Sir, I never in my life played upon a *gridiron*."[9] The vignette recalls C. P. E. Bach's refusal to play the Hamburg Michaeliskirche organ for Burney, not, like Smart, because he had never learned to use his feet, but precisely because he had. For his part, Smart had seen great German organists in person, and knew what it meant to play a German organ; but after his continental trip, he nonetheless had been unwilling, or unable, to train his feet to do what he had seen organists' feet do there.

By 1851 Smart's attitude counted as antiquated even in England, but there were many others marching with him in the anti-pedal rearguard. After touring some of the great organs of the continent, from Haarlem to Hamburg and Freiburg, the organist of York Minster, John Camidge, remained a devotee of the long English manual compass which extended down to GG, a fourth lower than the German compass. It was reported that Camidge favored this larger range because he "was not very brilliant on the pedals, but very brilliant with the left hand."[10] This defense of the left hand versus the pedal had an august pedigree: decades earlier Samuel Wesley, one of the fathers of the English Bach Revival, suggested that "pedals might be of service to those who could not use their fingers."[11] It is not as if Wesley was completely opposed to the use of the feet in organ-playing – he did, after all, introduce rudimentary pedal lines into his music. But he did

---

[8] George Thomas Smart, *Leaves from the Journals of Sir George Smart*, ed. H. Bertram Cox and C. L. E. Cox (London: Longmans, Green, and Co., 1907), p. 142.

[9] Charles W. Pearce, *The Evolution of the Pedal Organ and Matters Connected Therewith* (London: Musical Opinion, 1927), p. 57.

[10] Nicholas Thistlethwaite, *The Making of the Victorian Organ* (Cambridge University Press, 1990), pp. 97, 175.

[11] *Musical World*, 13 (1840), 315. See also Thistlethwaite, *The Making of the Victorian Organ*, pp. 14–15.

apparently believe that too heavy a reliance on the feet could be used to hide technical deficiencies in the left hand. This view was shared by many others. Even after the middle of the nineteenth century, serious proposals were made for extending the manual compass down a full octave beyond the German standard all the way down to CC, since such an arrangement would "in a great measure, if not altogether, do away with the necessity for a pedal organ."[12] When an instrument was equipped with some pedals they were used in ancillary fashion rather than for obbligato lines. W. T. Best, one of the great English pedal-players of the second half of the nineteenth century, would lampoon the style of one of the leading English organists of the early nineteenth century, Thomas Adams, who, claimed Best, added "droning pedal [to fugues from Bach's *Well-Tempered Clavier*] when his bunions were propitious."[13]

In the first half of the nineteenth century, English players and builders divided themselves into what Nicholas Thistlethwaite, in his magisterial study of the Victorian organ, calls the "Insular Movement," on the one hand, and proponents of the "German System," on the other, the former defending the GG compass for both manuals and pedals, while the latter pushed for the adoption of the layout of German instruments suited to the performance of Bach's music. Like Wesley, Insular organists were proud of their brilliant left hands, producing musical textures that could be buttressed by the pedal at key points, such as cadences. When an extra left hand was needed for obbligato lines or for complicated Bach works that a given organist could not manage with only two hands in play, the fingers of an assistant could be deployed on the lower part of the extended keyboard, or on a special separate keyboard sometimes placed next to the lower manual, which also operated the pedal pipes.

The Insular compass, then, was aimed at keeping the feet subservient to the hands, since freeing the feet required restricting the scope of the left hand. This much was clear to the English even before their wholesale conversion to the German System by about the middle of the nineteenth century. Already in the 1820s a writer for the Edinburgh *Gazetteer* expressed views shared with Forkel, whose Bach biography had appeared in English translation in 1820:[14]

Till within these [last] few years, pedals were scarcely known in England, and even now are generally what are termed "sham"; i.e. they are only a range of sticks for the feet, connected with the keys of the great Organ. Even these are such use, that a person accustomed to them, can scarcely endure the emptiness of the performance, which is manifest when they are wanting. They enable the Performer to double his

---

[12] *Musical Gazette*, 1 (1856), 44. See Thistlethwaite, *The Making of the Victorian Organ*, p. 97.

[13] Andrew McCrea, "A Note on Thomas Adams and his Showroom Demonstrations," *Journal of the British Institute of Organ Studies*, 25 (2001), 78–95, at 79.

[14] Michael Kassler (ed.), *The English Bach Awakening* (Aldershot, UK; Burlington, USA: Ashgate, 2004), p. 14.

bass, without being under the necessity of deserting the *tenore*, to which the left hand should be almost exclusively devoted. Indeed, an organ played with pedals, is as much superior to an organ played without them . . . as the modern Grand Piano-Forte is, to the Spinet of our Great Grandmothers.[15]

Pedal dependency of this kind had vexed many German writers of the eighteenth century, including Mattheson, Quantz, and C. P. E. Bach among others, who held the autonomy of the pedal to be fundamental to organ-playing, and indeed to German musical culture. Having overcome various levels of resistance from Wesley, Smart and others by the end of the nineteenth century, this ideology would become deeply embedded in Britain and across Europe.

THE ORGANS OF A GREAT CAPITAL

Though rare, pedals were not quite as novel in England as later English organists liked to remember as they reflected on the pedal revolution that had swept their country in the first half of the nineteenth century. The native organ-builder Renatus Harris published a pamphlet around 1712 in which he proposed a grandiose, never-realized scheme for a new west-end organ for St. Paul's, which, besides six (!) manual keyboards, would have had "Pedals for the Feet" and allowed the organist to "carry on three fugues at once."[16] Harris's wording suggests that he was thinking of the performance of contrapuntal trio textures, though it seems unlikely that he could have envisioned anything as ambitious as the Bach Trios, which would become the first organ works printed and widely disseminated in England, although not to be played on the organ and certainly not with the feet. In 1720 the organ-builder Christopher Shrider was paid for work on the St. Paul's organ, "adding 6 large Trumpet Pipes down to 16 ft Tone to be used with a pedal or without" and was paid for work on the "Pedal & Its movements."[17] Perhaps Handel's visits to St. Paul's were spurred by Shrider's additions, or perhaps these pedals encouraged him to visit the organ in the first place; a boisterous reed would have helped draw attention to Handel's feet when he "exercised" them of a Sunday afternoon, even if these pedals were not like those back in Germany.

These native English pedals not only had a shorter compass, but the individual keys were shorter and less sturdy than the German type, and in size more like those of the French classic organs of the seventeenth and eighteenth centuries; the keys seem generally to have been hinged at the

---

[15] Thistlethwaite, *The Making of the Victorian Organ*, p. 96.

[16] Stephen Bicknell, *The History of the English Organ* (Cambridge University Press, 1996), p. 160. See also Dominic Gwynn, "Lost Worlds: The English Organ Before 1700" in Thomas Donahue (ed.), *Music and its Problems: Essays in Honor of Peter Williams* (Richmond, Virginia: OHS Press, 2007), pp. 23–47.

[17] Bicknell, *ibid.*, p. 158.

Figure 5.2   "Toe" Pedals, Thomas Eliot, 1813, Scone Palace

front, rather than at the back as in German pedalboards; often there was no frame around the English pedalboard. Such pedalboards continued to be made into the 1820s, as that from the early nineteenth-century organ at Scone Palace shows (see Figure 5.2). Only the toe could be used on these small English pedals, and they were played more lightly, as if tapping them with the feet, unlike the more energetic approach of the German organists.

While most remembered Britain as pedal-less throughout the eighteenth century, a few instruments – like those at St. Paul's and Westminster Abbey – did have pedals.[18] Wesley recalled (inaccurately) that "the only Organ in London to which Pedals were affixed was that of the German Church of St. Mary-Le-Savoy in the Strand (also known as the Lutheran Chapel), built by Snetzler."[19] This instrument had an octave-and-a-half of German pedals up to c, but without any independent pipes. A cosmopolitan city with musicians from across Europe, London also attracted German organists, their unique way of playing having been advertised in advance by

---

[18] Nicholas Thistlethwaite has disproved the claim that an early seventeenth-century organ at Jesus College, Cambridge had pedals. See his "Organs and Arminians in Early Seventeenth-Century Cambridge" in John Ogasapian *et al.* (eds.), *Litterae organi: Essays in Honor of Barbara Owen* (Richmond, Virginia: OHS Press, 2005), pp. 27–50.

[19] *Ibid.*, pp. 14–15.

Burney's reports. The German émigré Carl Friedrich Baumgarten was organist at the church from 1783 to 1792, having been trained in the great organ city of Lübeck under Johann Paul Kunzen, one of Buxtehude's successors at the Marienkirche; Baumgarten was perhaps the first composer in England to publish a Voluntary with a simple pedal part written on a separate, third, staff.[20] The touring German virtuoso Johann Wilhelm Häßler, "a musical grandson of Bach," played in St. Mary-Le-Savoy to the "general astonishment" of those present, among them the King and Queen and many aristocrats, in 1791.[21] The feet are not mentioned in the surviving account published in Hamburg, but they doubtless came into play on this rare pedal instrument.

Thistlethwaite describes a "bewildering diversity" of pedal compasses and key-sizes in England in the early nineteenth century; most pedalboards were an octave or an octave-and-a-half, but there was no standard as far as range, width, or placement. Always at a premium for organists, adaptability was even more necessary in England. The 1819 edition of Rees's *Cyclopaedia* complained that "scarcely two organs in the kingdom have their pedals alike . . . so that every performer who comes to an organ (be he ever so skilful in the use of pedals), has the whole of his business to learn again."[22] The more robust keys for the feet introduced increasingly after 1820 were referred to as "German pedals" to differentiate them from the smaller toe pedals of the native tradition; but even if the newer designs resulted in more substantial pedalboards with longer keys, neither the range nor placement was standard.[23] This was a state of affairs that would have irked Schlick, just as it tested the German virtuosos who increasingly visited England in the nineteenth-century.[24] The opening installment of the *English Musical Gazette* of 1819 included a lengthy article on the organ at St. Paul's, and reported that "the pedals to the great organ being very short are of little use: we have heard this frequently complained of by foreigners, who have played upon the instrument, but could not manage them after the German style."[25] As one would expect, the organ at St. Paul's was a destination for visiting organists, as it would be for Mendelssohn. Those "foreigners" playing in the "German style" were clearly Germans equipped with impressive pedal

---

[20] Pearce, *The Evolution of the Pedal Organ*, p. 31.   [21] *BD*, 3: 506–507.

[22] Quoted in Thistlethwaite, *The Making of the Victorian Organ*, p. 23.

[23] Among countless examples, see the advertisement by the firm of Longman & Bates from the London *Examiner*, Sunday, May 8, 1825: "An Organ suitable for a place of Worship, two rows of keys, mahogany case, long octaves GG to F, in all the great Organ contains eight stops, the Swell four stops, to F, below middle G; three shifting movements, octave of German pedals, &c. Allowed by several eminent Professors to be one of the finest toned Organs ever made." For a list of the ranges of English pedalboards before 1820, see Thistlethwaite, *The Making of the Victorian Organ*, pp. 16–17.

[24] *Ibid.*, pp. 97–101.

[25] *The English Musical Gazette*, 1 (1819), 8/Plate 1. The engravings devoted to the organ in Rees's *Cyclopaedia* of 1814 show the St. Paul's pedalboard with what seem to be very short keys. See also Thistlethwaite, *The Making of the Victorian Organ*, p. 22.

techniques; hoping to draw on the sublime power of the feet in the cavernous acoustic of Christopher Wren's masterpiece, these visitors were disappointed at what they encountered.

One such complainer may have been August Frederic Christopher Kollmann, a north German like Baumgarten; Kollmann held the position at the German Chapel in St. James where there was another Snetzler organ, probably also with pedals. Arriving in London the year before Baumgarten, Kollmann published his influential *Essay on Practical Musical Composition* in 1799. In the *Essay* Kollmann takes it upon himself to inform the musical public and British organists as to what was really possible with a full set of pedals of two octaves arranged and played according to the German manner. Kollmann admits that such elaborate performance was hardly possible in his adopted country because such pedalboards were "not very frequently met with," and those that did exist were largely inadequate to the kind of techniques and music he went on to describe.[26] Kollmann allowed that the pedals could be used merely for doubling of the bass, but their higher purpose was for obbligato lines, or even tenor treatment of hymn and psalm tunes. Kollmann's modern examples were drawn from Häßler, but the highest levels of organ-playing were represented in the *Essay* by Bach's trios; the three movements of Bach's first sonata, BWV 525 close the volume as a sort of summation of the soloist's art: "pieces of this kind, when properly executed, exceed everything else in the art of organ-playing."[27] But how were such pieces to be heard, not to mention practiced, in a land where the organs lacked pedals? Kollmann explains that three hands can be used on a two-manual English organ. Bach's Trios demonstrated not only how one German organist could do what three string or wind players could, but also how he could do alone what it took two Englishmen to accomplish at an organ or piano. The German organist fully using his feet, was, as Kollmann would later put it of Bach, "many musicians in one."[28]

The most extreme contrast between the self-sufficient German organist and the three-handed approach of the English was to be seen in the London Apollonicon organ completed by Benjamin Flight and Joseph Robson in 1817.[29] This famed attraction could be played from one or more of its five separate consoles; the instrument could also be operated mechanically by means of a pinned barrel. Unusually for the time, the Apollonicon had two octaves of "German pedals," but these began not at C but at GG.

[26] August Frederic Christopher Kollmann, *An Essay on Practical Musical Composition* (London: the author, 1799; reprint, New York: Da Capo Press, 1973), p. 98.
[27] *Ibid.*, p. 99.
[28] August Frederic Christopher Kollmann, *Quarterly Register*, reprinted in Michael Kassler (ed.), *A. F. C. Kollmann's Quarterly Musical Register (1812); an Annotated Edition with an Introduction to his Life and Works* (Aldershot, UK; Burlington, USA: Ashgate, 2008), p. 33.
[29] Rachel Cowgill, "The London Apollonicon Recitals, 1817–1832: a Case-Study in Bach, Mozart and Haydn Reception," *Journal of the Royal Musical Association*, 123 (1998), 190–228, at 196.

Among the early spectacles presented in this secular setting was the ten-handed performance, by "five professors," of Bach's *Magnificat*, BWV 243, in 1819. The English were accustomed to having many organists busy at one organ.

A decade later the north-German immigrant Karl Friedrich Horn and the Bach devotee (and distruster of the pedal) Samuel Wesley began issuing the Bach Trio Sonatas separately in arrangements for three hands at one keyboard, effectively domesticating organ music for a chamber setting. The astonishing image of four-limbed performance figures prominently in the "Advertisement" for the first installment of the project, the E flat Trio Sonata, BWV 525:

The Trio was designed for the Organ, and performed by the matchless Author in a very extraordinary Manner; the first and second Treble Parts he played with both Hands on two Sets of keys, and the Bass (wonderful as it appears) he executed entirely upon the Pedals, without Assistance.

Such a physical act itself was hardly to be believed, especially when the kinds of instruments that allowed for it were literally foreign to the English. That an independent, solitary player could manage such things on his own is presented as something approaching the superhuman. Failing independent feet, however, another hand was required.

In the *Quarterly Musical Register* of 1812 Kollmann was for the most part less forgiving about the deficiencies of English organs, and by extension English organists and their need for a third hand to play *pedaliter* music, than he had been in the *Essay on Practical Musical Composition*. Kollmann summarily dismisses Burney's spurious, if unforgettable, portrait of J. S. Bach at the organ performing contrapuntal miracles with a stick between the teeth; the absurdity of that picture is adduced by Kollmann as evidence of English incredulity at real organ-playing and as a manifestation of the eccentric English appreciation of Bach's finest achievement – the organ works. Mere study of the scores of Bach's organ music or their transcription for domestic amusement and private edification were simply not enough:

It is evident, that no true idea can be formed of S. Bach's *organ-playing*, except by hearing his works expressly composed for the *organ*, performed in the manner in which *he* played them, viz: those for the *full* organ, on a good *large organ*, and the pedal part on a double bass stop; those for *solo* stops, on as many sets of keys with different stops as they contain parts, and the bass part on a suitable double bass stop.[30]

Bach's organ music required pedals and a player proficient in using them – this was the German view now being hammered into those English readers who cared to take this to heart. Kollmann implicitly criticized Samuel Wesley's music because it was "for manual keys only" and therefore did

---

[30] Kollmann, *Register*, p. 35.

not "[promote] the use of obligato [sic] pedals." But real progress was being made thanks to an increasing adoption of the German ideal: ". . . a true idea [of obbligato pedal-playing] begins now to become pretty general, by the increasing circulation of Sebastian Bach's Organ Trios, and of his other works for Organ."[31] Kollmann also acknowledged, though did not name, "numerous able performers" committed to playing with the feet and therefore to a manner of performance more fitting for the organ. Among these musicians may have been William Russell (1777–1813), who published two sets of voluntaries; the first, from 1805, included trio textures with simple, but unambiguously obbligato, pedal parts; the second set, from 1812, even dedicates a third staff to the pedal line.[32] In spite of such signs of "improvement," Kollmann lamented the lack of appropriate instruments in England for the greatest of organ works – those of J. S. Bach. Such a deficiency was more than simply a musical matter, but reflected poorly on the standing of a great nation: "In regard to *organs*, it is remarkable, that throughout the whole British Empire, and in the most opulent city on the face of the globe, London, there is, according to the best of our enquiries, *not one* organ equal to those which are *frequent* in the principal cities of Germany, Holland, and the Netherlands." Compared to the politically divided Germany, Britain was a global power, but it had no organs worthy of its geopolitical standing.

BACH'S FEET ON "CRIPPLED" ORGANS: MENDELSSOHN
AND THE ENGLISH LEARN TO WALK

As Holmes was rambling across Europe, organists back at home could not approach the virtuosity of a Schneider in Dresden. Still, a few English musicians were already performing Bach's organ works using their own feet on instruments with pedalboards of distinctly un-German dimensions. Writing in the *Musical World* in 1838, the lawyer-turned-organist John Henry Gauntlett, the "pedallist of London" and an ardent devotee of Bach, claimed that "Bach's pedal fugues, and their public performance in the Metropolis, took its rise about ten or twelve years ago," that is, around the time of Holmes's trip.[33] In October of 1827 Gauntlett and several others competed for the organist's position at St. Stephen's, Coleman Street in London. Among the applicants was Samuel Sebastian Wesley, son of Samuel Wesley. As befits someone named after Bach, the younger Wesley had learned to play with his feet, as his famous *Variations* on the National

---

[31] *Ibid.*, p. 15.
[32] Andrew McCrea, "British Organ Music after 1800" in Nicholas Thistlethwaite and Geoffrey Webber (eds.), *The Cambridge Companion to the Organ* (Cambridge University Press, 1999), pp. 279–298, at pp. 280–283.
[33] *Musical World*, 9 (1838), 208; Thistlethwaite, *The Making of the Victorian Organ*, p. 184.

Example 5.1   Samuel Sebastian Wesley, *God Save the King*, Variation 9, first half

Anthem, written in 1829, showed (see Example 5.1).[34] Throughout his life, however, the younger Wesley remained committed to the extended manual compass favored by his father because it encouraged a roaming and virtuosic left hand; a contemporary reviewer doubted any English organist other than Wesley himself could play the pedal part of the third variation – showy, but by no means excessive for a German organist.[35] *The Morning Post* reported that:

> On Wednesday the inhabitants of St. Stephen's Coleman Street, were highly gratified with a fine display of organ performances by the various candidates for the situation of Organist of their Parish Church. The organ, built by Avery [in 1775], had undergone a thorough repair for the occasion; and is, in every respect, a beautiful instrument. Where many acquitted themselves well, it would seem invidious to particularise; but we cannot pass by the masterly execution of a magnificent Pedal Fugue, the composition of J. Seb. Bach, which was severally performed by Messrs. Gauntlett and S. Wesley, jun. . . . It was, in the opinion of Mr. Attwood [organist at St. Paul's and celebrated student of Mozart], one of the Umpires, an extraordinary performance, and did the greatest credit to the talents and industry of these two gentlemen.[36]

The piece singled out for praise was the "St. Anne", BWV 552, the most popular Bach fugue among English organists of the time, perhaps because it had been the only *pedaliter* fugue published during Bach's lifetime, but more likely still because it was widely available in England after its

---

[34] For some of the quantities of praise heaped at Wesley's feet for his talents as an organist, and for his pedal-playing in particular, see Peter Horton, *Samuel Sebastian Wesley: A Life* (Oxford University Press, 2004), pp. 114, 174, 180.

[35] *Harmonicon*, 9 (1831), 196. Thistlethwaite, *The Making of the Victorian Organ*, p. 104.

[36] *The Morning Post*, October 17, 1827. See also Thistlethwaite, *The Making of the Victorian Organ*, p. 173.

Figure 5.3   St. James Bermondsey, console, James Bishop, 1829

publication in London in 1823.[37] The St. Stephen's organ dated from 1775 and had neither the pedal compass, nor the separate stops, of Bach's organs. Undaunted, the St. Stephen's candidates played the fugue anyway. Wesley senior had done duo performances at the Hanover Square music rooms nearly two decades before, but Gauntlett claimed that these were the first solo organ performances of the "St. Anne" fugue in England.[38]

Diversity continued to reign in England on native organs and in the performance of Bach's great organ works. The 1829 dedication of the organ at St. James, Bermondsey, prompted another performance of Bach's "St. Anne"; although the instrument had a small pedal division, three players performed at the console, one presumably using the manual keyboard to activate the pedal registers (see Figure 5.3). This extra pedal-manual, oxymoronic from a German point of view, provided a safe haven

[37] *Organ Voluntaries Consisting of Preludes & Fugues Selected from the Works of John Sebastian Bach*, ed. George Drummond (London: Royal Harmonic Institution, 1823).
[38] *Musical Times*, 37 (1896), 723.

for the left hand against the prerogatives of the feet.[39] On this manual the left hand could do exactly what the pedal did without committing what Forkel and so many others would have viewed as a crime against the organ. Imagine Schneider in Dresden asking for assistance from an underling or, for that matter, from a musical visitor in order to play a full obbligato pedal line because he couldn't; never! But few English organists were capable of performing Bach's obbligato pedal works by themselves, and such an extra manual was deemed a clever solution for deficient pedal-players. It allowed for more of Bach's music, even if, as Kollmann had put it, these performances were not in his "manner."

At the competition for the Bermondsey post that followed later in 1829, Gauntlett played the Fugue in B minor, BWV 544, and the fiendishly difficult final movement of the C minor Trio Sonata, BWV 526/3, as well as the Prelude in E flat, BWV 552/1, all without the assistance of a third hand. The Bermondsey pedal had a two-octave range but was displaced down a fourth from that of Bach's organs, from GG to g; Gauntlett and others would have had to make major adjustments to the pedal lines. This testifies to the impressive adaptability with which native organists navigated through the "bewildering diversity" of pedalboards in their performances of Bach's music.[40] There was no other way. Organs like that at Bermondsey represented a compromise in bass territory between devotees of the left hand and those committed to defending that terrain on behalf of the feet; playing Bach on such ambivalent instruments required courage and skill.

The adaptability summoned by English organists like Gauntlett was in still greater demand from German visitors, for whom such compasses and layouts were in every sense foreign. The most famous of these tourists was Felix Mendelssohn, and his contribution to the popularity of pedal-playing in England as a result of his many trips to that country was remembered as decisive by the English. Fresh from the triumphs of his performance of Bach's *St. Matthew Passion* in Berlin in the spring of 1829, the twenty-year-old genius Mendelssohn set off for England from the great organ city of Hamburg. On April 13 he wrote to his family that before he left he hoped "to snarl" [*anschnauzen*] at the organ in the Michaeliskirche with "some Seb. Bach," though in the event he was enjoined to play quietly because it was Holy Week and so he could not unleash the pedal's roar of this famous instrument. Seen historically, the Michaeliskirche is a fitting place for a German organist to embark for England, since it was here that C. P. E. Bach had refused to play for Burney because he could not use the pedal: the Michaeliskirche instrument had been central to the Anglo-German dialogue about the nature of the organ and the status of the pedals. From this very same instrument,

---

[39] *Ibid.*   [40] Thistlethwaite, *The Making of the Victorian Organ*, pp. 445–446.

the largest in Germany, Mendelssohn would travel directly to an organ culture he would in large part transform.[41]

Given his own defensive contempt for the pedals, George Smart might well have been gratified to see that on his visit to Mendelssohn's home in Berlin in 1825, when Felix played "a clever fugue pastorale, and a fantasia" on a house organ, the "very difficult part for the pedals" was taken by his sister, Fanny, on a nearby piano.[42] The Mendelssohns, and other drawing room devotees of Bach's organ music, including Franz Liszt, also used the three-handed approach long practiced by the English.[43] While Mendelssohn's feet may not have been fully trained when he set off on his Grand Tour, he would have appreciated the near holy importance of the pedals in organ-playing. In 1831, Mendelssohn's mentor Zelter had written to his friend Goethe that the pedals were the foundation not only of the organ but also of Bach's musical intellect (see Chapter 2, p. 106).[44]

From early on, Mendelssohn recognized the exalted status of German pedals; his teacher August Wilhelm Bach was organist in the Marienkirche in Berlin with its famous organ by Joachim Wagner, a student of Gottfried Silbermann; Mendelssohn is also known to have played Bach on the large Wagner organ in the city of Brandenburg, fifty miles from Berlin, in the year before he went to England. When vacationing with his family in Switzerland as a thirteen-year-old, Mendelssohn expressed disappointment at the limited compass of southern organs, like that he encountered in the small town of Bulle: "The pedals reach only to high A; B and C are missing, so that nothing of Bach's can be played on it."[45] Mendelssohn's feet would encounter even greater irregularities in English pedalboards. Yet before the English journey his repertoire was modest: mainstays were the E minor Fugue, BWV 533, one of the least demanding of Bach's free works, and the Pastorale, BWV 590, which Mendelssohn also played at the Wagner organ in Brandenburg; the latter was Bach's attempt at southern style, in which the left foot alone can move between the long pedal points of the first

---

[41] Mendelssohn to Lea and Fanny Mendelssohn Bartholdy, April 13/14, 1829. Felix Mendelssohn Bartholdy, *Sämtliche Briefe*, ed. Helmus Loos and Wilhelm Seidel, 12 vols. (Kassel: Bärenreiter, 2008–), vol. I, pp. 263–265.

[42] George Thomas Smart, Hugh Bertram Cox, and C. L. E. Cox, *Leaves from the Journals of Sir George Smart* (London: Longmans, Green & Co., 1907; reprint, New York: Da Capo, 1971), p. 173.

[43] Russell Stinson, *The Reception of Bach's Organ Works from Mendelssohn to Brahms* (Oxford University Press, 2006), p. 105.

[44] Zelter to Goethe, May 7, 1831, in *Goethe's Letters to Zelter: with Extracts from those of Zelter to Goethe*, trans. A. D. Coleridge (London: George Bell and Sons, 1892), pp. 451–452. See Stinson, *The Reception of Bach's Organ Works*, p. 18. Mendelssohn would impress Goethe in 1830 in Weimar with a performance of the Toccata in D minor, BWV 565. See also Mendelssohn to Zelter, June 22, 1830, *Sämtliche Briefe*, vol. I, pp. 558–561. For the identification of the "D Minor Toccata" referred to by Mendelssohn, see Stinson, *The Reception of Bach's Organ Works*, p. 19. For a more detailed account of Mendelssohn's formative early encounters with, and study of, the organ, including his trips to England and across the continent, as well as his relationship with Goethe, see Wm. A. Little, *Mendelssohn and the Organ* (Oxford University Press, 2010), pp. 21–50.

[45] Letter of September 13, 1822, quoted in Stinson, *ibid.*, p. 13.

Example 5.2   Felix Mendelssohn, *Volles Werk* in C minor, bars 1–16

movement (the rest of the piece is *manualiter*). Mendelssohn's earliest organ works presented little difficulty in the pedal; the *Volles Werk* in C minor from 1823 (see Example 5.2), composed at the age of fourteen, is based on Bach's great *Passacaglia*, BWV 582, but in contrast to its model the pedal never bursts out to display an independent virtuosity or contrapuntal independence from, not to mention equality with, the manuals. There was much practice to be done before Mendelssohn's feet would be capable of approaching Schneider's pedaling in Dresden.[46]

Mendelssohn was somewhat dubious of, or at least timid about, his skills as an organist, and made no great claims for his own standing as a public virtuoso on the instrument. Zelter, however, had little doubt about Mendelssohn's potential as an organist and perhaps unwittingly predicted the beneficial influence the English trip would have on the young man's interest in the organ. Just three days after Mendelssohn had ventured to the Michaeliskirche, Zelter wrote to Goethe, on Good Friday, April 17, 1829, "Felix is swimming on the high seas [to England] . . . As he plays the organ well, and there the organs are better than the organists, I think he may try his hand there too."[47] Where and how Zelter, who had never been to England, came to these judgments is unclear, but they reflect the long-standing dismissal of English organists by the Germans. Edward Holmes had visited Zelter in Germany and, given the Englishman's progressive view of German organs, and their potential for enriching English musical culture, he was perhaps responsible at least in part for informing Zelter's views of England. Zelter is prescient about the striking irony attending

[46] For more on Schneider, Mendelssohn, and other German organists of the period, see Little, *Mendelssohn and the Organ*, pp. 173–175.
[47] Zelter to Goethe, April 17, 1829, in *Goethe's Letters to Zelter*, p. 357.

Mendelssohn's role in the export of German pedaling – that the supremely gifted Mendelssohn would establish his reputation as an organist, and indeed work to build up his own technique, in a country with instruments of widely varying quality and with minimal pedals at best. It is not that Mendelssohn the organist was shunned in Germany, but his many public organ performances in England over a decade-and-a-half stand in stark contrast to his profile in Germany, where he would play only one official public organ recital in his entire career, and that would come much later, in 1840 at the Thomaskirche in Leipzig. Instead, it was on foreign turf that Mendelssohn's organ zeal would be ignited. Seen by Zelter and the Germans to be ill-supplied with organists, England was the perfect place for a young, would-be organist from Germany to improve himself in informal, accommodating settings surrounded by musicians such as Gauntlett, likewise bent on transforming their own organ-playing, not to mention reforming organ culture as a whole.

Mendelssohn's trip to England and the continuation of his tour to the continent between 1830 and 1832 was a journey of self-education, a *Bildungsreise*. He would try to practice Bach assiduously in England and then on the rest of his travels – in France, south Germany, Austria, Switzerland, and even in Italy where he "did not find a single [organ] in good order," as he reported to Goethe.[48] As Mendelssohn knew, the best instruments for his program of self-improvement were to be found back home. Yet the greater part of that personal training occurred abroad. Mendelssohn's own deficiencies at the pedal were no secret to English organists. Gauntlett recalled:

from [Mendelssohn's] remarks upon some hear-say of Schneider's playing at Dresden, we learn that [Mendelssohn's] notion of pedal-playing was very limited, and that then he had not seen the "not well known" organ music of Bach, which Marx, either then or soon after, sent to the press. I believe when staying with the Horsleys at this end of the town [west London] he had access to a small organ at St. Matthew's – "*a crippled*" organ as he called the G pedal and keyboard – upon which he might certainly gain some sort of facility.[49]

While Gauntlett's memory is somewhat faulty here on the publication and dissemination of Bach's organ music, his recollection confirms the widespread feeling that in the person of Mendelssohn, the English had an example of someone willing and able to remake himself as a "true" organist,

---

[48] Mendelssohn to Goethe, August 28, 1831, *Sämtliche Briefe*, vol. ii, pp. 375–378. See also Stinson, *The Reception of Bach's Organ Works*, p. 21, and Günter Schulz, *Felix Mendelssohn Bartholdy: Glückliche Jugend (Briefe des jungen Komponisten)* (Bremen: Jacobi Verlag, 1971), p. 193. For an account of Mendelssohn's practicing on his continental tour, see Stinson, *The Reception of Bach's Organ Works*, pp. 17–30.

[49] Gauntlett to George Grove, November 30, 1864, reprinted in *Musical Times*, 46 (1905), 456. One of the founders of the Philharmonic Society, William Horsley, was a London composer and organist who befriended Mendelssohn on his first trip to England.

a masterful pedal-player. In Gauntlett's view the greatest musician of the age, recognizing his weakness at the King of Instruments, had used the limping organs of England to climb to heights never before achieved in that country. There were many who had no intention of renovating their technique and attitudes: Smart is one of many examples of such defensiveness. Nor was Mendelssohn by any means the only reason English organists began to play Bach with their feet. But as the most illustrious musician of the period, he was a vital motivating force in the transformation of English organ culture.

During his early sojourns in England, Mendelssohn's organ performances were marked by their informality: these were not set-piece concerts, but often came about as open-practice sessions, or postludes to services. He often played the postlude at St. Paul's Cathedral at Sunday services. In a letter to his father of July 10, 1829, Mendelssohn wrote that he would go to St. Paul's "to play the organ for the last time, since it will be my last Sunday in London," "exercising" his feet where Handel had done the same a century earlier.[50] With its German compass, the pedalboard in St. Paul's as Mendelssohn encountered it seems to have been conducive to German organ-playing; the organ had been finished in 1826 by James Bishop, who would complete the organ in Bermondsey three years later. The progression from "Insular" compass to the "German System" was not a linear one; Bishop began the pedal at C at St. Paul's, but at GG in Bermondsey. In any case, for Mendelssohn, practicing the pedals in England meant amplifying his technique on all sorts of pedal compasses. In August of 1829, near the end of his first English sojourn, Fanny Mendelssohn wrote to her brother about her wedding and her desires for the recessional, which was to be "in G major, beginning in the pedals."[51] Pedals were on the minds of the Mendelssohn virtuosos: what better way to walk out of the church than to be urged on by the vigorous display of the organist's feet in action?

Mendelssohn remained intent on developing his pedal technique after leaving England as he continued his Grand Tour on the continent. In September of 1831 he was again practicing intensively, admitting in a letter to his family from Switzerland: "it is actually a shame that I cannot play Sebastian Bach's major works." Johann Schneider's playing remained the standard; having heard that the Dresden organist, whom Mendelssohn greatly admired, could even play the scalar flourish of the D Major fugue

---

[50] Felix Mendelssohn to Abraham Mendelssohn and to the Mendelssohn family, July 10, 1829, *Sämtliche Briefe*, vol. I, pp. 331–333; and Mendelssohn to his Family in Berlin, June 11/12, 1829, *Sämtliche Briefe*, vol. I, pp. 308–312, at p. 311. See also Rudolf Elvers (ed.), *Felix Mendelssohn: A Life in Letters*, trans. Craig Tomlinson (New York: Fromm, 1986), pp. 75–76.

[51] Fanny Hensel to Felix Mendelssohn, August 25, 1829, in Marcia J. Citron (ed.), *The Letters of Fanny Hensel to Felix Mendelssohn* (Hillsdale, New York: Pendragon Press, 1987), p. 77. Mendelssohn never wrote the piece.

Example 5.3   J. S. Bach, Fugue in D from *The Well-Tempered Clavier, Book 1*, BWV 850/2, with pedal playing bassline, bars 6–7

from *The Well-Tempered Clavier*, BWV 850/2, in the pedal (see Example 5.3), Mendelssohn set about mastering what had seemed to him to be an impossible task, and then working on the similarly acrobatic subject of the organ fugue in the same key, BWV 532.[52] After an entire morning spent at the organ, he could proudly pun on the "steps forward" he had made while still "sitting at the organ."[53] Later that afternoon he returned to the church and "practiced on the organ until dusk, trampling furiously on the pedals." This feverish practice came after his time in Italy, where he claimed not to have found a single organ up to his standard. Moving on from Switzerland to Munich, he continued to practice but complained that "unfortunately I cannot practice as I wish because the pedalboard lacks the five highest notes."[54] Nonetheless his efforts while traveling, on organs with a wide variety of often-limited pedalboards, advanced his skill considerably. Soon he had a number of major works in his arsenal and extended his technique to include double pedal.

Mendelssohn's next trip to England over the spring and summer of 1832 demonstrates the raised visibility commanded by his expanded organ art, one gaining confidence in Bachian footwork. On June 10 in his beloved St. Paul's, Mendelssohn played "fugue music . . . to the amazement of all the listeners."[55] In a letter written after his return to Berlin, he described organ-playing as his greatest triumph, or at least his most enjoyable musical activity. He now had a taste for the sublime that came with the pedal as it resounded in Christopher Wren's great cathedral:

My greatest joy in London was that every Sunday after the service in St. Paul's I could play the organ, as long as I wanted. As the people heard of this and came to hear the Bach fugue in A minor, whose conclusion shakes the church's pillars, other organists offered me the opportunity to play their organs during the week, so that I

[52] Andreas Sieling, "Der Dresdner Hoforganist Johann Gottlob Schneider" in Hermann J. Busch and Michael Heinemann (eds.), *Zur deutschen Orgelmusik des 19. Jahrhunderts* (Sinzig: Schewe, 1998), pp. 185–192, at p. 187. See also Wm. A. Little, *Mendelssohn and the Organ*, p. 366.

[53] Mendelssohn to Franz Hauser, August 30 to September 5, 1831, *Sämtliche Briefe*, vol. ii, pp. 380–390, at p. 387. For diagrams of the short south-German/Austrian pedalboard and the English G-compass pedalboard, see Little, *Mendelssohn and the Organ*, p. 35.

[54] Mendelssohn to his family, October 6 and 7, 1831, *Sämtliche Briefe*, vol. ii, pp. 402–406.

[55] Wolfgang Lampadius, *The Life of Felix Mendelssohn-Bartholdy*, trans. W. L. Gage (Boston: Oliver Ditson Company, 1887), pp. 193–194.

could play to my heart's content. There [in London] the organs are mostly very good and so I was able there to practice diligently Sebastian Bach.[56]

This is a rather different view of at least some English organs than is suggested by Gauntlett's comment about their lameness. While there were only two organs with German pedal compass in London in the 1820s, Mendelssohn may have been simply too polite to complain much, as other touring German organists would do. He couched these performances at St. Paul's as attempts to hone his technique in what amounted to open rehearsals. A four-month return trip in 1833 included more demonstrations at St. Paul's, often for surreptitious visitors, like "two female patrons of the Philharmonic who had stolen in and listened unseen" to his performance of Bach.[57] The effect of Mendelssohn's playing on others must have been obvious to him.

By the time of Mendelssohn's visit to England in 1837 his organ performances had acquired a much more public dimension. The St. Paul's postlude remained his prized moment. At the end of the service on September 10, 1837 he launched into what appears to have been a staple, the Prelude and Fugue in A minor, BWV 543, mentioned in the letter of 1832. For this 1837 postlude, all the leading musicians in London joined the large congregation to hear him. But to the shock of all those present, the bellows pumper, having already labored through the preceding service, left his post prematurely so that the wind gave out as Mendelssohn came to the fugue's daunting final pedal solo. As he departed the cathedral, Mendelssohn looked on as a mob of congregants shouted "Shame! Shame!" at the errant pumper for what they saw as his dereliction of duty, committed within a few bars of the end of one of Bach's greatest fugues. Mendelssohn's letter home describes this confrontation ironically as an "opportunity to observe something of the 'public spirit' of a crowd of Englishmen."[58] Gauntlett was among those in attendance and wrote a rapturous article for *The Musical World* entitled "Mendelssohn as Organist," in which he described the scene: "Just as Mendelssohn had executed a storm of pedal passages with transcendent skill and energy, the pumper was seduced from his post and farther supply of wind forbidden, and the composer was left to exhibit the glorious ideas of Bach in all the dignity of dumb action." The momentum of four-limbed performance carries through to the end of the piece, but without any sound from the instrument itself, the thunder of the largest pipes dying in the echoing church and leaving behind only the clacking of the action to the "dismay and disappointment" of the audience. Gauntlett enthused at how

---

[56] Mendelssohn to Marie Cathérine Kiéne, July 28, 1832, *Sämtliche Briefe*, vol. ii, pp. 577–580, at p. 578.

[57] Mendelssohn to Abraham Mendelssohn, June 23, 1833, quoted in Stinson, *The Reception of Bach's Organ Music*, p. 36.

[58] Walter Salmen, *Calcanten und Orgelzieherinnen: Geschichte eines "niederen Dienstes"* (Hildesheim: Olms Verlag, 2007), pp. 96–97.

the power of the performance more than made up for the collapsing of the wind: "We had never previously heard Bach executed with such energy – never witnessed a composition listened to with greater interest and gratification."[59]

Two days later Mendelssohn gave the first official public organ recital of his life, and many from the St. Paul's debacle came to hear the completion of Bach's A minor Fugue at Christ Church, Newgate Street. It was a set-piece encounter in which a proponent of the future of four-limbed performance met the greatest figure of the old-guard defenders of the left hand. The elder Samuel Wesley, "trembling and bent," as Mendelssohn put it in a letter home, sat next to the visiting German on the organ bench and "improvised with great artistry and splendid facility, so that I could not but admire."[60] Wesley's daughter was moved to tears at the sight of this succession of organists in England. Gauntlett had arranged the performance, and his account reflects the English admiration of Mendelssohn's skills of adaptability, his ability to fit a high-speed fugue on the Christ Church pedal, which probably had a compass of only one and a half octaves:

M. Mendelssohn performed six extempore fantasias, and the pedal fugue he was not allowed to go through with at St. Paul's. Those who know the wide range of passages for the pedals with which this fugue abounds, may conceive how perfectly cool and collected must have been the organist who could on a sudden emergency transpose them to suit the scale of an ordinary English pedalboard.[61]

That Mendelssohn's expansive organ-pedaling was the focus of general astonishment and a marker of his self-transformation can be seen in Gauntlett's account of the Christ Church performance. No one was more surprised at Mendelssohn's playing at Christ Church than his friend, the piano virtuoso Ignaz Moscheles, then residing in London. As Gauntlett would later relate it, "[Moscheles] evidently was quite unaware of [Mendelssohn's] mastery over the instrument, for he took me on one side and asked me about, 'Where did he practise?' 'Could it be gained without practice on the organ?' 'Was it too late for him (Moscheles) to begin?' 'Would I teach him?' It was plain the playing of that morning was an unexpected thing to the pianist."[62] Here was an enthusiasm utterly unlike Smart's intransigence.

[59] John Henry Gauntlett, "Mendelssohn as Organist," *Musical World*, 7 (September 15, 1837), 8–10. See Stinson, *The Reception of Bach's Organ Music*, pp. 45–46.

[60] Peter Ward Jones, *The Mendelssohns on Honeymoon: the 1837 Diary of Felix and Cécile Mendelssohn Bartholdy Together with Letters to Their Families* (Oxford: Clarendon Press, 1997), p. 103.

[61] *Ibid.*

[62] Gauntlett to George Grove, November 30, 1864, reprinted in *Musical Times*, 46 (1905), 456.

Mendelssohn's 1837 sojourn culminated in triumph at the Birmingham Festival with seven performances in four days; the last of these was a concert at Birmingham Town Hall that concluded with Mendelssohn's performance of Bach's Prelude and Fugue in E flat on William Hill's new organ with German compass; the virtuoso couldn't help but complain that the instrument's pedal keys did not "have the breadth which feet and boots usually require."[63] A review of Mendelssohn's performance in the *Manchester Times and Gazette* focused on the feet: "the finale, with the pedal movements, was a fine exhibition of power."[64] Mendelssohn made many more trips to England, the last in 1847, the final year of his life; these visits were filled with demonstrations of the German organ art, more and more often on instruments with familiar compasses, as the German System was increasingly introduced in England after 1840. The ascendancy of the German ideal can be seen in the 1842 meeting of Mendelssohn with Prince Albert, who was an amateur organist and hailed from the heart of Bach country, Gotha in Thuringia.[65] Each played for the other in Buckingham Palace on the one-manual Gray and Davison organ of 1841. The royal amateur knew that the organ art of the homeland was built on the feet, and played a chorale from memory for Mendelssohn, making sure to use the pedal. Prince Consort and visiting virtuoso were doubtless proud of the ascendancy of the German System, although the royal instrument in Buckingham Palace had only an octave compass in the pedal. If the Prince could not become King, he could watch as the King of Instruments attained its true (German) character in the British Isles through adoption of full German pedal compasses and the increasing ability of organists to play Bach's *pedaliter* works alone. Albert would also have been proud that that transformation was driven in no small measure by the efforts of the German organist, Mendelssohn.

Many others besides Mendelssohn were crucial to these developments: English organists, critics, other traveling virtuosos, the influx of foreign organ tutors, and the activities of players who had studied in Germany with Schneider and Rinck. Mendelssohn's heroics of 1837 were only some of the contributions to organ culture in a year described by Thistlethwaite as the *annus mirabilis* for Bach's music and for pedal performance. Before Mendelssohn's arrival in the Fall of that year the eighteen-year-old Elizabeth Stirling was playing major Bach works – chorales, preludes and fugues, trios – in full Victorian ladies' clothes on organs with widely

---

[63] Mendelssohn to Joseph Moore, July 24, 1845, in Elise Polko, *Reminiscences of Felix Mendelssohn-Bartholdy: a Social and Artistic Biography*, trans. Lady Grace Wallace (London: Longmans, Green, and Co., 1869), p. 235.

[64] "Birmingham Musical Festival" in *The Manchester Times and Gazette*, issue 470, September 23, 1837. See also Wm. A. Little, "Mendelssohn in Birmingham: the Composer as Organist, 1837 and 1840," *The American Organist*, 43 (March 2009), 73–79.

[65] Roland Smith, "Prince Albert," *The American Organist*, 41(5) (May 2007), 96.

Example 5.4   Egerton Webbe, Prelude and Fugue in A; beginning of fugue, bars 53–64

varying pedalboards ill-suited to Bach's music. Also in her repertoire was the massive Prelude and Fugue in A by the critic and composer Egerton Webbe, who also happened to be the brother-in-law of that devotee of German organ-playing, Edward Holmes. Webbe's piece was published by Novello the year after Stirling's debut, and, although not particularly demanding for the feet, nonetheless demonstrates that English musicians were indeed grasping the potential of obbligato pedaling (see Example 5.4). As for Stirling's performances, Holmes's glowing reviews stressed her technical accomplishment, and concentrated on her Bachian economy of motion and skilful use of the feet, as well as on her powers of adaptability:

Miss Stirling possesses a most correct and brilliant manual execution, and her system of pedal-playing, which we believe is peculiar to herself, enables her to preserve a graceful and quiet seat at the instrument. The *aplomb* and precision of her execution is remarkable in so young a person. Consider that the compass of the pedals at St. Katherine's [Regent's Park] differs materially from the organ on which she practices, it might well be a matter of surprise that throughout the performance there was scarcely an error, or slip.[66]

Mendelssohn's were perhaps not the best-practiced or most accurate feet in England.

The growth of English pedal divisions in London and across England served to answer the complaint made several decades earlier by the German émigré Kollmann. By the 1840s English pedal organs were ready for export

---

[66] See Judith Barger, *Elizabeth Stirling and the Musical Life of Female Organists in Nineteenth-century England* (Aldershot, UK; Burlington, USA: Ashgate, 2007), p. 77.

to the far reaches of the empire. In 1844 George French Flowers, who had been a student of Rinck, was demonstrating instruments built according to the German System that were headed for Calcutta; while still cleaving to the ad hoc approach to pedaling, Thomas Adams played a showroom concert in 1846 on a Gray & Davison organ with German compass intended for Trinidad Cathedral.[67]

Even if the contributions of Stirling, Flowers, and others to this trans-formation of English organ culture were diverse and important, it was Mendelssohn who was seen to be the critical figure. An 1838 *Musical World* article by Edward Holmes summed up the results, confirming the attitude of Gauntlett and others, as it took stock of how the triumphs of 1837 had helped the English re-imagine the performance of Bach on full organs, without suppressing the essential role of the feet:

Mendelssohn introduced Bach to the English, as an organ composer. Our native artists had known and appreciated him as a writer for the clavichord … but we had yet to venerate him as the inventor of a set of totally new effects upon the organ. It was not that [Samuel] Wesley was unacquainted with his Fantasias, Passacaglias, Preludes, and Coda, that he did not introduce them to the English: but never having heard a German organ, with its ponderous pedal, he could not realize the inventions of the author.[68]

As is clear from so many of his writings on the organ, Holmes considered hearing and seeing the "real" pedal in Germany vital to understanding the instrument's full potential. But not everyone could get to Dresden. For Holmes, Mendelssohn had brought – had "invented" – all the "new effects" of pedal-playing for the English; that is, he had made it possible for them to gain a vivid sense of "true" organs and organ-playing. But the relationship between Mendelssohn and England was a complementary one; the English organ scene in this crucial period of transition provided an encouraging milieu in which the progress of the visitor could be followed and his new-found organ mastery, and therefore Bach's music, "venerated," as Holmes put it.[69] The transformation of English organ culture required a new concept of what it was to be an organist, and Mendelssohn was a symbol of that metamorphosis.

It was only fitting that the English publisher Charles Coventry should commission a set of organ works from Mendelssohn that would, whether intended to do so or not, serve as a commemoration of his role in the introduction of pedal-playing in England. Coventry was a devotee of Bach's music and had published many of his free organ works in the 1830s in the midst of Mendelssohn's English triumphs. In a letter to Mendelssohn of 1844, Coventry congratulated himself for having "first … published [Bach's] pedal fugues in this country about eight years since. At that time

[67] McCrea, "A Note on Thomas Adams," 94.   [68] *Musical World*, 8 (1838), 101–102.
[69] *Ibid.*, 102.

Example 5.5   Felix Mendelssohn, Sonata in F minor, Op. 65, No. 1, first movement, bars 1–24

most of the organs here had but few pedals, since that time all the organs in this country have been improved, and, *of course*, [there is] a greater demand for Bach."[70] Mendelssohn duly supplied Coventry with copies of other major Bach works, and in 1844 Mendelssohn began assembling his Six Sonatas, Op. 65, which, after their publication by the firm of Coventry & Hollier in London in 1845, became fixtures of the organists' repertoire not only in England but in Germany, and everywhere else, too.[71]

The First Sonata, in F minor, sets out the ambitions of the collection as if cataloging the expanded scope of the remade organist's art. The opening figure of the sonata begins firmly in the English tradition with ceremonial, annunciatory chords (see Example 5.5, bars 1–2). The feet double the little

---

[70] Wm. A. Little, "Felix Mendelssohn and J. S. Bach's *Prelude and Fugue in E Minor* (BWV 533)," *The American Organist*, 39(2) (February 2005), 73–83.

[71] For a thorough treatment of the chronology, genesis, reception, and performance indications – among other topics – of the Six Sonatas, see Little, *Mendelssohn and the Organ*, pp. 243–343.

Example 5.5   (cont.)

finger of the left hand at the octave, an enrichment of the sonority by the pedal that had long been the basic task of the English organ. This sort of doubling was by no means unknown in Germany and was used without reservation by the great German pedal-players of the period; nonetheless the doubling admits to a subservience of the pedal to the manuals. Forkel frowns from beyond the grave. Quantz, Mattheson, and Bach, who left virtually no music that indulges in this kind of doubling, shake their heads as the feet proceed chained to the manual. Such ideals can be sacrificed for fullness of sound, but the longstanding contest between left-hand and pedal that marks English organ culture in the first half of the nineteenth century seems at the outset of Mendelssohn's sonatas to have been decided in favor of the little finger. On playing through the opening bars of this piece for the first time after its publication in 1845, a contemporary organist could be forgiven for asking: has a German organist capitulated to English partisans of the left hand?

The answer to this question comes quickly and resoundingly. After the opening chords of the first two bars the pedal becomes more active and independent, though still not too adventurous, seeking refuge twice in pedal points in bars 4–6 and 11–13 of Example 5.5. But then the feet unloose themselves through the most effective and archetypally German means of attaining independence: counterpoint. A fugue intrudes after ten bars, intermingling with, or perhaps disguised by, the cadence to the pedal point at bar 12. When the feet take up the fugue subject in bar 17, the pedal is now clearly more than a thickening agent: the feet have become contrapuntal. Whereas the hands had presented the subject with a bar-and-a-half of alternating rising thirds, the pedal takes this figure – a typical one for the feet – and carries it away in an extended display of its new-found autonomy. The movement then proceeds to juxtapose this full texture with pedal, often furiously contrapuntal, with reverent *manualiter* interludes of homophonic, half-note calm. When the pedal intervenes again it is raucous, disjointed, filled with churning figures and awkward intervals that require a commanding confidence over the pedalboard. Towards the end of the movement the building force of this pedal energy is released in what amounts to an accompanied pedal solo with the high chords in the manual, and playable by the right hand alone so that the left hand could, if necessary or desired, grab the bench. (see Example 5.6). This pedal exhibition includes many of the familiar interlocking thirds, but climaxes in a bravura chromatic scale extending from low D flat, tucked far away in the corner of the pedalboard, and ascending to the highest b flat – an upwelling that spans almost two octaves.

The sonata's closing movement makes an even more emphatic statement about the German way of using the feet. Tempestuous F minor gives way to triumphant F Major, with slow-moving pedal notes below rapidly broken chords and scales in the manuals. The opening is dominated by several pedal points, whose effect is to convey the instrument's gravity and sustaining power (see Example 5.7). Eventually freeing itself from the glorious inertia of these long-held notes, the pedal begins to mark the half-bar harmonic rhythm, providing a regular and resolute underpinning to the manual figuration. At the midpoint of the piece, Mendelssohn quickens the pace in the bass by involving the feet in the treatment of a new, quarter-note theme first heard in the manuals; thus the feet's supporting role over the first half of the piece eventually gives way to equal dialogue between manuals and pedal. The active elaboration of the new theme in the bass leads to an epic pedal point on the dominant C over bars 96 through 107, held for eight bars on the lowest note of the pedalboard, until the figuration of the manuals comes to a halt on a G–B flat diad in each hand (see Example 5.8). Then at bar 108 the pedal jumps up to (or very near) the top of the pedalboard of the German System to c¹ and traverses the entire length of the compass back down to the low C with a chromatically inflected scale in eighth-notes. This cadenza encompasses precisely the range of the pedal at the organ of St. Paul's that Mendelssohn had played so often and so famously; he marks off the full compass of the pedal as self-consciously as Schlick had done in his *Tabulaturen* more than three centuries earlier. Over the course of this thrilling movement, the overall pedal rhythm has moved from half-notes, to quarters, to eighths, these three distinct time values also reflecting different aspects

Example 5.6   Felix Mendelssohn, Sonata in F minor, Op. 65, No. 1, first movement,
"accompanied pedal solo," bars 91–106

of obbligato pedaling: harmonic foundation, contrapuntal equality, and fleet-footed display. After this pedal outburst, a reprise of the contrapuntal working-out of the quarter-note theme in closer imitation ensues, before a cadence to the tonic lands on a long tonic pedal point (see Example 5.8,

Example 5.7   Felix Mendelssohn, Sonata in F minor, Op. 65, No. 1, third movement, bars 1–10

bars 122–133). Beginning in bar 134 Mendelssohn then replays the descending scale, this time in purely diatonic form and pulling up short of its apparent goal on the low D, making the ultimate return to the dominant pedal on C after waiting two bars, all the more dramatic and final. A sonata that began without an independent pedal ends in an unabashed display of what the feet are capable of.

The collection was originally advertised by Coventry as "Mendelssohn's School of Organ Playing," and though this title was suppressed at the composer's request, the movement purposefully tests the skills of English organists with a program of graduated velocity and an exploration of diverse techniques, framed by expansive pedal points that exalt in the foundational grandeur of the organ. At the opening of Mendelssohn's "English" sonatas – also published simultaneously by Breitkopf & Härtel in Germany, as well as being issued in Milan by Ricordi and by

Example 5.8   Felix Mendelssohn, Sonata in F minor, Op. 65, No. 1, third movement, bars 90–144

Schlesinger in Paris, where such pedal demonstrations were no less ground-breaking – the composer demonstrated that this was music that demanded that organists saddled with "crippled" organs would have to throw away their crutches. The instruments, too, would have to be able to

Example 5.8   (cont.)

run. Here was demanding music to inspire individual refashioning and to bolster collective confidence in the path set for English organists and organs. New standards had been established for virtuosic organ performance in the British Isles.

Example 5.8 (cont.)

THE "HIGHER TRUTH" OF JOHANN SCHNEIDER
IN DRESDEN AND LONDON

Even while Mendelssohn was playing the organs of England for himself and for others, Holmes continued to instruct English audiences on the German dominance at the King of Instruments. In an 1835 article entitled "The Actual Organists of Germany," printed in *The Atlas*, a periodical encompassing literature, science, politics, and music, Holmes claimed that Johann Schneider surpassed his eminent German colleagues, including Mendelssohn, especially in independent pedal-playing and the performance of the music of Bach. This was a view shared by Mendelssohn.[72] The most striking attribute of Schneider's prowess, and the first one mentioned by Holmes in the article, is his pedaling: "His masterly certainty as a solo player in the most hazardous exploits of pedal execution has been attained by hard practice and still costs the most unwearied application." Holmes

[72] Edward Holmes, "The Actual Organists of Germany," *The Atlas*, 10 (1835), 792.

hammers home the importance of pedal-playing in organ performance; it is a high-wire act conducted over the vast abyss of the pedal's profundity, and takes great skill and courage: "No feet but that of a consummate master can venture among the deep and rolling pedal of a gigantic first-rate [organ], where a mistake would be fatal." In spite of the advances in organ culture in England, Holmes remains clear about who the world leader is: "Let us turn in short, in what directions we may, Germany is still, in all that concerns the organ supreme." And the first among its players was Schneider, ranked by Holmes above his brother Friedrich Schneider (organist in Dessau and author of an organ tutor, perhaps the first translated into English, in 1832),[73] then Mendelssohn, Mendelssohn's teacher August Wilhelm Bach, and the Austrian virtuoso Sigismund Neukomm, whom Holmes praised for the "facility of his pedaling" but criticized because his fugue-playing "did not savour of profundity."[74]

Published reports like this one along with personal connections and recommendations sent at least one young musician from the British Isles, the Scot, Adam Hamilton, to study with Schneider in Dresden for four years around 1840.[75] Like so many other musical travelers to Dresden, the American Lowell Mason heard Schneider play in 1837, ten years after Holmes's visit. Mason placed Schneider and Mendelssohn's teacher A. W. Bach at the top of his list of organists, but judged that "Mr. Schneider used the pedals with greater execution than Mr. Bach."[76] As usual, the feet decided the matter. Mason thought both Germans far surpassed any other organists he had heard, including Thomas Adams in London, he of "propitious bunions" – and inferior pedaling. Schneider demonstrated the organ at the Sophienkirche for Mason, improvising on a chorale tune for forty-five minutes, using "Obligato Pedals," as Mason makes sure to point out, noting also that the technique was just taking hold in England, too. Mason had first heard this style of playing at St. Sepulchre's in London, but that performance by Sigismund Neukomm had not matched the "strength and execution" of Schneider.

The most rapturous of all accounts of Schneider, published fifteen years after Holmes's *Ramble* and exceeding that already reverential description, comes from the third volume of *Music and Manners in France and Germany* of 1844 by Henry Fothergill Chorley. Music critic for *The Times* and long-time contributor to the *Athenaeum*, a widely read travel writer, friend of

---

[73] Friedrich Schneider, *Handbuch des Organisten*, 4 vols. (Halberstadt: Brüggeman, 1830–1832), trans. as *Frederick Schneider's Complete Theoretical and Practical Instruction for Playing the Organ, with Numerous Exercises for Acquiring the Use of the Pedals* (London: Novello, 1832). In 1828 Edward Holmes had written that "At Dessau Schneider's brother similarly holds forth with much command of the pedals, and mixes five or six parts together with great contrapuntal knowledge." Holmes, *A Ramble*, p. 244.

[74] Holmes, "The Actual Organists of Germany," 792.   [75] *Musical World*, 17 (1842), 38.

[76] Lowell Mason, *A Yankee Musician in Europe: the 1837 Journals of Lowell Mason*, ed. Michael Broyles (Ann Arbor, Michigan: UMI Research Press, 1990), p. 66.

Mendelssohn and many other important musicians, Chorley was a musical cosmopolitan, a proponent of German music and especially of the organ. He was one of the few people to hear Mendelssohn both in England and in Germany; in 1839 Chorley accompanied Mendelssohn as he took a break from his busy schedule as conductor and pianist at the Braunschweig music festival to visit the city's cathedral, where Mendelssohn made "the sadly out of tune [organ] ... speak most gloriously, winding up nearly an hour's magnificent playing [with] one of Bach's grand fugues."[77] Chorley was with Mendelssohn when he visited the "poor little organ" in Ringgenberg, Switzerland, just a few months before Mendelssohn's death in 1847; it was the very last time Mendelssohn played an organ.[78] Having heard of Schneider's fame, through Holmes, Mendelssohn and probably many others, Chorley made his way in 1840 to Dresden's Sophienkirche, the crucial destination for true devotees of the German organ art. On coming face to face with the legendary Schneider, Chorley admits that he felt as if he had already met him, having pictured him playing in this extraordinary way for so long: "I had seen him 'out of the body' years ago, during the whole time that I was occupying myself in tracing the imagined character of a German organist."[79] The real display far surpasses such imaginings. The visit to the Sophienkirche proves to be one of the most memorable excursions ever made by the much-traveled Chorley, who likens Schneider's organ-playing to "oracular utterances, as it were, in which musical Truth and Poetry, of the highest order, make themselves known."[80] Schneider's performance claims a metaphysical status beyond the physical display that also enthralls Chorley. As in Holmes, and in contrast to Burney, Chorley emphasizes the economy and ease of this German organist playing at an instrument with heavy action:

Those who treat organ-playing as "a black business," to which they bend themselves with frowning brows, and coat-sleeves turned up half-way to the shoulders – the school of kickers, and swingers to and fro, who make much exertion cover up very little skill – might have taken a lesson from this admirable artist, whose hands as they glided away over the keys ("*worked away*" is the established phrase), were bringing out into their fullest glory all those magnificent chains of sound – all those replies, and suspenses, and accumulations, which, with a calm but never-tiring munificence, the noble old *Cantor* of the *Thomas-Schule* has lavished in his compositions."[81]

Comparisons between home and abroad are crucial: "only a few weeks before I had been listening to our own noble organs at Christchurch in London and in the Town-hall at Birmingham."[82] Both venues hosted

---

[77] Henry Fothergill Chorley, *Modern German Music*, 2 vols. (London: Smith, Elder and Col., 1854), vol. I, p. 39.

[78] *Ibid.*, vol. II, pp. 395–396.

[79] Henry Fothergill Chorley, *Music and Manners in France and Germany*, 3 vols. (London: Longman, Brown, Green and Longmans, 1844), vol. III, p. 165.

[80] *Ibid.*, p. 163.   [81] *Ibid.*, p. 170.   [82] *Ibid.*, p. 169.

triumphs by Mendelssohn, but the Sophienkirche instrument and its renowned master are for Chorley superior to all those organs in the major metropolitan centers of Europe. Though this two-manual organ is the smallest Silbermann in Dresden it is the perfect instrument, in Chorley's eyes and ears, for the display of the German art: "This is one of the great Silbermann's organs; and never heard I pipes of such a ripe and fascinating sweetness of tone, from the lowest *elephant* pedal C to the *skylark* C *altissimo*."[83] Chorley's account combines praise for the organ with awe at the multitasking brilliance of its organist: "In all that regards hand, and foot, and mind, – firmness of the first, brilliancy of the second, and concentration of the third, – Herr Schneider is to me as unrivalled as his organ."[84] The "brilliant" feet are the focus of technical display.

Schneider knows not only what the best music is, but what the tourists have come to hear: Bach. Indeed, after sensing the presence of the "noble old Cantor of the Thomas-Schule," Chorley is ready to be in communion with Bach and his music at the side of the greatest organist in the world and in the shadow of one of its greatest organs: Schneider's "artistic exhibitions were a delight to the ear … [and] a gratification to the mind," especially since they came as a "sequel to the traces of Bach I had been exploring at Leipsic [sic]."[85] Schneider is a sort of medium for the spirit of Bach, his body enacting what Bach's body enacted a century earlier at the great organs of Dresden. After beginning with the Fugue in B minor (probably BWV 544/2, perhaps preceded by the Prelude), Chorley's Saturday evening visit to the organ loft culminates in a performance of Bach's Fugue in E minor, BWV 548/2, its subject "spreading in form like a wedge, offers such excellent scope for the amplification of science and the arrangement of climax." In the twilight, Chorley withdraws to a distant corner of the gallery as Bach and Schneider merge into pure "Music" and Chorley himself is transported back to "a childish feeling of mystery and delight."[86] The performance is of such intensity and transport, that one could well be in an E. T. A. Hoffmann short story. The "Wedge" is followed by "one or two more glorious displays of entire mastery of the key and pedalboard." At last vision begins to fail: "It is too dark for us to see any more of Bach," says Schneider, who asks for forgiveness for venturing into a vast improvisation. He moves from the noble past to the fervent present of spontaneous invention. The physical performance, now receding into the gathering dark, is impressive, but Chorley feels the presence of a still higher power:

Till then, the remarkable mental energy demanded for an exhibition like this never struck me in all its fullness. And yet, not only must the performer originate thoughts, but, by new and happily-successive admixtures, contrive effects totally, of course, beyond the reach of him who has only before him the plain and immovable keys of a piano-forte. Taken merely in its most matter-of-fact sense

---

[83] *Ibid.*, p. 168.   [84] *Ibid.*, p. 169.   [85] *Ibid.*, pp. 163–164.   [86] *Ibid.*, p. 171.

as a display which proved nothing, here were memory, combination, promptitude, invention, and mechanical skill, united. I may be laughed at, but I could not help imagining that the exercise of a power at once implying thought, self-mastery, and a patient use of physical strength, could hardly have been carried to so high a perfection without its favorable moral influences; and that if it were so, herein, and not from their being erected in churches, might lie the superior sacredness of organs beyond other instruments – herein the holiness of the performance of the music written for them.[87]

This is a classic exposition of the sublime as secularized religious experience; it is made possible by a surrogate Bach in whom mind and body are in perfect concert and evoke something far bigger, far more mysterious than can truly be grasped. For English converts to the German way of playing, the trip to the Sophienkirche to hear Schneider was a pilgrimage. The organ heard in "the comparative quiet of a German town" was all the more unforgettable when compared to the furor caused by a Paganini or a Liszt in a thrumming city.[88] Bach and the instrument he and his followers commanded were beyond fad and favor. Touring organists, chief among them Mendelssohn, could come to England and shine on British instruments, but the German organ destinations remained holy for devotees of the German organ art.

Visited and venerated in his own country, Schneider must have recognized his export value. He also knew that Mendelssohn and other German virtuosos were making big impressions beyond German borders; German accounts of Schneider's organ-playing stressed his credit to his own city and nation, but also documented his international appeal.[89] Yet it was only late in his career that Schneider journeyed to England, when in 1853, he accompanied the Cologne Choral Union on its English tour. The enthusiasm of Chorley and Holmes might well have garnered Schneider the invitation, or at least encouraged him to make the trip, and to allow the German virtuoso the chance to show English audiences the kind of pedal heroics – parallel octaves, scalar patterns, rocking figures, leaps, and arpeggios – heard, for example, in Schneider's impressive *Dank- und Jubelpräludium* ("Prelude of Praise and Exultation") on the Lutheran hymn *Nun danket alle Gott* ("Now Thank We All Our God")[90] (see Example 5.9). But hearing and seeing Schneider on his own organ in one of the revered sites of Germany was very different from experiencing his playing in England. On June 13 he performed on the Walker organ in the Exeter Hall (see Figure 5.4); the instrument had a German pedal compass, but it also extended down to FF on both manuals. In this foreign environment, on an instrument laid out in a manner unlike that of his beloved Silbermann, Schneider exposed himself to technical difficulties and to

---

[87] *Ibid.*, p. 173.   [88] *Ibid.*, p. 163.
[89] Sieling, "Der Dresdner Hoforganist Johann Gottlob Schneider," 185–192.
[90] Schneider's *Jubelpräludium* was a staple of mid-century German organ music. See, for example, *Allgemeine musikalische Zeitung*, June 29, 1864, col. 455.

Example 5.9   Johann Gottlob Schneider, *Dank- und Jubelpräludium*, bars 75–85

suspicions that his German intellectualism could become impenetrable, charges that had also been visited on Mendelssohn from time to time:

A warm reception was given to Herr Schneider, organist of the Protestant Church, Dresden, and attached to the Court of Saxony. The fame of this artist extends over all musical Germany, and the promised performance of several ancient choral melodies peculiar to his own country, with accompaniment in counterpoint and fugue by F. S. Bach, [sic] drew a large concourse of the professors of that noblest of all instruments – the organ – to the Hall. The composition was so learnedly profound that the ordinary listener was soon in a fog. Herr Schneider aimed at great effects, but was evidently bothered in the management of an organ so different to that on which he is accustomed to operate. In a second solo the player felt

Figure 5.4   Anti-Slavery Meeting of 1841 with Walker organ in background, Exeter Hall, The Strand, London

more at home; he started with an understandable theme, and then extemporized with such a fertility of imagination that three-quarters of an hour elapsed before he got into the marrow of it. Great as this organ-playing undoubtedly was, the audience thought that "enough was as good as a feast," and many rose from the table, indicating satiety. Less agreeable demonstrations of enough succeeded, and at last the player, doubtlessly "lost in himself," was informed by a friend that the plaudits were more in derision than otherwise – a circumstance that many regretted.[91]

How ironic it was that the man held to be the greatest German organist by Mendelssohn, didn't come close to winning the kind of approval from English organists that his admirer had. The Walker organ was not a Silbermann; the metaphysical, even magical, qualities of Schneider's performance cataloged by Chorley and others, heard in Bach country in the "town" of Dresden, could not be recaptured in the crowded hall on The Strand in teeming London. A sublime fantasy, which escapes time in Dresden, is yanked back to earth in London.

[91]   *The Era*, London, Issue 769, Sunday, June 19, 1853.

The crucial distinction between Mendelssohn and Schneider, one that fundamentally colored their engagement with English organ culture, was that Schneider was a professional organist and Mendelssohn was not. Mendelssohn's public profile as an organist in Germany did not approach that of Schneider. In contrast to Schneider, Mendelssohn never held a church position, and played few formal recitals: Mendelssohn is perhaps best thought of as the greatest amateur organist in history. As the review of Schneider's Exeter Hall performance makes clear, with its impatient attitude towards Bachian complexity and long-winded display, the possibility of informal demonstration, of trying things out while people eavesdropped (or strolled through the church back in Dresden), was not one afforded Schneider on this leg of his English tour. A concert was a concert, founded on certain norms of length and decorum. The kind of fervent, quasi-religious transport of Dresden was heard as self-indulgent in London by the skeptical critic. Thrust into a foreign cultural and musical environment, Schneider could neither rely on what Holmes had called Silbermann's "magnificence" nor could he convince his audience through the profundity of his invention or the display of pedal technique. The great German virtuoso would not return to London. Rather, it was as a distant prophet of pedaling to be visited in the Holy Land of Bach country and reported on back home in England by pilgrims, that Schneider's reputation helped spread the gospel of Bachian organ performance.

THE MOST FAMOUS FEET IN EUROPE

The most widely-traveled proselytizer of four-limbed performance across Europe, the man whom Holmes considered "the artist [most] celebrated for command of the pedals,"[92] was the Breslau organist Adolf Friedrich Hesse. Like Schneider, Hesse was a tourist attraction, renowned in his native Breslau, but also across Germany and beyond. The fame of his feet preceded him across Europe. Hesse's reports on his organ travels appeared in Breslau's newspapers, and in music journals such as the *Neue Zeitschrift für Musik* and the *Allgemeine musikalische Zeitung* which were disseminated across German-speaking Europe. His accounts were also printed in periodicals such as the monthlies *Euterpe* and *Urania* directed at Germany's schoolteachers.[93] Appearing in this broad range of publications, descriptions of Hesse's travels both molded and reflected German attitudes towards organ culture among professionals and amateurs, from the village

---

[92] *The Atlas*, 10 (1835), 775.

[93] The village organist was typically also a schoolteacher; even as renowned an organist as Kittel's student, Johann Christian Heinrich Rinck, had held these two jobs simultaneously for a large part of his career, though not without considerable disillusionment. J. C. H. Rinck, *Selbstbiographie* (Breslau: Aderholz, 1833) in Christoph Dohr (ed.), *Johann Christian Heinrich Rinck: Dokumente zu Leben und Werk* (Cologne: Dohr, 2003), pp. 27–29.

schoolroom to the bourgeois salon, from universities to churches, small and large. These journeys were not simply musical; they were exercises of musical patriotism in a nation not yet formed. Germany was the land of the real organists, and Hesse's reports helped to bolster organ pride on the home front and abroad. Like so many others before him, Hesse assumed that the way forward for foreign organ cultures lay in their transformation along German lines.

Hesse's confrontation with foreign organ cultures is marked by incredulity at the stunted pedals he encountered on his travels. This dominant reaction in his accounts sometimes comes across as feigned and exaggerated, given his wide experiences abroad. Yet each time he encounters substandard pedals, his reaction is a mixture of shock, condescension and impatience. An 1853 article by Hesse in the *Neue Zeitschrift für Musik*, written after the majority of his great successes in foreign countries, is one of the clearest of his many ideological statements: "So bad are organs, and for the most part the organists, in Catholic countries that it hardly needs mentioning." The playing in these places was decadent, the pedal enslaved to operatic fashion, dogging the left hand and poking out notes rather than pursuing true contrapuntal independence. The result was degrading to the organ's honor: the sonority lacked the requisite grandeur and the playing pandered to fashion. Appalling taste and poor pedal technique were symptoms of the same underlying deficiencies: true understanding of contrapuntal potential required independent pedal, agility of feet and mind. On trips across Catholic Europe, from Rome to Paris to Vienna to Prague, the fundamental problem was the pedal compass: it either began too low (as in France) or did not extend high enough (in Bavaria and Austria). In a more vehement reprise of eighteenth-century travel writers like Keyßler (see Chapter 4, p. 153) and others, Hesse praises the countless "glorious churches" of Italy, but excoriates their organs and organists. Invited by leading musicians to play in Vienna and other cultural centers, Hesse repeatedly complained that he was often forced to make do with poor pedals. He lambasted foreign organs for making "a mockery of every reasonable use of the pedal," and this made it "[clear] how little could have been known of German organ compositions."[94] The real music was German and Protestant, and it could not be played without pedal.

In a testimony printed in the widely circulating music periodical *Cäcilia* in 1829, when Hesse was just twenty, Rinck had anointed him a successor to the Bach tradition, emphasizing above all that the twenty-year-old's technical skill was built from the feet up: "With particular joy I can testify to the fact," wrote Rinck, "that he plays the organ with great accomplishment, and in particular handles the pedal in a way that earns him esteem and admiration."[95] Hesse's first major trip away from Breslau was to important

[94] *Neue Zeitschrift für Musik*, 39(6) (1853), 53–56, at 53. [95] *Cäcilia*, 10 (1829), 45.

musical centers in Germany including Dresden, Leipzig, Merseburg, Weimar, Frankfurt, Hamburg, and Berlin where organs had full pedal compasses. But it was when Hesse journeyed beyond central and northern Germany that his own reports register the difficulties of adaptation required of organ virtuosos whose music-making is built on the feet. On his first trip to Vienna in 1831, Hesse complained bitterly in a communication to *Eutonia*, yet another pedagogical periodical for schoolteachers and organists, of how the southerners "neglected the queen of all instruments"; in the famous Cathedral of St. Stephen, the limited range of the pedals and the lack of independent pedal stops forced him to hold his concert, featuring major preludes and fugues of Bach, on a smaller organ in the city's Protestant Church, where there was a rare instrument with a complete pedal.[96] Immediately following Hesse's report in *Eutonia*, the magazine reprinted a review of his concert by the Viennese conductor and critic Ignaz Seyfried, hailing the recital as a huge success; even the ambitious program did not exhaust the "physical power and endurance of the artist brimming with undiminished fullness of youth." In spite of Hesse's complaint that he had been unable to achieve anything truly lofty on this small organ, Seyfried enthused that Hesse's registration, contrapuntal facility, and manual dexterity were indeed astonishing, "but what was still more surprising was the awesome precision of his powerful pedal-playing."[97]

An account of a subsequent 1835 trip to Austria and south Germany printed in the *Allgemeine Musikalische Zeitung* once again strikes the incredulous tone favored by Hesse: "on his entire trip from Vienna and beyond, including Salzburg, Munich, Augsburg, Ulm and Stuttgart, Mr. Hesse found not a *single organ* on which something tolerable could have been achieved; all were in the most pitiful condition, and in addition all have only the so-called French pedal, which encompasses not even an octave-and-a-half completely, because c-sharp, d-sharp, f-sharp and g-sharp are missing."[98] (These notes were missing on account of the short octave Hesse despised.) Without full pedals the instruments in the major cities of south Germany and Austria did not even rate as organs at all. In spite of these obstacles, Hesse played Bach's fugues and his own improvisations across Europe, where his powers of adaptation were put to extreme tests.

Hesse's most famous foreign trip came in 1844 when he was invited to participate in the dedication of the large new organ at St. Eustache in Paris. The *Neue Zeitschrift für Musik* describes Hesse's performances as a national triumph, on a large French-built organ whose substantial pedal could only be managed by a German:

---

[96] *Eutonia*, 6 (1831), 150. See also Hans Jürgen Seyfried, *Adolph Friedrich Hesse als Orgelvirtuose und Orgelkomponist* (Regensburg: Gustav Bosse, 1965), p. 19.
[97] *Eutonia*, ibid., 152.   [98] *Allgemeine musikalische Zeitung*, 52 (December, 1835), 367.

The exceptional pedal had been conceived by the makers not only fittingly but excessively. Because of the typical ways of playing the organ here [in Paris] there was no organist capable of using this division of the organ with uncompromising aptitude, and it was decided to call on a recognized master from Germany. The choice fell on Mr. Hesse. The excitement of the local organists was enormous and the expectation was increased through his reputation, which was discussed intensely among his French colleagues.[99]

Reports in the French press of Hesse's prowess dated back at least to 1837; seven years later, he was summoned by the French as a German prophet of the pedal.[100]

Hesse's own account was sent to the *Breslauer Zeitung* and subsequently reprinted in *Euterpe* in August of 1844, two months after the St. Eustache dedication. Now all schoolteachers and organists across Germany could read of Hesse's triumph in Paris. As expected, Hesse's description of the situation in Paris focuses on the possibilities for the organist's feet.[101] He visits other recent organs in advance of the St. Eustache dedication. On his arrival in the city, Frédéric Chopin seeks Hesse out at his hotel so that these two great contemporary keyboardists, each an admirer of the other's abilities, can hasten to the organ in the famed cathedral of St. Denis. Hesse dramatizes his disappointment and disregard for the non-German approach by having his readers picture him confronting the console for the first time after he has been impressed with the façade: "Just as I wanted to sit down and try it out, oh, what a Shame!, I noticed that the installation of the pedal rendered organ performance impossible."[102] The problem with the St. Denis organ was that the pedal was based on the FF compass.[103] Given the newness of this important organ, finished by Cavaillé-Coll only three years earlier, Hesse had expected something more "modern," more "German" in the pedal. Chopin had apparently had no idea that such a large and costly organ as that at St. Denis could be lacking in anything at all. It took a German to show him as much.

Hesse visits other churches to hear other organists, too, and he is for the most part dismissive of what he sees and hears in Paris: transcriptions of Italian opera were the rage in performances marked by fast and brilliant manual passages and little use of the pedal, which is played only by "one toe tapping about ... in short staccato notes while the other foot comfortably relaxes on an iron bar." The dominant mode of performance is both intellectually and physically lazy, which, from the German perspective,

---

[99] August Gathy writing in *Neue Zeitschrift für Musik*, 10(21) (1844), 26, 31.

[100] *Revue et Gazette de 1837*, pp. 251, 343, 351, 519, 535. See also Josef Burg, "Quelques remarques sur les séjours d'Adolf Friedrich Hesse à Paris," *L'Orgue Francophone*, 13 (1992), 42–58, at 43.

[101] "Aus dem Schreiben von Adolph Hesse," in *Euterpe*, 4 (1844), 140–142. The *Breslauer Zeitung* article appears in issue no. 145 from the same year.

[102] *Neue Zeitschrift für Musik*, 39(6) (1853), 53–56, at 54.

[103] Fenner Douglass, *Cavaillé-Coll and the Musicians: A Documented Account of His First Thirty Years in Organ Building*, 2 vols. (Raleigh, North Carolina: Sunbury, 1980), vol. I, p. 27.

meant the same thing. The one-footed organist is a silly sight and produces a silly sound – decadent, facile, childish. Hesse claims that almost nothing is known of the strict style in France; the "faulty" construction of the short French pedals did not allow for proper performance, the strict style requiring, in his view, use of both heel and toe, "as we do it in Germany." Hesse tells German readers that he has been assured by Parisians that "he is the first to play this way here." Only the "old and worthy" organist Alexandre Böely, by then almost sixty years old and generally rebuked for the austerity of his playing and his interest in old music, is cited by Hesse for playing Bach as best he could on the French pedalboards.[104]

Hesse participated in the dedication of the huge organ by Daublaine-Callinet for St. Eustache on June 18; according to some accounts in the press as many as 8,000 listeners, including King Louis Philippe, were in attendance. (Later German reports expanded the already overblown estimates of the crowd to a still more unbelievable 10,000.) Lefébure-Wély and colleagues played in what Hesse characterized as the "gallant style," but "as a German musician" Hesse could not "praise the quickly released accompaniment of the left hand and pedal" – the staccato oom-pahs he so often maligned. Böely was also one of the performers at the dedication and played in a "strict style" [*gebundener Styl*]; all others sought operatic effects. One of these gentlemen, also lacking in pedal skill, produced a great effect on the public by elaborating on a Swiss cowherd's tune, then conjuring a terrible thunderstorm, and, after the sky had again turned blue, concluding with a return to the Alpine melody – all of this to Hesse's dismay.[105] For his contribution, held by him and the German press to be the decisive one of the evening and a watershed moment in the history of organ-playing in France, Hesse performed several original works including what he referred to in his reports as "new Fantasie in d." This was probably the "Grand Fantasy for Use at Organ Concerts and Festive Occasions" [*Grosse Fantasie zum Gebrauch bei Orgel-Concerten und festlichen Gelegenheiten*] subsequently published as Op. 73 (Breslau, 1844), and dedicated to Félix Danjou, organist of Notre Dame in Paris.[106] The St. Eustache dedication program also included an improvisation, and then closed with one of the most athletic of Bach's free works, the Toccata in F, BWV 540. As a flurry of accounts by Hesse and others stressed, his style was built on an often impressive – to some intrusive – use of the feet. One can get a sense of this approach, one which manifested itself not only in his printed music but also in his famous improvisations, from his Prelude and Fugue, Op. 66, published by Breitkopf in 1841 a few years before the Paris trip. Hesse was fond of pedal runs and leaps, and one of his favorite conceits was to play in

---

[104] *Euterpe*, 4 (1844), 140–142.　　[105] *Ibid.*

[106] The appearance of the publication was announced in the *Intelligenzblatt* (no. 8, December 1844) of the *Neue Zeitschrift für Musik*.

Example 5.10   Adolf Friedrich Hesse, Prelude and Fugue in D, Op. 66, bars 125–148

octaves, which not only made for a bigger sonority, but also showed that each of his feet could play rapidly on its own (see Example 5.10). The climax is a brash display of pedal technique, as physically demanding as anything then being played on the organ.

Nothing had ever been heard in Paris at this level of physical difficulty, and only in passing does Hesse mention that the compass of this new organ started at AA and went to c1.[107] Hesse's powers of adaptability were indeed staggering: he not only succeeded, but triumphed, in playing the pedal part of this toccata – which spans the range, extraordinary in its time, C to f1 – with its exposed and breathless pair of solos, on an enormous organ in a huge space before thousands of listeners, with little practice time (if any), on a pedalboard foreign in every sense, its lowest note shifted downward a disorienting minor third and with keys that were shorter than those on which Hesse played in Breslau and elsewhere in Germany; in addition to all this, the upper notes of the demanding pedal part, especially important in the second pedal solo, were lacking. In spite of these difficulties, the triumph was nearly absolute, though a few local voices were raised against the display of "the king of the pedal" as one reviewer sarcastically called Hesse.[108] Many claimed that his were the first *pedaliter* performances of Bach's fugues in Paris.[109] François-Charles Widor – father of Charles-Marie, composer of another famous Toccata in F, the last movement of his Fifth Organ Symphony – came to Paris a few months after Hesse and boasted that he could play the pedals as well as the German had done, but the blustery claim could hardly have been true.[110] Writing in the *Journal des debats*, Hector Berlioz noted that "a veritable congress of musicians had come above all to hear M. Hesse, the celebrated organist of Breslau ... He is a giant, who plays with his feet that which would have put the playing of others' hands to shame."[111] Here was the old trope of J. S. Bach's Obituary, one repeated by generations of Bach devotees: that well-trained feet could outdo mediocre hands. Most impressive for Berlioz was Hesse's performance of Bach's music, because the true sublimity of the counterpoint could only be heard with fully independent pedal. Hesse's performance would never be displaced as the greatest Bach-playing on the Daublaine-Callinet organ in St. Eustache. Six months after the inauguration the organ was destroyed by fire.

Hesse carried his efforts at exporting the German pedal to Bohemia as well. In 1853 he dedicated the new organ by the German firm of Buckow in St. Michael's, the Lutheran Church in Prague. Having visited the city two decades earlier and, as usual, been disappointed by the lack of pedals, Hesse was delighted by this new instrument; though small, four of its sixteen stops were given to the pedal, which, being of German manufacture, had a full compass. This modest instrument would, hoped Hesse, serve as an "enduring monument" for the transformation of Bohemian organ-building along German lines, and might also set reforms "in motion in Austria as well."[112]

[107] Douglass, *Cavaillé-Coll and the Musicians*, vol. I, p. 36.
[108] Orpha Ochse, *Organists and Organ Playing in Nineteenth-Century France and Belgium* (Bloomington: Indiana University Press, 1994), p. 39.
[109] F. J. Fétis, *Biographie universelle des musiciens*, 2nd edn., 8 vols. (Paris: Firmin-Didot, 1860–1865), vol. IV, pp. 321–322.
[110] *Ibid.*, p. 41.   [111] Hector Berlioz, writing in *Journal des debats*, June 25, 1844, p. 2.
[112] *Neue Zeitschrift für Musik*, 6 (1853), 56.

An organ did not have to be huge, like the one in St. Eustache, but it needed to allow the organist to undertake polyphony involving hands and feet in all its clarity, majestic even without the thunderous sound of 32′ stops. Astonishing not only amateurs but the "artistic nobility of Prague" with his abilities, Hesse had to play his concert three times in St. Michael's to overflowing audiences.[113] The local and foreign press reported on the landmark recital and what it foretold of organ culture in Bohemia and elsewhere. In a visit to Prague the next year to see the organ that he had read about from Hesse's own reports, the young Dresden organist Karl August Fischer confirmed that Bohemian organs were indeed backward. But Fischer could now reassure the readers of *Euterpe* that, in addition to the instrument in St. Michael's, the Director of the Organ Institute in Prague, Herr Pietsch, at last had a practice organ installed with a "complete pedal." The evangelist of obbligato playing received the credit: "the lion's share of this transformation is to be credited to Herr Hesse, who through word and deed used his stay in Prague to work for a better future for organ culture in Bohemia."[114] By July of 1854 advanced pupils at the Organ Institute were studying "real" German music – Bach fugues and Mendelssohn sonatas – with the zeal of new converts. According to the Germans, the "better future" of organ-playing had dawned in Bohemia.[115]

Long postponed, Hesse's first trip to England finally came in 1851 for the Great Industrial Exhibition; it was the first of three journeys there, the last coming in 1862. In "The Actual Organists of Germany" of 1835 Holmes feared that Hesse had already given up touring and perhaps playing the organ altogether. Nonetheless, he praised Hesse as the greatest proponent of the pedal in terms familiar from reports on his playing in his homeland and the other countries of Europe: "During the time of his organic ambition … there was not an artist living more celebrated for command of the pedals. It was objected against him that he drowned his audience in a flood of bass. This borders on what is known as a good fault." Holmes, it seems, could hardly get enough pedal, and Hesse supplied it in great quantities of sound and speed. In 1851 Hesse played at various London churches and was praised repeatedly in *The Times*.[116] But the high point of the tour came at the Crystal Palace for the Industrial Exhibition; all the nations of western Europe were represented by instruments with full pedals, except for Italy, which exhibited only a small positiv dismissed by Hesse, echoing Forkel at the distance of the half-century, as irrelevant.[117] On the organ by Ducroquet (the successors to the firm that had made the instrument he had played at St. Eustache), Hesse presented a

[113] *Euterpe*, 17 (1857), 28.   [114] *Euterpe*, 14 (1854), 43–45, at 44.
[115] E. S. Fischer, "Ein Beitrag zur Geschichte des Orgelwesens in unserem Nachbarlande Böhmen," *Euterpe*, 14 (1854), 43–45.
[116] See *Euterpe*, 17 (1857), 28.   [117] *Morning Chronicle*, London, July 25, 1851.

program dominated by Bach fugues, including the "Wedge," with piano virtuosos Johann Baptist Cramer, Sigismond Neukomm, Ferdinand Hiller, and Sigismond Thalberg in attendance, as Hesse himself would once again proudly remember in print shortly before his death.[118] Others at the same exhibition, like the stalwart George Smart, might have been frightened of the advance of German pedaling into their native land. Here at mid-century, in the age of train travel and international industrial exhibitions, was a historic tableau of the new and future course of organ culture in which a French organ with German pedals could be demonstrated by a leading German organist for a group of international virtuosos in the cultural capital that was London – where only a few decades earlier it had been almost impossible to find an organ whose keyboards for feet and hands allowed unaltered contrapuntal performance of Bach's organ works.

Soon after his return from London, Hesse reported to bemused Germans how on arriving at the entrance gallery of the Crystal Palace "someone began Bach's G minor Fugue" on the large Willis organ erected there. "I was curious, how far he would get with this," writes Hesse clearly expecting that the natives were not up to the task of one of Bach's trickiest fugues.[119] His doubts were quickly confirmed when "the pedal came in a bar too soon," the confusion lasting about eight bars, at which point the organist broke off and segued frantically into a tune from Donizetti's operetta *Daughter of the Regiment*.[120] With the cutting sarcasm that he was known for among friends and foes, Hesse concluded his account of this alarming juxtaposition with a rhetorical question: "Which German can boast of such a diverse and quickly changing repertoire?" In fact, as Hesse must have known, the "someone" attempting the Bach G minor Fugue was in fact two people. A single player could not have kept the pedal line following one bar behind the manual for so long. The assistant – the third hand responsible for the pedal – had simply missed his cue and come in too late. Here was a flagrant example of three-handed performance living on in English organ-playing to be scoffed at by a German virtuoso touring England. Visiting German feet, and those of native Englishmen and Englishwomen, had largely chased the cheating left hand from the pedal's territory. Only a few brave, or foolish souls, tried on occasion to sneak past the guardians of Bachian performance.

VICTORIOUS FEET AND REDISCOVERED HANDS

The last great battle between the left hand and feet in the history of English organ design came a few years later, and was played out at the large instrument built by Willis for St. George's Hall, Liverpool. The organ was

---

[118] *Euterpe*, 22 (1862), 108.   [119] "Orgelspiel in London," *Euterpe*, 11 (1851), 99–100.
[120] The piece (noted by Hesse in another version he told of the story in the *Neue Zeitschrift für Musik*, 39 (1853), 55) is the first-act arietta "Chacun le sait."

designed by Samuel Sebastian Wesley and Thomas Attwood Walmisley, both proponents of Bach but organists aligned with the indigenous tradition of extended keyboards on the manuals. Wesley had been asked as early as 1843 for a scheme that ultimately produced an organ, which, when it was completed in 1855, had a pedal compass of German range running from C to f1. The manuals, however, extended down to GG.[121] In a forceful letter published in the *Liverpool Mercury* on March 19, 1853, the vociferous proponent of the German System, John Henry Gauntlett, aired his support of the instrument's four keyboards and "large and independent pedal," but fumed at the prospect of the massive, but in his view redundant, pipes that were to be made for the bass of the extended manual keyboards; he complained that these would "add nearly TWO THOUSAND POUNDS to the estimate." This figure was about a fifth of the entire cost of the organ. Gauntlett's reasoning drew on a cosmopolitan attitude at odds with that of the tenacious Insular Tradition:

Now, as we must look entirely to the great continental organs for true ideas respecting the compass, &c, &c., of a large instrument, we invariably find that the keyboards never descend *lower* than CC; first *no* 'Organ' music is written for the left hand *lower* than CC; secondly, on an organ with a pedalboard containing separate stops (as in the present instance), the deep notes are assigned to, and *ought* to be played by the feet alone.[122]

Here was Forkel's attitude in all its glory: if a piece did not employ obbligato pedal it was not real organ music at all; the corollary of this axiom was that the bass belonged to the feet not the left hand. The dedication of the St. George's organ took place more than a year later, in September of 1854, with the extended compass fully in place. Years later Gauntlett was still complaining about the organ's designers since "the £10,000 laid out on the Liverpool organ was spent on the wrong keyboard, Master Wesley carrying it against me. I believe it cost £1,500 to put that organ right."[123] The remedies were presumably made in the renovations of 1867, by which time the German System had thoroughly prevailed in British organ-building. The implementation of Wesley's scheme for St. George' Hall was a Pyrrhic victory for the proponents of the extended manual range.

The first musician chosen to serve as organist on the newly finished instrument was William T. Best, who remained in the post until 1894. His *The Art of Organ-Playing* was begun in 1869; the second part of the treatise was devoted to "Studies for the Pedal," and included not only original compositions and exercises but many examples taken from the great German pedal-players, Bach, Rinck, Hesse, Mendelssohn and others. The final study piece is the third movement of Bach's Trio Sonata in C minor, BWV 526/3, which Gauntlett had played – without a third hand – back in

---

[121] See Thistlethwaite, *The Making of the Victorian Organ*, pp. 135–149.
[122] Gauntlett, Letter to the Editor, *Liverpool Mercury*, March 19, 1853.
[123] Gauntlett to George Grove, November 30, 1864, reprinted in *Musical Times*, 46 (1905), 456.

the 1820s. In this treatise the gruff pedagogue, Best, makes clear that "the characteristic of Organ music is, that it demands the simultaneous use of both hands and feet, a matter involving a different employment of the Left Hand, which does not play the Bass, as in Pianoforte music, except where the Pedal part ceases."[124] This is how Best would play the St. George's Hall organ over his four decades at its bench, pursuing more readily the German ideal of pedal independence once the low manual keys of the original scheme had been removed.

Yet the extent to which the older view of the English organ as something operated with the hands alone was retained in the popular imagination can be seen in a cartoon in an 1854 issue of *Punch* (Figure 5.5): captioned "Te Deum," the image is, it seems, meant to send-up the bloodthirstiness of Tsar Nicholas I and his armies in the ongoing Crimean War fought against the English and French. The Pickelhaube helmet was associated then both with the Russian and Prussian armies but would have brought to mind the latter much more readily for *Punch* readers. Unless one had happened on the short poem much earlier in the issue in which the Tsar sings his "Thanks for murder, havoc, ruin," one would have more likely figured this organist as a German. In the end, it hardly matters whether this organist is German or Russian; he is a symbol of militarism wrapped in religion, and that is the connection that places him at the organ. While the pipes and stops make the image organologically unambiguous, the organ now strikes us as incomplete since it has no pedals. The pedal-less instrument of the kind pictured in *Punch* was still not at all uncommon in England, in spite of the efforts at modernizing its organs that had been pursued energetically for little more than a decade. The image is roughly contemporaneous with, and inadvertently sympathetic to, the conservative views of Smart and others. But for the majority of younger English organists – and progressive, older ones as well – looking at the image in 1854 would have recalled the old days of the English organ. By the end of the century the organ in the *Punch* cartoon would have been seen as equally incomplete by the English, so thorough and quick had been the transformation of the organ to an instrument in which the pedals had become essential.

This newer, Germanic notion of the organist is encapsulated in a famous cartoon from a century later by Gerard Hoffnung, who fled Germany and the Nazis in 1939 to become one of England's most cherished humorists. Hoffnung's image of the diminutive organist caught speeding by the police lampoons the technological excess and physical overload of German-style organ performance (Figure 5.6). Nearly dwarfed by his console, this myopic musician peers up from his hymnal and the profusion of keyboards into the rearview mirror in which he would expect to follow the movements of a choir director, minister, or bride marching down the aisle only to see a

---

[124] W. T. Best, *Studies for the Pedal* (London: Novello, 1914), preface.

Figure 5.5 "Te Deum," *Punch*, 1854

police car pursuing him. The image would be incomplete and far less funny without the visually prominent pedals and dangling, gangly feet. The cartoon corresponds to the image of the organist in a wider culture: busy with both hands and feet, he operates a technological, sprawling console with his entire body; he is a kind of musical jet pilot, absurdly busy at his array of controls. Burney might have added a stick to his mouth to push down yet another note (see Chapter 4). Hoffnung's organist wins much of his comic effect by seeming barely up to the task of discharging the multiple

The Organ

Figure 5.6   "The Organ," Gerard Hoffnung, 1959

responsibilities that such a machine demands. The organist, whether British or not, needs his feet; without them he can't play the organ and, worse, he's not funny.

Like cartoons, the stories told by the English about the pre-pedal days and the advent of the new "German" organ often took on an overtly comic quality. Faced with the choice of either transforming their technique or sticking to their old ways, organists were the object of occasional ridicule, even if tenderly dispensed. Dr. W. H. Longhurst, who had a long tenure as assistant organist and then organist and choirmaster at Canterbury Cathedral between 1846 and 1898, related how "German pedals" connecting to a grand total of seven independent pedal pipes had been added by his organ-building father to the cathedral instrument around 1825; these were supposedly "the first examples of their kind introduced into Kent." Longhurst's teacher and longtime organist at Canterbury, Thomas Jones, had himself been a chorister under Highmore Skeats, junior, organist at Canterbury in the first three decades of the nineteenth century when this embryonic pedal was first added; Longhurst related how the old-fashioned Skeats had an "aversion [to the pedals], and would not use them. When anybody wished to hear [them] he would call his pupil Jones saying, 'Here, Jones, come and show these things off, I never learned to *dance*.'"[125] A fear of the new, and perhaps, of the contortions of the body, prevented the old-timer from making even slight concessions to new developments, which in the few pipes added at Canterbury could only have allowed pedal points or minimal bass support rather than making possible a trio or similarly challenging contrapuntal texture that might have resembled a musical activity even close to dancing. Humor was their defensive refuge against real and threatening change. The 1899 memoir of the Irish organist Sir Robert Stewart – the book was written by the Anglican cleric, Olinthus Vignoles – claimed that:

[pedals] were only introduced in the "thirties" into Ireland, and the Dublin organs had a pedal compass at the most from low G on the bass clef to middle C, and many of them only an octave from F to F. Moreover, the executants of those days (like Mendelssohn in his early period of organ-playing) were far from skilful in the use of pedals. Sir Robert, at a meeting of his colleagues, once [said] in his youthful days he often heard organists execrating the pedals while playing the opening or closing voluntaries. He remembered one performer more ingenious than the rest, who got over the difficulty by employing a boy to press down the pedals with his hands, while the organist gained all the credit![126]

Here was a variant of the three-handed approach and that curious English addition of a manual keyboard for the pedals installed alongside the lowest manual. Even with limited access to viable instruments, Stewart made himself into an excellent pedal-player, learning "to dance" rather than retreating to join the wallflowers, as the aged George Smart had done. A century after the German pedal compass and four-limbed performance had become standard in England, even a hardly athletic sixty-six-year-old knight, Australian-born George Thalben-Ball, would throw himself into dance-till-you-drop numbers, none more flamboyant than his own *Variations on a Theme by Paganini for Pedals* of 1962, an etude for feet alone to the tune of the notorious violinist's celebrated showpiece, the 24th Caprice, with its double-stops, harmonics, octaves, and left-hand pizzicato. Thalben-Ball answered Paganini's bravura with his own pedal glissandi, ankle-contorting chords, hip-swiveling chromatics, and

---

[125] John E. West, *Cathedral Organists Past and Present* (London: Novello, 1899), pp. 9–10. A footnote adds: "at the time of the completion of these large open wood pipes, Dr. Longhurst was a small boy, six or seven years old; he distinctly remembers being made to crawl into one or two of the largest of the pipes and therein sing a little song. It is not every Cathedral Organist who could say that he had sung a song in one of his own organ pipes!" This was cited as chief among the "amusing anecdotes" in a review of the book in the *Birmingham Daily Post*, Issue 12971, Monday, January 8, 1900.

[126] Olinthus J. Vignoles, *Memoir of Sir Robert P. Stewart* (London: Simpkin, Marshall, Hamilton, Kent, & Co., 1899), pp. 10–11.

Example 5.11   George Thalben-Ball, *Variations on a Theme by Paganini for Pedals*, incipits of each variation

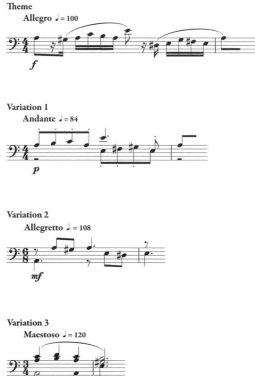

sprinting figuration. Example 5.11 gives the first bar of each variation, showing the range of conceits dreamt up by Thalben-Ball. However fun and difficult the variations are, none of them, with the possible exception of the glissandi of number 6, would have struck Bach, Petri and Knecht or even

Example 5.11   (cont.)

Variation 6
Maestoso ♩ = 76

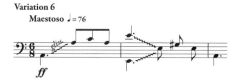

ff

Variation 7
Allegro ♩ = 136

p

Variation 8
Adagio ♩ = 69

pp

Variation 9
Adagio ♩ = 76

mp

fixed drone

pp

Variation 10
Vivace ♩ = 160

MANUAL

ff

PEDAL

Schlick as anything particularly new or daring from a technical point of view, as the demonic Paganini is made to dance the devil's dance with feet alone.

After a century of equipping their organs with pedals and retrofitting even their indigenous keyboard music of earlier times with pedal parts, some English organists began at last to reflect on what had been lost, or at least submerged, in the conversion to the German ideal. One of these was

Charles Pearce, an expert on old churches of London and their organs; his *Notes on Old City Churches: Their Organs, Organists and Musical Associations* appeared in 1909; *Notes on English Organs of the Period 1800–1810* came out in 1912.[127] Pierce's antiquarian interests led him to try to exhume an older performance practice from the newly solidified strata of ubiquitous pedal performance. In 1919 he gave a "recital of old English organ music played exactly as written, and with only scanty use made of the pedalboard a century ago."[128] The Wednesday afternoon concert at Trinity College of Music in London included a brief lecture to provide the proper historical context for something as unlikely as playing the organ without the feet. Such seeming austerity – what would now be called "authenticity" or "historically informed performance" – had acquired the status of novelty. Withholding the feet even from music originally written for hands alone had become eccentric. The English organ past had itself become a foreign country. *The Times* could similarly report of the Dolmetsch family's 1952 Haslemere Festival that "the special attraction of the first concert was a little eighteenth-century organ without pedal-board, made by Snetzler."[129] Ralph Downes played the Handel Concerto Op. 4, No. 2, in B flat without the feet, just as Handel himself had done, and in contrast to settings of these works by Best that had converted them into virtuosic solo organ music with obbligato pedal (see Examples 5.12a and 5.12b). Also presented were solos by Henry Purcell, Matthew Locke, and John Blow. How odd it now seemed to see and hear an organist perched before his instrument like the organist in *Punch* in 1854. The attitude prevails to this day, though the early music movement has reclaimed pedal-less organ repertories from Spain, Portugal, the Netherlands, Italy, Bohemia and other regions of Europe. Nonetheless,

Example 5.12a   G. F. Handel, Organ Concerto in B flat, Op. 4, No. 2, solo organ episode, bars 19–22

[127] Charles Pearce, *Notes on English Organs of the Period 1800–1810* (London: Vincent Music Co., and Boston: T. J. Donland, 1912).
[128] *The Times*, Thursday, January 9, 1909, p. 9.
[129] *The Times*, Monday, July 21, 1952, p. 6. See also *Musical Times*, 93 (1952), 420.

Example 5.12b   G. F. Handel, Organ Concerto in B flat, Op. 4, No. 2, solo organ episode, bars 19–22, transcribed by W. T. Best (London, 1858)

current plans for the restoration of the well-preserved 1735 Richard Bridge organ in Christ Church, Spitalfields, one of the last surviving remnants of English eighteenth-century organ-building, include a detachable pedalboard on which one can play Bach. One can have it both ways: sit at the organ with feet on the floorboards, or roll in a pedal board with compass of the Weissenfels organ for which Bach wrote the F Major Toccata and let loose in a manner that would have flabbergasted Richard Bridge. His original instrument had no pedals whatsoever.

While reclaiming something of his country's pedal-less past, Pearce remained loyal to the view of history that embraced the adoption of the German System as a necessary, indeed inevitable, advance. In 1927 Pearce published *The Evolution of the Pedal Organ and Matters Connected Therewith*, in which he admitted that "the evolution of pedal *playing* in England was as slow as the progress of the pedal organ itself." His diagnosis had a venerable pedigree: "Old fashioned organists were such skilful *left hand players* that it took time to convince them of any necessity for playing with their feet." By the end of the book the humble beginnings of English feet at the organ have been more than overcome by "such brilliant pedalists as Best, Stainer, and others." Pearce could confidently pronounce that the "evolution of pedals and pedaling is complete." He then cast a proud glance across the British Empire stretching over the globe from the Royal Albert Hall in London to Sydney Town Hall in Australia, the specifications of both these great organs occupying pride of place in his book. Also included in this dominion was the United States. As Churchill would do later, Pearce brought the Americans into the empire culturally under the

red-white-and-blue umbrella of "English-speaking."[130] Having mastered
the pedal – indeed, says Pearce, excelled at it – the "English-speaking race is
once more in the ascendancy, all the world over."[131] Without pedal power a
people cannot count themselves as truly powerful. As the German émigré
Kollmann had pointed out more than a century earlier, an empire should
have great organs – with massive pedals to be skillfully played by imperial
organists. Over the nineteenth century the British had expanded their
empire and with it the imperial reach of the organ pedals: it was through
the missionary zeal and military might of the British, along with the lesser
colonial powers, that German feet had conquered the world.

[130] Winston Churchill, *History of the English-speaking Peoples*, 4 vols. (New York: Dodd, Mead, 1956–1958).
[131] Pearce, *The Evolution of the Pedal Organ*, pp. 57, 69.

CHAPTER 6

Bach's Feet

It is as an organist in musical motion that Bach comes most vibrantly to life in the surviving historical documents describing him in performance. Yet his body is a ghost in the scholarly literature devoted to him; indeed, it has been absent from these pages, even though his feet are precisely the focus of contemporary and near-contemporary accounts of his music-making. The tendency for Bach's body to vanish from descriptions of his own life and works begins early on, in the account provided by his first biographer, Johann Nikolaus Forkel, himself an organist who knew what it feels like to play Bach's music. This chief apostle of the transcendent Bach claimed that the organ works "disdained everything common";[1] Forkel then went on to argue that because of the unique nature of his music, "[Bach] does not appear a man, but as a true disembodied spirit, who soars above everything mortal." There is no shortage of similarly lofty metaphysical statements from other Bach devotees. However seductive such rhetorical flourishes may be, I believe that it is by appreciating the physicality of Bach's organ music that we can better understand and value his achievement, even while we embrace the unique qualities of the organ as a sonic and visual work of art. In revisiting these well-known accounts of Bach's pedaling, I hope to restage the drama of the organist's dynamic performance at the monumental instrument he plays. By returning Bach to the organ loft we bring him back down to earth.

BACH'S SHOE BUCKLES

Since the organist's shoes are crucial to the act of playing, let's begin to reanimate Bach at the organ by thinking first about what he wore on his feet. The connection of the feet to the pedal is through the sole and heel of the organist's shoes, typically still today made of leather as they were in Bach's time; this material provides a sufficiently rigid and even platform for the supple bottom of the foot, and also allows one to slide along the pedal key, a maneuver that is often crucial in pedaling since one foot often has to dart behind or in front of the other. Several factors are important to the

---

[1] *NBR*, 438.

Figure 6.1   Men's Shoes. Central German, c. 1680

effectiveness of an organist's shoes, including: the pliability of the leather; the shoes' bulkiness, fit and comfort; and the height of the heel (on average about 2.5 inches tall in the eighteenth century). For Justin Heinrich Knecht, writing in the last decade of that century, the preferred approach to pedal-playing involved the heel and toe, and for this technique he recommended "a high heel in both shoes."[2] German shoes of Bach's day were made mostly from leather, with heels either of built-up strips of hide or of wood; the so-called quarter (the rear part of the upper) came from the heel around either side of the ankle and then narrowed into flaps (called "latchets" in English, "ears" [*Ohren*] in German); the shoes could be tightened around the top of the foot either with cloth bands (as in Figure 6.1) or the straps could be fed through a buckle.[3] Shoes such as these were generally good for walking in wet and muddy conditions, and for long journeys over country roads. But they would have been used for playing the organ, too, even for performing Bach's music in all its finesse and bravura.

Only on rare occasions does a discussion of the organist's footwear arise in the musicological literature. In the preface to the first modern edition of

[2] Justin Heinrich Knecht, *Vollständige Orgelschule für Anfänger und Geübtere*, 3 vols. (Leipzig: Breitkopf, 1795; reprint, Wiesbaden: Breitkopf & Härtel, 1989), vol. III, p. 47. The émigré Johann Paul Aegidius Martini (born Schwarzendorf) abundantly plagiarized Knecht in his *École d'orgue* published in Paris in 1804. In the material drawn from Knecht on polyphonic pedaling, Martini recommends a heel of 15 to 18 *lignes*, that is, up to about 1.5 inches, rather smaller than on many eighteenth-century shoes. Martini notes the widely varying compasses of French pedalboards; indeed on many of these French instruments, in contrast to those of Martini's homeland, it would have been impossible to play Knecht's pedal exercises, or to use the heel at all. J. P. A. Martini, *École d'orgue* (Paris: Imbault, 1805; reprint, Geneva: Minkoff, 1974), p. 42.

[3] "Schuh,"in Zedler, *Universal-Lexicon*, vol. XXXV, cols. 1333–1341, at col. 1337.

Schlick's *Ascendo ad patrem meum* from 1954, the Spanish musicologist,
Marco Kastner, who edited much Iberian organ music (all without pedal),
wondered what the blind organist might have had on his feet: "Schlick
proposes six voices for the manuals and four for the pedal. This is an
excellent etude in quadruple pedal ... Evidently the cut and form of the
shoes of Schlick's time rendered the playing of chords on the pedal easier
than those of the present day, especially in the case of the flat boots of many
country organists."[4] The particular country where such boots are worn is
not made clear by Kastner. The feminine figure pictured playing the organ
on the frontispiece of Schlick's *Tabulaturen* (Figure 6.2) sports shoes not so
unlike those made nowadays by the small Massachusetts company,
Organmaster (see Figure 6.3). But Schlick's female organist has shoes that
appear to have smaller heels than those of her modern counterparts.
Without heels, the shoes of the female organist of the *Tabulaturen* would
indeed have made two polyphonic parts in each foot difficult, not to say
impossible, although a slipper allows the foot to bend much more than a
cumbersome shoe. This is not the place to launch into a history of the organ
shoe, but suffice it to say that until the founding of Organmaster in 1976
there seems to have been no specially designed and manufactured footwear
for the organist,[5] although the vigorous exercise program laid out by Mark
Lendon Bennett in his *The Organist's Callisthenics or Gymnastic Exercises –
For the Development of the Muscles Brought into Action in Organ Pedal
Playing* from 1899 includes recommendations for minimal, form-fitting
boots (with heels) or shoes; these, too, resemble the Organmasters (see
Figures 6.3 and 6.4).[6] (Also similar to the Organmasters are the shoes seen
on the cover of this book, which were made by the Capezio company in
1979; they are tap-dance shoes without the metal taps. Recall that in a letter
of 1837, Mendelssohn had complained that the pedal keys of the
Birmingham Town Hall organ were too narrow for boots.) During the
long history of pedal-playing before the twentieth-century and the increasing specialization of footwear, the organist simply wore street shoes to play
in, as any number of historic photos of early twentieth-century virtuosos at
the console will confirm. Changing shoes before commencing to play – not
something every modern organist does, and a few even play in stocking
feet – seems to be a relatively recent phenomenon. We can probably assume
that Bach played Buxtehude's organ in Lübeck wearing the same shoes (like
those in Figure 6.1) he made his long journey in.

---

[4] Arnolt Schlick, *Hommage à L'Empereur Charles-Quint*, ed. M. S. Kastner (Barcelona: Boileau, 1954),
preface.
[5] See http://store.organmastershoes.com/
[6] Mark Lendon-Bennett, *The Organist's Pedal Callisthenics or Gymnastic Exercises – For the Development
of the Muscles Brought into Action in Organ Pedal Playing* (London: Guild of Church Musicians, 1899).
For Mendelssohn's references to the boots of organists, see Chapter 5, p. 210.

Figure 6.2   Arnolt Schlick, *Spiegel der Orgelmacher und Organisten*, frontispiece

Aside from their utility, shoes could also serve as a symbol of the organist's skill. In the early years of the nineteenth century, a musician named Böse withdrew from the competition for the organist's post in the north-German town of Altenburg (with its wonderfully preserved baroque organ) when he learned that Johann Kittel, one of Bach's last students, was also an applicant; Böse believed himself "unworthy to unfasten Kittel's shoe

Organmaster Shoes

YOU'LL PLAY BETTER! Highest quality, genuine leather shoes for organists make your pedaling elegant and sure. Leather sole has special finish for just the right amount of **slide** and **grasp**. Insole is slim foam layer with lining to cushion your feet yet allow **feel through**. Matching heel is 1 1/8 inches high for perfect legato playing of thirds. Steel shank gives the leverage you need for operating the stiffest swell pedals. No breaking-in is needed — these organ shoes are perfect for playing when new! Available in colors to match your vestments and professional clothes.

Enjoy the benefits of wearing the right shoe — a long-wearing all leather shoe made with the features most sought after by organ teachers and students.

WOMEN'S SHOE — a dressy style with narrow toe and sleek lines. Elasticized strap insures a no-slip fit and gives foot muscles complete freedom to **play**! Sizes 4-10, N, M, W.

Black Bone White Navy Lt. Blue
Brown Yellow Red Pink Royal Blue
$20.00 per pair plus $1 postage.

MEN'S SHOE weighs only half as much as a regular men's shoe! Slims and trims the foot while giving maximum comfort from soft fine leather and knit-fit lining. Sizes 6-12 N,M,W.

Black Brown Tan White
$22.00 per pair plus $1 postage.

RECITALISTS! We also offer these shoes in gold and silver to compliment the most beautiful long dresses.

$21.00 per pair plus $1 postage.

Black and some colors shipped immediately. Some colors and sizes are 3-6 weeks delivery.

Organmaster Shoes
90 Fowler Avenue
Meriden, Connecticut 06450

Name _____
Street _____ Zip _____
City _____ State _____

Men's/Women's	Color	Width	Size	Price	Postage

___ Personal Check ___ Money Order
___ Master Charge ___ Visa (BankAmericard)
Card Number _____
Exp. Date _____

Signature _____

Total for Shoes	
Conn. res. add 7% Tax	
Total for Postage	
AMOUNT ENCLOSED	

Organ shoes are tax-deductible on Form 1040, Schedule A, Line 33.

Canadians should send checks drawn on U.S. funds. (203) 235-5284
© Organmaster Shoes, 1977

You **must** be satisfied or return in 7 days for any reason.
Order usual size — whole and half sizes available.

Figure 6.3 First advertisement for Organmaster Shoes. *The American Organist*, January 1978

straps" [*er [war] nicht würdig, Kittels Schuhriemen aufzulösen*].[7] To be sure, this is a figure of speech in German (sometimes translated into English with the more demeaning language "not worthy to lick one's boots"), but in this context has particular resonance. The image of Böse kneeling down before

[7] *Urania*, 1(1844), 11.

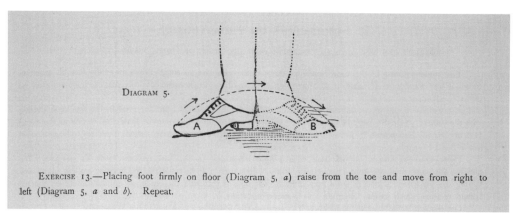

EXERCISE 13.—Placing foot firmly on floor (Diagram 5, *a*) raise from the toe and move from right to left (Diagram 5, *a* and *b*). Repeat.

Figure 6.4   Exercises for the properly clad foot. Mark Lendon-Bennett, *Organ Callisthenics*, London, 1899

his elder colleague's shoes can be read not only as expressing a recognition of the senior applicant's overall superiority at the organ, but also brings to mind Kittel's renowned skills with the feet – as in the pedal arpeggios and tremolo thirds and trills of a showpiece prelude for full organ from his method, *Der angehende praktische Organist* (Erfurt, 1808), which appeared the year before the author's death (see Example 6.1). Kittel's shoes were a metonym for the broader ability of an accomplished German organist and in turn for the gravity and power of the German organ he played.[8] The symbolic power of Bach's shoes was greater still. After praising Bach's chorale preludes for two manuals and obbligato pedal, Jakob Adlung concluded that "there was only one Bach in the world, and ... few are worthy of his shoes."[9] Whether or not this too is simply a figure of speech, it serves to draw attention towards the feet that symbolize the great organist in action.

After Bach's death in 1750, a detailed specification of his estate was prepared for purposes of probate. The specification lists: his collection of coins and medals; the petty cash on hand; his silverware and other valuables; the household wares of pewter, copper, and brass; his furniture and musical instruments; and his theological books. The document's ninth section concerns itself with the deceased's clothing and accessories. Listed are a silver sword [*Degen*],[10] a walking stick with silver mounting, a coat for funerals, two jackets, and a pair of silver shoe buckles [*paar silberne Schuh-*

---

[8] Forkel considered Kittel merely a "solid" [*gründlich*] but not very "dexterous" [*fertig*] organist. Forkel, *Ueber Johann Sebastian Bachs Leben, Kunst und Kunstwerke*, p. 43.

[9] Jakob Adlung, *Anleitung zu der musikalischen Gelahrtheit* (Erfurt: J. D. Jungnicol, 1758; reprint, Kassel: Bärenreiter, 1953), p. 692. See also *BD*, 2: 122.

[10] Martin Geck characterizes the sword as "a relic from his Lüneburg days." M. Geck, *Johann Sebastian Bach: Life and Work*, trans. John Hargraves (Boston: Houghton Mifflin Harcourt, 2006), p. 53.

Example 6.1   Johann Kittel, *Der angehende praktische Organist* (Erfurt, 1808), *Preludio pro Organo pleno* No. 1, bars 61–75

Schnallen],[11] perhaps the very ones Bach wore when he played the organ for the great German princes of the age: in Dresden for Augustus father and son, in turn Saxon Elector and Polish King; and in Potsdam for Frederick the Great.

Shoes began to be equipped in the 1660s with buckles, which attained an increasingly important function in the fashion of the eighteenth century because of the relative lack of variation in the shoes themselves, whose design remained largely unchanged in the period.[12] With the standardization in men's shoes, buckles became a crucial accessory for the projection of social status and fashion consciousness, and a given style could quickly become old-fashioned.[13] These accoutrements were common enough for members of the middle-class, but would have demonstrated that Bach had arrived at a certain station in life, rising from orphan to become one of the

---

[11] *NBR*, 250–256, at 252–253; see also *BD*, 2: 490–498, at 494.

[12] Giorgio Riello, *A Foot in the Past: Producers and Footwear in the Long Eighteenth Century* (Oxford University Press, 2006), p. 75.

[13] Penelope Byrd, *Male Image: Men's Fashions in England, 1300–1970* (London: Batsford Academic, 1979), p. 197; see also Riello, *A Foot in the Past*, p. 77.

Figure 6.5   Men's shoe with silver buckle, c. 1690

leading civic musicians in eighteenth-century Germany. Silver shoe buckles also enhanced the visual effect of Bach's organ performances, when bystanders' attention to the feet was at its most heightened; this was not the only reason for Bach to wear them, but he was doubtless aware of how his feet looked. For amazed onlookers the silver shoe buckles did more than secure the shoe around the foot; they drew the eye to pedal display. Such buckles could be affixed to the basic, functional shoes of Figure 6.1, or to fancier versions with the same basic design as in Figure 6.5, which shows a fine shoe from around 1690. There were much more lavish shoes than these, as in the design from 1730 in Figure 6.6 marked as exclusively aristocratic by its red heel; this color was forbidden to a man of Bach's social standing not only by custom but also by sumptuary law, but the height of these heels was quite common in men's shoes in the eighteenth-century.[14] One could entertain the image of Bach the famous organist, long since ascended to the top of his profession, wearing shoes of a similar shape.

It is a curious coincidence that the 1783 will of another of Bach's last students, Johann Gottfried Müthel, lists a pair of silver shoe buckles of an "old-fashioned small appearance" [*von altmodischer kleiner Façon*].[15] What did Anna Magdalena do with her late husband's buckles? Is it too wild a conjecture to ask if she could have used them as an in-kind payment for musical services Müthel might have provided soon after Bach's death,

---

[14] Riello, *A Foot in the Past*, pp. 63–64.

[15] Zane Gailíte, "Johann Gottfried Müthel, die Bach-Familie und die 'Wahre Art, das Clavier zu Spielen' in Riga" in Ulrich Leisinger and Hans-Günter Ottenberg (eds.), *Die Verbreitung der Werke Carl Philipp Emanuel Bachs in Ostmitteleuropa im 18. und 19. Jahrhundert* (Frankfurt an der Oder: Mess- und Veranstaltungs GmbH, 2002), pp. 480–514, at p. 487.

Figure 6.6   Aristocratic men's shoe with silver buckle, c. 1730

which the terms of Bach's employment dictated were to be paid for by his widow?[16] What a talisman Bach's buckles would have been for an organist. As can be seen in his so-called *Technische Übungen* ("Technical Exercises"), a collection of autograph manuscript pages apparently intended for a treatise on keyboard composition and performance, Müthel significantly expanded the possibilities of Bachian pedaling, demanding virtuosic facility with the feet that went beyond the techniques his teacher had asked for.[17] One of Müthel's innovations can be seen in the pedal solo found in Figure 6.7, which is written on the lower of the two staves, as is typical of eighteenth-century notation of pedal parts. In this passage the left foot jumps over the right to repeat the high b flat on the pedalboard in a maneuver that is analogous to hand-crossing on the manuals. A melancholic and solitary figure, Müthel spent his career far to the east of the Bach heartland in the Baltic city of Riga; his *Technische Übungen* were never published, and the innovations they contained were perhaps to be heard and seen only in Müthel's own performances. These passages counted as new

[16] See David Yearsley, "Women at the Organ: a Fragment" in Thomas Donahue (ed.), *Music and Its Questions: Essays in Honor of Peter Williams* (Richmond, Virginia: Organ Historical Society Press, 2007), pp. 119–141, at pp. 125–126. Although Müthel studied with Bach for only two months prior to his teacher's death he had close ties with the family. After Bach's death, Müthel continued his studies with J. C. Altnickol (Bach's son-in-law) in Naumburg. In May 1751, Müthel and Anna Magdalena Bach served as godparents to Altnickol's daughter Augusta Magdalena. *BD*, 3: 9–10. See Christoph Wolff, *Johann Sebastian Bach: The Learned Musician* (New York: Norton, 2000), p. 407.

[17] J. G. Müthel, *Technische Übungen*, in the Staatsbibliothek zu Berlin, Mus. ms. 15762/i–ii. For a modern edition of fragments, fantasias, and chorale preludes, including gymnastic pedal solos with multi-voice writing, see J. G. Müthel, *Orgelwerke*, 2 vols., ed. Rüdiger Wilhelm (Innsbruck: Helbling, 1985).

Figure 6.7   Johann Gottfried Müthel, *Technische Übungen*, Staatsbibliothek zu Berlin, Mus. ms. 15762/i, p. 11

physical research into the potential of the pedal, valuable in their own right, even if they never found a wider audience of colleagues and students. Though Forkel's lists of organists from the 1780s present diminishing numbers, there were other players pushing into new territory. Witness the high-speed double-pedal antics of Samuel Petri, a student of Wilhelm Friedemann Bach. These include full chords, grabbing sixteenth-note thirds in the right foot alone, even two accidentals – d-sharp and f-sharp – simultaneously (in the second bar of the first staff on page 329 of Figure 6.8; the number 1 indicates the right toe; 2 the left toe; 3 the right heel; 4 the left heel). Petri's footwork is proof that the German pedalboard continued to be explored in adventurous ways after the death of the pedal master, Bach.[18]

Using the admittedly minimal information available in the estate specification, we can add some other items to our image of Bach at the organ. Besides the buckles, he had other silver accessories: a silver-mounted walking stick and a silver sword at his side. In the famous assemblage of the various peoples of Europe, the so-called *Völkertafel* – "Table of Peoples" (see Figure 6.9a) painted by an unknown artist in Austria in the first decades of the eighteenth century – the German man standing fourth from the left has these three accoutrements.[19] The jacket this German wears (see Figure 6.9b) is also not too different from the fancier one described in Bach's estate. Bach's garment (called *Kleid* in the estate specification) was of fine fabric, *gros du tour* (that is, *gros du Tours*) – a close-woven silken ribbed fabric, generally black, as seen on the German man in the *Völkertafel*;[20]

[18] Knecht gives a much easier example of this technique in his *Vollständige Orgelschule* (1795), Pt. 1, p. 47, exercise 13.

[19] Franz Grieshofer, "Die Tracht der Kleidung: Bermerkungen zur Darstellung der europäischen Nationen auf der 'Völkertafel'" in Franz K. Stanzel (ed.), *Europäischer Völkerspiegel: Imagologisch-ethnographische Studien zu den Völkertafeln des frühen 18. Jahrhunderts* (Heidelberg: Universitätsverlag C. Winter, 1999), pp. 45–60.

[20] For more on the silk threads, see Kate Heintz Watson, *Textiles and Clothing* (Chicago: American School of Home Economics, 1907; reprint, Charleston, South Carolina: BiblioBazaar, 2009), pp. 91–92. For a contemporaneous tutorial in pedaling, see Daniel Gottlob Türk, *Von den wichtigsten Pflichten eines Organisten* (Halle: Schwickert, 1787), pp. 158–160.

Figure 6.8 Virtuosic multi-voiced pedaling. Johann Samuel Petri, *Anleitung zur praktischen Musik* (Leipzig, 1782), pp. 328–329

Figure 6.9a   *Völkertafel*, Steiermark, c. 1720

Bach's jacket is described in the specification as "turned" [*gewendet*], which generally indicated elaborate, textured piping or brocade.[21] The figure of eight Thaler assigned to this jacket in the estate specification makes it the second most valuable item in the clothing section, four Thaler less than the sword and of the same value as Bach's Stainer violin. Clothes were relatively more expensive in the eighteenth century than now, but it is clear from his estate that when he wanted to, Bach could look more than simply respectable.

A sword figures in the account of the youthful brawl between Bach and an affronted student named Geyersbach in Arnstadt in the summer of 1705. Insulted by Bach as "greenhorn bassoonist" [*Zippel Faggotist*], Geyersbach accosted the young organist, who was coming from the direction of the castle; as Bach went for his sword [*Degen*], Geyersbach fell upon him and the hot-tempered pair rolled around in the dusty square until separated by

---

[21] Jane Conlon, *Fine Embellishment Techniques: Classic Details for Today's Clothing* (Newtown, Connecticut: Taunton, 2001), p. 126.

Figure 6.9b   Detail of the German man

Figure 6.10   The organist at the console, Dom Bédos de Celles, *L'art du facteur d'orgues*,
vol. I, Paris, 1766, Plate LII

the other students.[22] There in the shadow of the New Church, its organist
seems to have worn his sword of a Tuesday evening. Perhaps we could
surmise that the sword was part of Bach's usual sartorial ensemble, as in the
famous image of the organist, with sword and buckled shoes, from the first
volume of Dom Bédos, *L'art du facteur d'orgues* of 1766 (Figure 6.10). Did
Bach have his *Degen* at his side when he sat at the organ bench?

BACH AT THE ORGAN

The most vivid contemporary accounts of Bach find him at the organ,
where his feet are the object of intense fascination. What history's witnesses
to Bach the organist would have seen was a slightly taller-than-average man,
apparently still vigorous late in life, since he could manage such late works as
the "St. Ann" Prelude and Fugue, BWV 552 – printed when he was in
his mid-fifties.[23] The pedalboards Bach knew had keys generally wider
than those of modern instruments. By modern standards, Bach was a
small man at large consoles, seated at benches that were generally higher

---

[22] Proceedings of the Arnstadt Consistory, August 5, 1705; *NBR*, 43.

[23] If the nineteenth-century "scientific" accounts of Bach's skeleton are to be believed, he was about
5'5", a bit taller than the average Saxon army recruit of the early eighteenth century. Wilhelm His,
"Johann Sebastian Bach's Gebeine und Antlitz," *Abhandlungen der königlich-sächsischen Gesellschaft
der Wissenschaft*, 37 (1895), 381–420. See also John Komlos and Francesco Cinnirella, "European
Heights in the Early 18th Century," Discussion Paper, April 2005 (Department of Economics,
University of Munich; see http://ideas.repec.org/p/lmu/muenec/572.html).

than present-day ones. He apparently favored a refined ergonomic layout with shorter manual keys; nonetheless, playing with feet and hands was an often aerobic activity that required a good deal of stretching, swiveling, and balancing.[24] Getting around on such an apparatus with the velocity and accuracy emphasized by contemporary accounts of his playing was a physical feat unparalleled in other modes of music-making.

Professionals and princes were swept away by Bach's pedal skill, as in a contemporary report probably stemming from his 1732 visit to Kassel to test a renovated organ:

Bach deserves to be called the miracle of Leipzig, as far as music is concerned. For if it pleases him, he can by the use of his feet alone while his fingers do either nothing or something else, achieve such an admirable, agitated, and rapid concord of sounds on the church organ that others would seem unable to imitate it even with their fingers. When he was called from Leipzig to Kassel to pronounce an organ properly restored, he ran over the pedals with this same facility, as if his feet had wings, making the organ resound with such fullness, and so penetrate the ears of those present like a thunderbolt, that Frederick, the legitimate hereditary Prince of Kassel, admired him with such astonishment that he drew a ring with a precious stone from his finger and gave it to Bach as soon as the sound had died away. If Bach earned such a gift for the agility of his feet, what, I ask, would the Prince have given him if he had called his hands into service as well?[25]

The most famous of musical feet are a complete musical entity capable alone of garnering lavish gifts. They fill up the church, dazzle the eye, and imprint themselves unforgettably on the memory. This prince was then a boy of twelve years, but adults too were happily willing to be awed by Bach.

Bach taught his students not only precision and finesse, but also how to impress listeners and viewers like the Landgrave of Kassel, who had the opportunity to watch Bach from the organ loft. The virtuosity recounted in anecdotes such as this brings to mind the same qualities evident in a famed musical fragment for feet alone from the Bach circle, the so-called *Pedal Exercitium*, BWV 598. This extended pedal solo survives on a single manuscript page in the hand of C. P. E. Bach, and is perhaps a sketch of an improvisation by his father[26] (Figure 6.11). A later student of J. S. Bach added the title along with an ascription to his teacher (or at least to "Bach") in the mid-1730s (soon after the trip to Kassel). The leaf remained in Leipzig after C. P. E. Bach left home in 1734, and the title suggests that the *Pedal Exercitium* was added to J. S. Bach's teaching materials as a model of the

---

[24] For an account of studies of eighteenth-century keyboards, see Jean-Claude Zehnder, "Organ Articulation in the Seventeenth and Eighteenth Centuries," Pt 1, *The American Organist*, 17 (1983), 30–31. See also Quentin Faulkner, *J. S. Bach Keyboard Technique: A Historical Introduction* (St. Louis: Concordia, 1984), p. 47.

[25] The author of this tribute is the school rector of Minden, Constantin Bellermann. For the Latin original, see *BD*, 2: 410. English trans. taken from *NBR*, 334–335.

[26] See *Carl Philipp Emanuel Bach: Organ Works*, series 1, vol. ix, ed. Annette Richards and David Yearsley (Los Altos: Packard Humanities Institute, 2008), pp. 121–123.

Figure 6.11   *Pedal Exercitium*, Staatsbibliothek zu Berlin, Mus. ms. Bach P 491

bravura pedal solo, and also, perhaps, an invitation to further improvisation, with the full manual chords sketched at the bottom of the page beckoning the player into a harmonic labyrinth; the pedal solo itself does not come to a close but ends on a half-cadence. With the breathless energy of its perpetual motion figure, the jagged leaps that send the feet vaulting across the pedals, the repeated notes exchanged between the feet culminating in a scale traversing nearly the entire compass (in the opposite direction to the descent

Example 6.2   J. S. Bach, *Nun komm, der Heiden Heiland*, BWV 599, bar 1

in BWV 564), the solo offers an example of how demonstrative, even demonic, Bachian pedaling could be. In modern times the *Pedal Exercitium* is generally performed as a *pedaliter* etude,[27] without the ensuing chords. In this form the piece remains a testament to the caché still associated with Bach's pedal technique. It was and is music meant primarily to astonish, visually and aurally. The pedal solo was a staple of the north-German *stylus phantasticus*, and, to judge from contemporary accounts, the most attention-getting weapon in Bach's technical arsenal.

However fantastical the *Pedal Exercitium* may have been, and however crucial its lessons of astonishment were to Bach's students, the core of Bach's organ pedagogy was the *Orgelbüchlein*. The title-page of the collection promised to help the beginner learn to develop a chorale in "diverse ways, and at the same time acquire facility in the study of the pedal since in the chorales contained [in the collection] the pedal is treated as wholly obbligato."[28] In contrast to the outpourings of so many of Bach's free works, the pages of the *Orgelbüchlein* presented perfected miniatures: the typical prelude from the collection was shorter than the fragmentary *Pedal Exercitium* and took up merely a page of the diminutive book. Bach begins the collection with the chorale, *Nun komm, der Heiden Heiland*, BWV 599 (see Example 6.2). In a seeming contradiction of the nearby words of the dedication proclaiming the importance of obbligato pedaling, the opening texture is *manualiter*, in four parts in the decorated arpeggiations of the so-called *style brisé* – the broken style. The hands take apparent control of the texture in the manner of a French harpsichordist as if defying the German feet to fulfill the obligation set out for them on the title-page. Meanwhile, the feet stand by, concerned perhaps, over the first half-bar, about how they might contribute to this already complete tonic harmony. The unresolved neighboring tone of d-sharp, coming midway through the bar and just before the pedal entry, makes the thicket still more impenetrable. Unfazed, the pedal strides into the fray, moving resolutely from the tonic a to the dominant e to clash directly with the manual d-sharp. The pedal will assert

---

[27] This view of the *Pedal Exercitium* is perpetuated, for example, in Peter Williams, *The Organ Music of J. S. Bach*, 2nd edn. (Cambridge University Press, 2002), pp. 225–226.

[28] *NBR*, 80–81.

its independence even if this requires the boldest of forays into the teeth of the crowded texture above. It is as if, in the opening bar of the collection, Bach makes it as difficult as possible for the pedal to find a way in in order to demonstrate all the more clearly how fervently he will pursue his commitment to the integrity of the pedal. The opening bar of the *Orgelbüchlein* is an ideological statement as much as a pedagogical one, and it speaks even louder than the bombast of the *Pedal Exercitium*. From the first bar of *Nun komm der Heiden Heiland*, Bach brings the hands and feet into contest and cooperation.

As rector of the Thomasschule in the early 1730s, the classical scholar Johann Matthias Gesner had had the chance to see and hear Bach on many occasions; four years after leaving Leipzig for a professorship in Göttingen in 1734, Gesner produced a florid Latin tribute to his former colleague. Gesner is transfixed by Bach's velocity; Bach is more than just "many" musicians in one, he is hundreds, and the sight is more astonishing even than the sound:

> If you could see Bach ... either playing our clavier, which is many citharas in one, with all the fingers of both hands, or running over the keys of the instrument of instruments [the organ], whose innumerable pipes are brought to life by bellows, with both hands and, at utmost speed, with his feet, producing by himself the most various and at the same time mutually agreeable combinations of sounds in orderly procession. If you could see him, I say, doing what many of your citharists and six hundred of your tibia players together could not do, not only, like a citharist, singing with one voice and playing his own parts, but watching over everything and bringing back to the rhythm and the beat, out of thirty or even forty musicians, the one with a nod, another by tapping with his foot, the third with a warning finger, giving the right note to one from the top of his voice, to another from the bottom, and to a third from the middle of it – all alone, in the midst of the greatest din made by all the participants, and although he is executing the most difficult parts himself, noticing at once whenever and wherever a mistake occurs, holding everyone together, taking precautions everywhere, and repairing any unsteadiness, full of rhythm in every part of his body – this one man taking in all these harmonies with his keen ear and emitting with his voice alone the tone of all the voices. Favorer as I am of antiquity, the accomplishments of our Bach, and of any others who may be like him, appear to me to effect what not many Orpheuses, nor twenty Arions, could achieve.[29]

Gesner contrasts the self-sufficiency of the organ and organist with the fragile interdependence of orchestra and chorus with their conductor, who must not only discharge his continuo function, but also fill holes in the music by singing, signaling, or playing missing parts when his musicians have gone astray. The complementary images Gesner summons of the performing musician as organist and then as conductor suggest that Bach becomes the perfect *Capellmeister* when at the organ: his limbs do what a

---

[29] For the Latin original, see *BD*, 2: 332. English trans. in *NBR*, 328–329. This passage would be translated in shortened form by Charles Burney for his article on J. S. Bach in Rees's *Cyclopaedia* of 1819. See also *BD*, 3: 943.

group of individual musicians – singers and players at their own instruments – can do if they execute their parts properly. If in good working order, Bach's organ is his private orchestra, following instantaneously his every command without complaint or error: the 600 tibia players of this symphony respond to his movements with unfailing accuracy. As an organist, Bach rules over the most responsive, all-encompassing, powerful, and advanced musical technology. In Gesner's account, Bach the conductor must keep his subordinates in line and his music together; Bach's organ, by contrast, is a symphony of obedient virtuosos, each answering precisely to the movements of his fingers and feet, performing exactly what he desires of them, from thrilling passagework to the largest and most complex contrapuntal constructions. At the instrument of instruments, he is the musician of musicians. Bach is not only supremely alive at the organ, he is supremely in control.

Bach's astounding technical ability provided a kind of unattainable standard, and his students were as awed by his skill as were the untrained. In a 1729 letter of application for an organist post in Görlitz, Bach's student Johann Caspar Vogler rather immodestly wrote that, "As regards virtue on the organ and speed of hands and feet, I come closest to [Bach] here in Saxony."[30] To have the second fastest feet in the land was quite a claim, though the Görlitz position went to another Bach pupil, David Nicolai, also apparently fleet of foot. The Görlitz church was home to Eugenio Casparini's most famous opus in the north, completed in 1703 after the builder's return from Italy, and several decades after his work on the organ in Santa Maria Maggiore in Trent. One wonders what speeds Vogler and Nicolai would have been able to attain on the Görlitz instrument, reportedly criticized by J. S. Bach as "A horse of an organ" [*eine Pferds-Orgel*] because of its heavy action.[31] If, as Burney had it, the workout on the Silbermann organ in the Frauenkirche in Dresden was a ten-mile run in the heat of summer, then to play a Bach Prelude and Fugue on the Görlitz organ was a musical marathon.

During Bach's lifetime, even his critics buffed his shoes with praise. Johann Adolph Scheibe, a Bach student who vexed his former teacher for years with his criticisms, praised Bach in the opening salvo of his infamous polemical attack: "One can hardly conceive how it is possible for [Bach] to achieve such agility with his fingers and with his feet, in the crossings, extensions, and extreme jumps that he manages without mixing in a single wrong tone, or displacing his body by any violent movement."[32] Here was a vision of corporeal efficiency that provided the model for Bach's students

---

[30] *NBR*, 320; *BD*, 2: 195–196.
[31] Marc Schaefer (ed.), *Das Silbermann-Archiv* (Winterthur: Amadeus, 1994), p. 170.
[32] J. A. Scheibe, *Der critische Musicus*, Pt. 6, May 14, 1737 (Hamburg: Thomas von Wiering's Heirs, 1738), p. 46. *NBR*, 338.

and later epigones, such as Johann Schneider in Dresden, into the nineteenth century.

After Bach's death his pedal prowess was magnified through the lens of hagiographic adulation. Ernst Ludwig Gerber, whose father had studied with Bach in Leipzig, describes superhuman technical deeds enacted with machine-like precision and ease:

On the pedals his feet had to imitate with perfect accuracy every theme, every passage that his hands had played. No appoggiatura, no mordent, no short trill was suffered to be lacking or even to meet the ear in less clean and rounded form. He used to make long double trills with both feet, while his hands were anything but idle.[33]

Here the astounding prospect of both feet oscillating at trilling speed monopolizes the attention. Gerber's tableau of Bach at the organ console also demonstrates that by the end of the eighteenth century – if not before – Bach's feet had attained heroic status. The eighteenth-century reception of Bach as organist emphasizes the visual spectacle of his performances, and suggests just how interested he may have been in impressing his listeners watching him in the organ loft. Double trills and big pedal solos again suggest that Bach understood and exploited the impact his playing had on bystanders. For all their possible distortions, these scenes capture the way Bach deployed the big, flashy gesture that could dumbfound the spectators close by while simultaneously thrilling the people down below in the church as he grappled with the colossal sound of the pedals. That extremes of unrestrained energy such as double trills are not to be found in any of Bach's surviving music might suggest that in performance he would let himself go further than composerly decorum might otherwise allow, that he would, as it were, let his feet run away with him even more unrestrainedly than in the flamboyant *Pedal Exercitium*.

The still-dominant picture of Bach, inherited from the nineteenth century, as an austere and devout figure, ignores the demanding physicality of his organ music made clear in these accounts of his performances.[34] If eyewitness reports are to be believed, Bach at the organ went beyond the figure of the musician devoted above all to the encouragement of religious devotion; he was a self-consciously impressive performer, and the sight of him at full tilt on the organ bench, his feet doing incredible things, was one of the great musical acts of the age.

---

[33] E. L. Gerber, *Historisch-biographisches Lexicon der Tonkünstler*, 2 vols. (Leipzig: Breitkopf, 1790), vol. i, col. 90. Gerber also cites J. A. Hiller's 1784 Bach biography which restates the claim made in the 1754 Obituary that Bach could play things with feet that others could not manage with their hands. See *BD*, 3: 402. English trans., *NBR*, 372.

[34] See Philipp Spitta's comparison of Bach and Handel in his *Johann Sebastian Bach*, 3 vols. (Leipzig, 1873–1888; English trans. by Clara Bell and J. A. Fuller-Maitland, London, 1889; reprint, New York: Dover, 1979), pp. 25–30.

FIREWORKS, EAGLES, AND CATHEDRALS OF LIGHT

Even for those not privileged to watch Bach up close in the organ loft, there was much to see. To get a sense of these thrills, let's revisit with Bach the large Silbermann organ in the Frauenkirche, recently completed when he played a famous recital on the afternoon of December 1, 1736 (see Chapter 4, p. 168), performing for two hours "in the presence of the Russian Ambassador, Von Keyserlingk, and many Persons of Rank, also a large attendance of other persons and artists," as the *Dresdner Nachrichten* informed its readership.[35] The instrument of three manuals and 43 stops had a large pedal division with a 32′ Untersatz capable of immense *Gravitas*. In contrast to the comparable organs in north Germany, Silbermann's instruments had no Rückpositiv, a feature that became rare in central Germany in the eighteenth-century. The Frauenkirche organ was placed at the front of the church, high above the altar (see Figure 6.12). From the uppermost of the three balconies in this church, which rises up to considerable heights above a relatively small footprint, the organist's back is visible, his hands, too, when they play high or low in the manual compass. The use of the pedals would have been suggested indirectly by some movement in the organist's upper body, even from a player of Bach's vaunted poise. For listeners in the other balconies and in the pews on the ground floor, less and less is seen of the organist as one goes lower in the church: from the second balcony head and shoulders are visible; from the first just the head; and then from all the way below, perhaps only the top of Bach's wig was apparent. Still, without the cover provided by the Rückpositiv, the organist would have had a sense of his own exposure to the audience, which would have been able to see at least something of the player seated at the organ.

From out in the Frauenkirche the eye would have been drawn up from Bach at the console to the long parallel lines of the case and its pipes; the sense of uplift was augmented by the organ's placement as a higher extension of the altar. This Silbermann organ was an immovable spectacle producing sound of immense sonic variety and dynamism: its polished pipes gleamed in the natural light streaming through the church's many windows, or reflected the candlelight at evening services. The pedal was massive and deep; the high sounds glittered and shimmered. The organ's verticality appeared in immovable counterpoint to the ephemeral and dynamic quality of the music it produced (see Figure 6.13).

---

[35] *NBR*, 188; *BD*, 1: 279. In the meticulous reconstruction of the bombed Frauenkirche completed in 2005, only the organ's façade was reconstituted; behind that façade is an "eclectic" organ of the twenty-first century. That the reconstruction of a Silbermann masterpiece could be rejected and with it an essential part of the history of the church, might be interpreted as confirming the continued unique status of the organ in Germany – at least for those responsible for the decision in the Frauenkirche – as a site of experimentation and ingenuity.

Figure 6.12   Interior of the Frauenkirche, Dresden

The Frauenkirche organ sparkled and shone like exploding fireworks captured at their climax. An engraving of 1747 of the fireworks for the Saxon royal wedding of Princess Maria Josepha and the French Dauphin, Louis Augustin, in Dresden depicts exactly this moment, a visual effect strikingly like that of the Silbermann organs of the city built during the

Figure 6.13   Facade of Frauenkirche organ, Gottfried Silbermann

same period; even the central niche of the structure evokes an organ console (see Figure 6.14). Silbermann himself could well have seen these or similar fireworks, which might well have put him in mind of his own dazzling pipework. The center of both organ and fireworks is marked by luminous grandeur: the pedal pipes and the huge Roman candle bursting above the

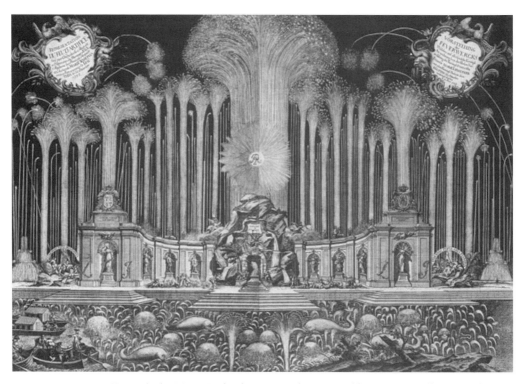

Figure 6.14   Moritz Bodenehr, *Feuerwerk zur Vermählung Maria Josephas von Sachsen mit dem Dauphin von Frankreich* (Fireworks Display for the Marriage of Maria Josepha of Saxony with the French Dauphin), 1747

insignia of the Saxon ruling house. These tall pipes similarly defied gravity even while they produced a sound that was itself described using that very term – *Gravitas*. The sonic and visual impression of the instrument was both fundamentally grounded and exuberantly aerial; the organ's façade implied power, mass, and profundity, but also a soaring weightlessness, the giant pipes somehow resisting collapse.

This may be the visual effect of the instrument out in the church, but the organist up in the balcony can also partake of some of this architectural uplift. In Chapter 2, I argued that it is impossible for an organist at the console to get a complete sense of the instrument that encompasses him. But he can see something of it. For an organist's-eye perspective let's move from the Frauenkirche back to the larger of the two instruments in Lübeck's Marienkirche, Buxtehude's church, where Bach arrived in the late Fall of 1705 after his long walk north from Thuringia in those sturdy German shoes (see Chapter 3, p. 110). When Bach played at a Sunday morning service or at the close of Vespers on a Saturday night by candlelight, and looked up from the console to the instrument stretching above him, his perspective shifted from the human-scaled keys and stops nearby to the towering pipes of the organ and its architecture.

Directly above the keyboard the organist saw the biggest pipe rising towards the vaulted ceiling, the pipe mouths decorated as fearsome faces. This upward view is the one Buxtehude would have had if he had made those vain, but occasionally irrepressible, attempts to take in the immense scope of the instrument around and above him. It is an uncomfortable, even awkward position to assume: head back, arms reaching over the keyboards, feet at the pedals. The pose cannot be held for long, especially if the music being played is physically involved. With ears directed upward and not straight into the console, one hears more of the organ and its immediate effect, and also more of the echo out in the church; one experiences a greater awareness of the monumentality of the instrument, but also a keener sense of the mass and character of the sound. This posture and view can also lead to vertigo. The feeling of power beyond human scale, enjoyed by all organists at the controls of these giant constructions, is magnified by the visual impression of these stolen, neck-straining views: to the player, also, the organ is larger than life. Dating from the sixteenth century, the façade of Buxtehude's organ was clearly a relic of distant origins. The central pedal pipes with curious scowling faces proclaimed to the organist looking upward from his bench that the organ's past, present, and future was founded on the pedals.

Perhaps because of the evocation of Germanic paganism in the decoration of these pedal pipes, as well as the impressive length stretching towards the ceiling, this vertiginous view from the Marienkirche organ bench was chosen for the cover of the book, *Die Orgel in der Gegenwart* (*The Organ of Today*) published in 1939 (Figure 6.15). The volume has several articles by the organ historian Gotthold Frotscher celebrating the "German ideal" that combines "gravity with intensity, richness with lightness" [*Gravität und Intensität, Fülle mit Helligkeit*].[36] For Frotscher, as for so many before him, the independence of the pedal, especially for Bach's music, was essential; however, in his attempt to provide historical and intellectual support for integrating the organ into the ritual worship of fascism, Frotscher makes much in this frightening book of the importance of smaller organs in the meeting places of the Hitler Youth.[37] The pre-Christian, Germanic faces on the cover also resonated with Frotscher's program for liberating the organ

---

[36] Gotthold Frotscher, "Orgelideale aus vier Jahrhunderten" in Frotscher (ed.), *Die Orgel in der Gegenwart* (Wolfenbüttel and Berlin: Geòrg Kallmeyer, 1939), pp. 17–23, at p. 21.

[37] For a powerful account of the organ's status as a Nazi symbol, along with an analysis of ideological tensions between the secular and sacred, and between small and huge instruments, see Albrecht Riethmüller, "Die Bestimmung der Orgel im Dritten Reich" in Hans Heinrich Eggebrecht (ed.), *Orgel und Ideologie: Bericht über das fünfte Colloquium der Walcker-Stiftung für orgelwissenschaftliche Forschung 5.–7. Mai 1983 in Göttweig* (Musikwissenschaftliche Verlags-Gesellschaft: Murrhardt, 1984), pp. 28–61. The definitive study of the Nazis and the organ is Stefan Zöllner, *Orgelmusik im nationalsozialistischen Deutschland* (Frankfurt: Peter Lang, 1999).

Figure 6.15   Cover of *Die Orgel in der Gegenwart.* Organist's view of largest pedal pipes, Marienkirche, Lübeck

from its ecclesiastical legacy and placing it at the center of the Nazi cult. The largest pipe bellowing out of its pagan mouth provides a disturbingly accurate representation of German organ triumphalism in which the pedal emerges out of myth and memory; the organ has a glorious German past that will be renewed in the new Nazi present. Quoting the later nineteenth-century Hegelian aesthetician, Friedrich Vischer, Frotscher writes in his article on "The Organ in Political Celebration" that the instrument can become a vital element of Nazi ceremonies only by remaining at odds with all "fashion and virtuosity, all hypocrisy, sentimentality and mawkishness."[38] Virile and pure will be the organ and its music in the Thousand Year Reich. In closing, Frotscher argues that the organ must be true to itself, to its power and independence, in order to further "the idea of the society in which we are rooted." The German organ is planted in German soil; it grows from the ground up.

Along with its praise of modest organs for the inculcation of young Nazis, *Die Orgel in der Gegenwart* also asserts that the monuments of the past must define and defend the higher purpose of the instrument against degenerate Wurlitzers and kindred abominations. If one wants to learn about real organs and organ music, writes the organist and early music pioneer Joachim Altemark in his contribution to the volume, then one needs to be taken to an instrument by Gottfried Silbermann or Arp Schnitger.[39] To be convinced of this, claims Altemark, one had only "to have Bach's E flat Major Prelude and Triple-fugue or the great F Major Toccata with Fugue played for him" on these German organs. The essence of what Altemark calls the "German organ art" can be truly heard only on large German instruments with massive, independent pedals capable of projecting the erudition and athleticism of Bach's polyphony, performed with well-trained precision of arms and legs.[40]

The German organ arts inspired not only Nazi musicologists, but Nazi designers as well. The notorious tourism poster of 1935 by Lothar Heinemann draws on a long tradition of organ design (Figure 6.16). Given its cultural status in Germany, the organ is an obvious choice to represent "Deutschland, Das Land der Musik" – "Germany, the Land of Music."[41] Heinemann's glowering, steely blue Nazi Eagle has a cluster of organ pipes as its plumage. On either side, slightly canted from, and somewhat darker than, the bright vertical organ pipes at the center of the image, beams of light extend upward to form the wings. The design seeks the same impact as Nazi architect Albert Speer's infamous light displays, albeit on the minimal space of a poster rather than on the infinity of the night sky. Speer's searchlight beams trace their lineage back to pyrotechnic displays like that of Bodenehr. In contrast to Speer's "Cathedral of Light" staged at the 1937 Party Congress in Nuremberg (see Figure 6.17), which might well have

---

[38] Gotthold Frotscher, "Die Orgel in der politischen Feier" in *Die Orgel in der Gegenwart*, pp. 5–8.

[39] The photograph (taken by Walter Kurka) of the Marienkirche organ used for the cover of *Die Orgel in der Gegenwart* had appeared in an earlier 1937 article by Altemark about early music in Lübeck. See Altemark, "Alte Musik in einer alten Stadt," *Musik in Jugend und Volk*, (1937), 21–26, at 24. For a historical and visual analysis of this photograph, see Zöllner, *Orgelmusik im nationalsozialistischen Deutschland*, pp. 13–15.

[40] Joachim Altemark, "Gedanken bei leisem Orgelspiel" in Gotthold Frotscher (ed.), *Die Orgel in der Gegenwart*, pp. 23–26, at p. 26.

[41] Equally unsurprising, when considered from this same point of view, is the fact that England for so long should have had organs without pedals and be "The Land without Music."

Figure 6.16   Lothar Heinemann, *Deutschland, das Land der Musik*, 1935

been partly inspired by the poster, Heinemann's image adopts the classic framing towers of large northern organs, taken by so many German writers we have encountered as evidence of their preeminence in the development of the instrument and its crucial pedals. Accordingly, the gigantic organ of more than two hundred stops built by the Walcker firm at the time of the 1936 Olympic games for Speer's Nazi Congress Hall [*Luitpoldhalle*] in

Figure 6.17   Albert Speer, *Cathedral of Light*. Photograph by Heinrich Hoffmann,
Nuremberg 1937

Nuremberg was praised by Eduard Kissel, Music Director in Munich, for its thunderous pedal – "the fundamental and enormous rolling basses" [*die grundgewaltige rollende Bässe*].[42] In Heinemann's poster Germany is not only the master of the organ, but the organ is the musical symbol of the master race. The bird attains its menace from the sweep of the largest, framing vertical columns; the eagle threatens flight with the wing feathers that are the visual equivalent of pedal pipes.

What these comparisons of Nazi eagles and Speer's spotlight cathedrals with Silbermann organs and Saxon fireworks suggest is not only that luminous displays and organ imagery share a long visual tradition, but also that the largest metal pipes and columns of light conveyed a sense of transcendent power, frequently in this book described by witnesses in the language of the divine, or its surrogate, the sublime. This capacity for terror is capitalized on by Heinemann, but also, in benign forms, by many composers, not least Bach himself in pieces such as the *Pedal Exercitium*. It was the pedals that could summon thoughts of the Last Judgment; the thunder of the bass could inspire devotion, but could also be criticized for

---

[42] Quoted in Riethmüller, "Die Bestimmung der Orgel im Dritten Reich," 41. See also Zöllner, *Orgelmusik im nationalsozialistischen Deutschland*, pp. 35–40, 83–90.

degrading the organ and its higher purpose by disrupting pious thoughts of congregants through the inappropriate overuse of such effects.[43] Bigger meant lower in sound, more imposing and awe-inspiring: the organ as edifice was framed and articulated by pedals, just as it was musically founded on what the feet could do with them.

My intention in reflecting on the organ's exploitation as a Nazi image is not intended to poison the history of the instrument and many of the themes explored in this book; supreme manipulators of symbol, the Nazis distilled their own twisted message from historical antecedents with chilling potency. Heinemann's design exploits the privileged position of the organ in German culture across many centuries; it was a symbol of German music long before the Nazis. While I am confident that these associations will not taint the historical and thematic connections pursued in this book, I nonetheless maintain that the instrument and its music did significant cultural work, not only in German musical life but also in contributing to a sense of national pride and cohesion. The triumph of the German model of organ-playing throughout Europe and the world not only offers a case study in cultural and technological exchange across borders and over time, but also in the uses and abuses of the symbolic power of the instrument that made the unprecedented expansion of that ideal possible. Nowhere is this connection clearer than in Forkel's seminal biography (see Chapter 4), where Bach's mastery of the pedal is a vital aspect of his identity as a German hero, both musically and in uniting a people. The organ's power is both visual and sonic, and while I hope to have shown at least some of the antecedents for German political representations of the instrument, it is the dual spectacle of dynamic organ performance and static organ architecture that I want to stress by tracing some of the fraught history extending from Silbermann and Bodenehr to Heinemann and Speer.

BACH BEGINS

In all the historical accounts of Bach making music, the feet are singled out for their velocity: there is nothing sedentary or lethargic about them. As we've seen, Bach was also a master at drawing on the sustaining power of the lowest tones: he understood the immense drama of the pedal point or the fugal subject in augmentation in the bass. But in the eyewitness reports, the feet fly across the pedalboard: motion is their marker. While Bach was able – and, one supposes, more than willing – to impress those watching his performance with his extravagant virtuosity, he also would have been fully aware, as all organists must be, that his movements had to be projected from the console out into the church, both through the big gesture and through tightly controlled counterpoint: he could impress distant listeners with both

---

[43] *Euterpe*, 6 (1844), 190.

his fantastical playing and his polyphonic brilliance. Though their visual attention can wander around the churches, as they themselves do when promenading to the music, auditors often look up at the organ – an impressive visual presence, though a static one in contrast to the kinetic organist often unseen in the loft. Like all organists, Bach would have rejoiced in the aura of the organ, which in many respects was even more impressive from afar. Organs are to be looked at and listened to.

This was never more true than at Bach's celebrated concert at the Hamburg Katharinenkirche in November of 1720 (see Chapter 2, p. 94). He had seen the organ and listened to it from down in the church during his teenage visits to Hamburg to hear Reincken; two decades later, and at the height of his powers as organist, he played for Reincken and other musical and political leaders of the city. As we've seen, the Obituary relates that "at the request of those present, [Bach] performed extempore the chorale *An Wasserflüssen Babylon* at great length (for almost half an hour) and in different ways." Some twenty years earlier at the Lüneburg home of his teacher Böhm, the teenage Bach had copied in its entirety Reincken's epic treatment of the same melody. The Obituary, presumably retailing the story that J. S. Bach had told C. P. E. Bach, also stresses the historical resonance of the event, the anointing of the next generation. After Bach has finished and descended to the nave of the church, Reincken tells him: "I thought that this art was dead, but I see that in you it still lives."[44] That art is founded on the pedals.

Before he began his concert on that autumn evening, Bach himself would have had the chance to look up at the organ at some point before his program began; the instrument was a monument of the German organ art, its central fields framed to each side by giant pedal towers (Figure 6.18).[45] To arrive at the console, hidden from view behind the Rückpositiv that mimicked the central part of the main case above it, Bach would have had to climb up three stories by a staircase behind the organ. (The staircase seen in the photograph leading directly to the organ loft from the lower balcony is a nineteenth-century addition, although if a similar construction were in existence in Reincken's day it would have accorded with his well-known flair for the theatrical.) Perhaps Bach personally greeted the most important of his auditors – the city fathers and clergy, and the musical luminaries, chief among them the aged Reincken – before going to the back of the church to the staircase.

As he climbs the hidden stairs, Bach knows he is the best at the best instrument. Those out in the church either already know this, too, or soon will. Bach has never left Germany, yet he has mastered the great national

[44] *NBR*, 302.
[45] Christoph Wolff and Markus Zepf, *Die Orgeln J. S. Bachs: Ein Handbuch* (Leipzig: Evangelische Verlagsanstalt, 2006), pp. 51–55.

Figure 6.18   Organ, Katharinenkirche, Hamburg

styles of France and Italy while transforming them for his own purposes. In this vibrant city of Hamburg, full of immigrants and visitors and imported institutions, from English coffee houses to public opera, the audience assembled in the Katharinenkirche understands that the most German of musical arts is about to be on display. The Germans invented the "modern" organ with its proliferation of stops and keyboards and fully independent pedal. Johann Mattheson is down in the audience, probably not far from where Reincken sits. Mattheson already believes that Germany produces the greatest organists and that Bach and Handel are at the head of the list, but he is twenty years from saying this in his masterpiece, *Der vollkommene*

Capellmeister (*The perfect Capellmeister*). This concert will cement Bach's reputation for Germany's greatest music critic, and for many others as well. But of all those present, Bach is perhaps the most acutely aware of the historical importance of the music about to unfold: he is at the very organ that so captivated him when he heard it played by the hands and feet of the old man now down below in the church, a musician who is now nearly one hundred years old and can probably no longer even make it up those stairs. Many in the audience, Mattheson among them, know history has been made before the first note is played.

After completing his climb and gaining the organ loft, Bach perhaps comes to the rail to the side of the Rückpositiv and takes one more look at those assembled below in the church – maybe he even bows – before he again disappears from view. The ritual of taking one's place at the organ is like an inverted entrance onto an opera stage, an exit aria in reverse: only after the star has disappeared from view can he begin to shine. The listeners down below in the Katharinenkirche experienced the most demonstrative of musical acts as pure sound emanating from an opulent piece of scenery – the glittering, but immobile, facade of the organ. The listeners were to be moved by something that seemed not to: for the duration of the performance there will be no external sign of human agency.

What may be one of the most welcome aspects of listening to a recording in your living room or ambling along with your iPod – the abstracted enjoyment of disembodied sound – rarely works to the advantage of the organists of the present day. In a modern world obsessed by the moving image, not to mention the visual appeal of a star performer, the hidden organist plays as if from another cultural world. But audiences of Bach's time and before must have thought it miraculous that such a giant and dynamic music could radiate from a gleaming instrument operated by an unseen organist. These listeners must have been thrilled by the very notion of a giant color machine whose unlimited combinations of sonorities were conjured invisibly from behind a bank of pipes, like the firemaster behind his fireworks display, or even the Wizard of Oz behind his curtain. What a feat of late-Gothic remote control it was that thousands of pipes, many of them thirty, forty, or even fifty feet from the fingers and feet of the organist, could be supplied with wind and brought to speak with split-second finesse and accuracy through a highly evolved technology commanded by an expert organist, the astronaut of his time.[46] Ranging in size from the massive pedal pipes to those of the tiny and brilliant mixture stops, the organ's registers

---

[46] For a brilliant take on the fantasies of technological power associated with organ-playing, see "Men at the Keyboard: Liminal Spaces and the Heterotopian Function of Music" in Daniel Goldmark, Lawrence Kramer, and Richard Leppert (eds.), *Beyond the Soundtrack: Representing Music in Cinema* (Berkeley: University of California Press, 2007), pp. 277–291, at p. 278.

explored the upper and lower reaches of human perception, the infinite nuances of timbre.

But it was the enormous gravity of the lowest tones emanating from the largest pipes that most frequently elicited praise. In the German Jesuit Athanasius Kircher's 1650 allegory of creation found in his encyclopedic *Musurgia universalis*, God is himself an organist; on the first day he pulls the lowest stop on his world organ [*Welt-Orgel*] and this Subbass provides the foundation not just of music but of all things.[47] More than a century before Kircher, the south-German organist Hans Buchner had praised the "forceful and truly German gravity" [*vis et vere germana gravitas*] of the organ.[48] Following in this long tradition, Bach viewed the organ's *Gravitas* as an essential, and essentially German, value, one that extends through Forkel into the nineteenth century and transporting metaphysics of Romantic sensibility, as in Jean Paul's 1825 observation that "the pedal tones of the organ pull us deeper into the romantic realm of evening than do the tones of the discant."[49]

Having retreated from the rail and secluded himself in the musical compartment that is the organ loft, Bach perhaps props his walking stick against the back of the Rückpositiv, then unbuttons his jacket and sits down at the bench. If he wears his sword, maybe he keeps it on. Bach takes stock of the controls at his musical command: these are the most sophisticated and complex of any on the planet. Four manuals are stacked in front of him, a full pedalboard below, the monumental case and its pipes are all around him. The possible combinations of stops, the knobs in matrices spreading to his right and left on either side of the keyboards, are virtually unlimited. One by one he draws the registers he will use for his opening, finally pulling the knob marked "Calcant" that rings a bell for the organ pumper to raise the wind from the row of large bellows hidden behind the organ; like the organist's labors, the Calcant's will also be invisible.

Bach readies himself on the bench: he is in balance, feet poised above the pedalboard, his entire body ready to spring into action. Forkel tells us that Bach would often begin his performances outside the context of the divine service with a prelude and fugue: on this historic occasion, playing for experts and amateurs, something big and bold is certainly called for, as it had been in the presence of the Landgrave of Kassel.

There is an echoing silence during which the audience continues to stare up at the organ although all have seen its unchanging façade uncountable times before. Yet each rediscovers the organ anew every time he or she turns to

---

[47] Athanasius Kircher, *Germaniae redonatus: sive artis magnae de consono et dissono ars minor*, trans. Andreas Hirsch (Schwäbisch Hall: Hans Reinhold Laidigen and Johann Christoph Gräter, 1662), p. 253.

[48] Ingeborg Rücker, *Die deutsche Orgel im Oberrhein* (Freiburg: Eberhard Albert Universitäts-Buchhandlung, 1940), p. 7.

[49] Jean Paul, *Kleine Bücherschau*, 2 vols. (Breslau, 1825), vol. II, p. 16.

gaze at this vertical half-acre of gilded wooden sculptures and brilliant tin-foiled pipes.

As Hamburg's most august personages continue to look on in rapt anticipation, the church is suddenly filled with a swell of sound three stories high, conjured from the full organ, those thousands of pipes ranging in height from thirty-two feet to a few inches – those hundreds of eager tibia players waiting for the *Capellmeister*'s signal. The Katharinenkirche organ, whose 32′ open Principal stop was admired by Bach for its prompt speech and gravity, surges to life from the bottom up, and a low rumble shimmering with a halo of heaven-high sonorities rushes down the length of the church. Reincken and the others below have not seen the flash of silver shoe buckles up in the organ loft that preceded this wave of sound, but from the depth and brilliance of the sonority and the impetuous profile of the echoing flourish, the listeners know almost immediately what the organist is doing.

Bach has begun with a pedal solo.

Select bibliography

Adlung, Jakob. *Anleitung zu der musicalischen Gelahrtheit*. Erfurt: Jungnicol, 1758;
    reprint, Kassel: Bärenreiter, 1953.
Musica mechanica organoedi. 2 vols. Berlin: Friedrich Wilhelm Birnstiel, 1768;
    reprint, Kassel: Bärenreiter, 1931.
Alpenburg, Johann Neopomuk Ritter von. *Deutsche Alpensagen*. Vienna: Wilhelm
    Braumüller, 1861.
Altemark, Joachim. "Gedanken bei leisem Orgelspiel." In *Die Orgel in der
    Gegenwart*. Ed. Gotthold Frotscher, pp. 23–26. Wolfenbüttel and Berlin:
    Georg Kallmeyer, 1939.
Anthes, F. C. *Die Tonkunst im evangelischen Cultus*. Wiesbaden: Friedrich, 1845.
Apel, Willi. *The History of Keyboard Music to 1700*. Trans. and rev. Hans Tischler.
    Bloomington: Indiana University Press, 1972.
Archbold, Lawrence and William J. Peterson, eds. *French Organ Music: From the
    Revolution to Franck and Widor*. New York: University of Rochester Press,
    1995.
Atkinson, Catherine. *Inventing Inventors in Renaissance Europe: Polydore Vergil's
    "De inventoribus rerum" (1499 and 1521)*. Tübingen: Mohr Siebeck, 2007.
Bach, Carl Philipp Emanuel. "Auszug eines Schreibens aus – – – vom 27sten Febr.
    1788." *Allgemeine deutsche Bibliothek*, 81 (1788), Pt. 1, 295–303.
Organ Works. Series I/9. Ed. Annette Richards and David Yearsley (Los Altos
    Hills, California: Packard Humanities Institute, 2008.
Bach, Johann Sebastian. *Clavierübung Dritter Theil*. Leipzig: the author, 1739;
    reprint, Paris: Fuzeau, 1989.
Musicalisches Opfer / Musical Offering, BWV 1079. Book 1: *Ricercari*. Ed.
    Christoph Wolff. Leipzig: Deutscher Verlag für Musik,1981.
Neue-Bach-Ausgabe: Orgelwerke. 11 vols. Kassel: Bärenreiter, 1957–2007.
Sechs Choräle von verschiedener Art. Zella: Schübler, 1746; reprint, Innsbruck:
    Helbling, 1985.
Baclawski, Karen. *The Guide to Historic Costume*. London: Batsford, 1995.
Barger, Judith. *Elizabeth Stirling and the Musical Life of Female Organists in
    Nineteenth-century England*. Aldershot, UK; Burlington, USA: Ashgate, 2007.
Beckmann, Klaus. *Repertorium Orgelmusik: Komponisten, Werke, Editionen,
    1150–2000*. 3rd edn. Mainz: Schott, 2001.
Bédos de Celles, Francois. *L'art du facteur d'orgues*. 3 vols. Paris: L. F. Delatour,
    1766–1778; reprint, Kassel: Bärenreiter, 1963–1966.
*Kurzgefaßte Geschichte der Orgel aus dem französischen des Dom Bédos de Celles
    nebst Herons Beschreibung der Wasserorgel*. Trans. and ed. J. C. Vollbeding.
    Berlin: Ernst Felisch, 1793.

Beißwenger, Kirsten. "Zur Chronologie der Notenhandschriften Johann Gottfried Walthers." In *Acht kleine Präludien und Studien über BACH: Georg von Dadelsen zum 70. Geburstag*. Ed. Collegium of the Bach Institute, Göttingen, pp. 11–39. Wiesbaden: Breitkopf & Härtel, 1992.

Belotti, Michael. "Buxtehude und die norddeutsche Doppelpedaltradition." In *Dietrich Buxtehude und die europäische Musik seiner Zeit*. Ed. Arnfried Edler, and Friedhelm Krummacher, pp. 235–244. Kassel: Bärenreiter, 1990.

Bendeler, Johann Philipp. *Organopoeia*. Frankfurt and Leipzig: Calvisius, 1690; reprint, Amsterdam: Knuf, 1972.

Best, William T. *Studies for the Pedal*. London: Novello, 1914.

Bicknell, Stephen. *The History of the English Organ*. Cambridge University Press, 1996.

Böhm, Georg. *Sämtliche Orgelwerke*. Ed. Klaus Beckmann. Wiesbaden: Breitkopf & Härtel, 1986.

Boyvin, Jacques. *Premier Livre d'Orgue*. Paris: Christophe Ballard, 1689–90. 2 vols. Ed. Jean Bonfils. Paris: Les Éditions Ouvrères, 1969.

Brahms, Johannes. *Briefwechsel mit Philipp Spitta*. Ed. Carl Krebs. Berlin: Verlag der Deutschen Brahms-Gesellschaft, 1920.

Bruhns, Nicolaus. *Sämtliche Orgelwerke*. Ed. Harald Vogel. Wiesbaden: Breitkopf & Härtel, 2008.

Buchner, Hans. *Sämtliche Orgelwerke*. Ed. Jost Harro Schmit. 2 vols. Frankfurt: H. Litolff, 1974.

Bünting, Heinrich. *Itinerarium Sacrae Scripturae*. Magdeburg: Ambrosius Kirchner, 1589.

Burg, Josef. "Quelques remarques sur les séjours d'Adolf Friedrich Hesse à Paris." *L'Orgue Francophone*, 13 (1992), 42–58.

Burkholder, J. Peter. "The Organist in Ives." *Journal of the American Musicological Society*, 55 (2002), 255–310.

Burney, Charles. *An Account of the Musical Performances in Westminster-Abbey, and the Pantheon, May 26th, 27th, 29th; and June the 3d, and 5th, 1785*. Dublin: Moncrieffe, Jenkin, White, H. Whitestone, Burton, and Byrne, 1785.

  A General History of Music. 4 vols. London: Becket, Robson, and Robinson, 1776–1789.

  The Present State of Music in France and Italy. London: T. Becket and Co., 1771; reprint, New York: Elibron Classic, 2005.

  The Present State of Music in Germany, the Netherlands, and United Provinces. 2 vols. 2nd edn. London: Becket, Robson, and Robinson, 1775.

Bush, Douglas E. "Musicus Consummatissimus: the Biography and Organ Music of Arnolt Schlick." *Organ Yearbook*, 16 (1985), 26–46.

Buxtehude, Dieterich. *Dieterich Buxtehude: Collected Works*. Vol. xv, Pt. 1. Ed. Michael Belotti. New York: Broude Trust, 1998.

Byrd, Penelope. *Male Image: Men's Fashions in England, 1300–1970*. London: Batsford Academic, 1979.

Cave, William. *Scriptorum ecclesiasticorum historia literaria*. London: Chiswell, 1688–1698.

Chase, Mary Ellen. *Life and Language in the Old Testament*. New York: Norton, 1955.

Chorley, Henry Fothergill. *Modern German Music*. 2 vols. London: Smith, Elder, and Co., 1854.

Music and Manners in France and Germany. 3 vols. London: Longman, Brown, Green, and Longmans, 1844.

Coppy, Joseph and Jean Willy Kunts. *Helmut Walcha: Nuit de lumière*. Paris: Broché, 2007.

Dähnert, Ulrich. *Der Orgel- und Instrumentenbauer Zacharias Hildebrandt*. Leipzig: Breitkopf & Härtel, 1960.

David, Hans T. and Arthur Mendel, eds., rev. Christoph Wolff. *The New Bach Reader: A Life of Johann Sebastian Bach in Letters and Documents*. New York: Norton, 1998.

Dohr, Christoph, ed. *Johann Christian Heinrich Rinck: Dokumente zu Leben und Werk*. Cologne: Verlag Dohr, 2003.

Douglass, Fenner. *Cavaillé-Coll and the Musicians*. 2 vols. Raleigh: Sunbury, 1980.

Dürer, Albrecht. *Hierinn sind begriffen vier Bücher von menschlicher Proportion*. Nuremberg: Albrecht Dürer's Widow, 1528.

Edler, Arnfried. "Arnolt Schlick – Musicus consummatissimus ac organista probatissimus." In *Von Isaac bis Bach: Festschrift Martin Just zum 60. Geburtstag*, ed. Frank Heidlberger, Wolfgang Osthoff and Reinhard Wiesend, pp. 115–126. Kassel: Bärenreiter, 1991.

Edwards, Lynn. "The Thuringian Organ 1702–1720: ein wohlgerathenes gravitätisches Werk." *Organ Yearbook*, 22 (1991), 119–150.

Eggebrecht, Hans Heinrich. "Zwei Nürnberger Orgel-Allegorien des 17. Jahrhunderts." *Musik und Kirche*, 27 (1957), 170–181.

Ehrenhofer, Walter Edmund. *Taschenbuch des Orgelbau-Revisors*. Graz: Universitäts-Buchdruckerei, 1908; reprint, Buren, The Netherlands: Fritz Knuf, 1980.

Eichler, Anja. *Albrecht Dürer, 1471–1528*, trans. Fiona Hulse. Cologne: Könemann, 1999.

Faulkner, Quentin. *J. S. Bach Keyboard Technique: a Historical Introduction*. St. Louis: Concordia, 1984.

"*Musica Mechanica Organoedi* and the 'Bach Organ.'" *BACH: Journal of the Riemenschneider Bach Institute*, 21 (1991), 42–59.

Fétis, François-Joseph. *Biographie universelle des musiciens et bibliographie générale de la musique*. 8 vols. Brussels: Melines, Cans et Compagnie, 1837–1844.

Biographie universelle des musiciens, 2nd edn. 8 vols. Paris: Firmin-Didot, 1860–1865.

Fischer, Carl August. "Ein Beitrag zur Geschichte des Orgelwesens in unserem Nachbarlande Böhmen." *Euterpe*, 14 (1854), 43–45.

Flade, Ernst. "Literarische Zeugnisse zur Empfindung der 'Farbe' und 'Fabrigkeit' bei der Orgel." *Acta musicologica*, 22 (1950), 97–127.

Fock, Gustav. *Arp Schnitger und seine Schule*. Kassel: Bärenreiter, 1974.

Forkel, Johann Nikolaus. *Allgemeine Geschichte der Musik*. Leipzig: Schwickert, 1788–1801; reprint, Graz: Akademische Druck- u. Verlagsanstalt, 1967.

Musikalischer Almanach für Deutschland auf das Jahr 1782. Leipzig: Schwickert, 1782; reprint, Hildesheim: Olms Verlag, 1974.

Ueber Johann Sebastian Bachs Leben, Kunst und Kunstwerke. Leipzig: Hoffmeister & Kühnel, 1802; reprint, Kassel: Bärenreiter, 1999.

Freylinghausen, Johann Anastasius. *Geistreiches Gesang-Buch*. Halle: Verlegung des
Waysenhauses, 1741.

Friedel, Robert and Paul Israel. *Edison's Electric Light: Biography of an Invention*.
New Brunswick, New Jersey: Rutgers University Press, 1987.

Frotscher, Gottfried. *Geschichte des Orgelspiels und der Orgelkomposition*. 2 vols.
Berlin: Max Hesse, 1935.

"Orgelideale aus vier Jahrhunderten." In *Die Orgel in der Gegenwart*. Ed.
Frotscher, pp. 17–23. Wolfenbüttel and Berlin: Georg Kallmeyer, 1939.

Ed. *Die Orgel in der Gegenwart*. Wolfenbüttel and Berlin: Georg Kallmeyer,
1939.

Gailíte, Zane. "Johann Gottfried Müthel, die Bach-Familie und die 'Wahre Art,
das Clavier zu Spielen' in Riga." In *Die Verbreitung der Werke Carl Philipp
Emanuel Bachs in Ostmitteleuropa im 18. und 19. Jahrhundert*, ed.
Ulrich Leisinger und Hans-Günter Ottenberg, pp. 480–514. Frankfurt an
der Oder: Mess- und Veranstaltungs GmbH, 2002.

Gauntlett, John Henry. "Mendelssohn as Organist." *Musical World*, 7 (1837),
8–10.

Geck, Martin. *Johann Sebastian Bach: Life and Work*. Trans. John Hargraves.
Boston: Houghton Mifflin Harcourt, 2006.

Gerber, Ernst Ludwig. *Historisch-biographisches Lexicon der Tonkünstler*. 2 vols.
Leipzig: Breitkopf, 1790–1792.

Goethe, Johann Wolfgang von. *Goethe's Letters to Zelter: with Extracts from those of
Zelter to Goethe*. Ed. A. D. Coleridge. London: George Bell and Sons, 1892.

Grieshofer, Franz. "Die Tracht der Kleidung: Bermerkungen zur Darstellung der
europäischen Nationen auf der 'Völkertafel.'" In *Europäischer Völkerspiegel:
Imagologisch-ethnographische Studien zu den Völkertafeln des frühen 18.
Jahrhunderts*. Ed. Franz K. Stanzel, pp. 45–66. Heidelberg: Universitätsverlag
C. Winter, 1999.

Gurgel, Anne Marlene, ed. *Dresdner Orgelmusik. Vol. 1: Orgelmusik des 19.
Jahrhunderts*. St. Augustin: Butz, 2002.

Gwynn, Dominic. "Lost Worlds: The English Organ Before 1700." In *Music
and its Problems: Essays in Honor of Peter Williams*, ed. Thomas Donahue,
pp. 23–47. Richmond, Virginia: OHS Press, 2007.

Handel, George Frideric. *Organ Concertos, Op. 4*. Arranged by W. T. Best.
London: Novello [1858]; reprint, New York: Dover, 2001.

Orgelkonzerte I. Hallische Händel Ausgabe. Ser IV/2. Ed. Terence Best and
William D. Gudger. Kassel: Bärenreiter, 2001.

Orgelkonzerte II. Hallische Händel Ausgabe. Ser IV/8. Ed. Eva Gerlach and
Ingeborg Schneider. Kassel: Bärenreiter, 1989.

Harrassowitz, Hermann. "Geschichte der Kirchenmusik an St. Lorenz in
Nürnberg." *Mitteilung des Vereins der Stadt Nürnberg*, 60 (1973), 1–15.

Häuser, Johann Ernst. *Geschichte der christlichen, insbesondere des evangelischen
Kirchengesanges und der Kirchenmusik*. Quedlinburg and Leipzig: Basse, 1834.

Heller, Morton A., ed. *Touch, Representation, and Blindness*. Oxford University
Press, 2000.

Hess, Joachim. *Dispositien der merkwaardigste kerk-Orgelen*. Gouda: Johannes
Vander Klos, 1774.

Hesse, Adolf Friedrich. "Aus dem Schreiben von Adolph Hesse." *Euterpe*, 4
(1844), 140–142.

"Orgelspiel in London." *Euterpe*, 11 (1851), 99–100.

Orgelwerke. Vol. I, ed. Otto Depenheuer. St. Augustin: Butz, 1989.

"Musikdirector A. Hesse in London und Paris." *Euterpe*, 21 (1862), 108–111.

Hill, Robert. *Keyboard Music from the Andreas Bach Book and the Möller Manuscript*. Cambridge, Massachusetts: Harvard University Press, 1991.

Holmes, Edward. "The Actual Organists of Germany." *The Atlas*, 10 (1835), 775–776, 792.

A Ramble among the Musicians of Germany. London: Hunt and Clarke, 1828.

Horton, Peter. *Samuel Sebastian Wesley: A Life*. Oxford University Press, 2004.

Hutchison, Jane Campbell. *Albrecht Dürer: a Biography*. Princeton University Press, 1990.

Joeres, Ruth-Ellen Boetcher. "The German Enlightenment (1720–1790)." In *The Cambridge History of German Literature*, ed. Helen Watanabe-O'Kelly, pp. 147–201. Cambridge University Press, 1997.

John, Hans. *Der Dresdner Kreuzkantor und Bach-Schüler Gottfried August Homilius*. Tutzing: Hans Schneider, 1980.

Johnson, Cleveland, ed. *Orphei organi antiqui: Essays in Honor of Harald Vogel*. Orcas, Washington: Westfield Center, 2006.

Jones, Peter Ward. *The Mendelssohns on Honeymoon: the 1837 Diary of Felix and Cécile Mendelssohn Bartholdy Together with Letters to Their Families*. Oxford: Clarendon Press, 1997.

Kassler, Michael, ed. *The English Bach Awakening*. Aldershot, UK; Burlington, USA: Ashgate, 2004.

Keyl, Stephen. *Arnolt Schlick and Instrumental Music circa 1500*. Ph.D. diss., Duke University, 1989.

Keyßler, Johann Georg. *Neueste Reisen durch Deutschland, Böhmen, Ungarn, die Schweiz, Italien und Lothringen*. 2nd rev. edn. 2 vols. Hannover: Heirs of Nicolai Förster and Son, 1751.

Kindermann, Johann Erasmus. *Harmonia organica*. Nuremberg: the author, 1645; Stuttgart: Cornetto, 2007.

Harmonia organica: 14 Præambulum in den Kirchentonarten, 5 Choralbearbeitungen, 4 Fugen, Magnificat im 4. und 8. Ton (Nürnberg, 1645). Ed. Rudolf Walter. Altütting: Coppenrath, c. 1960.

Kircher, Athanasius. *Germaniae redonatus: sive artis magnae de consono et dissono ars minor*. Trans. Andreas Hirsch. Schwäbisch Hall: Hans Reinhold Laidigen and Johann Christoph Gräter, 1662.

Musurgia universalis. Rome: Corbelletto, 1650; reprint, Kassel: Bärenreiter, 1988.

Kittel, Johann Christian. *Der angehende praktische Organist*. 3 vols. Erfurt: Beyer and Maring, 1801–1808; reprint, Buren: Knuf, 1981.

Vierstimmige Choräle mit Vorspielen . . . für die Schleswig-Hollsteinischen Kirchen. 2 vols. Altona: J. F. Hammerich, 1803.

Knecht, Justin Heinrich. *Vollständige Orgelschule für Anfänger und Geübtere*. Leipzig: Breitkopf, 1795; reprint, Wiesbaden: Breitkopf & Härtel, 1989.

Kollmann, August Frederic Christopher. *An Essay on Practical Musical Composition*. London: the author, 1799; reprint, New York: Da Capo Press, 1973.

A. F. C. Kollmann's Quarterly Musical Register (1812); an Annotated Edition with an Introduction to his Life and Works. Ed. Michael Kassler. Aldershot, UK; Burlington, USA: Ashgate, 2008.

Komlos, John and Francesco Cinnirella. "European Heights in the Early 18th Century." Discussion Paper, April 2005, Department of Economics, University of Munich. See http://ideas.repec.org/p/lmu/muenec/572.html

Komlós, Katalin. "Mozart and the Organ: Piping Time." *Musical Times*, 143 (2002), 59–61.

Krebber, Sabine. *Der Spaziergang in der Kunst*. Frankfurt: Peter Lang, 2002.

Lahee, Henry Charles. *The Organ and Its Masters*. Boston: L. C. Page, 1903.

Langley, Robin, ed. *The English Organ: An Anthology from Four Centuries in Ten Volumes*. Vol. VIII: 1740–1815. London: Novello, 1988.

The English Organ: An Anthology from Four Centuries in Ten Volumes. Vol. IX: Thomas Attwood to Thomas Attwood Walmisley. London: Novello, 1988.

Laukvik, Jon. *Orgelschule zur historischen Aufführungspraxis*, trans. Brigitte and Michael Harris. Stuttgart: Carus, 1996.

Leaver, Robin A. "Bach's 'Clavierübung III': Some Historical and Theological Considerations." *Organ Yearbook*, 6 (1975), 17–32.

Bach's Theological Library. Neuhausen-Stuttgart: Hänssler-Verlag, 1983.

Lendon-Bennett, Mark. *The Organist's Pedal Callisthenics or Gymnastic Exercises – for the Development of the Muscles Brought into Action in Organ Pedal Playing*. London: Guild of Church Musicians, 1899.

Leyding, Georg. *Sämtliche Orgelwerke*, ed. Klaus Beckmann. Wiesbaden: Breitkopf & Härtel, 1984.

Little, Wm. A. *Mendelssohn and the Organ*. Oxford University Press, 2010.

Lunelli, Renato. "Contributi trentini alle relazioni musicali fra l'Italia e la Germania nel Rinascimento." *Acta Musicologica*, 21 (1949), 41–70.

et al. I "bellissimi organi" della Basilica di S. Maria Maggiore in Trento. Trent: Comitato per le Manifestazioni Inaugurali, 1945.

Der Orgelbau in Italien in seinen Meisterwerken. Trans. Carl Elis and Paul Smets. Mainz: Rheingold, 1956.

Studi e Documenti di Storia Organaria Veneta. Florence: San Giorgio Maggiore, 1973.

Marchand, Louis. *Livre d'orgue*. Ed. Alexandre Guilmant and André Pirro. Paris: Durand, 1901–1904; reprint, New York: Schott, 1908.

Marpurg, Friedrich Wilhelm. *Abhandlung von der Fuge*. 2 vols. Berlin: Haube & Spener, 1753–1754; reprint, Hildesheim: Olms Verlag, 1970.

Critischer Musikus an der Spree. Berlin: Haube & Spener, 1749–1750; reprint, New York: Olms Verlag, 1970.

Historisch-Kritische Beyträge zur Aufnahme der Musik. 5 vols. Berlin: G. A. Lange, 1754–1758.

Marshall, Kimberly, ed. *Historical Organ Techniques and Repertoire*, vol. III: *Late-Medieval Before 1460*. Gen. Ed. Wayne Leupold. Colfax, North Carolina: Wayne Leupold Editions, 2000.

Martin, Dieter. "Vom 'unsterblichen Leipziger' zum 'vortreflicher Berliner': Ein unbekanntes Dokument: J. S. Bach und C. Ph. E. Bach als Exempla in einer Kritik F. Nicolais an J. J. Bodmer." *Bach-Jahrbuch*, 77 (1991), 193–198.

Martini, Johann Paul Aegidius. *École d'orgue*. Paris: Imbault, 1805; reprint Geneva: Minkoff, 1974.

Mason, Lowell. *A Yankee Musician in Europe: the 1837 Journals of Lowell Mason*. Ed. Michael Broyles. Ann Arbor, Michigan: UMI Research Press, 1990.

Mattheson, Johann. *Grosse General-Bass Schule*. Hamburg: J. C. Kißner, 1731; reprint, Hildesheim: Olms Verlag, 1968.

Grundlage einer Ehren-Pforte. Hamburg: the author, 1740. Modern edition, ed. Max Schneider. Berlin: Liepmannssohn, 1910; reprint, Kassel: Bärenreiter, 1969.

Der Musicalische Patriot. Hamburg: the author, 1728.

Philologisches Tresespiel. Hamburg: Johann Adolph Martin, 1752.

Der vollkommene Capellmeister. Hamburg: Christian Herold, 1739; reprint, Kassel: Bärenreiter, 1954. English trans. Ernest C. Harriss. *Johann Mattheson's "Der vollkommene Capellmeister": a revised translation with critical commentary*. Ann Arbor, Michigan: UMI Research Press, 1981.

Maul, Michael and Peter Wollny, eds. *Weimarer Orgeltabulatur: Die frühesten Notenhandschriften Johann Sebastian Bachs sowie Abschriften seines Schülers Johann Martin Schubart*. Kassel: Bärenreiter, 2007.

McCrea, Andrew. "British Organ Music after 1800." In *The Cambridge Companion to the Organ*, ed. Nicholas Thistlethwaite and Geoffrey Webber, pp. 279–298. Cambridge University Press, 1999.

"A Note on Thomas Adams and his Showroom Demonstrations." *Journal of the British Institute of Organ Studies*, 25 (2001), 78–95.

Mendelssohn Bartholdy, Felix. *Felix Mendelssohn: A Life in Letters*. Ed. Rudolf Elvers. Trans. Craig Tomlinson. New York: Fromm, 1986.

Felix Mendelssohn Bartholdy: Glückliche Jugend (Briefe des jungen Komponisten). Ed. Günter Schulz. Bremen: Jacobi Verlag, 1971.

Letters of Felix Mendelssohn Bartholdy from 1833 to 1847. Ed. Paul Mendelssohn Bartholdy and Carl Mendelssohn Bartholdy. Trans. Lady Wallace. London: Longman, Green, Longman, Roberts, & Green, 1863.

Neue Ausgabe sämtlicher Orgelwerke. Ed. Christoph Albrecht. 2 vols. Kassel: Bärenreiter, 1993–1994.

Sämtliche Briefe. Vol. I. Ed. Juliette Appold and Regina Back. Kassel: Bärenreiter, 2008.

Sämtliche Briefe. Vol. II. Ed. Anja Morgenstern and Uta Wald. Kassel: Bärenreiter, 2009.

Mersenne, Marin. *Harmonie Universelle*. 3 vols. Paris: Sebastien Cramoisy, 1636–1637; reprint, Paris: Éditions du Centre National de la Recherche Scientifique, 1963. English trans. Robert E. Chapman. *Harmonie Universelle: The Books on Instruments*. The Hague: Martinus Nijhoff, 1957.

Misson, Francois Maximilien. *Nouveau voyage d'Italie*. The Hague: Bulderen, 1691.

Morgan, Michael J. *Molyneux's Question: Vision, Touch, and the Philosophy of Perception*. Cambridge University Press, 1977.

Moser, Hans Joachim. *Die Musik der deutschen Stämme*. Vienna and Stuttgart: Wancura, 1957.

"Die Niederlande in der Musikgeographie Europas." In *International Society for Musical Research, Fifth Congress, Utrecht, 3–7 July 1952: Report*. Amsterdam: Alsbach, 1953.

Paul Hofhaimer. Stuttgart and Berlin: Cotta, 1929.

"Eine Trienter Orgeltabulatur aus Hofhaimers Zeit." In *Studien zur Musikgeschichte: Festschrift für Guido Adler, zum 75. Geburtstag*, pp. 84–86. Vienna: Universal Edition, 1930.

Mozart, Wolfgang Amadeus *et al.* *The Letters of Mozart and His Family*. 3rd edn. Ed. and trans. Emily Anderson. London: Macmillan, 1985.

Müthel, Johann Gottfried. *Orgelwerke*. Ed. Rüdiger Wilhelm. 2 vols. Innsbruck: Helbling, 1985.

Technische Übungen. Manuscript in Staatsbibliothek zu Berlin, Mus. ms. 15762/i–ii.

Natorp, Bernhard Christoph Ludwig. *Ueber Rinck's Präludien*. Essen: Bädeker, 1834.

Nemeitz, Joachim Christoph. *Nachlese besonderer Nachrichten von Italien, als ein Supplement von Misson, Burnet, Addisson, und andern*. Leipzig: Johann Friedrich Gleditsch, 1726.

Neubacher, Jürgen. "Johann Ernst Bernhard Pfeiffer und die Organistenproben." In *Critica musica: Studien zum 17. und 18. Jahrhundert: Festschrift Hans Joachim Marx zum 65. Geburtstag*, ed. Nicole Ristow, Wolfgang Sandberger and Dorothea Schröder, pp. 221–232. Stuttgart: Metzler, 2001.

Neukomm, Sigismund. *25 Grandes Études pour Orgues*. Ed. Francois Sabatier and Nanon Bertrand-Tourneur. Paris: Editions Publimuses, 1999.

Ochse, Orpha. *Organists and Organ Playing in Nineteenth-Century France and Belgium*. Bloomington: Indiana University Press, 1994.

Ornithoparchus, Andreas. *Musicae activae micrologus*. Leipzig: Schumann, 1517; reprint, New York: Dover, 1973.

Ottenberg, Hans-Günter, ed. *Carl Philipp Emanuel Bach Spurensuche: Leben und Werk in Selbstzeugnissen und Dokumenten seiner Zeitgenossen*. Leipzig: E. A. Seemann, 1994.

Owens, Jessie Ann. *Composers at Work: the Craft of Musical Composition, 1450–1600*. Oxford University Press, 1997.

Pearce, Charles W. *The Evolution of the Pedal Organ and Matters Connected Therewith*. London: Musical Opinion, 1927.

Notes on English Organs of the Period 1800–1810. London: Vincent Music Co.; and Boston: T. J. Donland, 1912.

Petri, Johann Samuel. *Anleitung zur praktischen Musik*. Leipzig: Breitkopf, 1782.

Polko, Elise. *Reminiscences of Felix Mendelssohn-Bartholdy: a Social and Artistic Biography*. Trans. Lady Grace Wallace. London: Longmans, Green, and Co., 1869.

Praetorius, Michael. *Syntagma musicum III: De organographia*. Wolfenbüttel: Elias Holwein, 1619; reprint, Kassel: Bärenreiter, 1985.

Printz, Wolffgang Caspar. *Historische Beschreibung der edelen Sing- und Kling-Kunst*. Dresden: Johann Georg, 1690; reprint, Graz: Akademische Druck- und Verlagsanstalt, 1964.

Phrynis Mitylenaeus, oder Satyrischer Componist. Dresden and Leipzig: Johann Christoph Mieth and Johann Christoph Zimmermann, 1696.

Quantz, Johann Joachim. *Versuch einer Anweisung, die Flöte traversiere zu spielen*. Berlin: Voss, 1752; reprint, Leipzig: Deutscher Verlag für Musik, 1983. Trans. as *On Playing the Flute*. 2nd edn. Trans. Edward R. Reilly. New York: Schirmer, 1985.

Rampe, Siegbert, ed. *Orgel- und Claviermusik der kaiserlichen Hofkapelle, Wien, 1500–1700*. Kassel: Bärenreiter, 2006.

Ribeiro, Aileen. *Dress in Eighteenth-Century Europe, 1715–1719*. New York: Holmes & Meier, 1985.

A Visual History of Costume: The Eighteenth Century. London: Batsford, 1983.

Richter, Tobias. *Keyboard Works.* In *Denkmäler der Tonkunst in Österreich.* Vol. xxvii. Ed. Hugo Botsbiber. Graz: Akademische Druck- und Verlagsanstalt, 1959.

Riello, Giorgio. *A Foot in the Past: Producers and Footwear in the Long Eighteenth Century.* Oxford University Press, 2006.

Riethmüller, Albrecht. "Die Bestimmung der Orgel im Dritten Reich." In *Orgel und Ideologie: Bericht über das fünfte Colloquium der Walcker-Stiftung für orgelwissenschaftliche Forschung 5.–7. Mai 1983 in Göttweig.* Ed. Hans Heinrich Eggebrecht, pp. 28–61. Musikwissenschaftliche Verlags-Gesellschaft: Murrhardt, 1984.

Rinck, Johann Christian Heinrich. *Selbstbiographie.* Breslau: G. P. Aderholz, 1833.

Ritter, A. G. *Zur Geschichte des Orgelspiels.* Leipzig: Hesse, 1884.

Sabellicus, Antonius Coccius. *Enneade X.* In *Operibus omnibus.* 4 vols. Basel: Johannes Hervagius, 1560.

Salmen, Walter. *Calcanten and Orgelzieherinnen: Geschichte eines "niederen Dienstes."* Hildesheim: Olms Verlag, 2007.

Scheibe, Johann Adolf. *Der critische Musicus.* 2nd edn. Leipzig: Breitkopf, 1745; reprint, Hildesheim: Olms Verlag, 1970.

Scheidt, Samuel. *Tabulatura nova (1624).* Ed. Harald Vogel. 3 vols. Wiesbaden: Breitkopf & Härtel, 1994–2002.

Schlick, Arnolt. *Gaude dei genitrix, Ascendo ad patrem meum.* Manuscript. Archivio Principato Vescovile, Sezione tedesca Miscellanea 105, Archivio di Stato Trento.
  Hommage à L'Empereur Charles-Quint. Ed. M. S. Kastner. Barcelona: Boileau, 1954.
  Orgelkompositionen. Ed. Rudolf Walter. Mainz: B. Schott's Söhne, 1969.
  Spiegel der Orgel-macher und Organisten. Mainz: Peter Schöffer, 1511. Parallel trans. Elizabeth Berry Barber. Buren: Knuf, 1980.
  Tabulaturen Etlicher lobgesang und lidlein uff die orgeln und lauten. Mainz: Peter Schöffer, 1512; reprint, Leipzig: Zentralantiquariat, 1979.

Schneider, Friedrich. *Handbuch des Organisten.* 4 vols. Halberstadt: Brüggeman, 1830–1832. English edn., *Frederick Schneider's Complete Theoretical and Practical Instruction for Playing the Organ, with Numerous Exercises for Acquiring the Use of the Pedals.* Trans. Charles Flaxman. London: Novello, 1832.

Schubart, Christian Friedrich Daniel. *Vermischte Schriften.* 2 vols. Ed. Ludwig Schubart. Zürich: Gessner, 1812.

Seyfried, Hans Jürgen. *Adolph Friedrich Hesse als Orgelvirtuose und Orgelkomponist.* Regensburg: Gustav Bosse, 1965.

Sieling, Andreas. "Der Dresdner Hoforganist Johann Gottlob Schneider." In *Zur deutschen Orgelmusik des 19. Jahrhunderts*, ed. Hermann J. Busch and Michael Heinemann, pp. 185–192. Sinzig: Schewe, 1998.

Smart, George Thomas. *Leaves from the Journals of Sir George Smart*, ed. H. Bertram Cox and C. L. E. Cox. London: Longmans, Green & Co., 1907; reprint, New York: Da Capo, 1971.

Smith, Rollin. "Pipe Organs of the Rich and Famous: Queen Victoria and Prince Albert". *The American Organist*, 41 (May, 2007), 96.

Snyder, Kerala. "Arnstadt to Lübeck." *Musical Times*, 127 (1986), 672–677.
  "Buxtehude's Organs: Helsingør, Helsingborg, Lübeck. 2: The Lübeck Organs." *Musical Times*, 126 (1985), 427–434.

Dieterich Buxtehude: Organist in Lübeck. 2nd edn. New York: University of Rochester Press, 2007.

Spitta, Philipp. *J. S. Bach*. Trans. Clara Bell and J. A. Fuller-Maitland. 3 vols. London: Novello, 1889; reprint, New York: Dover, 1951.

Sponsel, Johann Ulrich. *Orgelhistorie*. Nuremberg: G. P. Monath, 1771; reprint, Hilversum: Knuf, 1968.

Stainer, John. *The Organ*. London: Novello, 1877.

Stauffer, George. "Boyvin, Grigny, D'Anglebert, and Bach's Assimilation of French Classical Organ Music." *Early Music*, 21 (1993), 83–96.

and Ernest May, eds. *J. S. Bach as Organist: His Instruments, Music, and Performance Practices*. London: B. T. Batsford, 1986.

Steigleder, Johann Ulrich. *Compositions for Keyboard I. Corpus of Early Keyboard Music*, vol. XIII. Ed. Willi Apel *et al.* American Institute of Musicology, 1968.

Tabulatur Buch, darinnen dass Vatter Unser auf 2, 3, und 4, Stimmen Componiert, und Viertzig mal Varirt würdt. Strasbourg: Marx von der Heiden, 1627.

Stinson, Russell. *Bach: The Orgelbüchlein*. Oxford University Press, 1999.

The Reception of Bach's Organ Works. Oxford University Press, 2006.

"Some Thoughts on Bach's Neumeister Chorales." *Journal of Musicology*, 11 (1993), 455–477.

Stirling, Elizabeth. *Romantic Pieces for Organ*. Ed. Barbara Harbach. Pullman, Washington: Vivace, 1995.

Suchalla, Ernst, ed. *Carl Philipp Emanuel Bach: Briefe und Dokumente, Kritische Gesamtausgabe*. Göttingen: Vandenhoeck & Ruprecht, 1994.

Sykes, Ingrid. *Women, Science and Sound in Nineteenth-Century France*. Frankfurt: Peter Lang, 2007.

Tattershall, Susan and James Wyly. *The Brebos Organs of El Escorial*. Wilmington, Ohio: OHS Press, 2006.

Thalben-Ball, George. *Variations on a Theme by Paganini for Pedals*. London: Novello, 1962.

Thistlethwaite, Nicholas. *The Making of the Victorian Organ*. Cambridge University Press, 1990.

"Organs and Arminians in Early Seventeenth-Century Cambridge." In *Litterae organi: Essays in Honor of Barbara Owen*, ed. John Ogasapian, Scot L. Huntington, Len Levasseur and N. Lee Orr, pp. 27–50. Richmond, Virgina: OHS Press, 2005.

Todd, R. Larry. *Mendelssohn: a Life in Music*. Oxford University Press, 2003.

Tunder, Franz. *Sämtliche Orgelwerk*. Ed. Klaus Beckmann. 4th edn. Wiesbaden: Breitkopf & Härtel, 1985.

Türk, Daniel Gottlob. *Von den wichtigsten Pflichten eines Organisten*. Halle: Schwickert, 1787.

van der Straeten, Edmond. *La Musique aux Pays-Bas avant le XIXe Siècle*. Brussels: Van Trigt, 1878.

Vergil, Polydore. *De inventoribus rerum*. Venice: De Pensis, 1499.

Vignoles, Olinthus J. *Memoir of Sir Robert P. Stewart*. London: Simpkin, Marshall, Hamilton, Kent, & Co., 1899.

Eigentlicher Bericht, der Erfinder aller Ding. Trans. Marcus Tatius Alpinus. Frankfurt: Weygand Han, c. 1550.

On Discovery. Ed. and trans. Brian P. Copenhaver. Cambridge, Massachusetts: Harvard University Press, 2002.

Walther, J. G. *Musicalisches Lexicon*. Leipzig: Wolffgang Deer, 1732; reprint, Kassel: Bärenreiter, 1953.

    Sämtliche Orgelwerke. Ed. Klaus Beckmann. 4 vols. Wiesbaden: Breitkopf & Härtel, 1998.

Weckman, Matthias. *Choral-Bearbeitungen für Orgel*. Ed. Werner Breig. Kassel: Bärenreiter, 1977.

Werckmeister, Andreas. *Organum Gruningense redivivum*. Quedlinburg and Aschersleben: Struntz, 1705.

Wesley, Samuel Sebastian. *Original Compositions for the Organ*. Ed. G. M. Garrett. London and New York: Novello, Ewer and Co., c. 1900.

West, John E. *Cathedral Organists Past and Present*. London: Novello, 1899.

Williams, Peter. "BWV 565: A Toccata in D Minor for Organ by J. S. Bach?" *Early Music*, 9 (1981), 330–337.

    "Early References to the Organ in Presentday Southern Germany." In *Musicus Doctus: Festschrift für Hans Musch zum 65. Geburtstag*. Ed. Kay Johannsen, Georg Koch and Stephan Rommelspacher. Freiburg: Verlag Freiburger Musik, 2000.

    The European Organ. Bloomington and London: Indiana University Press, 1966.

    J. S. Bach: A Life in Music. Cambridge University Press, 2007.

    The Organ Music of J. S. Bach. Cambridge University Press, 2nd edn., 2002.

    and Barbara Owen, *The New Grove Organ*. London: Macmillan, 1988.

Wolff, Christoph. *Johann Sebastian Bach: The Learned Musician*. New York: Norton, 2000.

    Ed. *The Neumeister Collection of Chorale Preludes from the Bach Circle (Yale University Manuscript LM 4708)*. New Haven: Yale University Press, 1986.

    And Markus Zepf. *Die Orgeln Johann Sebastian Bachs: Ein Handbuch*. Leipzig: Evangelische Verlagsanstalt, 2006.

Yearsley, David. *Bach and the Meanings of Counterpoint*. Cambridge University Press, 2002.

    "In Buxtehude's Footsteps." *Early Music*, 35 (2007), 339–353.

    "An Ideal Organ and Its Experts across the Seventeenth Century." In *The Organ as a Mirror of Its Time*, ed. Kerala Snyder, pp. 93–112. Oxford University Press, 2002.

    "*Stylus Phantasticus* and the New Musical Imagination." In *GOArt Research Report*s, vol. ii, ed. Sverker Jullander, pp. 91–105. University of Gothenburg Press, 2000.

Zavarsky, Ernest. "Zum Pedalspiel des jungen Johann Sebastian Bach." *Musikforschung*, 18 (1965), 370–378.

Zedler, Johann Heinrich. *Grosses vollständiges Universal-Lexicon*. 64 vols. Leipzig: Zedler, 1732–1754; reprint, Graz: Akademische Druk- und Verlagsanstalt, 1961–1964.

Zehmen, Emanuel Leberecht von. *Reise des Erb-Prinzen Leopold zu Anhalt-Cöthen nach Holland vom Jahre 1710*. Köthen, Historisches Museum, Register 1734, Inventar-Nr. VS 462.

Zingerle, Ignaz Vincenz. *Sagen, Märchen und Gebräuche aus Tirol*. Innsbruck: Wagner, 1859.

Zöllner, Stefan. *Orgelmusik im nationalsozialistischen Deutschland*. Frankfurt: Peter Lang, 1999.

Index

DATE DUE
